MC

Microsoft Certified
Azure Data Fundamentals

Study Guide

MC

Microsoft Certified
Azure Data Fundamentals

Study Guide

EXAM DP-900

Jake Switzer

SYBEX®
A Wiley Brand

Acknowledgments

While I have been able to work on several exciting opportunities in my professional career at Microsoft, including delivering live presentations and working with some of the biggest brand name organizations the world, this was my first time tackling a technical book. This project was both intense and incredibly rewarding, as it allowed me to share what I believe are the fundamental skills anyone will need to start a successful career with the Microsoft data stack. However, this would not have been possible without the support from the following people.

First and foremost, I would like to thank my wife, Kaiya, for her love and support during the writing of this book. It is from her that I gather inspiration to be my best self every day. Thanks to my mom and dad for their unrelenting support and helping me make the most of every opportunity.

I would also like to thank my colleague Susanne Tedrick, author of *WOMEN OF COLOR IN TECH: A Blueprint for Inspiring and Mentoring the Next Generation of Technology Innovators*, (Wiley, 2020) for reaching out to me when this opportunity became available and to Kenyon Brown, the acquisitions editor, for helping me get it off the ground. Many thanks to Ayman El-Ghazali, the technical editor for this book and a mentor of mine throughout my time at Microsoft. Special thanks to Jon Flynn and Tash Tahir, two of my colleagues at Microsoft, for taking the time out of their busy schedule to review the content.

Finally, thank you to the entire team who made this book come together, including David Clark (project editor), Pete Gaughan (managing editor), Judy Flynn (copyeditor), and Barath Kumar Rajasekaran, who polished the rough content and made sure the project kept moving. Thanks also to all of the people who work behind the scenes with the production of this book.

About the Author

Jake Switzer has been using technology to build data-oriented solutions since his time as a student at the University of Alabama. He has held delivery and advisory roles at Microsoft for over nine years, including as a consultant and cloud solution architect. Jake has designed and developed data platform and advanced analytics solutions for an assortment of Microsoft enterprise customers to ensure that their specific business needs were met. Over the last few years, he has focused on advising Microsoft's sports customers how to design and build modern data solutions in Azure. His responsibilities in this role include providing architecture guidance, building proof of concepts, aiding in production deployments, and troubleshooting support issues. He is well-versed in a variety of data engineering technologies and frameworks such as SQL Server, Apache Spark, Azure Data Factory, Azure Databricks, Azure Synapse Analytics, and Power BI. In his free time, he enjoys spending time outdoors hiking and can be found most weekends cooking and sharing a scotch with his wife.

About the Technical Editor

Ayman El-Ghazali is a seasoned data and analytics professional, being in the industry since 2006. His passion for technology started when he was just a boy playing DOS games on his father's computer. From there, he pursued studies in computer science while attending high school in Egypt and continued his journey to earning both a bachelor of science and a master of science in Information Systems from Drexel University. On a personal note, Ayman enjoys playing and watching soccer, training in martial arts (mostly Brazilian Jiu Jitsu), and enjoying time with his wife, kids, friends, and family.

For more information about his background and his work, please visit his blog `thesqlpro.com` or `linkedin.com/in/aymansqldba`.

Contents at a Glance

Contents

Introduction

Hello! I am Jake Switzer, and as a data & advanced analytics cloud solution architect at Microsoft, I work with several Microsoft customers on designing and implementing data solutions in Azure. These questions vary day-to-day from very deep technical questions to questions like "What is the right data processing solution for a new data feed that I want to analyze?" or "Why should I move from my on-premises SQL Server solution to a cloud-based data solution?" While these questions vary in difficulty and specificity, they can all be traced back to one common topic: Azure data fundamentals.

If you are picking up this book for the first time, then I assume you are starting your journey as a data practitioner in Azure. The content in this book will not only prepare you for the DP-900 Microsoft Certified Azure Data Fundamentals exam, it will also give you a broad understanding of data solutions in Azure. This book is intended to help you understand the different approaches to storing data in Azure as well as how you can turn raw data into information used to make valuable business decisions. While this exam will not dive deep into specific technical features of the products listed in this book, you will need a broad understanding of these technologies, which will serve as a starting point for becoming more technical with each technology if you so choose.

Who Should Read This Book?

This book is appropriate for anyone who wants to understand Azure data fundamentals in a broad sense and prepare for the DP-900 exam. Technical individuals such as data engineers, data scientists, and DBAs who work with data can greatly benefit from Azure data fundamentals training. This will help them transition their existing skills, whether they are in on-premises data solutions or solutions in other cloud platforms, to a career in Azure. Along with understanding highly technical roles, this book can also help analysts and project managers understand how to use technologies such as Power BI and other Azure data services to help them in their roles. Technical sellers will also find value from this book as they will gain the necessary knowledge for sales discussions where Azure data services are critical to winning business with a potential customer.

What's Included in the Book?

This book consists of six chapters plus supplementary information: a glossary, this introduction, flashcards, and the assessment test after the introduction. The chapters are organized as follows:

- Chapter 1, "Core Data Concepts," covers the foundations of data storage and analysis techniques. It defines the different types of data, data processing patterns, and categories of data analytics.

- Chapter 2, "Relational Databases in Azure," covers the different relational database options in Azure and when to use which one. This includes IaaS and PaaS offerings such as SQL Server in a VM, Azure SQL Database, and Azure SQL Managed Instance. Chapter 2 defines best practices for deploying, migrating to, securing, managing, and querying relational databases in Azure. This chapter also includes the open-source relational database PaaS options that are available in Azure.

- Chapter 3, "Nonrelational Databases in Azure," covers the different types of NoSQL databases and how to implement them with Azure Cosmos DB. This chapter defines the different Azure Cosmos DB APIs and explores how Azure Cosmos DB provides security, high availability, and consistency for NoSQL data.

- Chapter 4, "File, Object, and Data Lake Storage," explores the file and object storage options in Azure Storage, including Azure Files, Azure Blob storage, and Azure Data Lake Storage Gen2 (ADLS). This chapter covers deployment, security, and management options for Azure Storage services.

- Chapter 5, "Modern Data Warehouses in Azure," explores common data processing patterns and features used by analytical workloads. This chapter covers several common Azure services that are used to build modern data warehouses, such as Azure HDInsight, Azure Databricks, Azure Data Factory, and Azure Synapse Analytics.

- Chapter 6, "Reporting with Power BI," explores the different components of Power BI, such as Power BI Desktop, Power BI service, and Power BI Report Builder. This chapter covers the common steps used in a Power BI workflow and the different aspects of interactive reports, paginated reports, and dashboards.

Each chapter begins with a list of the objectives that are covered in that chapter. The book does not cover the objectives in order, so you should not be alarmed at some of the odd ordering of the objectives within the book. At the end of the chapter, you will find the following elements that you can use to prepare for the exam:

- *Exam Essentials*—This section summarizes the most important information that was covered in the chapter. You should be able to answer questions relevant to this information.

- *Review Questions*—Each chapter concludes with review questions. You should answer these questions and check your answers against the ones provided after the questions. If you can't answer at least 80 percent of these questions correctly, go back and review the chapter, or at least those sections that seem to be giving you difficulty.

WARNING   The review questions, assessment test, and other testing elements included in this book are *not* derived from the exam questions, so do not memorize the answers to these questions and assume that doing so will enable you to pass the exam. You should learn the underlying topic, as described in the text of the book. This will let you answer the questions provided with this book and pass the exam. Learning the underlying topic is also the approach that will serve you best in the workplace.

To get the most out of this book, you should read each chapter from start to finish and then check your memory and understanding with the end-of-chapter elements. Even if you are already familiar with a topic, you should skim the chapter; Azure data services are complex enough that there are often multiple ways to accomplish a task, so you may learn something even if you are already competent in an area.

Recommended Home Lab Setup

There are multiple objectives in the DP-900 exam that will require you to download and install different desktop tools. These tools are described in their respective chapters, with instructions on where to download them and how to use them.

In addition to these tools, it is important to have access to a Microsoft Azure subscription. Because Microsoft Azure is a cloud-based offering, you only need a computer with a connection to the Internet to set up a free Azure subscription for experimentation. You can create a free Azure subscription by going to https://azure.microsoft.com/en-us/free and clicking *Start Free*. You will need to log in with a Microsoft account, such as a Hotmail, Live, or Outlook account. The Azure website will step you through the process of signing up for your free subscription. While you will need to provide contact information and a credit card number, Microsoft will not charge the credit card unless you upgrade to a paid subscription.

Like all exams, the Azure Data Fundamentals certification exam from Microsoft is updated periodically and may eventually be retired or replaced. In the event Microsoft is no longer offering this exam, the old editions of our books and online tools may be retired. If you have purchased this book after the exam was retired or are attempting to register in the Sybex online learning environment after the exam was retired, please know that we make no guarantees that this exam's online Sybex tools will be available once the exam is no longer available.

Interactive Online Learning Environment and Test Bank

We've put together some really great online tools to help you pass the MC Microsoft Certified Azure Data Fundamentals exam. The interactive online learning environment that accompanies this study guide provides a test bank and study tools to help you prepare for the exam. By using these tools, you can dramatically increase your chances of passing the exam on your first try.

The test bank includes the following:

Sample Tests   Many sample tests are provided throughout this book and online, including the assessment test, which you'll find at the end of this introduction, and the chapter review questions at the end of each chapter. In addition, there is a bonus practice exam. Use all of these practice questions to test your knowledge of the material. The online test bank runs on multiple devices.

Flashcards   The online text bank includes more than 100 flashcards specifically written to hit you hard, so don't get discouraged if you don't ace your way through them at first! They're there to ensure that you're really ready for the exam. And no worries—armed with the assessment test, review questions, practice exam, and flashcards, you'll be more than prepared when exam day comes! Questions are provided in digital flashcard format (a question followed by a single correct answer). You can use the flashcards to reinforce your learning and provide last-minute test prep before the exam.

Other Study Tools   A glossary of key terms from this book and their definitions is available as a fully searchable PDF.

Go to www.wiley.com/go/sybextestprep to register and gain access to this interactive online learning environment and test bank with study tools.

DP-900 Exam Objectives

MC Microsoft Certified Azure Data Fundamentals Study Guide: Exam DP-900 has been written to cover every exam objective at a level appropriate to its exam weighting. The following table provides a breakdown of this book's exam coverage, showing you the weight of each section and the chapter where each objective or subobjective is covered:

Subject Area	% of Exam
Describe core data concepts	15–20%
Describe how to work with relational data on Azure	25–30%
Describe how to work with nonrelational data on Azure	25–30%
Describe an analytics workload on Azure	25–30%
Total	100%

Domain 1: Describe Core Data Components

Subdomain 1a: Describe types of core data workloads

Exam Objective	Chapter
1-1 Describe batch data	1
1-2 Describe streaming data	1
1-3 Describe the difference between batch and streaming data	1
1-4 Describe the characteristics of relational data	1

Subdomain 1b: Describe data analytics core concepts

Exam Objective	Chapter
1-5 Describe data visualization (e.g., visualization, reporting, business intelligence (BI))	1
1-6 Describe basic chart types such as bar charts and pie charts	1
1-7 Describe analytics techniques (e.g., descriptive, diagnostic, predictive, prescriptive, cognitive)	1
1-8 Describe ELT and ETL processing	1
1-9 Describe the concepts of data processing	1

Domain 2: Describe How to Work with Relational Data on Azure

Subdomain 2a: Describe relational data workloads

Subdomain 2b: Describe relational Azure data services

Subdomain 2c: Identify basic management tasks for relational data

Subdomain 2d: Describe query techniques for data using SQL language

Domain 3: Describe How to Work with Nonrelational Data on Azure

Subdomain 3a: Describe nonrelational data workloads

Subdomain 3b: Describe nonrelational data offerings on Azure

Subdomain 3c: Identify basic management tasks for nonrelational data

Exam Objective	Chapter
3-10 Describe provisioning and deployment of nonrelational data services	3, 4
3-11 Describe method for deployment including the Azure portal, Azure Resource Manager templates, Azure PowerShell, and the Azure command-line interface (CLI)	3, 4
3-12 Identify data security components (e.g., firewall, authentication, encryption)	3, 4
3-13 Identify basic connectivity issues (e.g., accessing from on-premises, access with Azure VNETs, access from Internet, authentication, firewalls)	3, 4
3-14 Identify management tools for nonrelational data	3, 4

Domain 4: Describe an Analytics Workload on Azure

Subdomain 4a: Describe analytics workloads

Exam Objective	Chapter
4-1 Describe transactional workloads	5
4-2 Describe the difference between a transactional and an analytics workload	5
4-3 Describe the difference between batch and real time	5
4-4 Describe data warehousing workloads	5
4-5 Determine when a data warehouse solution is needed	5

Subdomain 4b: Describe the components of a modern data warehouse

Subdomain 4c: Describe data ingestion and processing on Azure

Subdomain 4d: Describe data visualization in Microsoft Power BI

 Exam domains and objectives are subject to change at any time without prior notice and at Microsoft's sole discretion. Please visit Microsoft's website for the most current information.

Assessment Test

1. Which of the four Vs of big data is related to the speed at which data is processed?

    A. Volume

    B. Velocity

    C. Value

    D. Variety

2. Which of the following components is not included in the Lambda architecture design pattern?

    A. Batch layer

    B. Serving layer

    C. Speed layer

    D. Transactional layer

3. Which of the following transactional database properties ensures that once a transaction is committed, it will remain committed even if there is a system failure?

    A. Consistency

    B. Atomicity

    C. Durability

    D. Resilience

4. Which of the following technologies can be used to orchestrate the flow of data in a data processing pipeline?

    A. Azure SQL Database

    B. Azure Data Factory

    C. Azure Data Lake Storage Gen2

    D. Azure Synapse Analytics dedicated SQL pools

5. Is the italicized portion of the following statement true, or does it need to be replaced with one of the other fragments that appear below? Azure Synapse Analytics dedicated SQL pools is an example of a *relational* database.

    A. Nonrelational

    B. NoSQL

    C. Object

    D. No change needed

6. Which of the following is not a core component of a relational database?

   A. Document

   B. Index

   C. Table

   D. View

7. Which of the following is the most optimal solution for storing images, telemetry data, and data that is used for distributed analytics solutions?

   A. Azure SQL Database

   B. Azure Blob Storage

   C. Azure Cosmos DB Gremlin API

   D. Azure Files

8. What data processing approach is typically used to process data for traditional business intelligence solutions?

   A. ELT

   B. Batch

   C. Streaming

   D. ETL

9. Data that is transformed so that it meets the schema requirements of a destination table is an example of what type of data processing strategy?

   A. Schema-on-upload

   B. Schema-on-read

   C. Schema-on-write

   D. Analytical processing

10. What technology in Azure allows data engineers to build data processing pipelines with a graphical user interface?

    A. Azure Data Factory mapping data flows

    B. SSIS

    C. Azure Databricks

    D. Azure Logic Apps

11. Which of the following methods is used to manage the order in which data processing activities are executed?

    A. Data flow

    B. Management flow

    C. Control flow

    D. Orchestration flow

12. You have been tasked with taking data stored as parquet files in Azure Data Lake Storage Gen2 and loading the most recent three years of data into an Azure Synapse Analytics data warehouse. However, you must first query the parquet data to determine which rows fall within the last three years. Which of the following options will allow you to query the parquet data without requiring you to physically store the data in the data warehouse first?

    A. Azure Synapse Analytic serverless SQL pools

    B. Synapse Pipelines

    C. Synapse Link

    D. Linked Service

13. Is the italicized portion of the following statement true, or does it need to be replaced with one of the other fragments that appear below? *Prescriptive* analytics involves examining historical data to determine why certain events happened.

    A. Predictive

    B. Diagnostic

    C. Cognitive

    D. No change needed

14. You are a data analyst for a company that sells different types of bicycles. For an upcoming review of this past quarter's sales, you would like to build a report that shows how well different types of bikes have done in the company's various sales territories. One requirement for this report is that it includes a visualization that displays total sales for each bike subcategory. Which of the following visuals best serves this requirement?

    A. Line chart

    B. Column chart

    C. Scatter plot

    D. Map

15. What type of index is optimal for database tables that are used in queries that perform large aggregations of data?

    A. Columnstore

    B. Clustered

    C. Nonclustered

    D. Unique

16. Which Azure SQL option is an example of an IaaS offering?

    A. Azure SQL Database

    B. Azure SQL Managed Instance

    C. SQL Server on an Azure Virtual Machine

    D. Azure Synapse Analytics dedicated SQL pools

17. Which Azure SQL option requires the least amount of administrative effort and is typically used when building modern cloud applications?

A. Azure SQL Managed Instance

B. Azure SQL Database

C. Azure Synapse Analytics Serverless SQL Pools

D. SQL Server on an Azure Virtual Machine

18. You are developing a database platform that will serve an OLTP system and will need to store more than 10 TB of data. The database platform will need to minimize administrative effort as much as possible. Which of the following database and service tier options is the most appropriate for this use case?

A. Azure SQL Database Hyperscale

B. Azure SQL Database Elastic Pool

C. Azure SQL MI, Business Critical

D. Azure Synapse Analytics dedicated SQL pools

19. Which of the following options will give specific IP addresses access to an Azure SQL Database's logical server?

A. Virtual network firewall rules

B. Private Link

C. Server-level IP firewall rules

D. Database-level IP firewall rules

20. What free tool can be used to determine potential compatibility issues when planning a SQL Server database upgrade or a migration to Azure SQL?

A. Data Migration Planner

B. Data Migration Assistant

C. Database Migration Recommender

D. Database Migration Service

21. Which of the following tools can be used to automate Azure resource deployments?

A. Azure PowerShell

B. Azure CLI

C. Azure Resource Manager templates

D. All of the above

22. How often does Azure perform a full database backup of an Azure SQL Database?

A. Once a month

B. Once a week

C. Once a day

D. Once an hour

23. Which of the following commands is an example of a DML command?

    A. SELECT

    B. CREATE

    C. ALTER

    D. DROP

24. Which SQL Server feature can be used to obfuscate sensitive data in different columns?

    A. Always Encrypted

    B. Transparent Data Encryption

    C. Dynamic data masking

    D. Column-Level Security

25. Which of the following open-source databases is available as a PaaS offering in Azure?

    A. PostgreSQL

    B. MySQL

    C. MariaDB

    D. All of the above

26. Which of the following describes Read Committed isolation for SQL Server?

    A. Transactions running with Read Committed isolation issue locks on involved data at the time of data modification to prevent other transactions from reading dirty data. This is the default isolation level for SQL Server–based database engines.

    B. Transactions running with Read Committed isolation issue read and write locks on involved data until the end of the transaction.

    C. Read Committed isolation is the lowest isolation level, only guaranteeing that physically corrupt data is not read.

    D. Read Committed isolation is the highest isolation level, completely isolating transactions from one another.

27. When following a star schema design pattern for a data warehouse, which of the following table types is used to store metrics?

    A. Measure table

    B. Dimension table

    C. Materialized table

    D. Fact table

28. When configuring a SQL Server instance on an Azure VM, what is the recommended storage configuration for the disk, log, and tempdb files?

    A. Place data and log files on the same disk and tempdb on a separate disk.

    B. Place data, log, and tempdb files on separate disks.

    C. Place log and tempdb files on the same disk and data files on a different disk.

    D. Place data and tempdb files on the same disk and log files on a separate disk.

29. Is the italicized portion of the following statement true, or does it need to be replaced with one of the other fragments that appear below? *Nonrepeatable* reads occur when a transaction reads the same row several times and returns different data each time.

A. Phantom

B. Dirty

C. Inconsistent

D. No change needed

30. What type of join will retrieve all data from the left table of a join condition and only data that meets the join condition from the table on the right?

A. Full inner join

B. Left inner join

C. Left outer join

D. Right outer join

31. Which of the following nonrelational database types is optimal for storing the relationships between multiple entities?

A. Graph database

B. Document database

C. Key-value store

D. Columnar database

32. Which of the following statements is not true about a document in a document database?

A. Different schemas can be used across multiple documents.

B. Documents are typically stored as semi-structured data formats, such as JSON, BSON, and XML.

C. Queries performing specific lookups or filters can only search by a document's key and not by one of the data values.

D. Documents can easily be distributed across multiple storage devices.

33. You are designing a data storage solution that will store transactions made on an e-commerce site. The schema for these transactions is very fluid and is typically different for each transaction. There is also a requirement for the database to be able to scale globally, with some of the replicated regions being able to be written to. Which of the following is the most appropriate?

A. Azure SQL Database

B. Azure Cosmos DB API for MongoDB

C. Azure Cosmos DB Cassandra API

D. Azure Cosmos DB Core (SQL) API

34. Which of the following is a difference between Azure Table storage and the Azure Cosmos DB Table API?

   A. Entities in Azure Table storage maintain a defined schema, while entities in the Azure Cosmos DB Table API have flexible schemas.

   B. Azure Table storage offers single region replication, while the Azure Cosmos DB Table API offers multi-region replication.

   C. Queries can only perform searches on keys when interacting with Azure Table storage, while the Azure Cosmos DB Table API allows queries to search on keys and values.

   D. The maximum entity size in Azure Table storage is 2 MB, while the Azure Cosmos DB Table API has a maximum entity size of 4 MB.

35. What is the unit of measure used to represent the throughput required to read and write data stored in Azure Cosmos DB?

   A. Database transaction units (DTUs)

   B. Request Units (RUs)

   C. Throughput units (TUs)

   D. Cosmos DB transaction units (CDTUs)

36. What type of keys does an Azure Cosmos DB account generate to provide access to its resources? How many are created?

   A. One read-write key and one read-only key

   B. Two read-write keys and one read-only key

   C. One read-write key and two read-only keys

   D. Two read-write keys and two read-only keys

37. Which consistency level guarantees that all reads will return the most recent version of a document while potentially resulting in slower write performance due to application connections being paused while transactions are committed?

   A. Session

   B. Bounded staleness

   C. Strong

   D. Eventual

38. What is the name of the field that is used to distribute Azure Cosmos DB data across storage?

   A. Partition key

   B. Distribution key

   C. Primary key

   D. Foreign key

39. You have been asked to isolate an Azure Cosmos DB account by associating it with a subnet in a virtual network. Which of the following services can you use to attach a private IP address from the subnet to the account?

   A. Private endpoint

   B. Service endpoint

   C. IP endpoint

   D. Access endpoint

40. As the data architect for your company, you have been tasked with designing a storage solution that is optimized for storing videos, images, audio files, and each file's associated metadata. Which type of data store should you use?

   A. Graph

   B. Document

   C. Object

   D. Columnar

41. Which of the following storage services is used to replace existing on-premises file shares and is accessible via SMB or NFS protocols?

   A. Azure Blob storage

   B. Azure Files

   C. Azure Data Lake Storage Gen2

   D. Azure Cosmos DB File API

42. Which of the following access tiers is available for file shares that are hosted on a standard Azure storage account?

   A. Transaction optimized

   B. Hot

   C. Cool

   D. All of the above

43. What object is used to organize data in Azure Blob Storage?

   A. Container

   B. Directory

   C. Blob

   D. Table

44. What storage service is optimized to serve data to big data analytics environments such as Azure HDInsight, Azure Databricks, and Azure Synapse Analytics due to how it structures data and its integration with the Hadoop Distributed File System?

   A. Azure Blob Storage

   B. Azure Files

   C. Azure Data Lake Storage Gen2

   D. Azure Table storage

45. Is the italicized portion of the following statement true, or does it need to be replaced with one of the other fragments that appear below? *Azure Data Lake Storage Gen2* provides users with the ability to grant granular access to storage objects and data with the use of POSIX-like access control lists.

A. Azure Blob storage

B. Azure Files

C. Azure Table storage

D. No change needed

46. You are designing an Azure Storage solution that will be used to store log files. One of the solution requirements is that the data must be replicated to a secondary storage account in a different Azure region in case of a region outage. Which of the following options should you enable on the storage account?

A. Geo-redundant storage (GRS)

B. Geo-zone-redundant storage (GZRS)

C. Zone redundant storage (ZRS)

D. Both A and B

47. What is the minimum number of storage accounts you need to create to host two blob containers, one file share, and one table?

A. One

B. Two

C. Three

D. Four

48. Which of the following Azure RBAC roles will grant users read, write, and delete access to an Azure Blob Storage container but will not give them full management rights over the container?

A. Storage Blob Data Owner

B. Storage Blob Data Contributor

C. Storage Blob Data Reader

D. Storage Blob Data Writer

49. Is the italicized portion of the following statement true, or does it need to be replaced with one of the other fragments that appear below? *AzCopy* is a stand-alone desktop application that can be used to create and delete Azure Storage resources such as blob containers and file shares. Users can also upload, download, and delete Azure Storage data with *AzCopy*.

A. Azure Data Factory

B. Azure Data Box

C. Azure Storage Explorer

D. No change needed

50. Which of the following open-source frameworks can be deployed with Azure HDInsight?

    A. Apache Hadoop

    B. Apache Storm

    C. Apache Kafka

    D. All of the above

51. Is the italicized portion of the following statement true, or does it need to be replaced with one of the other fragments that appear below? *Spark drivers* are installed on every worker node in a Spark cluster and are used to execute job tasks.

    A. Spark sessions

    B. Spark executors

    C. Cluster managers

    D. No change needed

52. Which of the following statements regarding Azure Databricks is true?

    A. Azure Databricks can be used for both batch and stream processing workflows.

    B. The Databricks File System (DBFS) is a built-in distributed file system that Azure Databricks uses to persist data after a Databricks cluster is terminated so that it is not lost.

    C. Azure Databricks provides an interactive development environment for data exploration.

    D. All of the above.

53. The cost of an Azure Databricks cluster consists of what two components?

    A. Azure VMs and Databricks Units (DBUs)

    B. Azure Kubernetes Service (AKS) and Databricks Units (DBUs)

    C. Azure Container Instance (ACI) and Databricks Units (DBUs)

    D. Azure Kubernetes Service (AKS) and Databricks Cost Units (DCUs)

54. You are configuring a new Azure Databricks cluster that will be used for nightly batch processing jobs. The cluster will be responsible for processing very large datasets and will need to be able to scale out horizontally to finish processing data within a few hours. Which of the following cluster modes is the most optimal for this workload?

    A. High concurrency

    B. Standard

    C. Single node

    D. Compute

55. Which of the following is not a type of analytical pool that is available with Azure Synapse Analytics?

    A. Serverless SQL pool

    B. Dedicated SQL pool

    C. Databricks pool

    D. Apache Spark pool

56. You are designing a data warehouse with an Azure Synapse Analytics dedicated SQL pool that will serve business intelligence applications and analytical queries. To optimize query performance, which of the following table types should you consider adding a clustered columnstore index to?

   A.   Large fact tables with more than 60 million rows

   B.   Small reference tables

   C.   Medium-sized dimension tables

   D.   All of the above

57. Is the italicized portion of the following statement true, or does it need to be replaced with one of the other fragments that appear below? In Azure Data Factory, *linked services* represent data structures within data stores, such as a SQL Server table or a set of files in Azure Data Lake Storage Gen2.

   A.   Dataset

   B.   Activity

   C.   Pipeline

   D.   No change needed

58. What Azure Data Factory resource is used to power pipeline runs?

   A.   Compute resources

   B.   Integration runtimes

   C.   Spark clusters

   D.   Hadoop clusters

59. Azure Databricks notebooks and Azure HDInsight Hive queries are examples of what Azure Data Factory activity type?

   A.   Control

   B.   Data movement

   C.   Data transformation

   D.   Data manipulation

60. Which of the following data movement mechanisms that are native to Azure Synapse Analytics dedicated SQL pools provide the most flexibility when loading data from Azure Storage?

   A.   PolyBase

   B.   COPY command

   C.   BCP

   D.   OPENROWSET

61. Is the italicized portion of the following statement true, or does it need to be replaced with one of the other fragments that appear below? *External tables* are used by services such as Azure Synapse Analytics to read data from files in Azure Storage without having to create an additional copy of the data.

   A. Materialized views

   B. SQL tables

   C. Virtual tables

   D. No change needed

62. When using PolyBase, which of the following T-SQL commands are used to define external tables in a dedicated SQL pool?

   A. CREATE EXTERNAL FILE FORMAT

   B. CREATE EXTERNAL TABLE

   C. CREATE EXTERNAL DATA SOURCE

   D. All of the above

63. What service is used to create Power BI paginated reports?

   A. Power BI Report Builder

   B. Power BI service

   C. Power BI Desktop

   D. Power BI Report Server

64. Which of the following Power BI data connectivity types cannot be used to establish a connection with an Azure SQL Database?

   A. Import.

   B. Live connection.

   C. DirectQuery.

   D. All of the above can be used to connect to an Azure SQL Database.

65. Power BI supports what formula language for building custom calculations such as measures, custom columns, and custom tables?

   A. M

   B. DAX

   C. F#

   D. SQL

66. Is the italicized portion of the following statement true, or does it need to be replaced with one of the other fragments that appear below? A Power BI *dashboard* provides a summarized view that enables business decision makers to monitor their business through a single page.

   A. Interactive report

   B. Paginated report

   C. Table

   D. No change needed

67. Which of the following Power BI service components can be used to explore data with natural language queries?

A. Power BI Quick Insights

B. Power BI Q&A

C. Power BI Natural Language Query

D. Power BI Dataflows

Answers to the Assessment Test

1. B. The velocity at which data is processed is defined as either being processed in scheduled batches or streamed in real time. See Chapter 1 for more information.

2. D. Lambda architectures have a batch and a serving layer for batch processed data and a speed layer for stream processed data. See Chapter 1 for more information.

3. C. When adhering to ACID properties, transactional databases must ensure that transactions are durable and will be available for querying after the database is brought back online from a database failure. See Chapter 1 for more information.

4. B. Azure Data Factory can be used to orchestrate the flow of data in a data processing pipeline. It can schedule the order of when different transformation activities need to occur, and allows users to incorporate error handling logic. See Chapter 1 for more information.

5. D. Azure Synapse Analytics dedicated SQL pools is a relational database offering that follows a distributed, multi-parallel processing architecture. See Chapter 1 for more information.

6. A. Documents represent user-defined content in a NoSQL database such as Azure Cosmos DB or MongoDB. Tables, indexes, and views are core components of a relational database. See Chapter 1 for more information.

7. B. Azure Blob Storage is optimized for storing objects such as images and telemetry data. It is also an optimal data store for data that is used by distributed analytics platforms such as Azure Databricks and Azure HDInsight. See Chapter 1 for more information.

8. D. The ETL, or Extract, Transform, and Load, approach has been used to build business intelligence solutions for years. This approach involved extracting data from source systems, transforming it to adhere to business rules, and loading it into a data model used for analysis. See Chapter 1 for more information.

9. C. Conforming data to a predefined schema is known as schema-on-write. Schema-on-read, on the other hand, is the process of defining a schema as data is read from a storage location. See Chapter 1 for more information.

10. A. Azure Data Factory mapping data flows is a graphical tool that gives data engineers the ability to extract data from one or more source systems, transform data through a series of different activities, and then load the data into a destination data store for reporting. See Chapter 1 for more information.

11. C. Control flows are used to enforce the correct processing order of data movement and data transformation activities. See Chapter 1 for more information.

12. A. Azure Synapse Analytics serverless SQL pools is an interactive service that allows developers to query data in ADLS or Azure Blob Storage. See Chapter 1 for more information.

13. B. Diagnostic analytics uses historical data to answer questions about why different events have happened, whereas prescriptive analytics answers questions about what actions should be taken to achieve a particular goal. See Chapter 1 for more information.

14. B. Column charts display aggregations for categorical data. See Chapter 1 for more information.

15. A. Columnstore indexes compress data in a column-wise format that is ideal for large-scale scans of data that is done when performing aggregations. See Chapter 2 for more information.

16. C. Virtual machines are an Infrastructure as a Service (IaaS) offering in Azure. These allow organizations to offload the management of their hardware infrastructure to Azure while providing a mirror image of how the service was hosted in their on-premises environment. The SQL Server on an Azure VM option allows organizations the ability to have full control over the OS and database engine while not needing to host any of the hardware. See Chapter 2 for more information.

17. B. Azure SQL Database is a fully managed PaaS relational database in Azure. The hardware, OS, and database engine are completely managed by Microsoft, allowing developers to focus on application development instead of needing to spend time implementing database features such as backup management, high availability, disaster recovery, and advanced threat protection. See Chapter 2 for more information.

18. A. Azure SQL Database Hyperscale is used for very large OLTP databases (>4 TB) and can automatically scale storage and compute. It uses a scale-out architecture to store data on filegroups across multiple nodes. See Chapter 2 for more information.

19. C. Server-level IP firewall rules for Azure SQL Database opens port 1433 for all databases on a logical server to a specified IP address. See Chapter 2 for more information.

20. B. The Data Migration Assistant can be used to detect compatibility issues between versions of SQL Server and make recommendations on how to address them. The Azure Database Migration Service uses the Data Migration Assistant to assess an on-premises SQL Server database's compatibility with the different versions of Azure SQL. See Chapter 2 for more information.

21. D. Resource deployments in Azure can be scripted out and automated with Azure PowerShell, Azure CLI, and Infrastructure as Code templates such as Azure Resource Manager templates. See Chapter 2 for more information.

22. B. Azure creates a full database backup once a week, while creating differential backups every 12 to 24 hours and transaction log backups every 5 to 10 minutes. See Chapter 2 for more information.

23. A. Data Manipulation Language (DML) commands are used to interact with data stored in a database. DML commands can be used to retrieve and aggregate data for analysis, insert new rows, or edit existing rows. See Chapter 2 for more information.

24. C. Dynamic data masking obfuscates sensitive data in a database table. It allows users to specify which columns to mask with one of several available masking patterns. See Chapter 2 for more information.

25. D. PostgreSQL, MySQL, and MariaDB are available on Azure as PaaS offerings. See Chapter 2 for more information.

26. A. Read Committed transactions issue locks on involved data at the time of data modification to prevent other transactions from reading dirty data. However, data can be modified by other transactions, which can result in non-repeatable or phantom reads. See Chapter 2 for more information.

27. D. Fact tables store measurable observations or events such as sales totals and inventory. See Chapter 2 for more information.

28. B. The recommended configuration for SQL Server storage is to place data, log, and tempdb files on separate drives. See Chapter 2 for more information.

29. D. Nonrepeatable reads occur when a transaction reads the same row several times and returns different data each time. See Chapter 2 for more information.

30. C. Left outer joins retrieve all data from the table on the left side of the join condition and data that meets the join condition from the table on the right. See Chapter 2 for more information.

31. A. Graph databases are specialized databases that focus on storing the relationship between data entities. Applications reading data from graph databases traverse the network of entities, analyzing their relationships. See Chapter 3 for more information.

32. C. Unlike key-value stores, documents can be queried by both their key and different data values. See Chapter 3 for more information.

33. D. Azure Cosmos DB Core (SQL) API is the native document database API for Azure Cosmos DB. It stores data in a JSON format, allowing documents storing transactions to maintain different schemas. Azure Cosmos DB can be globally distributed to multiple regions around the world, even allowing users to set one or more of the replicated regions to allow write operations. See Chapter 3 for more information.

34. B. Azure Table storage only supports one additional replica, which can optionally support read-only workloads. The Azure Cosmos DB Table API supports multi-region replication and supports both read-only and read-write replicas. See Chapter 3 for more information.

35. B. Request Units (RUs) are units of compute resources that are used to measure the throughput required to read and write data in Azure Cosmos DB. See Chapter 3 for more information.

36. D. Azure Cosmos DB provides primary and secondary keys for read-write and read-only access. This allows users to regenerate and rotate keys without requiring any downtime. See Chapter 3 for more information.

37. C. Strong consistency guarantees that reads will return the most recent version. This is at the expense of write performance as all application connections will be paused until a transaction is fully synchronized with every participating region. See Chapter 3 for more information.

38. A. Partition keys are data fields that are used to distribute data into logical partitions. Logical partitions are then distributed to physical storage partitions. See Chapter 3 for more information.

39. A. A private endpoint is a network interface that uses a private IP address from a virtual network. You can attach a private endpoint to a PaaS technology, such as Azure Cosmos DB, to isolate it in a virtual network. See Chapter 3 for more information.

40. C. Object storage is used to store large volumes of data in binary and text format. This can include videos, images, audio files, and metadata that is saved in text format. See Chapter 4 for more information.

41. B. Azure Files is a fully managed file share service in the Azure Storage suite of services. It is globally redundant and can be accessed using SMB or NFS protocols. See Chapter 4 for more information.

42. D. Transaction optimized, hot, and cool access tiers are available for file shares hosted on a standard Azure storage account. See Chapter 4 for more information.

43. A. Storage accounts allow users to organize their Blob storage data in container objects. See Chapter 4 for more information.

44. C. Azure Data Lake Gen2 (ADLS) uses a hierarchical namespace to organize data in a way that optimizes data access. Using the Azure Blob Filesystem (ABFS) driver allows Apache Hadoop to easily interact with ADLS. See Chapter 4 for more information.

45. D. Azure Data Lake Storage Gen2 (ADLS) implements an access control model that supports role-based access control (RBAC) and POSIX-like access control lists (ACLs). See Chapter 4 for more information.

46. D. GRS and GZRS are both valid disaster recovery options because they both replicate data to a secondary Azure region. See Chapter 4 for more information.

47. A. A single storage account can host multiple blob containers, file shares, tables, and queues. See Chapter 4 for more information.

48. B. Azure AD identities assigned the Storage Blob Data Contributor RBAC role are able to read, write, and delete blob containers and data. The Storage Blob Data Owner role also grants these rights, but it provides additional management access as well. See Chapter 4 for more information.

49. C. Azure Storage Explorer is a stand-alone desktop application that can be used to manage Azure Storage resources and data. See Chapter 4 for more information.

50. D. Azure HDInsight is a managed, open-source analytics service in Azure that can be used to deploy distributed clusters for Apache Hadoop, Apache Spark, Apache Interactive Query/LLAP, Apache Kafka, Apache Storm, and Apache HBase. See Chapter 5 for more information.

51. B. Spark executors are installed on every worker node and are assigned tasks from the Spark driver. The executor is then responsible for processing the task it is assigned. See Chapter 5 for more information.

52. D. Azure Databricks is a unified analytics platform that offers an optimized Spark runtime for big data batch and stream processing workflows. It uses a distributed file system called the Databricks File System (DBFS), similar to HDFS, to persist data after a Databricks cluster is terminated so that it is not lost. Through its interactive notebook environment, developers can analyze data with SQL, Python, R, Scala, or Java. See Chapter 5 for more information.

53. A. The cost of an Azure Databricks cluster can be broken down into two main components: Azure VMs and Databricks Units (DBUs). See Chapter 5 for more information.

54. B. The standard cluster mode is optimized for single-user clusters that run batch or stream processing jobs. It is ideal for processing large datasets at scale. See Chapter 5 for more information.

55. C. Azure Synapse Analytics has several categories of analytics pools, including dedicated and serverless SQL pools, Data Explorer pools, and Apache Spark pools. See Chapter 5 for more information.

56. A. Clustered columnstore indexes (CCIs) organize tables into a columnstore format, compressing data into rowgroups. This is ideal for analytical queries that aggregate large amounts of data. However, CCIs will not compress data until there are more than 60 million rows in a table (1 million in an SMP database like Azure SQL Database). For this reason, adding a CCI to a large fact table will optimize analytical queries that scan the table. See Chapter 5 for more information.

57. A. Datasets represent data structures within data stores, such as a table or a set of files. Datasets use a data store's connection information that is defined as a linked service to connect to the data store. See Chapter 5 for more information.

58. B. Integration runtimes provide the compute infrastructure where pipelines and pipeline activities either run or get triggered from. See Chapter 5 for more information.

59. C. Data transformation activities, such as Azure Databricks notebooks and Azure HDInsight Hive queries, perform transformation operations on the data. See Chapter 5 for more information.

60. B. The COPY command offers the most flexibility for high-throughput data ingestion into an Azure Synapse Analytics dedicated SQL pool. See Chapter 5 for more information.

61. D. External tables are vital components of data virtualization techniques such as PolyBase and logical data warehouses as they are used to read data from files in Azure Storage without having to create an additional copy of the data. See Chapter 5 for more information.

62. D. Defining external tables involves more than the external table definition. It also requires the connection to the data source and the format of the external data to be predefined. See Chapter 5 for more information.

63. A. Power BI Report Builder is a free Windows desktop application that is used to create traditional paginated reports. See Chapter 6 for more information.

64. B. While Power BI can establish a live connection with an Azure SQL Database through the DirectQuery connectivity type, the live connection connectivity type is exclusive to data stores that use the same storage engine as Power BI, such as Azure Analysis Services and SQL Server Analysis Services. See Chapter 6 for more information.

65. B. The Data Analysis Expression (DAX) formula language can be used to create custom calculations such as measures, calculated columns, and calculated tables in a Power BI data model. See Chapter 6 for more information.

66. D. A Power BI dashboard provides a clear, summarized view that allows them to monitor their business and see the most important metrics without having to dig through a mountain of reports. See Chapter 6 for more information.

67. B. Power BI Q&A is a tool in the Power BI service that allows users to explore their data with natural language queries. The visuals that are generated by Q&A can be added to a Power BI dashboard. See Chapter 6 for more information.

Chapter 1

Core Data Concepts

MICROSOFT EXAM OBJECTIVES COVERED IN THIS CHAPTER:

✓ **Describe types of core data workloads.**

- Describe batch data.
- Describe streaming data.
- Describe the difference between batch and streaming data.
- Describe the characteristics of relational data.

✓ **Describe data analytics core concepts.**

- Describe data visualization (e.g., visualization, reporting, business intelligence (BI).
- Describe basic chart types such as bar charts and pie charts.
- Describe analytics techniques (e.g., descriptive, diagnostic, predictive, prescriptive, cognitive).
- Describe ELT and ETL processing.
- Describe the concepts of data processing.

This chapter will focus on the first objective for the Microsoft Azure DP-900 exam certification: describe core data concepts. We will discuss the different types of data and how they are stored, data processing techniques, and categories of data analytics. Understanding the concepts covered in this chapter is critical to designing the most appropriate modern data solution in Azure for any business problem.

Describe Types of Core Data Workloads

The volume of data that the world has generated has exploded in recent years. Zettabytes worth of data is created every year, the variety of which is seemingly endless. Competing in a rapidly changing world requires companies to utilize massive amounts of data that they have only recently been exposed to. What's more is that with the use of edge devices that allow *Internet of Things (IoT)* data to seamlessly move between the cloud and local devices, companies can make valuable data-driven decisions in real time.

It is imperative that organizations leverage data when making critical business decisions. But how do they turn raw data into usable information? How do they decide what is valuable and what is noise? With the power of cloud computing and storage costs growing cheaper and cheaper every year, it's easy for companies to store all the data at their disposal and build creative solutions that combine a multitude of different design patterns. For example, modern data storage and computing techniques allow sports franchises to create more sophisticated training programs by combining traditional statistical information with real-time data captured from sensors that measure features such as speed and agility. E-commerce companies leverage click-stream data to track a user's activity while on their website, allowing them to build custom experiences for customers to reduce customer churn.

The exponential growth in data and the number of sources organizations can leverage to make decisions have put an increased focus on making the right solution design decisions. Deciding on the most optimal data store for the different types of data involved and the most optimal analytical pattern for processing data can make or break a project before it ever gets started. Ultimately, there are four key questions that need to be answered when making design decisions for a data-driven solution:

- What *value* will the data powering the solution provide?

- How large is the *volume* of data involved?

- What is the *variety* of the data included in the solution?

- What is the *velocity* of the data that will be ingested in the target platform?

Data Value

The first question that needs to be answered when designing a data-driven solution is, what value will be gained by processing, storing, and analyzing potential data sources? What answers are the business trying to solve? While it is true that having more data can provide new and more fine-grained insights, it can sometimes come at a cost. Organizations must give considerable thought to what data is valuable and what data is not, all the while trying to minimize the amount of time spent in the decision-making process.

Designing a data-driven solution requires everyone involved to focus on deriving value from every process in the solution. This means that data architects must know the business goal of the solution from the beginning. Is this going to be a transactional database that provides the backend for a business's e-commerce site? Will it be a data warehouse aggregating data from multiple source systems to provide a holistic view of a business's performance? Or will the data store need to be able to ingest bursts of IoT data for real-time analytics? To answer these questions, we first need to understand the different types of data stores and the scenarios for which each one is best suited.

Relational Databases

Relational databases organize data into tables that can be linked based on data common to each other. The relationship between tables allows users to easily query multiple tables in the same query by joining columns from multiple tables together. Database tables store data as rows and are organized into a set number of columns. Columns are defined by specific data types such as integer or string so that only specific types of data from new or modified rows of data is accepted. For example, if you have a database table with a name column that only accepts string values, then trying to insert a number into that column will fail. Relational databases allow designers to go a step forward and design constraints on columns so that data must meet predefined criteria. This predefined structure that data in relational databases must adhere to is called a schema and is fundamental to how users query relational data.

Users querying a relational database use a version of the *Structured Query Language (SQL)* to issue queries to the database. Depending on the vendor, most relational database management systems (RDBMSs) have their own variation of SQL that are based on the ANSI standardized version of SQL. For example, the Microsoft suite of RDBMSs (e.g., SQL Server, Azure SQL Database, Azure SQL Managed Instance) can be interacted with using Transact SQL (T-SQL). T-SQL provides four flavors of commands for query development:

- *Data Manipulation Language (DML)* commands are used to manipulate data in database tables. DML commands include SELECT, INSERT, UPDATE, and DELETE.
- *Data Definition Language (DDL)* commands are used to define RDBMS objects such as databases, tables, views, stored procedures, and triggers. DDL commands include CREATE, ALTER, and DROP.
- *Data Control Language (DCL)* commands are used to manage permissions and access control for users in a database. DCL commands include GRANT, REVOKE, and DENY.
- *Transaction Control Language (TCL)* commands are used to explicitly manage and control transaction execution to ensure that a specific transaction is successfully done without violating database integrity. TCL commands include BEGIN TRANSACTION, COMMIT TRANSACTION, and ROLLBACK TRANSACTION.

Relational database design considerations largely depend on what the database will be supporting. A database that's supporting a business's e-commerce site and needs to log every transaction made by a customer has vastly different requirements than a database that supports a report application. While there are many different design patterns for data-driven solutions, most of them fall into one of two broad categories: transactional processing systems or analytical systems.

Transactional Processing Systems

Transactional processing systems, also known as online transaction processing (OLTP) systems, are used to capture the business transactions that support the day-to-day operations of an organization. Transactions can include retail purchases logged to point-of-sale (PoS) systems as purchases are made, orders purchased through e-commerce platforms, or even ticket scans at a sport or concert venue. Transactions do not only consist of newly inserted data, but also include deletes and updates of data. While each transaction is a small and unique measurement of work, OLTP systems need to be able to handle millions of transactions a day. This requires OLTP systems to be designed in a way that optimizes how fast transactions are applied to them. To support this requirement, OLTP data stored in relational databases is split into small chunks and stored in separate database tables. Splitting data into multiple tables allows the system to only update the tables that need to be updated, all the while maintaining relationships to data in tables that are associated but not updated with that transaction. This is commonly referred to as normalizing data.

Transactional databases must adhere to *ACID properties* (atomicity, consistency, isolation, durability) to ensure that each transaction is reliable. These properties can be defined as follows:

- Atomicity guarantees that each transaction is treated as a single unit of work that either succeeds completely or fails completely. If any part of an insert, delete, or update operation in a transaction fails, the entire transaction fails and the database is left unchanged.

- Consistency ensures that data affected by a transaction is valid according to all predefined rules. Inserting or altering data will only be successful if it maintains the appropriate predefined data types and constraints of the affected columns.

- Isolation ensures that concurrent transactions do not affect one another.

- Durability guarantees that once a transaction has been committed, it will remain committed even if there is a system failure.

Adhering to ACID properties is critical for OLTP systems that support many concurrent users reading and writing from them at the same time. They need to be able to process transactions in isolation, all the while ensuring that users querying data can retrieve a consistent view of data even as it is being altered. Many RDBMSs implement relational consistency and isolation by applying locks to data when it is updated. A lock prevents other processes from reading data until the lock is released, and it is only released when the transaction is committed or is rolled back. Extensive locks caused by long-running queries can lead to poor query performance. To mitigate the issues caused by table locks, SQL Server and Azure SQL Database give database administrators (DBAs) the ability to specify the level of isolation to which one transaction must be isolated from data modifications made by other transactions. Isolation levels determine the acceptance rate for queries returning data that has not been committed by an insert, update, or delete for faster return times. More on isolation levels can be found in Chapter 2, "Relational Databases in Azure."

Analytical Systems

Analytical systems are designed to support business users who need to make informed business decisions from large amounts of data. For example, decisions made from analytical systems can drive the placement of an item in a retail store or an e-commerce site based on an item's seasonal popularity. Most analytical systems ingest data from multiple sources, such as OLTP systems, and perform transformations that leverage business rules that cleanse and aggregate data so that it is useful for decision making. Decision makers usually don't need all the details of a specific transaction, so data architects will design analytical systems that use data from OLTP systems to only include relevant information. Analytical systems are also denormalized so that users querying them are not burdened by having to develop complex queries that join multiple tables together. Analytical systems such as data warehouses are updated by either processing batches of data at the same time or aggregating data in real time from sources that can stream data. These different data-processing techniques are discussed further in the section "Data Velocity" later in this chapter.

The two types of analytical systems are *data warehouses* and *online analytical processing (OLAP)* systems. Data warehouses serve as the single source of truth for different functional areas within a business. Good data warehouses consolidate multiple disparate data sources and are optimized for reading data, making them perfect data sources for reporting applications. Data warehouses are typically relational data stores such as Azure Synapse Analytics dedicated SQL pool or Azure SQL Database. OLAP models are typically business intelligence (BI) models that apply business logic and pre-aggregations to data warehouse data to create a layer of abstraction between the data warehouse and a reporting platform. Azure Analysis Services and Power BI tabular models are examples of OLAP technologies that can create these types of data models.

> Something important to note is that data warehouses and OLAP models are not dependent on one another. While you can build an OLAP model from a data warehouse, reports can be built directly from data warehouse data, and OLAP models can be built from data sources other than a data warehouse. More on data warehouses and OLAP models in Chapter 5, "Modern Data Warehouses in Azure."

Typical data warehouses and OLAP tabular models will store data using a star schema. Star schemas make data easy to report against because of the way data is denormalized. Measurements and metrics are consolidated in fact tables. They are connected to tables that contain descriptive attributes for each measurement, also known as dimension tables. For example, an Internet sales fact table can be associated to multiple dimension tables, that include a date dimension that provides granular information on the date a purchase was made, a customer dimension that includes specific information about the customer that made the purchase, and a product dimension that describes the different attributes of the product that was sold. The inherent simplicity in a star schema's design allows analysts to easily create aggregations on fact tables while joining the necessary dimension tables to answer different business questions about the data.

Nonrelational Data Stores

There is a wide variety of data that doesn't fit in a relational model. Nonrelational data, also known as NoSQL (Not Only SQL), refers to data that doesn't fit into a relational model. Some solutions require more flexible data models than that of a relational database and can afford to trade ACID compliancy for speed and horizontal scale. NoSQL databases can handle volatile data that is written and read quickly better than relational databases because they don't force the data to conform to a specific structure.

Binary objects such as images, videos, and PDFs are also considered nonrelational data. While relational databases such as SQL Server can store files such as the PDF copy of this book using features such as FILESTREAM, it is not the most optimal solution for file storage. Object stores are optimized for binary file storage and can be easily accessed to serve these files to applications. They can also be used to create highly scalable data lake ecosystems for big data processing solutions.

NoSQL Databases

NoSQL databases do not impose a schema on data they store, allowing data to maintain its natural format as it is ingested. In fact, one of the primary benefits is that users who are designing a NoSQL database solution do not need to define the schema ahead of time. This flexibility makes NoSQL databases the ideal choice for solutions that require millisecond response times and need to be able to scale rapidly. Scenarios where NoSQL databases are potentially better options than relational databases include ingesting and analyzing bursts of data from IoT sensors, storing product catalog data for an e-commerce site's web search functionality, and storing user-generated content for web, mobile, and social media applications.

Instead of storing data as rows in a table as in a relational database, data is stored as entities in collections or containers. Unlike rows in a table, entities in the same collection can have a different set of fields. This flexibility allows for several different implementations of NoSQL databases depending on the solution requirements. Generally, these implementations fall into the following four categories:

- *Key-value stores* are the simplest types of NoSQL database for inserting and querying data (see Figure 1.1). Each piece of data contains a key and a value. The key serves as a unique identifier for the piece of data, and the value contains the data. Values can be scalar values or complex structures such as a JSON array. When applications are querying data from key-value stores, they issue queries that specify the keys to retrieve the values. Figure 1.1 is an example of a phone directory that stores one or more phone numbers per person in a key-value store. Examples of key-value stores include Python dictionary objects, Azure Table storage, and the Azure Cosmos DB Table API.

FIGURE 1.1　Key-value store

Key	Value
Pete	{(012) 123-4567}
Jim	{(987) 765-4321}
Kate	{(654) 879-1234, (123) 456-7890}

- *Document databases* are the most common types of NoSQL databases (see Figure 1.2). Pieces of data are defined as documents and are typically stored in JSON, XML, YAML, or BSON format. Each document includes a document key that serves as a unique identifier for management and query lookups. Unlike a key-value store that can only retrieve data by doing a search on the key, applications querying a document database can perform lookups on a document's key and/or one or more of its fields to retrieve specific sets of data. This feature makes document databases a better option for applications that need to be more selective. Figure 1.2 illustrates an example of customer orders stored as documents in a document database. Examples of document databases include MongoDB and the Azure Cosmos DB Core (SQL) API.

FIGURE 1.2　Document database

Key	Document

1001	{
	   "CustomerID": 101,
	   "OrderItems":[
	     {
	       "ProductID": 500,
	       "Quantity": 2,
	       "Cost": 350
	     },
	     {
	       "ProductID": 505,
	       "Quantity": 1,
	       "Cost": 50
	     }],
	   "OrderDate":"2021-07-14"
	 }

1002	{
	   "CustomerID": 102,
	   "OrderItems":[
	     {
	       "ProductID": 450,
	       "Quantity": 5,
	       "Cost": 650
	     }],
	   "OrderDate":"2021-07-15"
	 }

- *Columnar databases* appear like relational databases conceptually (see Figure 1.3). They organize data into rows and columns but denormalize data so that it is divided into multiple column families. Each column family holds a set of columns that are logically related. Figure 1.3 is an example of a bicycle company's product information stored in a columnar format. An example of a columnar database is the Azure Cosmos DB Cassandra API.

FIGURE 1.3   Columnar database

Row Key	Column Families	
ProductKey	**ProductInfo**	**Quantity Info**
500	Category: Bicycle Subcategory: Mountain Bike Color: Matte Black UnitPrice: 700	QuantityOnHand: 10 QuantitySold: 12 ProductRating: 8.2
505	Category: Helmet Subcategory: Standard Helmet Color: Orange UnitPrice: 30	QuantityOnHand: 30 QuantitySold: 40 ProductRating: 9.3

- *Graph databases* store data as entities and focus on the relationship that these entities have with each other (see Figure 1.4). Entities are defined as nodes, while the relationships between them are defined as edges. Applications querying a graph database do so by traversing the network of nodes and edges, analyzing the relationships between entities. While relational databases can accomplish similar goals, large graph databases can perform very traverse relationships very quickly bypassing the need to perform multiple join operations on many tables. Figure 1.4 illustrates an example of a graph database that stores an organization's personnel chart. The entities represent different job titles and departments, while the edges represent how each entity is related. Examples of graph databases include Neo4j and the Azure Cosmos DB Gremlin API.

FIGURE 1.4   Graph database

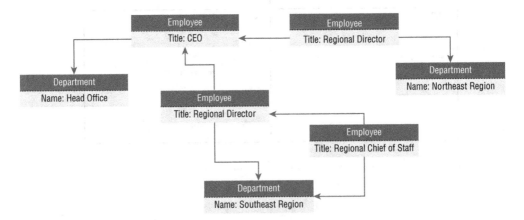

Chapter 3, "Nonrelational Databases in Azure," describes each of the Azure NoSQL Database options in further detail.

Object Storage

Object data stores such as Azure storage accounts store huge volumes of data in text and binary format. You can think of a storage account as being like a shared folder on an organization's local network. Unlike local file shares, storage accounts are highly scalable and allow organizations the freedom of being able to add whatever data they want without needing to worry about adding hardware. Azure-based solutions that rely on data stored in files leverage Azure storage accounts in some form, as in the following scenarios:

- Storing images or videos that are analyzed by deep learning models or that are served to a website
- Storing files such as JSON, Avro, Parquet, CSV, or TSV that are used for distributed processing in big data solutions
- Storing data for backup and restore, disaster recovery, and archiving
- Storing telemetry information as log files that can be used for near real-time analysis

Storage accounts can service a wide variety of object store use cases. Depending on the scenario, you may decide to use one of the following storage account services to store binary objects:

- *Azure Blob Storage* is the most common service for object storage in Azure. Solutions that require analysis, from images or videos, backup management, or files used for distributed processing solutions, can be stored in Blob Storage. It can store exabytes worth of data and offers different access tiers to store data in the most cost-effective manner.
- *Azure Data Lake Storage Gen2*, also known as ADLS, is a set of capabilities that are built on top of Blob Storage but specifically for distributed analytics solutions. The key feature of ADLS that allows for quick and efficient data access is its *hierarchical namespace*. Hierarchical namespaces organize files into a hierarchy of directories that enable you to store data that is raw, cleansed, and aggregated without having to sacrifice one copy for the next.
- *Azure Files* is a fully managed file share solution in Azure. File shares are accessible via the Server Message Block (SMB) protocol or the Network File System (NFS) protocol. They can be mounted concurrently by cloud or on-premises systems.

Chapter 4, "File, Object, and Data Lake Storage," describes the different Azure storage accounts services in detail and when each should be used.

Data Volume

Data volume refers to the amount of data that needs to be analyzed and processed. Access to larger datasets can provide just as many headaches as it does clarity. Large datasets that are stored in databases that use bad design practices or queried by poorly written queries can cause applications to perform so badly that they come to a screeching halt. Traditional relational databases such as SQL Server or Azure SQL Database can be used for large data warehouses if they are leveraging a well-thought-out data model design with appropriate indexes and partitions, and applications are reading data with well-written queries. However, there is a limit to the amount of data that traditional database technologies and processing patterns can handle.

It is critical that the right data storage technologies and processing patterns are chosen in the design phase, especially if the datasets are going to be large in volume. Even the most properly tuned relational databases will begin to perform poorly after a certain size threshold. *Symmetric multiprocessing*, or SMP, systems such as SQL Server and Azure SQL Database are characterized by a single instance of an RDBMS that shares all the resources (CPU, memory, and disk). SMP systems can scale up to serve gigabytes (GB) and terabytes (TB) worth of data but hit a wall when the resource limits are hit. *Massively parallel processing*, or MPP, systems such as Azure Synapse Analytics dedicated SQL pool are designed to process large datasets. MPP systems are designed to be distributed parallel processing solutions, meaning they are not only able to scale up by adding more compute resources but can also scale out by adding more nodes to the system.

MPP databases can be less performant and more costly than an SMP database when the dataset size is small. Consider using an SMP database if the data warehouse is never going to be more than 1TB and queries perform more lookups than large-scale aggregations.

You can think of data processing differences between SMP and MPP systems as how a grocery store goes about restocking its shelves. One employee of a store can efficiently restock shelves in a single aisle in a relatively short amount of time. However, restocking every aisle in a large store that has many aisles can take hours or even days if there is only one employee available for the task. In most cases, floor managers at a store will assign aisles to different employees. This drastically reduces the amount of time it takes to restock an entire store since there are many employees restocking shelves in parallel. This is how MPP systems such as Azure Synapse Analytics, Azure HDInsight, and Azure Databricks operate. The underlying architecture includes a driver/control node that divides large processing tasks into multiple operations and assigns them to different worker/compute node. Data is stored in a distributed file system that is split into chunks to be processed by the different worker nodes.

The ability to separate compute and storage allows MPP systems to scale very quickly. Adding nodes to an Azure Synapse Analytics dedicated SQL pool or an Azure Databricks cluster can happen without having to repartition data. Data is instead persisted in a distributed file system that shards it into partitions or distributions to optimize the performance of the system. Cloud-based object storage such as Azure Blob Storage or Azure Data Lake Storage Gen2 are generally used for the basis of distributed file systems. These technologies are highly scalable by design, making it easy to store massive amounts of data used by MPP systems.

While technologies such as Azure Synapse Analytics and Azure Databricks are ideal for modern data warehouse and data processing needs, they aren't designed to store highly transactional data. Distributed file systems are great for storing data that will be used to create aggregated analysis but are not optimized for transactional data that is inserted or optimized one at a time. In cases where large amounts of transactional data, such as many thousands of transactions per second, need to be stored and globally distributed, it can be beneficial to use a NoSQL database such as Azure Cosmos DB to store transactional data. Transactional systems that use NoSQL databases have relaxed ACID properties in favor of schema flexibility and horizontal scale across multiple nodes. This provides similar benefits to MPP systems in that there are more compute resources available for processing and storage. The trade-off here is that the process of maintaining transaction consistency will fall on application developers since NoSQL databases do not strictly follow ACID properties.

Data Variety

Data variety refers to the types of data involved. While you may think of data as just being entries in a spreadsheet, it can come in many different forms. Transactions captured from PoS systems, events generated from sensors, and even pictures can generate valuable insights that businesses can use to make decisions. Ultimately, data falls into three categories: structured, semi-structured, and unstructured.

Structured Data

Structured data can be defined as tabular data that is made up of rows and columns. Data in an Excel spreadsheet or a CSV file is known to be structured, as is data in a relational database such as SQL Server, Oracle, or MySQL. Structured data fits a well-defined schema, which means that every row in a table will have the same number of columns even if one or more of those columns do not have any values in the row. The process of every row in a structured dataset having the same number of columns is known as schema integrity. This is what gives users the ability to create relationships between tables in a relational database. More on this later in this chapter and in Chapter 2.

While schema integrity allows relational data to be easily queried and analyzed, it forces data to follow a rigid structure. This rigid structure forces users to consider how volatile their data will be over time. Considerations for how your schema will evolve over time or the differences between source data's schema and your target solution will force you to develop sophisticated data pipelines to ensure that this volatility does not negatively impact your solution.

Figure 1.5 illustrates an example of structured data. The data in the figure is product information from the publicly available AdventureWorks2019 database.

FIGURE 1.5   Structured data

	ProductID	Name	ProductNumber	MakeFlag	FinishedGoodsFlag	Color	SafetyStockLevel	ReorderPoint	StandardCost	ListPrice	Size
1	680	HL Road Frame - Black, 58	FR-R92B-58	1	1	Black	500	375	1059.31	1431.50	58
2	706	HL Road Frame - Red, 58	FR-R92R-58	1	1	Red	500	375	1059.31	1431.50	58
3	717	HL Road Frame - Red, 62	FR-R92R-62	1	1	Red	500	375	868.6342	1431.50	62
4	718	HL Road Frame - Red, 44	FR-R92R-44	1	1	Red	500	375	868.6342	1431.50	44
5	719	HL Road Frame - Red, 48	FR-R92R-48	1	1	Red	500	375	868.6342	1431.50	48
6	720	HL Road Frame - Red, 52	FR-R92R-52	1	1	Red	500	375	868.6342	1431.50	52
7	721	HL Road Frame - Red, 56	FR-R92R-56	1	1	Red	500	375	868.6342	1431.50	56
8	722	LL Road Frame - Black, 58	FR-R38B-58	1	1	Black	500	375	204.6251	337.22	58
9	723	LL Road Frame - Black, 60	FR-R38B-60	1	1	Black	500	375	204.6251	337.22	60
10	724	LL Road Frame - Black, 62	FR-R38B-62	1	1	Black	500	375	204.6251	337.22	62
11	725	LL Road Frame - Red, 44	FR-R38R-44	1	1	Red	500	375	187.1571	337.22	44
12	726	LL Road Frame - Red, 48	FR-R38R-48	1	1	Red	500	375	187.1571	337.22	48
13	727	LL Road Frame - Red, 52	FR-R38R-52	1	1	Red	500	375	187.1571	337.22	52
14	728	LL Road Frame - Red, 58	FR-R38R-58	1	1	Red	500	375	187.1571	337.22	58
15	729	LL Road Frame - Red, 60	FR-R38R-60	1	1	Red	500	375	187.1571	337.22	60
16	730	LL Road Frame - Red, 62	FR-R38R-62	1	1	Red	500	375	187.1571	337.22	62
17	731	ML Road Frame - Red, 44	FR-R72R-44	1	1	Red	500	375	352.1394	594.83	44
18	732	ML Road Frame - Red, 48	FR-R72R-48	1	1	Red	500	375	352.1394	594.83	48
19	733	ML Road Frame - Red, 52	FR-R72R-52	1	1	Red	500	375	352.1394	594.83	52
20	734	ML Road Frame - Red, 58	FR-R72R-58	1	1	Red	500	375	352.1394	594.83	58
21	735	ML Road Frame - Red, 60	FR-R72R-60	1	1	Red	500	375	352.1394	594.83	60

Semi-structured Data

Semi-structured data has some structure to it but no defined schema. This allows data to be written to and read from very quickly since the storage engine does not reorganize the data to meet a rigid format. While the lack of a defined schema naturally eliminates most of the data volatility concerns that come with structured data, it makes analytical queries more complicated as there isn't a reliable schema to use when creating the query.

The most popular examples of semi-structured datasets are XML and JSON files. JSON specifically is very popular for sharing data via a web API. JSON stores data as objects in arrays, which allows an easy transfer of data. Both XML and JSON formats have somewhat of a structure but are flexible enough that some objects may have more or fewer attributes than others. Because the structure of the data is more fluid than that of a database with a schema, we typically refer to querying semi-structured data as *schema-on-read*. This means that the query definition creates a sort of quasi-schema for the data to fit in. Figure 1.6 demonstrates how JSON can be used to store data for multiple customers while including different fields for each customer.

There are multiple ways that we can store semi-structured data, varying from NoSQL databases such as Azure Cosmos DB (see Chapter 3) to files in an Azure storage account (see Chapter 4). Relational databases such as SQL Server, Azure SQL Database, and Azure Synapse Analytics can also handle semi-structured data with the native JSON and XML data types. While this creates a convenient way for data practitioners to manage structured and semi-structured data in the same location, it is recommended to limit the amount of semi-structured data you store in a relational database to very little or none.

Semi-structured data can also be stored in other types of NoSQL data stores, such as key-value stores, columnar databases, and graph databases.

FIGURE 1.6   JSON example

```json
{
    "Customers":[
    {
        "CustomerID": "1",
        "Name": {
            "first": "John",
            "middle":"Stephen",
            "last":"Smith"
            },
        "SeasonTicketStatus": "Active",
        "Address": {
            "street": "Main Street",
            "number": "1111",
            "city": "Seattle",
            "state": "WA",
            "county": "King"
            },
        "SeasonTicketHolderSince": "02/28/2018"
    },
    {

        "ProductID": "2",
        "Name": {
            "title": "Mr.",
            "forename": "Jake",
            "surname":"Parker"
            },
        "SeasonTicketStatus":"NonActive",
        "Address":{
            "street": "A Street",
            "number": "222",
            "city": "London",
            "county": "London",
            "country-region": "UK"
        }
    }
    ]
}
```

Unstructured Data

Unstructured data is used to describe everything that doesn't fit in the structured or semi-structured classification. PDFs, images, videos, and emails are just a few examples of unstructured data. While it is true that unstructured data cannot be queried like structured or semi-structured data, deep learning and artificial intelligence (AI) applications can derive valuable insights from them. For example, applications using image classification can be trained to find specific details in images by comparing them to other images.

Storing unstructured data is easier today than it has ever been. As mentioned previously, Azure Blob Storage allows companies and individuals the ability to store exabytes of data in any format. While this exam does not cover the many applications of unstructured data, it is important to note that unstructured data is becoming more and more vital for companies to gain a competitive edge in today's world.

Data Velocity

The speed at which data is processed is commonly known as data velocity. Requirements for data processing are largely dependent on what business problem or problems we are trying to solve. Raw data such as football player statistics could be stored as raw data until every game for a given week is finished before it is transformed into insightful information. This type of data processing where data is processed in batches is commonly referred to as *batch processing*. We can also process data from sensors located on equipment that a player is wearing in real time so that we can monitor player performance as the game is happening. This type of data processing is called *stream processing*.

Batch Processing

Batch processing is the practice of transforming groups, or batches, of data at a time. This process is also known as processing data at rest. Traditional BI platforms relied on batch processing solutions to create meaningful insights out of their data. Concert venues would leverage technologies such as SQL Server to store batch data and SQL Server Integration Services (SSIS) to transform transactional data on a schedule into information that could be stored in their data warehouse for reporting. Many of the same concepts apply today for batch processing, but cloud computing gives us the scalability to process exponentially more data. Distributed computing paradigms such as Hadoop and Spark allow organizations to use compute from multiple commodity servers to process large amounts of data in batch.

Batch processing is typically done in a process of jobs automated by an orchestration service such as *Azure Data Factory (ADF)*. These jobs can be run one by one, in parallel, or a mix of both depending on the requirements for the solution these jobs are a part of. Automated batch jobs can be run after a certain data threshold is reached in a data store but are more often triggered one of two ways:

- On a recurring schedule—an ADF pipeline running every night at midnight, or on a periodic time interval starting at a specified start time.
- Event/trigger-based—an ADF pipeline running after a file is uploaded to a container in Azure Blob Storage.

It is also critical that batch processing includes error handling logic that acts on a failed job. A common architecture pattern that handles batch processing in Azure is illustrated in Figure 1.7.

FIGURE 1.7 Common architecture for batch processing in Azure

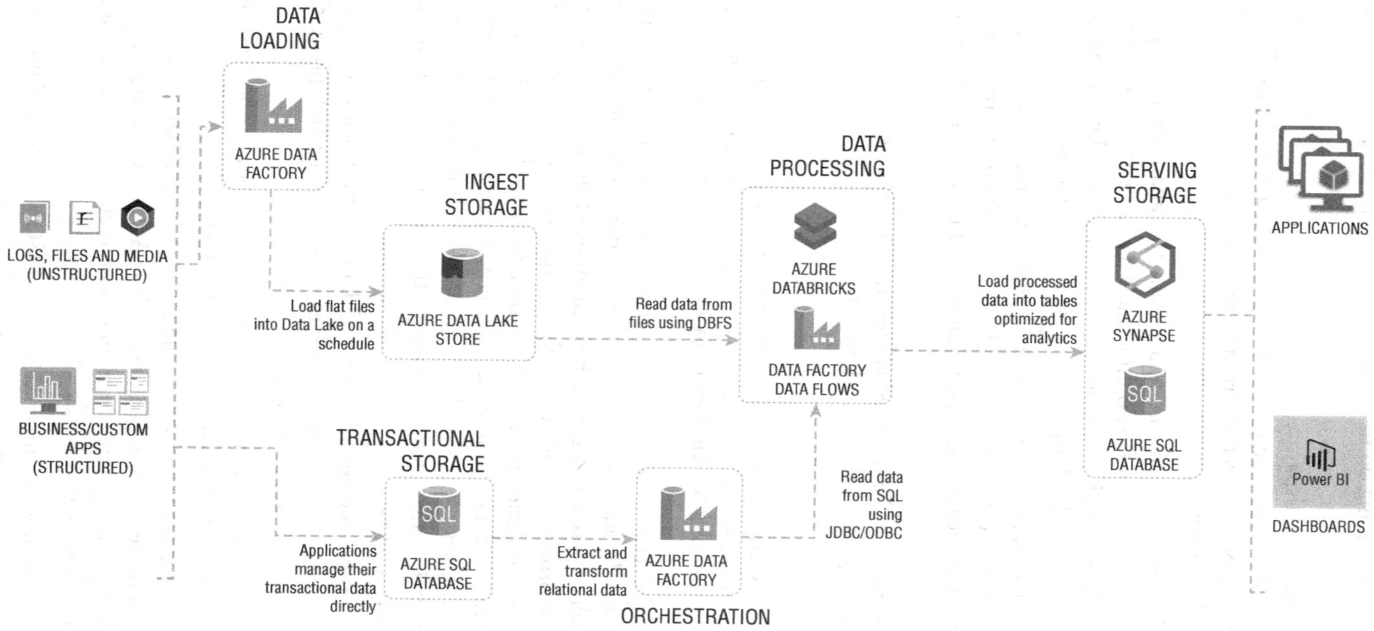

There is quite a bit going on in the diagram in Figure 1.7, so let's break it down step-by-step:

- Data is loaded from disparate source systems into Azure. This could vary from raw files being uploaded to a central data repository such as Azure Data Lake Storage Gen2 (ADLS) to data being collected from business applications in an OLTP database such as Azure SQL Database.

- Raw data is then transformed into a state that is analytics and report ready. Here, we can choose between code-first options such as Azure Databricks to have complete control over how data is transformed or GUI-based technologies such as Azure Data Factory Data Flows. Both options can be executed as activities in an ADF pipeline.

- Aggregated data is loaded into an optimized data store ready for reporting. Depending on the workload and the size of data, an MPP data warehouse such as Azure Synapse Analytics dedicated SQL pool can be used to optimally store data that is used for reporting.

- Data that is ready to be reported is then analyzed through client-native applications or a business intelligence tool such as Power BI.

Azure technologies such as Azure Data Lake Gen 2, Azure Data Factory, Azure Databricks, and Azure Synapse Analytics are discussed in detail in Chapter 5, "Modern Data Warehouses in Azure."

While the architecture in Figure 1.7 is a common pattern for batch processing data, it is by no means the only one. Deciding on the most appropriate technologies and strategies for processing batch data requires exploratory analysis of the data, knowledge of the source data that will be processed, and well-defined requirements for how the data will be used. You will also need to decide on an *extract, transform, and load (ETL)* or an *extract, load, and transform (ELT)* data manipulation pattern, depending on whether your storage and transformation engines are one and the same. The section "Data Processing Techniques" later in this chapter further examines each of these two patterns. Batch processing includes the following advantages:

- Accurately processing large volumes of data at a time. More compute power can be allocated to batch processing, and the time constraint for batch processing usually isn't as critical as it is with stream processing.

- Conveniently scheduling when data is processed. Batch processes can be scheduled whenever, which allows organizations to schedule their batch jobs to run off-peak hours.

- Easily creating complex analytics and aggregations of data. Because the data processed in batches is persisted in data stores such as ADLS, Azure SQL Database, and Azure Synapse Analytics, organizations can return to clean datasets repeatedly for reporting and machine learning purposes.

- Transforming semi-structured data such as JSON or XML data into a structured, schematized format that is ready for analytical queries.

Batch processing includes the following disadvantages:

- Latency between receiving data and being able to analyze it.

- Data that is processed in batch jobs must be ready before the batch can be processed. As mentioned previously, complex error handling checks need to be in place to ensure that problems with data, errors, or failed activities do not bring the entire process down.

Stream Processing

Instead of processing groups of data at scheduled intervals as you would with batch processing, stream processing performs actions on data in real time as it is generated. The proliferation of connected applications and IoT sensor devices in recent years has led to a boom in the amount of data sources that can stream data. Organizations that leverage data streams are able to innovate at an on-the-go pace, allowing them to instantly respond to the needs of their customers.

You can think of a stream of data as a continuous flow of data from some source, also known as a message producer. Each piece of data in a stream is often referred to as an event or a message and typically arrives in an unstructured or semi-structured format such as JSON. The following list includes some examples of stream processing:

- An e-commerce company analyzing click-stream data as consumers are browsing the company's website to provide product recommendations in real time

- Fitness trackers streaming heart rate and movement data to a mobile app and providing real-time updates of the wearer's workout efficiency

- Financial institutions tracking stock market changes in real time and automatically making portfolio decisions as stock prices change

- Oil companies monitoring the status of pipelines and drilling equipment

While these examples include the same transformation activities as many batch processes, they have vastly shorter latency requirements.

Stream processing is just one step in designing a real-time data processing solution. The following logical components will need to be considered when designing a real-time solution:

- *Real-time message ingestion*—The architecture must include a way to capture and store real-time messages regardless of the technology that is creating the stream of data. Message brokers such as Azure Event Hubs, Azure IoT Hub, and Apache Kafka are used to ingest millions of events per second from one or many message producers. These technologies will then queue messages before sending them to the next appropriate step in the architecture. Most of the time this will be a processing engine of some type, but some solutions will require sending the raw messages to a long-term storage solution such as Azure Blob Storage or ADLS for future batch analysis.

- *Stream processing*—Stream processing engines are the compute platforms that process, aggregate, and transform data streams. Technologies such as Azure Functions, Azure Stream Analytics, and Azure Databricks Structured Streaming can create time-boxed insights data that is queued in a real-time message broker. These technologies will then write the results to message consumers such as an analytical data store or a reporting tool that can display real-time updates.

- *Analytical data store*—Processed real-time data can be written to databases such as Azure Synapse Analytics, Azure Data Explorer, and Azure Cosmos DB that power analytical applications.

- *Analysis and reporting*—Instead of being written to an analytical data store first, processed real-time data can be published directly from the stream processing engine to report applications like Power BI.

While Azure Stream Analytics typically uses a message broker such as Azure Event Hubs or Azure IoT Hub as an input for data, it can also take static data from Azure Blob Storage or Azure Data Lake Store Gen 2 as an input and process it as a stream to an analytical data store or a reporting tool.

Using these steps, we have the flexibility to choose if we want to process data streams live, on demand, or a combination of both. The "live" approach is the most common method for processing data streams and involves analyzing data continuously as it arrives from a message broker such as Azure Event Hubs. This approach is what allows organizations to create calculations and aggregations against data streams for temporal analysis. Figure 1.8 illustrates this approach with a simple example of an IoT-enabled thermostat streaming temperature data to Azure for analysis.

FIGURE 1.8 Live stream processing

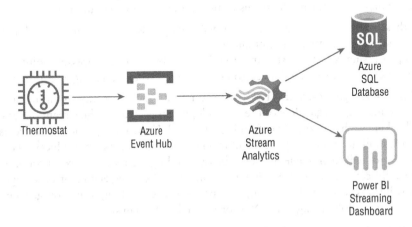

This approach produces a real-time streaming solution that creates temperature analysis on the fly while storing the transformed data in an Azure SQL Database for further analysis such as comparing one month's temperature data to the same month in the previous year.

While most streaming solutions will be designed with the live approach, there are some cases that call for processing stream data in micro-batches. This "on-demand" approach involves persisting incoming data into a data store like ADLS and processing the data when convenient. If the scenario does not require real-time analysis, then this can significantly cut computing costs. Figure 1.9 illustrates an example of this approach. While it is like the solution in Figure 1.8, the on-demand design adds an extra step that stores temperature data in ADLS before Azure Stream Analytics performs any computations on the data and outputs it to Power BI and Azure SQL Database.

FIGURE 1.9   On-demand stream processing

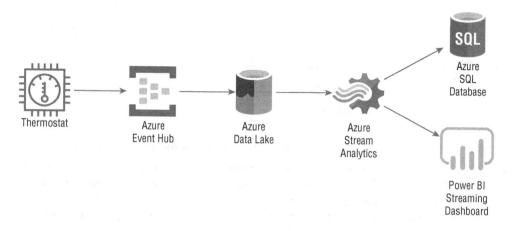

 Azure Stream Analytics can leverage static reference data stored in sources such as ADLS, Azure SQL Database, and Azure Cosmos DB to enrich the streamed dataset. This is true for both live and on-demand approaches.

Solutions such as this demonstrate how technologies that are typically used for batch processing scenarios can be used in stream processing solutions. In the next section, we will discuss how modern design principles can be used to leverage batch and stream processing in the same solution.

Leveraging Batch and Stream Processing Together

Until recently, most organizations were limited to how quickly they could process data by the hardware and network connectivity in their datacenters. They were often limited to the types of queries they could run with real-time data and were often left waiting for hours on stream processing activities to complete. However, the scalability of cloud-based solutions such as those in Azure empower organizations to process data whenever they want. This flexibility has given way to modern architectural designs that creatively analyze batch- and stream-processed data in the same solution. One of the most popular of these design patterns is the *Lambda architecture*. The Lambda architecture is a data processing architecture that separates batch and stream processing operations into a cold path and a hot path. Figure 1.10 illustrates the movement of this pattern.

FIGURE 1.10   Lambda architecture

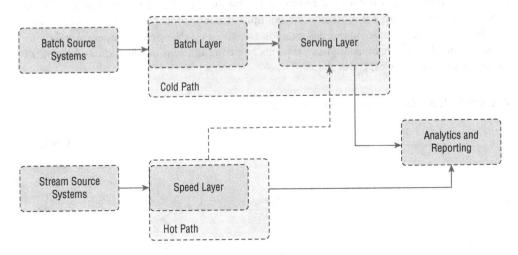

Solutions that use a Lambda architecture create two paths for data processing:

- The *cold path* is where the batch processing operations, also known as the batch layer, occur. Data flowing into this path is not constrained to low latency requirements, allowing for much larger datasets to be processed on a scheduled basis. Once data has been processed in the batch layer, the results are sent to a serving layer (e.g., data warehouse such as Azure Synapse Analytics or Azure SQL Database) for querying.

- The *hot path* is where speed processing operations, also known as the speed layer, occur. Data flowing into this path need to be processed as quickly as possible, at the expense of accuracy. Once processed, data from the speed layer either is sent directly to the analytics/report application for analysis or incrementally updates the serving layer based on the most recent data.

Eventually, data from the hot and cold paths will converge at the analytics/report application. If the application needs to display data in real time, it will acquire it from the hot path. Otherwise, the application will read data from the cold path to display more accurate analysis created from a larger dataset.

One of the core principles of the Lambda architecture is that raw data stored in the batch layer is immutable. New data is always appended to existing data, never overwriting older data. Changes to the value of a particular dataset are stored as a new time-stamped record. This allows for recompilation of computations at any point in time to provide more accurate historical analysis. Azure enables organizations to easily implement this design without needing to purchase and install new hardware. For example, Azure Data Lake Storage Gen2 can store petabytes worth of information, and with its native hierarchical namespaces (think of directories and folders in a file explorer), organizations can create directory trees corresponding to different dates that can store and maintain data that was generated on that date. Organizations are not burdened with scaling existing or installing new storage devices and can instead focus on implementing business logic.

Describe Data Analytics Core Concepts

The process of taking raw data and turning it into useful information is known as data analytics. Companies that invest in sophisticated, well-designed data analytics solutions do so to discover information that helps the overall performance of the organization. Finding new opportunities, identifying weaknesses, and improving customer satisfaction are all results that come from data analytics. This involves building a repeatable solution that collects data from the appropriate source systems, transforms it into dependable information, and serves it in a way that is easy to consume.

One example of an end-to-end data analytics solution is a sports franchise that would like to build a fan engagement solution to improve stadium attendance rates and in-stadium retail sales by retaining more season ticketholders and creating incentive-based programs for different fan groups. The first step to create this solution will be to identify the sources of data that will be most useful to answering questions related to who attends games and what external factors may influence attendance rates. The next step will be to take these disparate sources of data and transform them so that they present a reliable view of the data that can be easily read by consumers who are acting on the data. For example, consumers of the data could be data scientists who develop regression models that predict future stadium attendance or analysts who build reports and dashboards that display in-stadium trends for different fan groups. These actions are then used to create decisions that will enhance ticket sales and operational efficiency during a game.

Data Processing Techniques

The most critical part of a data analytics solution is that the result set is clean, reliable data. Consumers of the data must be able to retrieve the same answer from a question, regardless of how the question is presented to the data model. There cannot be a question of the quality of data being reported on. This is the goal of data processing.

Simply put, data processing is the methodology used to ingest raw data and transform it into one or more informative business models. Data processing solutions will ingest data either in batches or as a stream and can either store the data in its raw form or begin transforming it. Data can undergo several transformations before it is ready to be reported on. Some of the most common transformation activities are as follows:

- Filtering out corrupt, duplicated, or unnecessary data
- Joining data or appending it to other datasets
- Normalizing data to meet a standard nomenclature
- Aggregating data to produce summarizations
- Updating features to a more useful data type

Data processing pipelines must include activities that are repeatable and flexible enough to handle a variety of scenarios. Tools such as ADF, Azure Databricks, and Azure Functions can be used to build processing pipelines that use parameters to produce desired results.

These tools also allow developers to include error handling logic in their processing pipelines to manage how pipelines proceed if processing errors present themselves without bringing the pipeline to a screeching halt.

Cloud-based data processing solutions make it easy to store data after multiple stages of transformations. Storage solutions such as ADLS allow organizations to store massive amounts of data very cheaply in folders designated for raw data that was just ingested, data that has been filtered and normalized, and data that has been summarized and modeled for reporting. This allows data processing solutions to reuse data at any point in time to validate actions taken on the data and produce new analysis from any point in the data's life cycle.

There are two data processing approaches that can be taken when extracting data from source systems, transforming it, and loading the processed information into a data model. These approaches are extract, transform, and load (ETL) and extract, load, and transform (ELT). Choosing between them depends on the dependency between the transformation and storage engines.

Extract, Transform, and Load (ETL)

ETL pipelines process data in a linear fashion with a different step for each phase. They first collect data from different sources, transform the data to remove dirty data and conform to business rules, and load the processed data into a destination data store. This approach has been used in business intelligence (BI) solutions for years and has a wide array of established best practices. Each of the three phases requires an equal amount of attention when being designed. If properly designed and developed, ETL pipelines can process multiple sources of data in parallel to save time. For example, while data from one source is being extracted, a transformation activity could be working on data that has already been received, and a loading process can begin working on writing the transformed data to a destination data store such as a data warehouse. Figure 1.11 illustrates common Azure technologies used in each phase of an ETL workflow.

FIGURE 1.11   ETL workflow

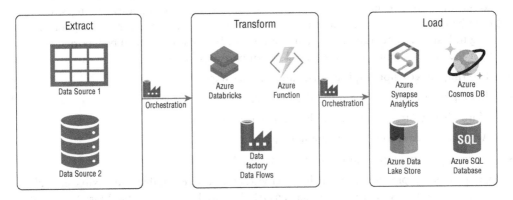

In this example, data is extracted from its source systems and transformed by one or more compute engines such as Azure Databricks, Azure Functions, or Azure Data Factory mapping data flows. After the necessary transformations are completed, the data is loaded into a destination data store such as Azure Synapse Analytics, Azure Cosmos DB, ADLS, or Azure SQL Database to power different types of applications. ADF automates this workflow and controls when each step is executed. Keep in mind that this is a rudimentary example and a typical ETL pipeline may include several staging layers and transformation activities as data is prepared. The following sections describe each phase and how each activity is managed in an ETL workflow.

Extract

The first phase of an ETL process involves extracting data from different source systems and storing it in a consolidated staging layer that is easier for the transformation tools to access. Data sources are typically heterogenous and are represented by a wide variety of data formats. The staging layer can be transient to cut back on storage demands or to eliminate personally identifiable information (PII) that may be present in the source systems or persisted if PII data is not present and storage is not a concern. The staging layer is typically persisted as files in an object store such as Azure Blob Storage or ADLS.

In Azure, tools such as Azure Logic Apps and ADF allow data engineers to drag and drop activities with a graphical user interface (GUI) that copies data from source systems and land them in the staging layer. These activities can be parameterized to dynamically adjust where the raw data is staged. Custom code options such as Azure Databricks and Azure Functions are also available to extract data with languages such as C#, Python, Scala, and JavaScript. The very nature of these custom code options gives data engineers more control over how extracted data is formatted and staged. Regardless of whether data extraction is done with a GUI-based or code-first tool, data extraction activities can be automated to run on a schedule or event driven based on when new data is added to the source system.

Data can be extracted from a source system a few different ways. Incremental extractions involve only pulling source data that has been recently inserted or updated. This can minimize both the time to extract the necessary source data and the time to transform the new raw records but requires additional logic to determine what data has been changed. For systems that are not capable of identifying which records have changed, a full data extraction needs to take place. This requires having a full copy of the source data being extracted. While that can result in an accurate copy of the source data, it could take longer to extract, and subsequent transformation activities will take longer to run.

Transform

The second phase of an ETL process involves transforming the extracted data that is cleansed and meets a set of business requirements. Data is scrubbed of dirty data and prepared so that it fits the schema of the destination data model. Transformations are split into multiple activities for optimal data pipeline performance. This modular approach allows transformation activities to run in parallel and provides an easier method for troubleshooting failed tasks. It also allows data engineers to easily implement additional transformation activities as new business requirements are added.

Depending on the complexity of the transformations, data may be loaded into one or more additional staging layers to serve as intermediary stages for partially transformed data. One example of this is splitting the different phases of data transformations into bronze, silver, and gold staging layers.

- The *bronze* layer represents raw data ingested from different sources in a variety of different formats. Some filtering may have happened to get the data to this stage, but there are minimal transformations to data in the bronze layer.

- The *silver* layer represents a more refined view of the data. Silver layer data is characterized by data that has been scrubbed of dirty records and entities made up of fields from multiple bronze layer datasets using join or merge operations. Data in the silver layer is typically used for machine learning activities since this data is cleansed but not summarized.

- The *gold* layer represents aggregated datasets that are used by reporting applications. Calculations such as weekly sales and month-over-month averages are included in gold layer datasets.

As in the extract phase, transformation activities can be built with GUI-based or code-based technologies. SQL Server Integration Services (SSIS) is an ETL tool that is involved in traditional, on-premises BI solutions. SSIS provides many connectors and transformation activities out of the box that allow developers to build sophisticated data engineering pipelines with a GUI. ADF provides a similar development experience for cloud-based ETL. ADF provides a drag-and-drop experience with several data transformation activities out of the box that can be chained together graphically. The core components of how ADF orchestrates ETL pipelines will be discussed in the section "Control Flows and Data Flows" later in this chapter, but as far as transformations are concerned, ADF can execute transformation activities in four ways:

- *External Compute Services*—ADF can be used to automate the execution of externally hosted transformation activities that are custom coded. These activities can be developed in several different languages and hosted on tools such as Azure Databricks and Azure Functions. Stored procedures hosted on Azure SQL Database or Azure Synapse Analytics can also be invoked by ADF using the Stored Procedure Activity. Transformations that are developed from scratch give engineers more flexibility on how to implement business rules and how to handle different scenarios. ADF allows engineers to pass results from previous steps in a data pipeline as parameters or static predefined parameters to a custom-developed transformation activity so that it can transform data more dynamically.

- *Mapping Data Flows*—ADF gives data engineers the option to build no-code transformation pipelines with the use of mapping data flows. These are very similar to data flow activities in SSIS, giving data engineers the ability to create transformation activities with a GUI. The benefit of a no-code solution like this is that the code performing the transformations and the compute running the code is obfuscated from the data engineer. This can greatly improve operational productivity by allowing engineers to purely focus on implementing business logic instead of optimizing code and compute infrastructure.

Just as with transformation activities that are hosted on external compute services, ADF can pass static parameters or results from previously executed activities as parameters to mapping data flows to dynamically transform data.

- *Power Query*—Previously known as wrangling data flows, ADF allows data engineers to perform no-code transformations on data using Power Query. Power Query is a native component of Power BI and gives analysts the ability to perform transformation activities in a scalable manner. Power Query in ADF enables citizen data analysts to create their own pipelines in ADF without needing to know how to build sophisticated data engineering pipelines.

- *SSIS*—Organizations have been building BI solutions for many years now, and if their solution involved SQL Server, then there is probably an SSIS component involved. Rebuilding existing SSIS with ADF pipelines could be very time consuming if the existing SSIS footprint is sophisticated. This can be a blocker for organizations migrating to Azure. To alleviate these concerns, customers can choose to migrate their SSIS projects to ADF. Data engineers can use the Execute SSIS Package activity in their data pipelines as singleton activities or chained to other ADF native activities. Running an SSIS project in ADF requires the use of a special compute infrastructure known as the Azure-SSIS integration runtime to run them. Chapter 5 will discuss the Azure-SSIS integration runtime and other types of runtimes in further detail.

ADF only supports SSIS packages that are deployed using the project deployment model.

Load

The last phase of an ETL process involves loading the transformed data to a destination data model. This data model can be a data warehouse such as Azure Synapse Analytics or Azure SQL Database, a database such as Azure Cosmos DB that serves highly distributed web applications, or an object store such as ADLS that is used as the golden copy of data for machine learning activities. This phase can also be handled by GUI-based tools such as ADF or custom code solutions.

Data can be loaded to a destination data store using a few different loading patterns. Incremental or differential loads involve adding new data or updating existing data with new values. This can reduce the amount of time it takes to load newly transformed data to the destination data store, allowing consumers of the data to analyze the new data as quickly as possible. Sometimes there is a need to load the destination data store with the entire dataset, requiring an erasure of the existing data store's data. For these use cases, it can be useful to have a staging table in the destination data store to serve as an intermediary between the final transformed copy of the data and production tables being analyzed. Since the staging tables are the tables being truncated, consumers would not experience any downtime from missing data. New records can be added to the production table through a process called partition switching.

Relational database tables that are loaded with data processed by an ETL pipeline must have their schemas prebuilt. Not considering the structure of a table's existing schema can result in load errors stemming from mismatched data types and incorrect column names. This requirement to shape data so that it conforms to a predefined schema is known as *schema-on-write*.

Control Flows and Data Flows

Many ETL tools employ two methods for orchestrating data pipelines. Tasks that ensure the orderly processing of data processing activities are known as *control flows*. Data processing activities are referred to as *data flows* and can be executed in sequence from a control flow. Data engineers that use ADF to orchestrate their data pipelines can use control flows to manage the processing sequence of their data flows.

Control flows are used to enforce the correct processing order of data movement and data transformation activities. Using precedence constraints, control flows can dictate how pipelines proceed if a task succeeds or fails. Subsequent tasks do not begin processing until their predecessors complete. Examples of control flow operations in ADF include Filter, ForEach, If Condition, Set Variable, Until, Web, and Wait activities. ADF also allows engineers to run entire pipelines within a pipeline after an activity has finished with the Execute Pipeline control flow activity. Figure 1.12 shows a simple control flow in ADF, where the Lookup task is retrieving table metadata from a SQL Server database that will be passed to a set of Copy activities to migrate those tables to a data warehouse hosted in Azure Synapse Analytics.

FIGURE 1.12   ADF control flow

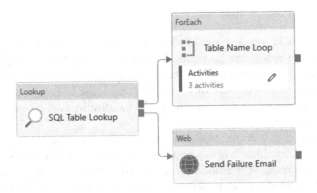

This control flow includes outcomes for successful lookups of table metadata and failures. If metadata is retrieved successfully, then the next step will be a ForEach loop that includes data movement tasks that will migrate each SQL Server table successfully retrieved to Azure Synapse Analytics. If the Lookup task fails for whatever reason, then the next step will be a Web activity that will send an email alerting an administrator of the failure.

Another example of a control flow is the order in which different mapping data flows are executed. Using the Data Flow activity, data engineers can chain together multiple mapping data flows to process data in the correct order. Figure 1.13 illustrates an example of a control flow that executes a series of data flows sequentially and in parallel.

FIGURE 1.13   Ordering data flow processing with a control flow

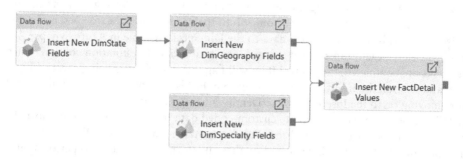

This pipeline begins by inserting new State fields followed by new geography fields in the State and geography destination tables, all the while inserting new specialty fields in parallel. Once these data flows are complete, the control flow will run a final data flow that inserts new detail fields into the destination detail table. Of course, these tasks only control what order ETL activities run in, not the underlying data transformation steps. ADF allows developers to build or edit specific mapping data flows by double-clicking their corresponding Data Flow control flow activity.

While control flows manage the order of operations for ETL pipelines, data flows are where the ETL magic happens. Data flows are specific tasks in a control flow and are responsible for extracting data from its source, transforming it, and loading the transformed data into the appropriate destination data stores. The output of one data flow task can be the input to the next one, and data flows without a dependency on each other can run in parallel. As mentioned in the section "Transform" earlier in this chapter, ADF can execute four types of transformation activities that can serve as data flows. This section will focus on two of those types: mapping data flows and external compute services that host custom code.

Mapping data flows are ETL pipelines that data engineers can design with a GUI. Developers begin by selecting a source to extract data from, then performing one or more transformation activities on the data, and finally loading the transformed data into a destination data store. The finished data flows are translated to code upon execution and use scaled-out Apache Spark clusters to run them. Figure 1.14 is a screenshot of the Insert New DimSpecialty fields data flow task from Figure 1.13.

FIGURE 1.14   ADF mapping data flow

This data flow begins by extracting data from a CSV file. Next, the CSV data undergoes a few transformations including the removal of duplicate rows, selecting only the columns needed, and creating new columns to conform to the destination data store's schema. Finally, the data flow loads the transformed data to the DimSpecialty table in Azure Synapse Analytics by inserting each transformed column into its associated destination column. Once these tasks are completed, the control flow will flag this data flow as being successfully completed and wait on the Insert New DimGeography Fields data flow to successfully complete before moving on to the Insert New FactDetail Values data flow.

ADF can also be used to automate custom-coded data flow activities that are hosted in external compute services such as Azure Functions, Azure Databricks, SQL Stored Procedures, or Azure HDInsight. Code hosted on these platforms can be used to perform one or more phases of an ETL pipeline. Running these tasks as activities in ADF allows them to run on a scheduled basis and alongside other activities such as mapping data flows or other custom-coded data flows. Figure 1.15 illustrates a control flow in ADF that executes external data flows that are hosted in Azure Databricks and Azure SQL Database.

FIGURE 1.15   Azure Databricks and SQL stored procedure control flow

This example is a part of a solution that analyzes American football players who are NFL football players. The destination data store is a data warehouse hosted on an Azure SQL Database that provides consumers with the ability to compare the current year's group of prospects with those in previous years. The pipeline in Figure 1.15 starts by running a Python notebook hosted in Azure Databricks that extracts information on when a prospect was selected in the current year's NFL Draft, cleanses the data, and loads the cleansed data in the data warehouse. The next step in the pipeline is to run a stored procedure in the data warehouse that associates a unique identifier that was assigned to them before the NFL draft. Finally, the pipeline executes another stored procedure that tells analysts if a prospect was not drafted. As you can see, each of these data flows is critical to the success of this data analytics solution. ADF makes it possible to run these activities that are developed on different technologies in sequential order and control when they should run.

A notebook is a web-based interface that contains runnable code, visualizations, and narrative texts. ADF can run notebooks that are hosted in Azure Databricks as well as code developed in Azure Databricks that is packaged as Jar or Python files.

Extract, Load, and Transform (ELT)

ELT workflows differ from ETL workflows solely in where the data transformation takes place. Instead of a separate transformation engine, the destination data store is used to load and transform data. This simplifies the design by removing extraneous components that would typically be used to transform data. Since the transformation and load components are one and the same, the destination data store must be powerful enough to efficiently complete both tasks at the same time. This makes large-scale analytics scenarios the perfect use cases for ELT workflows since they rely on the scalability of MPP technologies such as Azure Synapse Analytics or Azure Databricks. Figure 1.16 illustrates the common Azure technologies used in each phase of an ELT workflow.

FIGURE 1.16   ELT workflow

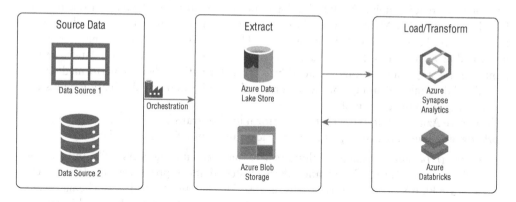

In this example, data is extracted from its source systems via ADF and stored as flat files in a raw data store such as ADLS or Azure Blob Storage. Next, data is virtually "loaded" into staging tables in the destination data store. *Data virtualization* is what enables ELT workflows to process massive amounts of data with relatively little overhead. Instead of data being physically stored in the destination data store, external tables are used to overlay a schema over the flat file data in ADLS or Azure Blob Storage. The data is then able to be queried like any other table, without taking up storage in the destination data store. MPP technologies such as Spark (using Azure Databricks or Azure Synapse Apache Spark pools) and Azure Synapse Analytics are typical data stores used for this approach because they have mechanisms for creating external tables and performing transformations on them. The following sections will describe each phase in further detail.

Extract

Collecting data from various sources is just as important in ELT workflows as it is in ETL. Unlike with ETL scenarios that might begin raw processing once the data is extracted, data involved in ELT scenarios is always consolidated in a central repository. These repositories must be able to handle large volumes of data. Scalable file systems that are based on the *Hadoop Distributed File System (HDFS)*, such as ADLS and Azure Blob Storage, are typically used in these scenarios.

Extracted data must also be in formats that are compatible with the loading mechanisms of the destination technology. Typical file formats include delimited text files, such as CSV or TSV, semi-structured files such as XML or JSON, and column compressed files such as AVRO, ORC, or Parquet. Column compressed file formats should be used for larger datasets as these are optimized for big data workloads because they support very efficient compression and encoding schemes. Parquet is widely used because of its ability to embed the data's schema within the structure of the data, thus reducing the complexity of data loading and transformation logic.

Load and Transform

The key to any ELT workflow is the destination data store's ability to process data without needing to store it in-engine. MPP technologies do this by fitting a schema over one or more files that are stored in ADLS or Azure Blob Storage. The destination data store only manages the schema of the data and not the storage of it. These external tables allow engineers to query and process data as they would a table that is stored in the destination data store but minimizes the amount of storage required by it. Transformations that are performed on the virtualized data take advantage of the features and capabilities of the destination data store but are applied to the data in object storage.

The three Azure technologies that can perform load & transform operations in an ELT workflow are Azure HDInsight, Azure Databricks, and Azure Synapse Analytics.

- *Azure HDInsight* is a managed cloud service that lets data engineers build and manage Hadoop, Spark, Kafka, Storm, and HBase clusters that can process stored data in ADLS or Azure Blob Storage. HDInsight clusters use Apache Hive to project a schema on data in object storage without needing to persist the data locally on the cluster. This decoupling of compute from storage allows clusters to process data at scale.

- *Azure Databricks* is a fully managed, cloud-based data platform that allows data engineers to build enterprise-grade Spark-powered applications. Databricks was built by the same team that built Apache Spark and provides a highly optimized version of the open-source version of the Spark runtime. Azure Databricks is a specific implementation of Databricks that includes native integration with a variety of Azure-based storage such as ADLS, Azure Blob Storage, Azure Synapse Analytics, Azure SQL Database, and Azure Cosmos DB. Azure Databricks provides a similar mechanism to decoupling compute from storage as Azure HDInsight but has a few key advantages. For one, Azure Databricks provides native integration with Azure Active Directory for identity and access management. Azure Databricks also provides easier ways to manage clusters by letting data engineers manually pause clusters or set an auto-shutdown after being idle for a fixed amount of time. Clusters can also be set to auto-scale to support different workload sizes.

- *Azure Synapse Analytics* is a comprehensive data analytics platform that includes tools for data ingestion, transformation, exploration, and presentation. For the purposes of this section, we will focus on the three tools that can be used for the load and transform phases: dedicated SQL pools, serverless SQL pools, and Apache Spark pools.

  - *Dedicated SQL pools*, formerly known as Azure SQL Data Warehouse, store data in relational tables with columnar storage. A dedicated SQL pool can scale up or down depending on how large the workload is and can be paused when it's not being used. Data engineers can choose to virtualize data that is stored in object storage with either PolyBase or the COPY statement. PolyBase uses external tables to define and access the data in Azure object storage. PolyBase requires the creation of a few external objects to be able to read data. These include an external data source that points to the data's location in either ADLS or Azure Blob Storage, an external file format that defines how the data is formatted, and finally the actual external table definition. The COPY statement is a newer command for loading data into a dedicated SQL pool. It simplifies the load process by requiring only a single T-SQL statement that needs to be run instead of needing to create multiple database objects. It also includes some additional features to what PolyBase offers. Going forward, the COPY statement should be used to load data from ADLS and Azure Blob Storage to a dedicated SQL pool.

  - *Serverless SQL pool* is an interactive service that allows developers to query data in ADLS or Azure Blob Storage. It is a distributed data processing system, built for large-scale data explorations. There is no infrastructure to set up or clusters to maintain since it is serverless. A default endpoint for a serverless SQL pool is provisioned for every Azure Synapse Analytics workspace that is deployed. Data engineers and data analysts can use the OPENROWSET function to query files in Azure object storage and can create external tables or views to maintain the structure of the data for later usage. Serverless SQL pools support T-SQL for users querying and processing data.

  - *Apache Spark pools* allow data engineers to deploy Spark clusters using the open-source version of Spark to process large volumes of data.

Azure Synapse Analytics serverless SQL pools and Apache Spark pools are also able to perform ELT actions on operational data that is stored in Azure Cosmos DB. Azure Synapse Link is a hybrid transactional and analytical processing (HTAP) capability that gives data engineers and developers the ability to use Synapse Spark or Synapse SQL to build analytics solutions without needing to transform data in Azure Cosmos DB first. More on HTAP for Azure Cosmos DB in Chapter 5.

Each of these technologies is an MPP system and is designed to handle big data scenarios. The key advantage of using an MPP technology like the ones just discussed for big data scenarios is that once the data is loaded, they will break the data down into smaller partitions and distribute the processing of the partitions across multiple machines in parallel. Instead of one job processing a mammoth sized dataset, transformations can occur in parallel on smaller subsets of the data, resulting in more efficient processing of the data. For more information on Azure HDInsight, Azure Databricks, and Azure Synapse Analytics and to better understand when to use which one or how to use them in tandem, see Chapter 5.

Describe Analytics Techniques

While it is important to spend considerable time planning and developing data processing pipelines, it is vital not to forget about the questions that drove the solution to be built in the first place. Being able to answer questions like the following is critical to the success of a business: What has happened? Why did certain events happen? What will happen? What should we do? and What might happen if different variables change?. Knowing how to answer these questions can help businesses understand their past successes and failures and predict what actions they should take in the future. These questions can be answered using the five types of analytics techniques, telling the story of a business's past, present, and future.

The five types of analytics include *descriptive, diagnostic, predictive, prescriptive*, and *cognitive analytics*. Each type of analytics represents a different stage of an organization's analytics maturity. For example, descriptive analytics techniques are based on decades of best practices that are easier to implement than prescriptive analytics but do not provide as much value. The relationship between the value provided by an analytics technique and its implementation complexity is known as the *Analytics Maturity Model*. This is illustrated in Figure 1.17.

FIGURE 1.17   Analytics Maturity Model

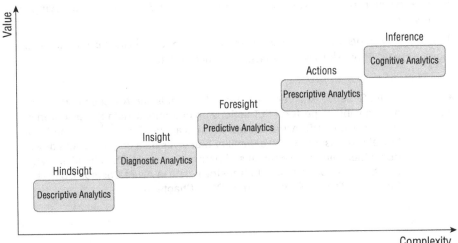

Descriptive

Descriptive analytics use historical data to answer questions about what has happened to the business. This is a great first step for conducting statistical analysis as it informs decision makers of any trends, data distribution, and if there are any outliers in the data. Key performance indicators (KPIs) allow analysts to summarize large datasets to track the success and failure of key objectives. This type of analysis is reactive and is typically the first analysis technique used by organizations making decisions based on data.

Data used for descriptive analytics is typically gathered and persisted in a central repository, such as a data warehouse. Well-designed data warehouses make it easy for OLAP models and BI tools to analyze performance metrics against a variety of scenarios. An example of descriptive analytics is generating reports to provide a view of an organization's sales data.

Diagnostic

Diagnostic analytics use historical data to answer questions about why different events have happened. While descriptive analytics use historical data to display past results, diagnostic analytics take this a step further by determining the root cause behind those results. This is the first technique that leverages machine learning to provide insights. Examples of diagnostic analytics include drilling down to focus on a particular facet of data, anomaly detection, data mining to get information from a massive set of data, and correlation analysis to pinpoint cause-and-effect relationships.

Predictive

Predictive analytics use historical data to build statistical and machine learning models to forecast what will happen in the future. This is the first type of analytics in the Analytics Maturity Model that answers questions regarding a business's future. Techniques such as neural networks, decision trees, and regression models allow predictive analytics solutions to make recommendations on the following scenarios:

- Whether or not a customer will leave for a competitor. Customer churn models use past trends to make predictions on the risk of a customer leaving. These models can help organizations make decisions on how to preemptively maintain high-risk customers' business.

- When to replace or repair a piece of equipment. Predictive maintenance models enable organizations that rely on machines to run their business (e.g., oil and gas companies or vending machine companies) to know when they should take proactive measures to repair or replace equipment.

- Whether or not a piece of data is fraudulent. Fraud detection models will alert organizations if they find any suspicious transaction activity.

While descriptive and diagnostic analysis can be completed using traditional BI techniques, predictive analysis requires developers to have a more specialized skillset. Along with the need to properly maintain the historical data warehouse, solutions involving predictive analytics must maintain and regularly revisit model performance to ensure that the models are making well-informed decisions. While not in scope for this book, it is important to understand the tools and mechanisms used to maintain a machine learning model's life cycle. Azure Machine Learning and Apache Spark's MLflow enable data scientists to train, deploy, automate, and manage their machine learning models. These technologies allow data scientists to deploy models using container-based technologies such as Kubernetes or Azure Container Instances, which can be used by applications to make batch or real-time predictions.

Prescriptive

Prescriptive analytics solutions are a step up from predictive analytics as they not only predict outcomes, but they also advise organizations on how to reach a desired outcome. These solutions use findings from descriptive, diagnostic, and predictive analytics techniques to answer questions about what actions should be taken to achieve a particular goal. Combinations of machine learning algorithms and business rules are used to simulate the outcomes of different input parameters. One example of the impact prescriptive analytics solutions can make is in the sports science field. Prescriptive analytics solutions not only predict when an athlete will experience a soft tissue injury but will also advise team doctors on what measures to take to prevent them. They can also be used to advise athletes on the most efficient training exercises for performing at their peak.

Cognitive

Cognitive analytics solutions combine several artificial intelligence and machine learning techniques such as deep learning and natural language processing to draw inferences from existing data and patterns. This type of analytics will provide information based on existing knowledge bases and then add this information back into the knowledge base for future inferences.

This type of analytics takes inspiration from the way the human brain processes information. Instead of retrieving data via a query or creating analysis using structured development methods, cognitive analytics solutions are developed to derive more accurate inferences over time by learning from each interaction with data.

Describe Data Visualization Techniques

Different analytics techniques provide a business with the information needed to make critical decisions moving forward but can be difficult to interpret if the findings are left as plain numbers. Data visualization refers to the process of graphically representing valuable information. The resulting infographics include charts, graphs, maps, and other objects that make information easy to read. Visualizations make it easy for analysts and business decision makers to see trends, outliers, and patterns in data. It is for this reason that using the most effective visualizations to represent information is critical to the storytelling process of data analytics.

Data visualization techniques come in a few different flavors. Depending on the purpose of the infographic and the skillset of the end users, data visualizations may be developed using one of the following three methods:

- *Analytical tools* allow users the ability to access and manipulate very granular levels of data. Tools like SQL Server Analysis Services (SSAS), Azure Analysis Services (AAS), and Power BI store data as OLAP models that can be filtered in a way that allow analysts to view calculated metrics for different scenarios. Data scientists can use tools such as Jupyter Notebooks to develop visualizations in a browser-based shell using Python or R. Using Python or R packages such as matplotlib or ggplot2, data scientists can build visualizations that are highly customized depending on what story they are trying to tell. Analysts and developers building infographics with analytical tools must have an intimate knowledge of the data that they are working with and must possess very specialized development skills. However, while analytical tools require the most complex set of skills to use, they provide users with the most flexibility in how they visualize information.

- *Reporting tools* give analysts the ability to organize data into informational summaries to monitor how different areas of the organization are performing. Traditional report tools such as SQL Server Reporting Services (SSRS) allow report builders to build static reports that use set filters to monitor business performance, only updating the displayed data when the dataset powering the report is refreshed. Modern technologies such as Power BI improve reporting capabilities by allowing users to dynamically alter the displayed data with filters, slicers, and interactive visualizations. This interactive capability empowers decision makers to consider multiple scenarios when determining the most appropriate course of action for their business. Reports are typically accessed by end users through an online portal such as `powerbi.com` and are only accessible to users with the appropriate level of access. You can learn more about Power BI security in Chapter 6, "Reporting with Power BI."

- *Dashboarding tools* provide quick overviews of the most relevant pieces of information. Dashboards are designed to be easy to consume, allowing decision makers to act shortly after the data exposes new opportunities or threats. Tools such as Power BI allow analysts to collect the most relevant parts of a report to a decision maker and pin them to a dashboard.

Once a decision has been made on the most useful data visualization technique, it is important to choose the visual or visuals most appropriately suited for the data being displayed. Poorly chosen visuals can be hard to interpret or, worse, convey the wrong message. Another important aspect is the design of each visual. It's not enough to choose the correct chart or graph for the job, analysts must also be consistent with the aspect and color scheme for their visuals. This will help keep end users focused on any insights that are displayed rather than being overwhelmed by clashing color patterns and inconsistent sizing. End users should be able to quickly interpret the message each visual is telling with little to no explanation. The following sections include common visualizations used in analytical, reporting, and dashboarding tools. While these visualizations are popular and easy to build, there are countless more available for storytelling.

The data used to develop each of the visualizations discussed in the following sections comes from the AdventureWorksDW2019 sample database. Please visit `https://docs.microsoft.com/en-us/sql/samples/adventureworks-install-configure?view=sql-server-ver15&tabs=ssms#download-backup-files` for instructions on how to download and restore a backup of this database.

Table

A table is a grid that contains data that is ordered in rows and columns. Tables work well with quantitative comparisons where you are evaluating many values for a single category. Technologies such as Power BI Paginated Reports and SSRS format large tables to fit onto multiple pages make them easier to read. This type of reporting is known as paginated and has been used in BI solutions for decades. Figure 1.18 is an example of a table that lists the quantity sold and total sales amount for different bike subcategories sold online in different US regions.

FIGURE 1.18   Table

Product Subcategory	Sales Territory Region	Order Quantity	Sales Amount
Road Bikes	Southwest	1475	$2,569,983.42
Mountain Bikes	Southwest	1058	$2,070,024.79
Road Bikes	Northwest	972	$1,716,135.51
Mountain Bikes	Northwest	683	$1,333,561.55
Touring Bikes	Southwest	463	$858,303.57
Touring Bikes	Northwest	244	$431,788.26
Mountain Bikes	Southeast	4	$7,455.89
Mountain Bikes	Northeast	2	$4,344.09
Road Bikes	Southeast	2	$1,565.98
Mountain Bikes	Central	1	$2,071.42
Road Bikes	Central	1	$539.99
Road Bikes	Northeast	1	$1,700.99
Touring Bikes	Southeast	1	$2,384.07
Total		**4907**	**$8,999,859.53**

Matrix

A matrix is a table that summarizes data into totals and subtotals for different groupings. In Figure 1.18 we can see that most bikes that are sold online in the United States are sold in the Northwest and Southwest sales territory regions. However, tables can become very hard to read if we start adding additional levels of granularity such as sales data for specific types of bikes. Matrices take care of this issue by providing a hierarchical structure that provides totals for multiple layers of granularity. Figure 1.19 is an example of a matrix that displays order quantity and sales totals for bikes, each bike subcategory, and each specific bike type sold online in the US Northwest and Southwest regions.

FIGURE 1.19   Matrix

Sales Territory Region	Northwest		Southwest		Total	
EnglishProductCategoryName	Sales Amount	Order Quantity	Sales Amount	Order Quantity	Sales Amount	Order Quantity
⊟ **Bikes**	**$3,481,485.32**	**1899**	**$5,498,311.78**	**2996**	**$8,979,797.10**	**4895**
⊞ **Mountain Bikes**	**$1,333,561.55**	**683**	**$2,070,024.79**	**1058**	**$3,403,586.34**	**1741**
⊞ **Road Bikes**	**$1,716,135.51**	**972**	**$2,569,983.42**	**1475**	**$4,286,118.94**	**2447**
⊟ **Touring Bikes**	**$431,788.26**	**244**	**$858,303.57**	**463**	**$1,290,091.83**	**707**
Touring-1000 Blue, 46	$45,297.33	19	$88,210.59	37	**$133,507.92**	56
Touring-1000 Blue, 50	$40,529.19	17	$76,290.24	32	**$116,819.43**	49
Touring-1000 Blue, 54	$35,761.05	15	$109,667.22	46	**$145,428.27**	61
Touring-1000 Blue, 60	$52,449.54	22	$78,674.31	33	**$131,123.85**	55
Touring-1000 Yellow, 46	$38,145.12	16	$83,442.45	35	**$121,587.57**	51
Total	**$3,481,485.32**	**1899**	**$5,498,311.78**	**2996**	**$8,979,797.10**	**4895**

Column and Bar Charts

Bar and column charts enable organizations to see how a set of variables change across different categories. Both chart types represent data with rectangular bars. The difference between the two is that if the rectangles are stacked horizontally, it is called a bar chart, and when they are aligned vertically, then it is a column chart. Figure 1.20 illustrates an example of a column chart that compares the total Internet sales amount for the different subcategories of bikes sold in the US Northwest and Southwest sales territories.

FIGURE 1.20   Column chart

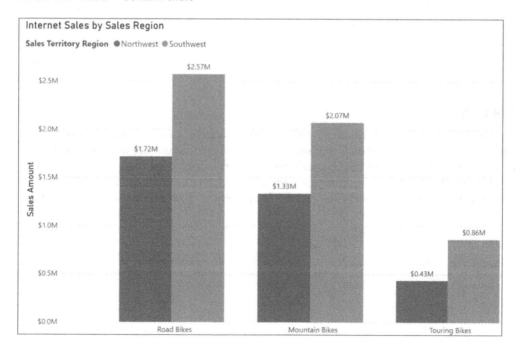

Line Chart

Line charts represent how a series of values change over time. Power BI enhances line charts by including a tooltip that provides more granular information for each data point on the x-axis. This is helpful if you are trying to prove a correlation between data points. Tooltips can be displayed by hovering your mouse over the x-axis value you would like to further analyze. Figure 1.21 illustrates an example of a line chart that compares monthly Internet bike sales in 2011, 2012, and 2013 in the US West sales territory. This line chart also includes a tooltip displaying the Internet sales totals for the month of July in each year.

FIGURE 1.21   Line chart

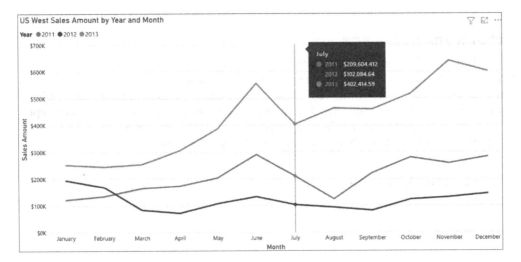

Pie Chart

Pie charts are useful for determining how responsible different categories are for a given value. Each category corresponds to a single slice of the pie, and the size of each slice indicates the percentage of the whole pie each category is responsible for. Figure 1.22 illustrates an example of a pie chart that displays the total Internet bike sales for each country where a sale occurred as well as the percentage of the total sales that each country is responsible for.

FIGURE 1.22   Pie chart

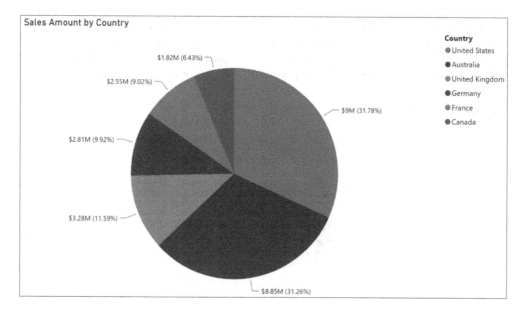

Scatter Plot

Scatter plots show the relationship between two numerical values. Power BI enhances scatter plots by including a tooltip that provides more granular information for each data point, or bubble. Tooltips can be displayed by hovering your mouse over the bubble you would like to further analyze. Figure 1.23 illustrates a simple example of a scatter plot chart that displays the correlation between the sales amount and order quantity for the different types of bikes sold online. The plot takes the analysis a step further by examining this correlation for the US Northwest and Southwest regions.

FIGURE 1.23   Scatter plot

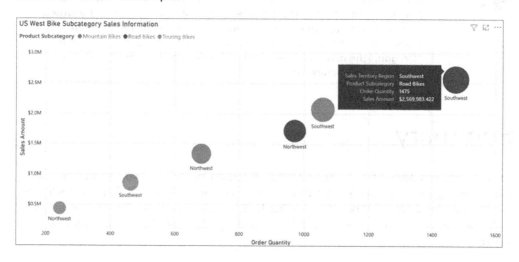

Map

Maps show the geographic distribution of data. These visualizations can show broad comparisons such as country or state sales information or very granular comparisons at the postal code, address, or latitude and longitude level. Figure 1.24 illustrates a map that displays cities in the US Pacific Northwest where bikes were bought online. The size of the bubble represents the total bike sales proportion that each city is responsible for.

FIGURE 1.24   Map

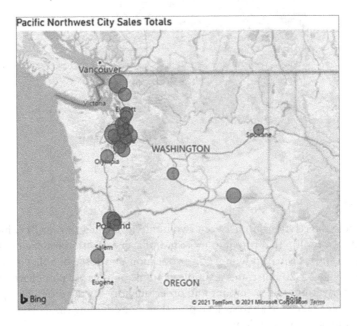

Pacific Northwest City Sales Totals

Take special care when building visualizations that map data points for cities. Be sure to include specific information such as the country, state/province, or postal code to mitigate the risk of plotting data in the wrong city. For example, if the data in the map in Figure 1.24 only provided sales information for "Salem" with no indication that the correct state is "Oregon," the map may have incorrectly assumed that the data referred to Salem, Massachusetts.

Summary

The concepts included in this chapter cover the different categories of data, storage options, and processing patterns. This chapter also covered common analysis techniques and when to use different visualizations depending on what business questions you are trying to answer. Understanding these core definitions will help you design data solutions in Azure for any scenario.

This chapter covered the following concepts:

Describe types of core data workloads.   The design strategy for a data solution comes down to what value will be provided by the solution, the volume of data the solution will store and process, the variety of data involved, and the velocity of the data being ingested. Solutions can be either a transactional workload, accounting for the business transactions that support the day-to-day operations of an organization, or an analytical workload that supports business users who need to make calculated business decisions from large amounts of data. These workloads can consist of structured, semi-structured, and unstructured data that can be stored in relational or nonrelational databases or as files in object storage. Cloud-based solutions can easily support requirements for data to be batch and stream processed.

Describe data analytics core concepts.   Data analytics is the process of turning raw data into information that is used to make important business decisions. First, raw data is extracted from source systems that are used to power a business and is either transformed first and then loaded into a destination data store or is loaded first and then transformed in the destination data store. Depending on the value being derived from the information, one or more analytics techniques can be applied to the processed data to view past performance and predict the most optimal actions to take advantage of future opportunities or prevent potential threats. Value is then exposed through several data visualization techniques so that decision makers can easily interpret the processed data and quickly make decisions that will ensure the success of their business.

Exam Essentials

Describe the characteristics of relational data.   Relational databases are data storage technologies that organize data into tables that can be linked based on data common to each other. Database tables store data as rows and are organized into a set number of columns. Relationships between tables allow users to easily query data from multiple tables at the same time. These databases also enforce schema integrity and maintain ACID rules, which makes them a good option for storing structured data. Relational databases are also critical for analytical workloads such as data warehouses because they structure data in a way that is easy to serve to reporting applications.

Describe the characteristics of nonrelational data.   Nonrelational data is data that requires flexibility in the way it is stored. Semi-structured data such as JSON and XML and unstructured data such as images or videos are some examples of nonrelational data. NoSQL databases can be used to store data with constantly changing schemas without forcing it to conform to a fixed structure. This allows queries that write and read data from these databases to potentially perform much faster than a relational database. Object storage can be used to store unstructured data such as binary files that cannot be stored in a database.

Describe batch data.   Batch processing is the practice of transforming groups, or batches, of data at rest. Data involved in batch processing solutions can come from any number of data stores, including relational, nonrelational, and files stored in object storage. Batch processing jobs can be scheduled to run at fixed time periods or when an event occurs, such as when a new transaction is added to a transactional data store. These jobs can process large amounts of data at a time and can be relied on to produce very accurate results since processing can take significant time to complete.

Describe streaming data.   Stream data is a continuous flow of data from some source. Data is processed in real time as it arrives in stream processing solutions. Each piece of data in a stream is often referred to as an event or a message and typically arrives in an unstructured or semi-structured format such as JSON. Streaming data solutions begin by ingesting data from a source such as an IoT sensor into a real-time message engine system that queues data for live processing or into an object store for on-demand processing. A stream processing engine such as Azure Stream Analytics is then used to transform the data, typically by time window, and write the transformed data either to an analytical data store or directly to a dashboard. Stream processing is ideal for solutions that require real-time analytics and do not need to process a large amount of data at once.

Describe the concepts of data processing.   Data processing is the methodology used to ingest raw data and transform it into one or more informative business models. Data processing solutions will either ingest data in batches or as a stream and can either store the data in its raw form or begin transforming it. Data can undergo several transformations such as being filtered, normalized, and aggregated before it is ready to be reported on. Data processing pipelines must include activities that are repeatable and flexible enough to handle a variety of scenarios.

Describe extract, transform, and load (ETL) and extract, load, and transform (ELT) processing.   Extract, transform, and load (ETL) is a data processing technique that extracts data from various sources, transforms the data according to business rules, and loads it into a destination data store. Data transformation takes place in a specialized technology and includes multiple operations. Before data is loaded into production tables, the data is typically stored in staging tables to temporarily store it as it is being transformed.

Extract, load, and transform (ELT) is like ETL but differs from ETL workflows only in where the transformations occur. Instead of using a separate transformation engine, ELT workflows transform data in the target data store. Data that is stored as flat files in scalable object storage such as Azure Data Lake Store Gen2 is mapped to a schema in the destination data store. This schema-on-read approach allows the destination data store to perform the necessary transformations on the data without needing to duplicate data. In these scenarios, the destination data store is typically a massively parallel processing (MPP) technology such as Spark or Azure Synapse Analytics, which are capable of processing large amounts of data at a time.

Describe how analytics tell the story of a business's past, present, and future.   The maturity of an organization's data analytics journey can be summarized by how well they are able to implement each category of analytics. From easiest to hardest, the analytics categories are descriptive, diagnostic, predictive, prescriptive, and cognitive. Descriptive analytics answer questions about what has happened, diagnostic analytics answer why things have happened, predictive analytics answer questions about what will happen, prescriptive analytics answer questions about what actions should be taken to achieve a target, and cognitive analytics derive inferences from existing data and patterns.

Describe data visualization techniques. Data visualization techniques can be broken down into three core categories: analytical, reporting, and dashboarding. Analytical tools allow users the ability to access and manipulate very granular levels of data. Data scientists can use these tools to create highly customized visualizations to display insights over several different scenarios. Reporting tools give analysts the ability to organize data into informational summaries to monitor how different areas of the organization are performing. Reports built with these tools can be either static or dynamic depending on how interactive analysts want their reports to be. Dashboarding tools provide quick overviews of the most relevant visuals to decision makers. Dashboards empower decision makers to quickly act on opportunities or threats as they arise.

Choosing the right type of infographic to display information is critical to the success of a data analytics solution. Poorly chosen visualizations can be hard to interpret or, worse, convey the wrong message. Another important aspect is the design of each visual. It's not enough to choose the correct chart or graph for the job, but analysts must also be consistent with the aspect and color scheme for their visuals. This will help keep end users focused on any insights that are displayed rather than being overwhelmed by clashing color patterns and inconsistent sizing.

Review Questions

1. Which of the following technologies is not an example of a real-time message ingestion engine?

   A. Azure IoT Hub

   B. Azure Event Hubs

   C. Azure SQL Database

   D. Apache Kafka

2. Is the underlined portion of the following statement true, or does it need to be replaced with
   one of the other fragments that appear below?

   DML statements include <u>INSERT, UPDATE, and DELETE</u> commands.

   A. GRANT, DENY, and REVOKE.

   B. SELECT, INSERT, UPDATE, and DELETE.

   C. BEGIN TRANSACTION, COMMIT TRANSACTION, and ROLLBACK TRANSAC-
   TION.

   D. No change is needed.

3. You are the data architect for a game company and are designing the database tier for a new
   game. The game will be released globally and is expected to be well received with potentially
   millions of people concurrently playing online. Gamers are expecting the game to be able
   to integrate with social media platforms so that they can stream their sessions and in-game
   scores in real time. Which of the following database platforms is the most appropriate for
   this scenario?

   A. Azure Cosmos DB supports millisecond reads and writes to avoid lags during gameplay
   and can easily integrate with social features.

   B. Azure SQL Database is necessary because this workload is transactional by nature.

   C. Azure Synapse Analytics dedicated SQL pool is necessary to analyze millions of user
   data at the same time.

   D. Azure Cache to support in-memory storage of each player and their related gamer metadata.

4. You are developing a real-time streaming solution that processes data streamed from different brands of IoT devices. The solution must be able to retrieve metadata about each device
   to determine the unit of measurement each device uses. Which of the following options
   would serve as a valid solution for this use case?

   A. Process the IoT data on demand and store it in micro-batches in Azure Blob Storage
   with the static reference data. Azure Databricks Structured Streaming can process both
   datasets from Azure Blob Storage to retrieve the required information.

   B. Process the IoT data live and use static data stored in Azure Blob Storage to provide
   the necessary metadata for the solution. Azure Stream Analytics supports Azure Blob
   Storage as the storage layer for reference data.

   C. This cannot be done in real time.

   D. Either A or B will work.

5. Which of the following is an example of a nonrelational data store?

   A. Azure Blob Storage

   B. Azure Cosmos DB

   C. MongoDB

   D. All of the above

6. You are a data architect at a manufacturing company. You were recently given a project to design a solution that will make it easier for your company's implementation of Azure Cognitive Search to analyze relationships of employees and departments. Which of the following is the most efficient solution for this project?

   A. Use the Azure Cosmos DB Gremlin API to store the entities and relationships for fast query results.

   B. Store the departments and employees as values in an Azure SQL Database relational model.

   C. Store the data as Parquet files in Azure Data Lake Store Gen2 and then query the relationships using Azure Databricks.

   D. Denormalize the data into column families using the Azure Cosmos DB Cassandra API.

7. You are designing a solution that will leverage a machine learning model to identify different endangered species that inhabit different wildlife reservations. Part of this solution will require you to train the model against images of these animals so that it knows which animal is which. What storage solution should you use to store the images?

   A. Azure SQL Database's FILESTREAM feature

   B. Azure Blob Storage

   C. Azure Data Lake Storage Gen2

   D. Azure Cosmos DB Gremlin API

8. You are the administrator of a data warehouse that is hosted in an Azure Synapse Analytics dedicated SQL pool instance. You choose to transform and load data using ELT to eliminate the number of hops data must go through to get from your data lake environment to the data warehouse. Which of the following technologies provides the most efficient way to load data into the Azure Synapse Analytics dedicated SQL pool instance through ELT?

   A. Azure Databricks

   B. Azure Stream Analytics

   C. COPY statement

   D. Azure Data Factory

9. Is the underlined portion of the following statement true, or does it need to be replaced with one of the other fragments that appear below?

Azure SQL Database is an example of an MPP system.

   A. Azure Data Factory.

   B. Azure Synapse Analytics dedicated SQL pool.

   C. Azure Batch.

   D. No change is needed.

10. You are a data engineer for a retail company that sells athletic wear. Company decision makers rely on updated sales information to make decisions based on buying trends. New data must be processed every night so that reports have the most recent sales information by the time decision makers examine the reports. What type of processing does this describe?

   A. Transactional processing

   B. Stream processing

   C. Scheduled processing

   D. Batch processing

11. As the data architect for your retail firm, you have been asked to design a solution that will process large amounts of customer and transaction data every night and store it in your Azure Synapse dedicated SQL pool data warehouse for analysis. There are multiple sources of data that must be processed to ensure that analysts are able to make the most appropriate business decisions based on these datasets. The solution must also be easy to maintain and have the minimal operational overhead. Which of the following is the most appropriate choice for this solution?

   A. Create Azure Data Factory mapping data flows to process each entity and add them to a control flow in ADF to be processed in the correct order every night.

   B. Develop the data flows in Azure Databricks and schedule them through an Azure Databricks job to run every night.

   C. Create SSIS jobs in an Azure VM to process each entity and add them to a control flow in SSIS to be processed in the correct order every night.

   D. Create workflows in Azure Logic Apps to process each entity every night.

12. Is the underlined portion of the following statement true, or does it need to be replaced with one of the other fragments that appear below?

   Descriptive analytics answer questions about why things happened.

   A. Predictive.

   B. Cognitive.

   C. Diagnostic.

   D. No change is needed.

13. Is the underlined portion of the following statement true, or does it need to be replaced with one of the other fragments that appear below?

   Matrices can be used to display totals and subtotals for different groups of categorical data.

   A. Tables.

   B. Bar charts.

   C. Scatter plots.

   D. No change is needed.

14. You are responsible for designing a report platform that will provide your leadership team with the information necessary to build the company's long-term and short-term strategy. Analysts must be able to build interactive visualizations with the least amount of complexity to provide executives recommendations based on business performance and customer trends. Analysts will also need to be able to create views of the most critical pieces of information for executives to consume. These views are the only pieces of the platform that executives need to have access to. Which of the following is the most appropriate choice given the requirements?

   A. Give analysts the ability to create and interact with reports in Power BI while also having them create dashboards for executives. Executives will only need access to Power BI dashboards.

   B. Give analysts and executives the ability to create and interact with reports in Power BI. This will give executives the ability to build dashboards for time-sensitive decision making.

   C. Recommend that analysts build infographics in a Jupyter Notebook with Python or R as this is the only way to build the dashboards the executives require.

   D. Give analysts the ability to build static reports with SSRS and pin the most important SSRS visualizations to a Power BI dashboard.

15. You are a report designer for a retail company that relies on online sales. Your boss has requested that you add a visualization to the executive performance dashboard that will show sales patterns over the last three years. Which of the following is the most appropriate options?

   A. Column chart

   B. Line chart

   C. Scatter plot

   D. Matrix

16. As the chief data scientist of a large bike company, you have been tasked with designing a bot service that customers can use to receive guidance on their bike maintenance. The bot must be able to learn as new queries are issued to it so that it can improve the quality of its responses. What type of analytics is this an example of?

   A. Cognitive analytics

   B. Prescriptive analytics

   C. Predictive analytics

   D. Diagnostic analytics

Chapter

2

Relational Databases in Azure

MICROSOFT EXAM OBJECTIVES COVERED IN THIS CHAPTER:

✓ Describe relational data workloads.

- Identify the right data offering for a relational workload.
- Describe relational data structures (e.g., tables, indexes, views).

✓ Relational Database Offerings in Azure.

- Describe Azure SQL database services such as Azure SQL Database, Azure SQL Managed Instance, and SQL Server on Azure Virtual Machine.
- Describe Azure Synapse Analytics.
- Describe Azure Database for PostgreSQL, Azure Database for MariaDB, and Azure Database for MySQL.

✓ Identify basic management tasks for relational data.

- Describe provisioning and deployment of relational data services.
- Describe method for deployment including the Azure portal, Azure Resource Manager templates, Azure PowerShell, and the Azure command-line interface (CLI).
- Identify data security components (e.g., firewall, authentication).
- Identify basic connectivity issues (e.g., accessing from on-premises, access with Azure VNets, access from Internet, authentication, firewalls).
- Identify query tools (e.g., Azure Data Studio, SQL Server Management Studio, sqlcmd utility, etc.).

✓ **Describe query techniques for data using SQL language.**

   ■ Compare Data Definition Language (DDL) versus Data Manipulation Language (DML).

   ■ Query relational data in Azure SQL Database, Azure Database for PostgreSQL, and Azure Database for MySQL.

Relational databases have been critical components to organizations' IT infrastructure for the last few decades. They are the most common way to store data due to their ease of use, the wide variety of solutions they can support, and the well-established best practices with which they are designed. Relational databases are useful for storing data elements that are related and must be stored in a consistent manner. This chapter will discuss the key features of a relational database, the different relational database offerings in Azure, basic management tasks for relational databases, and common query techniques for relational data.

Relational Database Features

Relational databases store data as collections of entities in the form of tables. In the context of data, entities can be described as nouns, such as persons, companies, countries, or products. Tables contain structured data that describes an entity and are composed of zero or more rows and one or more columns of data. Some of the columns might be special columns that are used to uniquely identify each row or act as a reference to another table that they might be related to. Rows might not include values for each column, but because relational databases are designed with a rigid schema, the row will still include that column in its definition. Default or null values are used when a value is not provided for a row. This organized approach to data storage allows relationships between entities that can easily be queried by a data analyst or a data processing solution. Let's examine the features of a relational database, starting with design considerations.

Relational Database Design Considerations

Design considerations for relational databases largely depend on what type of solution the database will be powering. As discussed in Chapter 1, "Core Data Concepts," relational databases are commonly used to power online transaction processing (OLTP) and analytical systems. Solutions that are powered by OLTP databases have different write and read requirements than that of an analytical database. Even though OLTP databases often serve as data sources for data warehouses or online analytical processing (OLAP) systems, these requirements make it necessary to distribute and store data differently in each system.

OLTP Workload Design Considerations

Transactional data that is stored in an OLTP database involve interactions that are related to an organization's activities. These can include payments received from customers, payments made to suppliers, or orders that have been made. Typical OLTP databases are optimized to handle data that is written to them and must be able to ensure that transactions adhere to ACID properties (see Chapter 1 for more information on ACID properties). This will guarantee the integrity of the records that are stored. Relational database management systems (RDBMSs) typically enforce these rules using locks or row versioning.

Regardless of whether a transaction is reading, inserting, updating, or deleting data, the data involved in the transaction must be reliable. This becomes even more true as the number of users running transactions concurrently on the same pieces of data increases, resulting in the following issues:

- Dirty reads can occur when a transaction is reading data that is being modified by another transaction. The transaction performing the read is reading the modified data that has not yet been committed. This potentially results in an inaccurate result set if the transaction modifying the data is rolled back to the original values.

- Nonrepeatable reads occur when a transaction reads the same row several times and returns different data each time. This is the result of one or more other transactions being able to modify the data between the reads within the transaction.

- Phantom reads occur when two identical queries running in the same transaction return different results. This can happen when another query inserts some data in between the execution of the two queries, resulting in the second query returning the newly inserted data.

To mitigate these issues, a transaction will request locks on different types of resources, such as rows and tables, that the transaction is dependent on. Transaction locks prevent dirty, nonrepeatable, and phantom reads by blocking other transactions from performing modifications on data objects involved in the transaction. Transactions will free their locks from a resource once they have finished reading/modifying it. While locks are critical for ensuring consistency, they can cause long wait times for users that have issued transactions that are being blocked. The following isolation levels can be assigned to a transaction to balance consistency versus performance depending on its requirements:

- *Read Uncommitted* is the lowest isolation level, only guaranteeing that physically corrupt data is not read. Transactions using this isolation level run the risk of returning dirty reads since uncommitted data is read.

- *Read Committed* transactions issue locks on involved data at the time of data modification to prevent other transactions from reading dirty data. However, data can be modified by other transactions, which can result in nonrepeatable or phantom reads. This is the default isolation level for SQL Server and Azure SQL Database.

- *Repeatable Read* transactions issue read and write locks on involved data until the end of the transaction. No other transaction can modify data involved by a repeatable read transaction until the transaction has completed. However, other transactions can insert new rows into tables involved in a repeatable read transaction. This could possibly result in phantom reads occurring.

- *Serializable* is the highest isolation level and completely isolates transactions from one another. Statements cannot read data that has not yet been committed by a transaction with serializable isolation. What's more is that statements cannot modify data that is being read by a transaction whose isolation is set to serializable.

SQL Server and Azure SQL Database also allow users to use row versioning to maintain versions of rows that are modified. Transactions can be specified to use row versions to view data as it existed at the start of the transaction instead of protecting it with locks. This allows the transaction to read a consistent copy of the data while mitigating performance concerns from locking. The following isolation levels support row versioning:

- *Read Committed Snapshot* is a version of the Read Committed isolation level that uses row versioning to present each statement in the transaction with a consistent snapshot of the data as it existed at the beginning of the statement. Locks are not used to protect the data from updates by other transactions. To enable Read Committed Snapshot, set the READ_COMMITTED_SNAPSHOT database option to ON.

- *Snapshot* isolation uses row versioning to return rows as they existed at the start of the transaction, regardless of whether another transaction modifies those rows. To enable Snapshot isolation, set the ALLOW_SNAPSHOT_ISOLATION database option to ON.

 Since each version is stored in `tempdb`, special maintenance considerations must be taken into consideration. Please refer to the following link for more information on isolation levels based on row versioning: `https://docs.microsoft.com/en-us/sql/relational-databases/` `sql-server-transaction-locking-and-row-versioning-` `guide?view=sql-server-ver15#Row_versioning`.

Maintaining ACID compliancy while also ensuring a premium performance experience is no easy task. Design best practices for OLTP databases are able to accomplish this by breaking up data into smaller chunks that are less redundant, also known as *data normalization*. There are a few rules for data normalization, which can be defined as follows:

- First normal form (1NF) involves eliminating repeating groups in individual tables, creating separate tables for each set of related data, and identifying each set of related data with a primary key. This is essentially stating that you should not use multiple fields in a single table to store similar data. For example, a retail company may have customers that make multiple orders at different periods of time. Instead of duplicating the customers' information each time they place an order, place all customer information in a separate table called Customers and identify each customer with a unique primary key.

- Second normal form (2NF) takes 1NF a step further. Along with the rules that define 1NF, 2NF also involves creating separate tables for sets of values that apply to multiple records and then relating those tables via a foreign key. For example, if a customer's address is needed by the Customer, Order, and Shipping tables, separate the addresses into a single table such as the Customer table or their own Address table.

- Third normal form (3NF) builds on 1NF and 2NF by including a requirement to eliminate fields in tables that do not depend on the key. For example, let's assume that each product being sold by the retail company includes several subcategories. If each subcategory is stored in the Products table, then each product will be duplicated numerous times to include each subcategory. In this case, it is more efficient to create a Product Subcategory table and relate it to the Products table.

The more normalized a database is, the more efficiently the database will handle write operations. This is because normalized data avoids extra processing for redundant data. Typical OLTP databases follow 3NF to ensure that database writes are as efficient as possible. Figure 2.1 is a partial example of the AdventureWorks OLTP entity relationship diagram (ERD), focusing on entities that are related to products manufactured and sold by AdventureWorks. The entire ERD can be found at `https://dataedo.com/download/AdventureWorks.pdf`.

FIGURE 2.1   OLTP ERD

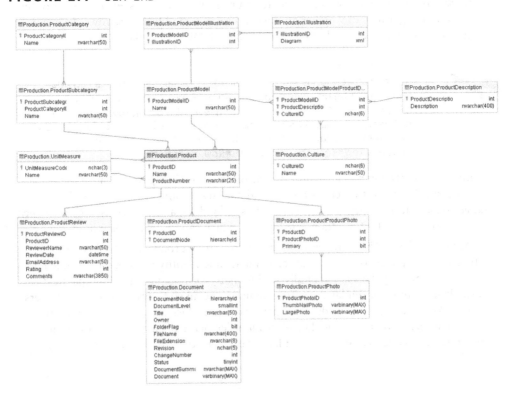

In this diagram, every entity that has multiple records is broken up into multiple tables to avoid redundant data storage. Entities that are related to one another can be related one or many times. For example, each product category has multiple product subcategories. Therefore, the relationship between the ProductCategory table and the ProductSubcategory table is one-to-many. The *crow's feet* shape in the relationship signals that there are many product subcategories for each product category.

While this level of data normalization is highly efficient for writing and storing individual transactions, it can be less efficient for applications that perform large numbers of read operations. Queries that are issued from read-heavy applications (e.g., reporting and analytical applications) potentially require many joins to de-normalize the data, making these queries very long and complex. Read operations that perform aggregations over large amounts of data are also very resource intensive for OLTP databases and can cause blocking issues for other transactions issued against the database. It is for these reasons that analytical databases carry different design best practices than their OLTP counterparts.

Analytical Workload Design Considerations

Data warehouses and online analytical processing (OLAP) systems are optimally designed for read-heavy applications. While OLTP systems focus on storing current transactions, data warehouses and OLAP models focus on storing historical data that can be used to measure a business's performance and predict what future actions it should take.

Data warehouses serve as central repositories of data from one or more disparate data sources, including various OLTP systems. Not only does this eliminate the burden of running analytical workloads from the OLTP database, it also enriches the OLTP data with other data sources that provide useful information for decision makers. Data warehouses can store data that is processed in batch and in real time to provide a *single source of truth* for an organization's analytical needs. Data analysts commonly run analytical queries against data warehouses that return aggregated calculations that can be used to support business decisions.

Data warehouses can be built using one of the SMP database offerings on Azure, such as Azure SQL Database, or on the MPP data warehouse Azure Synapse Analytics dedicated SQL pools. The choice largely depends on the amount of historical data that is going to be stored and the nature of the queries that will be issued to the data warehouse. A good rule of thumb is that if the size of the data warehouse is going to be less than 1 terabyte, then Azure SQL Database will do the trick. However, this is a general statement, and more consideration is needed when deciding between SMP or MPP. Chapter 5, "Modern Data Warehouses in Azure," covers more detail on what to consider when designing a modern data warehouse.

OLAP models extract commonly used data for reporting from data warehouses to simplify data analysis. Like data warehouses, OLAP models are used for read-heavy scenarios and typically include the following predefined features to allow users to see consistent results without having to write their own logic:

- Aggregations that can be immediately reported against
- Time-oriented calculations

OLAP models come in two flavors: multidimensional and tabular. Multidimensional cubes such as those created with SQL Server Analysis Services (SSAS) were used in traditional business intelligence (BI) solutions to serve data as dimensions and measures. Tabular models such as Azure Analysis Services and models built in Power BI serve data using relational modeling constructs (e.g., tables and columns) while storing metadata as multidimensional modeling constructs (e.g., dimensions and measures) behind the scenes. Tabular models have become the standard for OLAP models as they use similar design patterns to relational databases, make use of columnar storage that optimally compresses data for analytics and leverages an easy-to-learn language (DAX) that data analysts can use to create custom metrics. Chapter 6, "Reporting with Power BI," will describe in detail tabular models and how they are used in Power BI.

Data warehouses and OLAP models store data in a way that is designed to be easy for analysts and developers to read. Tables in analytical systems are defined to be easily understood by business users so that they do not have to rely on IT every time they need to produce new analysis against historical data. Instead of using strict nomenclature and normalized rules that make OLTP systems ideal for storing transactional data, analytical systems flatten data so that business users can easily query data without having to join several tables together.

One common design pattern for data warehouses and OLAP models is the *star schema*. Star schemas denormalize data taken from OLTP systems, resulting in some attributes being duplicated in tables. This is done to make the data easier for analysts to read, allowing them to avoid having to join several tables in their queries. While de-normalization is not optimal for write-heavy, transactional workloads, it will increase the performance of read-oriented, analytical workloads.

Star schemas work by relating business entities, also known as the nouns of the business, to measurable events. These can be broken down into the following classifications that are specific to a star schema:

- *Dimension tables* store information about business entities. Dimension tables store descriptive columns for each entity and a key column that serves as a unique identifier. Examples include date, customer, geography, and product dimensions. Dimension tables typically store a relatively small number of rows but many columns, depending on how many descriptors are necessary for a given dimension.

- *Fact tables* store measurable observations or events such as Internet sales, inventory, or sales quotas. Along with numeric measurements, fact tables contain dimension key columns for each dimension that a measure or observation is related to. These relationships determine the granularity of the data in the fact table. For example, an Internet sales fact table that has a dimension key for date is only as granular as the level of detail stored in the date dimension table. If the date dimension table only includes details for years and months, then queries performing time-based calculations will only be able to drill down to monthly sales. However, if it includes details for years, quarters, months, weeks, days, and hours, then queries will be able to perform more fine-grained analysis of the data.

Figure 2.2 is a partial example of the AdventureWorks DW star schema, focusing on dimensions and facts related to Internet sales for products manufactured and sold by

AdventureWorks. The entire diagram can be found at `https://dataedo.com/samples/html/Data_warehouse/doc/AdventureWorksDW_4/modules/Internet_Sales_101/module.html`.

FIGURE 2.2   Star schema

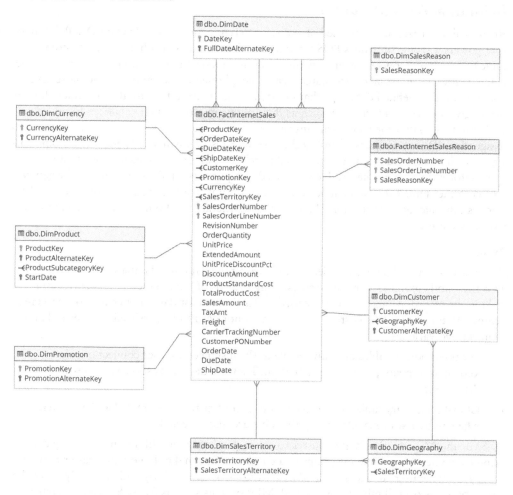

This diagram shows the relationship between the *nouns* involved in an online sale and the associated metrics. While not illustrated in the image, if you go to the link in the preceding paragraph, you will find more details on each dimension table and will see that they have many columns that provide high granularity for the sales metrics.

OLAP models take star schemas a step further by including business logic and predefined calculations that are ready to be used in reports. This level of abstraction that allows users to focus on building business-critical reports without needing to write SQL queries that perform aggregations and joins over the underlying data is known as a *semantic layer*. Semantic layers are typically placed over data pulled from a data warehouse. Along with the business-friendly names that come with a star schema, semantic layers store calculations that allow users to easily filter and summarize data.

Relational Data Structures

Relational databases are composed of several different components. Take an OLTP database that powers a retail company's POS for example. This database probably has a customer table that contains rows for every customer that has made a purchase. The table can include columns for each customer's first name, last name, phone number, address, and more. Every column has a predefined data type that inserted values must adhere to. If a customer chooses not to give a piece of information such as their phone number, a null value can be added as a placeholder so that the row maintains the structure of the table's schema. Every row is also assigned an ID that uniquely identifies the customer, also known as a *primary key*. Some columns, such as the ID column, are also used to relate to other tables such as one that stores more information about the products involved in a purchase. This is known as a *foreign key*. The customer table can also include *indexes* that optimize how the data is organized so that queries can quickly retrieve data. These database structures and others are defined in the following sections.

Tables

Tables are structured database objects that store all the data in a database. Data is organized into rows and columns, with rows representing records of data and columns representing a field in the record. Along with user-defined tables that persist data, users can choose to create temporary tables that briefly store data that does not need to be persisted long term. These come in two varieties:

- Local temporary tables are only visible to the instance of a user connection, also known as a session, that they are built in. They are deleted as soon as the session is disconnected.

- Global temporary tables are visible to any user after they are created and are deleted when all user sessions referencing the table are disconnected.

SMP and MPP databases allow users to create partitions on tables to horizontally distribute data across multiple filegroups in a database. This makes large tables easier to manage by allowing users to access individual partitions of data quickly and efficiently while the integrity of the overall table is maintained. MPP systems such as Azure Synapse Analytics dedicated SQL pools take this a step further. Along with being able to partition data across filegroups, MPP systems spread data across multiple *distributions* on one or more compute nodes. The types of distributed tables available in Azure Synapse Analytics dedicated SQL pools and when to use each are covered in Chapter 5, "Modern Data Warehouses in Azure."

Views

Views are virtual tables whose contents are defined by a query. The rows and columns of data in a view come from tables referenced in the query that define the view. They act as a virtual layer to filter and combine data from regularly queried tables. Users can simplify their queries since views handle the complex filtering and joining of data that would normally need to be handled by the user. They are also useful security mechanisms as users do not need permission to the underlying tables that make up the views.

Figure 2.3 is an example of a view definition taken from the AdventureWorks OLTP database. This view queries the ProductModel, ProductModelProductDescriptionCulture, and ProductDescription tables to compile a list of products sold and their descriptions in multiple languages.

FIGURE 2.3   View definition

```
CREATE VIEW [Production].[vProductAndDescription]
AS
SELECT
        p.[ProductID]
       ,p.[Name]
       ,pm.[Name] AS [ProductModel]
       ,pmx.[CultureID]
       ,pd.[Description]
FROM [Production].[Product] p
    INNER JOIN [Production].[ProductModel] pm
    ON p.[ProductModelID] = pm.[ProductModelID]
    INNER JOIN [Production].[ProductModelProductDescriptionCulture] pmx
    ON pm.[ProductModelID] = pmx.[ProductModelID]
    INNER JOIN [Production].[ProductDescription] pd
    ON pmx.[ProductDescriptionID] = pd.[ProductDescriptionID];
GO
```

This view allows users querying product description information to simplify their queries from performing joins on multiple tables to only reading from one database object.

A special type of view that can be used to improve the performance of complex analytical queries that are issued against large data warehouse datasets are *materialized views*. Unlike regular views that are generated each time the view is used, materialized views are preprocessed and stored in the data warehouse. The data stored in a materialized view is updated as it is updated in the underlying tables. Materialized views that are defined by complex analytical queries improve performance and reduce the amount of time required to prepare data for analysis by pre-aggregating data and storing it in a manner that is ready to be used in reports.

To create a materialized view in Azure Synapse Analytics dedicated SQL pools, you will need to issue a CREATE MATERIALIZED VIEW statement instead of a CREATE VIEW statement that you would with a normal view. Materialized views also require an explicit distribution type, like tables stored in dedicated SQL pools. More on distribution types in Chapter 5, "Modern Data Warehouses in Azure."

Indexes

Consider the index at the end of this book. Its purpose is to sort keywords and provide each keyword's location in the book. Database indexes work very similarly in that they sort a list of values and provide pointers to the physical locations of those values. Ideally, indexes are designed to optimize the way data is stored in database tables to best serve the types of queries that are issued to them.

Depending on the workload, indexes physically store data in a row-wise format (rowstore) or a column-wise format (columnstore). If queries are searching for values, also known as seeks, or for a small range of values, then rowstore indexes such as clustered and nonclustered indexes are ideal. On the other hand, columnstore indexes are best for database tables that store data that is commonly scanned and aggregated. The following are descriptions of the three commonly used types of indexes:

- *Clustered indexes* physically sort and store data based on their values. There can only be one clustered index because clustered indexes determine the physical order of the data. Columns that include mostly unique values are ideal candidates for clustered indexes. Clustered indexes are automatically created on primary key columns for this reason.

- *Nonclustered indexes* contain pointers to where data exists. There can be more than one nonclustered index on a database, and each one can be composed of multiple columns depending on the nature of the queries issued to the database. For example, queries that return data based on specific filter criteria can benefit from a nonclustered index on the columns being filtered. The nonclustered index allows the database engine to quickly find the data that matches the filter criteria.

- *Columnstore indexes* use column-based data storage to optimize the storage of data stored in a data warehouse. Instead of physically storing data in a row-wise format like that of a clustered or nonclustered index, columnstore indexes store data in a column-wise format. This provides a high level of compression and is optimal for analytical queries that perform aggregations over large amounts of data.

Proper index design can be the difference between a poorly performing database and one that runs like a charm. While index design best practices are out of scope for this book, I recommend the following article for guidelines on choosing an index strategy: `https://docs.microsoft.com/en-us/sql/relational-databases/sql-server-index-design-guide?view=sql-server-ver15`.

Stored Procedures

Stored procedures are groups of one or more T-SQL statements that perform actions on data in a database. They can be executed manually or via an external application (e.g., custom .NET application, Azure Data Factory). They can also be scheduled to run at predetermined periods of time with a SQL Server Agent job, such as every hour or every night at midnight. Stored procedures can accept input parameters and return multiple values as output parameters to the application calling them.

Code that is frequently used to perform database operations is an ideal candidate to be encapsulated in stored procedures. This eliminates the need to rewrite the same code repeatedly, which also reduces the chances of errors from code inconsistency. The application tier is also simplified since applications will only need to execute the stored procedure instead of needing to maintain and run entire blocks of T-SQL code.

Functions

Functions are like stored procedures in that they encapsulate commonly run code. The major difference between a user-defined function in SQL and a stored procedure is that functions must return a value. Stored procedures can be used to make changes to data without ever returning a response to the user running the stored procedure. Functions, on the other hand, can only return data that is typically the result of a complex calculation. Functions accept parameters and return values as either a single scalar value or a result set.

Triggers

Triggers are T-SQL statements that are executed in response to a variety of events. These events can be DDL, DML, or login related. Triggers are typically used when you want to do the following:

- Prevent certain changes to columns in tables.
- Perform an action based on a change to database schemas or underlying data.
- Log changes to the database schema.
- Enforce relational integrity throughout the database.

Relational Database Offerings in Azure

Until recently, most organizations hosted their database systems in on-premises datacenters that they owned or leased. They were responsible for applying updates to the database software and had to make sure that the hardware hosting the databases was properly maintained. Business continuity aspects such as database backup management, high availability (HA), and disaster recovery (DR) standards would need to be implemented to ensure minimal downtime in case of database corruption or server downtime. Scalability is also a concern, as database servers that outgrow compute allocated to them require someone to physically add compute to the server. All these items require additional hardware and levels of expertise from employees, thus increasing the total cost of ownership (TCO) for a database.

Cloud-based hosting has fundamentally shifted how organizations calculate TCO for their relational databases. Many operations that surround database upgrades or patching, business continuity, and scalability are handled by the cloud company. This allows organizations to shift their focus from maintaining hardware and managing business continuity concerns to being able to purely focus on the needs of the database users. Provisioning and scaling a database is also much easier as almost every requirement is preconfigured. Shortly put, databases can be easily deployed in Azure with the click of a button and scaled up and down with a slider (more on this later in the chapter).

Before getting into the different relational databases offerings in Azure, it's important to understand the three types of cloud computing services. Having a foundational knowledge of how each of these are implemented is paramount to understanding the responsibilities and the TCO for hosting a database on Azure.

▪ *Infrastructure as a Service (IaaS)* offerings in Azure provide customers with the ability to create virtual infrastructure that mirrors an on-premises environment. IaaS offerings give organizations the ability to easily migrate their on-premises infrastructure to similar IaaS-based offerings in Azure without needing to completely redesign their applications using a cloud native approach. This is a typical first step for moving to the cloud as it allows organizations to offload the management of their hardware to Microsoft using a *lift-and-shift* strategy. While IaaS deployments allow organizations to no longer worry about maintaining the hardware powering an application, they will still need to manage maintenance at the operating system (OS) and application level. IaaS offerings include virtual machines that host services that would typically be hosted in a customer's on-premises environment, such as SQL Server, and are connected via an Azure Virtual Network (VNet). These services can easily connect to an organization's existing network infrastructure, allowing them to utilize a hybrid cloud strategy.

▪ *Platform as a Service (PaaS)* takes IaaS a step further by abstracting the OS and application software from the user. When deploying a PaaS offering, organizations can specify the resources they would like deployed, an initial size and compute tier depending on the intensity of the workload, what Azure region they would like them deployed to, and other optional or service-specific requirements. Azure will then provision the necessary resources to meet those specific requirements. Once deployed, all OS and software maintenance such as business continuity, upgrades, and patches are handled by Azure. This allows organizations to minimize the amount of effort required to maintain these services and instead focus on using them to build solutions that impact the business. Like IaaS offerings, PaaS offerings can also be interconnected via a VNet and connected to an organization's existing on-premises network infrastructure. PaaS services include Azure SQL Database, Azure SQL Managed Instance (MI), and all the open-source relational database offerings that are hosted on Azure SQL.

▪ *Software as a Service (SaaS)* offerings represent the highest level of abstraction available to an organization hosting its infrastructure and applications on the cloud. Organizations simply purchase the number of licenses required for the service and then use it. Typical examples of SaaS offerings include Power BI Online and Office 365. None of the relational database offerings discussed in this chapter are SaaS offerings.

IaaS, PaaS, and SaaS are critical components of the Microsoft Azure Fundamental AZ-900 exam. If you would like to learn more about the three types of cloud computing services, please read Jim Boyce's *Microsoft Certified Azure Fundamental Exam Guide* (Wiley, 2021). This book provides a fundamental knowledge of Azure and provides further in-depth information on IaaS, PaaS, and SaaS applications.

Azure SQL

Azure SQL is a broad term used to describe the family of SMP relational database products in Azure that are built upon Microsoft's SQL Server engine. These include one IaaS option with SQL Server on Azure Virtual Machines (VM) and two PaaS options with Azure SQL MI and Azure SQL Database. Azure SQL Database can be broken down even further into two different options: single database and elastic pool. There are also several service tiers available for each offering that best suit different types of workloads. With so many options available, organizations must weigh several factors when deciding which Azure SQL option is the most appropriate for their use cases:

- *Cost*—All three options include a base price that covers underlying infrastructure and licensing. Each option also includes hybrid licensing benefits that allow organizations to apply on-premises SQL Server licenses to reduce the cost of the service. Keep in mind that hosting a database in a virtual machine will require additional administration overhead that the PaaS options don't require.

- *Service-level agreement (SLA)*—All three options provide high, industry-standard SLAs. PaaS options guarantee a 99.99 percent SLA, while IaaS guarantees a 99.95 percent SLA for infrastructure, meaning that organizations will need to implement additional mechanisms to ensure database availability. You can refer to the following documentation for more information regarding Azure SQL SLAs: `https://docs.microsoft.com/en-us/azure/azure-sql/azure-sql-iaas-vs-paas-what-is-overview#service-level-agreement-sla`.

- *Migration timeline*—This is a factor that must be considered if an organization is migrating to Azure as opposed to building an application from scratch with a cloud native design. Organizations may consider one option over the other depending on how long the timeline is. For example, databases can be migrated to a virtual machine in a relatively short amount of time because virtual machines can host the same version of SQL Server as an on-premises SQL Server instance. Azure SQL MI also provides nearly the same feature parity as an on-premises SQL Server, but some changes may need to be applied, especially if the database that will be migrated is hosted on an older version of SQL Server.

- *Administration*—Azure SQL Database and Azure SQL MI minimize overhead by managing typical database administration activities such as database backups, patches, version upgrades, HA, and threat protection. However, this also limits the range of custom administrative activities that can be performed.

- *Feature parity*—Because Azure SQL Database abstracts the OS and database server components from the user, there are certain features of SQL Server that are not supported in Azure SQL Database. These include cross-database joins, CLR integration, and SQL Server Agent. Azure SQL MI is nearly 100 percent feature compatible with SQL Server but still maintains a few differences such as features that rely on Windows-related objects. SQL Server on Azure VMs provides 100 percent feature parity because it is the same as a SQL Server instance hosted on an on-premises virtual machine. However, because of potential SQL Server version differences, there could be feature differences when migrating from an old version of SQL Server to a newer version of SQL Server on Azure VM or one of the PaaS options. Deprecated features and features that are incompatible with the PaaS options can be discovered using the Data Migration Assistant (DMA). The DMA will be covered in further detail later in this chapter.

Most differences between SQL Server and Azure SQL Database are focused on server-related differences. Because Microsoft manages the backend server for an Azure SQL Database, features such as logins, server-level permissions, and EXECUTE AS LOGIN are not available. Instead, users can use database-scoped features such as database-level permissions and EXECUTE AS USER. More information on SQL Server and Azure SQL Database differences can be found at `https://docs .microsoft.com/en-us/azure/azure-sql/database/transact- sql-tsql-differences-sql-server`.

The various Azure SQL offerings come with different levels of abstraction and management. Figure 2.4 illustrates the relationship between abstraction and administrative effort for each option.

FIGURE 2.4 Azure SQL abstraction vs. administrative effort

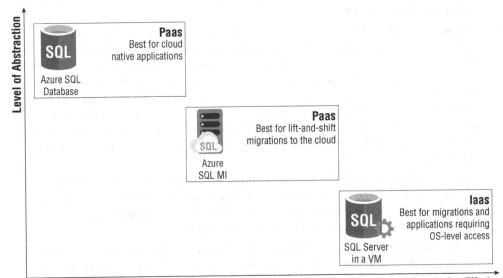

As seen in the diagram, a SQL Server on Azure VM requires the most administrative effort because it provides full control over the SQL Server instance and the underlying OS. This is ideal for situations that require highly customized OS and/or database images

or scenarios requiring very granular control over the SQL Server engine. Azure SQL MI removes the OS layer from the user's point of view but is more like an on-premises SQL Server instance than Azure SQL Database in that it provides a fully isolated environment encapsulated in a VNet and includes system databases. Users hosting their databases on Azure SQL MI still benefit from using a PaaS database in that patching, SQL Server version upgrades, backups, HA, DR, data encryption, auditing, and threat protection are all handled behind the scenes by Microsoft. Azure SQL Database completely abstracts the OS layer and database engine from users. Greenfield solutions that are developed using cloud native best practices typically use Azure SQL Database as their backend relational database.

Ultimately, choosing the right Azure SQL option comes down to the solution requirements and how much control is needed over the OS and database engine. The following sections explore each option in further detail.

SQL Server on Azure Virtual Machine

There are several reasons why an organization would want to migrate its applications to the cloud. Perhaps the most common reason is to offload the maintenance of hardware and networking equipment that it either owns or leases to a cloud provider. Expiring datacenter leases or aging hardware force many companies to rethink how they manage their IT infrastructure. While many organizations will work to modernize their applications to be cloud native, most of them still use legacy applications that rely on features of SQL Server that are not available in the PaaS offerings of Azure SQL. There could also be specific situations that require fine-grained control over the database engine and the OS that it sits on. For these reasons, organizations may decide to migrate their existing SQL Server footprint to Azure SQL's IaaS offering: SQL Server on Azure VMs.

As far as the database engine is concerned, a SQL Server on Azure VM is no different than a SQL Server instance hosted on a physical server in an on-premises environment. This allows developers and database administrators to acclimate quickly to working with SQL Server in Azure. Engineers deploying a SQL Server on Azure VM can choose one of three approaches for doing so:

- Choose one of the available SQL Server VM images from the Azure marketplace. These images allow you to easily deploy a specific version of SQL Server on the OS of your choosing.

- Install your own SQL Server license on a VM. Users with existing VMs in Azure can choose to install SQL Server with an existing license to save the need of deploying a new VM.

- Lift-and-shift existing VMs from an on-premises environment to Azure with Azure Migrate. Azure Migrate is a tool that can be used to assess and migrate on-premises infrastructure to Azure. VMs hosting SQL Server can be migrated to Azure using Azure Migrate without needing to deploy a new VM through the Azure Marketplace. More information on migrating VMs to Azure with Azure Migrate can be found at `https://docs.microsoft.com/en-us/azure/migrate/migrate-services-overview#azure-migrate-server-migration-tool`.

Taking advantage of the ready-made images available in the Azure Marketplace greatly reduces the amount of time needed to provision a SQL Server VM in Azure. There are two licensing types available for SQL Server VMs: pay-as-you-go and bring your own license (BYOL). Pay-as-you-go simplifies licensing costs by billing you for the per-minute usage of the instance. Table 2.1 outlines the available pay-as-you-go SQL Server images in Azure.

TABLE 2.1 Available Pay-As-You-Go SQL Server images

Version	Operating System	Edition
SQL Server 2019	Windows Server 2019	Enterprise, Standard, Web, Developer
SQL Server 2019	Ubuntu 18.04	Enterprise, Standard, Web, Developer
SQL Server 2019	Red Hat Enterprise Linux (RHEL) 8	Enterprise, Standard, Web, Developer
SQL Server 2019	SUSE Linux Enterprise Server (SLES) v12 SP5	Enterprise, Standard, Web, Developer
SQL Server 2017	Windows Server 2016	Enterprise, Standard, Web, Express, Developer
SQL Server 2017	Red Hat Enterprise Linux (RHEL) 7.4	Enterprise, Standard, Web, Express, Developer
SQL Server 2017	SUSE Linux Enterprise Server (SLES) v12 SP2	Enterprise, Standard, Web, Express, Developer
SQL Server 2017	Ubuntu 16.04 LTS	Enterprise, Standard, Web, Express, Developer
SQL Server 2016 SP2	Windows Server 2016	Enterprise, Standard, Web, Express, Developer
SQL Server 2014 SP2	Windows Server 2012 R2	Enterprise, Standard, Web, Express
SQL Server 2012 SP4	Windows Server 2012 R2	Enterprise, Standard, Web, Express
SQL Server 2008 R2 SP4	Windows Server 2008 R2	Enterprise, Standard, Web, Express

Organizations who have already purchased SQL Server licenses can also apply those licenses to reduce the VM's SQL Server cost component. This is known as bring your own license, or BYOL for short. Table 2.2 outlines the available BYOL SQL Server images in Azure.

TABLE 2.2 Available bring your own license SQL Server images

Version	Operating System	Edition
SQL Server 2019	Windows Server 2019	Enterprise BYOL, Standard BYOL
SQL Server 2017	Windows Server 2016	Enterprise BYOL, Standard BYOL
SQL Server 2016 SP2	Windows Server 2016	Enterprise BYOL, Standard BYOL
SQL Server 2014 SP2	Windows Server 2012 R2	Enterprise BYOL, Standard BYOL
SQL Server 2012 SP4	Windows Server 2012 R2	Enterprise BYOL, Standard BYOL

You can deploy an older version of SQL Server that is not available in the Azure Marketplace with PowerShell. To view available images, run the following command in a PowerShell window:

```
Import-Module -Name Az
$Location = <Azure Region the SQL Server VM will be deployed to>
Get-AzVMImageOffer -Location $Location -Publisher`
'MicrosoftSQLServer'
```

The available pay-as-you-go and BYOL SQL Server images are liable to change as new versions of SQL Server are introduced and older versions are deprecated. You can stay up to date on the available SQL Server VM images by referring to the tables in the following link: https://docs.microsoft.com/en-us/azure/azure-sql/virtual-machines/windows/sql-server-on-azure-vm-iaas-what-is-overview#get-started-with-sql-server-vms.

VM size and storage configuration must also be considered when creating a SQL Server Azure VM. There are multiple VM sizes available that include different virtual CPU quantities, memory sizes, and different disk sizes. Additional disks can be added to the VM depending on what is hosted in addition to SQL Server. There are also different categories of VM sizes that provide different baselines for performance, including these:

- *Memory optimized*—These provide stronger memory-to-vCPU ratios and are the Microsoft-recommended choice for SQL Server VMs on Azure.

- *General purpose*—These provide balanced memory-to-vCPU ratios and best serve smaller workloads such as development and test, web servers, and smaller database servers.
- *Storage optimized*—These are designed with optimized disk throughput and input-output (I/O) and are strong options for data analytics workloads.

These are general recommendations and should be used with application performance metrics to make the most appropriate VM choice for different workloads. Keep in mind that VMs use a pay-as-you-go cost model and can be stopped when not needed so that you are not charged during those times. However, most SQL Server VMs will need to stay online unless the SQL Server instance is a test instance. Organizations that will be using one or more SQL Server VMs for one or three years can purchase *Azure Reserved Virtual Machine Instances*. Once applied to a VM, Azure Reserved Virtual Machine Instances discount the cost of the virtual machine and compute costs.

 It is important to determine the right VM size before purchasing a reservation. The following link provides more information on Azure Reserved Virtual Machine Instances and determining the right VM size: `https://docs.microsoft.com/en-in/azure/virtual-machines/prepay-reserved-vm-instances?toc=/azure/cost-management-billing/reservations/toc.json#determine-the-right-vm-size-before-you-buy.`

Deploying a ready-made SQL Server VM image from the Azure Marketplace will include a default storage configuration for data, log, and tempdb files. While these configurations are optimal for general workloads, many workloads may benefit from different ones. There may also be a need to optimize for cost versus performance for non-production workloads. Regardless of workload type, these are some general checklist items that should be considered when configuring storage for a SQL Server VM on Azure:

- Place data, log, and tempdb files on separate drives.
- Place tempdb on the local SSD drive. This drive is ephemeral and will deallocate resources when the VM is stopped.
- Consider using standard HDD/SDD storage for development and test workloads.
- Use premium SSD disks for data and log files for production SQL Server workloads.

  - Use P30 and/or P40 disks for data files to ensure caching support.
  - Use P30 through P80 disks for log files.

Collecting storage performance metrics for workloads that will be migrated to Azure will help determine the most appropriate disk configuration. More information on SQL Server on Azure VM storage configurations can be found at `https://docs.microsoft.com/en-us/azure/azure-sql/virtual-machines/windows/performance-guidelines-best-practices-storage.`

Business Continuity

There are multiple solutions available in Azure to ensure that data hosted on SQL Server VMs is highly available in the event of several outage scenarios, ranging from planned downtime to datacenter-level disasters. These include solutions that provide database backup management at the database level and high availability and disaster recovery (HADR) capabilities at both the VM and database levels.

Azure provides business continuity for disk storage by creating copies of the data stored on disk and storing them on Azure Blob storage. This type of redundancy can be broken down with the following options:

- *Locally redundant storage (LRS)* creates three copies of the data stored on disk and stores them in the same location in the same Azure region.

- *Geo-redundant storage (GRS)* stores three copies of the disk data in the same Azure region as the VM and then stores an additional three copies in a separate region.

While these services provide redundancy for data stored on Azure VMs, they should not be relied on as the only business continuity solution for SQL Server data. Database backups should also be taken to protect against application or user errors. Also, GRS does not support the data and log files to be stored on separate disks. Data from these two files is copied independently and asynchronously, creating a risk of losing data in the event of an outage.

Organizations can choose to set up their own database backup strategy through maintenance plans that are run as a SQL Server Agent job on a scheduled basis. Backups can be stored on local storage or in Azure Blob storage. Azure also allows organizations to offload this process by using a service called *Automated Backup*. This service regularly creates database backups and stores them on Azure Blob storage without requiring a database administrator to set up the job on the database engine.

For true database-level HADR, organizations can add databases hosted on SQL Server VMs to a *SQL Server Always On availability group*. Availability groups, or AGs for short, replicate data from a set of user databases to one or more secondary SQL Server instances that are hosted on different VMs. The VMs, or server nodes, that host the primary and secondary SQL Server instances are clustered at the OS level. The cluster monitors the health of the server nodes and will promote a secondary server node to the primary if the existing primary experiences a failure.

Typical AG configurations include at least one secondary node in the same region as the primary to maintain HA and at least one secondary node in a different region for DR. Database connections will move, or failover, to the HA node during planned downtime for the primary node. If the primary node and the secondary nodes in the same region as the primary are down at the same time, database connections will failover to the DR node in the other region.

AG configurations are not limited to Azure-only VMs. Hybrid scenarios are possible, allowing organizations to add on-premises SQL Server instances to the solution. This requires VPN connectivity between the Azure network that SQL Server Azure VM is in and the on-premises network that the on-premises SQL Server is in. Network requirements for SQL Server VMs on Azure and hybrid scenarios will be discussed in the next section.

> While these are common solutions used to create business continuity solutions for SQL Server on Azure VMs, there are more specific patterns designed to serve different scenarios. Refer to the following link to learn more about setting up HADR solutions for SQL Server on Azure VMs: https://docs.microsoft.com/en-us/azure/azure-sql/virtual-machines/windows/business-continuity-high-availability-disaster-recovery-hadr-overview.

Network Isolation

A critical component of any IaaS offering is its ability to be completely self-isolated within a virtual network. Virtual networks in Azure, otherwise known as VNets, provide the backbone for isolating communication between different services. A VNet can include one or more subnets depending on the services that it is hosting. VNets can connect to other Azure VNets using a service called VNet peering as well as connect to on-premises networks through a point-to-site VPN, site-to-site VPN, or an Azure ExpressRoute. Hybrid connections are critical for organizations that have a presence in Azure and continue to maintain some of their applications in their on-premises environment.

VNets enable organizations to block specific IP address ranges and network protocols from being able to access resources connected to them. This includes blocking access to and from the public Internet. Databases hosted on SQL Server VMs on Azure are therefore restricted to only being able to communicate with applications that have been approved by an organization's network security team.

Deploying through the Azure Portal

Deploying services in Azure can be done manually on the Azure Portal or automated using a scripting language (e.g., PowerShell or Bash) or an *Infrastructure as Code* template. SQL Server on Azure VMs are no different than any other service in this aspect, providing users multiple options for managing the deployment of their SQL Server databases on Azure. This section will cover the steps on how to manually deploy a SQL Server Azure VM through the Azure Portal. See the section "Deployment Scripting and Automation" later in this chapter to learn more about scripting and automating the deployment process for relational databases in Azure.

Use the following steps to create a SQL Server on Azure VM using the Azure Portal:

1. Log into `portal.azure.com` and search for *SQL virtual machines* in the search bar at the top of the page. Click *SQL virtual machines* to go to the SQL virtual machines page in the Azure Portal.

2. Click *Create* to start choosing the configuration options for your SQL Server on Azure VM.

3. Navigate to the SQL virtual machines option on the *Select SQL deployment option* page and select the VM image you would like to deploy. Figure 2.5 shows how this page is displayed and some of the options available after you click the *Image* drop-down arrow. Once you have selected an image, click the *Create* button to continue configuring the VM.

FIGURE 2.5 Select a SQL virtual machine image.

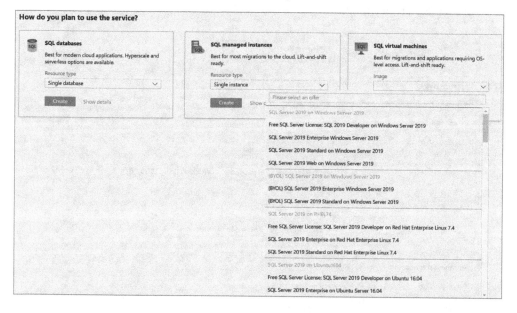

4. The *Create a virtual machine* page includes eight tabs with different configuration options to tailor the SQL Server VM to fit your needs. Let's start by exploring the options available in the Basics tab. Along with the following list that describes each option, you can view a completed example of this tab in Figure 2.6.

   a. Choose the subscription and resource group that will contain the SQL Server VM. You can create a new resource group on this page if have not already created one.

   b. Enter a name for the VM.

   c. Choose the Azure region you wish to deploy the image to.

   d. Select whether you would like to enable high availability for the VM by using an Availability Zone or an Availability Set. Note that this is high availability for the VM and not for the SQL Server instance.

   e. Review the VM image selected and change it if necessary.

   f. Choose the VM size.

   g. Set a username and password for the administrator account.

h. Set any inbound network ports that you wish to be accessible from the public Internet.

i. The last optional step on this page is whether you would like to apply an existing Windows Server license to the VM to reduce its cost.

FIGURE 2.6   Create a SQL virtual machine: Basics tab.

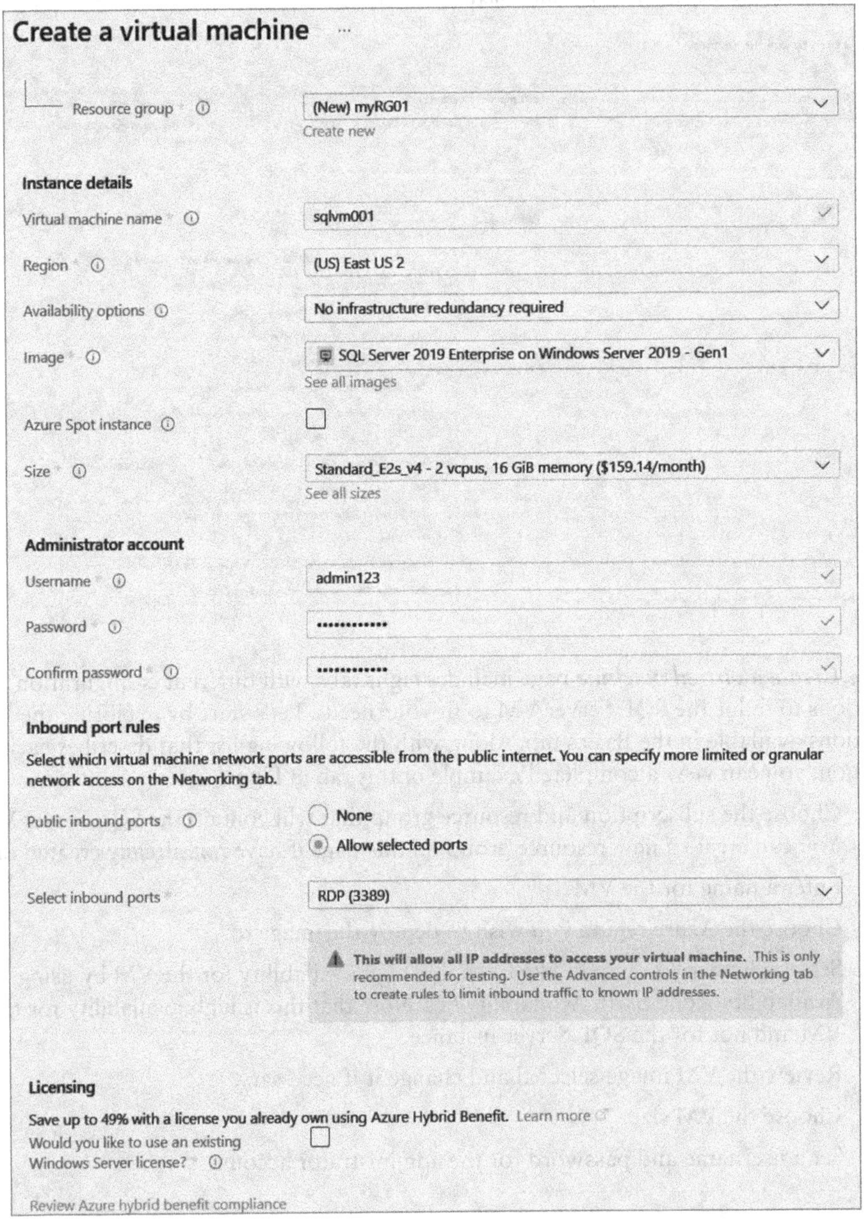

Create a virtual machine   ...

Resource group ⓘ	(New) myRG01 ▽
	Create new

Instance details

Virtual machine name * ⓘ	sqlvm001 ✓
Region * ⓘ	(US) East US 2 ▽
Availability options ⓘ	No infrastructure redundancy required ▽
Image * ⓘ	🖳 SQL Server 2019 Enterprise on Windows Server 2019 - Gen1 ▽
	See all images
Azure Spot instance ⓘ	☐
Size * ⓘ	Standard_E2s_v4 - 2 vcpus, 16 GiB memory ($159.14/month) ▽
	See all sizes

Administrator account

Username * ⓘ	admin123 ✓
Password * ⓘ	•••••••••••• ✓
Confirm password * ⓘ	•••••••••••• ✓

Inbound port rules

Select which virtual machine network ports are accessible from the public internet. You can specify more limited or granular network access on the Networking tab.

Public inbound ports ⓘ	◯ None
	◉ Allow selected ports
Select inbound ports *	RDP (3389) ▽

> ⚠ **This will allow all IP addresses to access your virtual machine.** This is only recommended for testing. Use the Advanced controls in the Networking tab to create rules to limit inbound traffic to known IP addresses.

Licensing

Save up to 49% with a license you already own using Azure Hybrid Benefit. Learn more ↗
Would you like to use an existing   ☐
Windows Server license? ⓘ

Review Azure hybrid benefit compliance

5. The Disks tab focuses on the disk configuration for the OS. You can choose to change this from a Premium SSD to another disk type as well as change the encryption type used for the disk.

6. The Networking tab provides the following network configuration options for the VM. A completed example of this tab can be seen in Figure 2.7.

    a. Choose the virtual network that the VM will be located in.

    b. Choose a subnet within that virtual network for the VM.

    c. Optionally choose a public IP address to be used for communication outside of the virtual network.

    d. If needed, revise the open inbound ports selected in the Basics tab.

FIGURE 2.7   Create a SQL virtual machine: Networking tab.

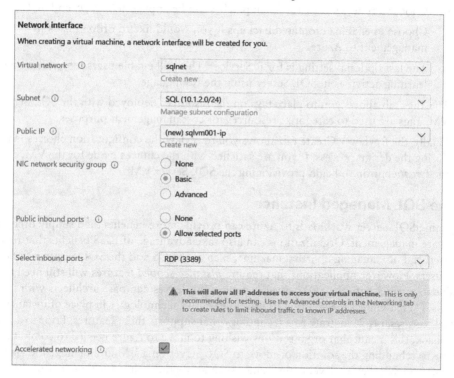

7. The Management tab allows you to customize features such as Azure Security Center monitoring, enabling automatic shutdown for the VM, and when OS patches should be applied.

8. The Advanced tab allows you to add any extensions or scripts to further customize the VM as it is being provisioned.

9. The SQL Server settings tab provide the following configuration options for the SQL Server instance hosted on the VM. Figure 2.8 illustrates a completed view of this tab.

   a. Choose the level of network isolation for SQL. The default for this option is limiting communication to applications that are connected to the VNet the VM is in. However, there are options to further lock the SQL Server instance down so that only applications in the VM can communicate to it and to relax security by allowing any application communicating over the public Internet to access it.

   b. Choose whether you would like to enable SQL Authentication and Azure Key Vault Integration.

   c. Review the default storage configuration for SQL Server's data, log, and tempdb files. Edit the configuration if the default options do not meet your requirements.

   d. Choose to apply an existing SQL Server license to reduce the cost of SQL.

   e. Choose a time window for when patches can be applied to the OS and SQL.

   f. Choose to enable automated backups if you would like to offload backup management to Azure.

   g. The last optional setting is for R Services. This will enable users to perform machine learning activities in SQL Server using the R language.

10. The Tags tab allows you to place tags on the resources deployed with the SQL Server VM. Tags are used to categorize resources for cost management purposes.

11. Finally, the Review + Create tab allows you to review the configuration choices made during the design process. If you are satisfied with the choices made for the VM, click the *Create* button to begin provisioning the SQL Server VM.

Azure SQL Managed Instance

Migrating SQL Server workloads to Azure can provide more benefits than simply offloading hardware management. Organizations can also take advantage of PaaS benefits that remove the overhead of managing a virtual machine, such as the OS and the SQL Server instance from users. However, applications that require *instance-scoped* features will still need to be able to interact with the SQL Server instance. This leaves database architects with two options: (1) rearchitect the solution to use cloud native technologies in place of instance-scoped features, or(2) migrate to a technology that supports these features. Prior to a few years back, this meant that organizations wishing to move to Azure needed to commit a lot of time to rebuilding the solution or move to SQL Server on a VM and manage the virtual machine and SQL Server–level maintenance such as upgrades. It is for these reasons that Microsoft introduced Azure SQL Managed Instance.

Azure SQL Managed Instance, or Azure SQL MI for short, is a PaaS database offering on Azure. It abstracts the OS but includes a SQL Server instance so that users can continue using their existing SQL Server processes without having to manage hardware or virtual machines. This makes it the ideal solution for customers looking to migrate many databases to Azure with as little effort as possible. Azure SQL MI also includes many system databases such as model, msdb, and tempdb. It can be used to host a distribution database for transactional replication, SSRS databases, and SSIS data catalog databases.

FIGURE 2.8   Create a SQL virtual machine: Settings tab.

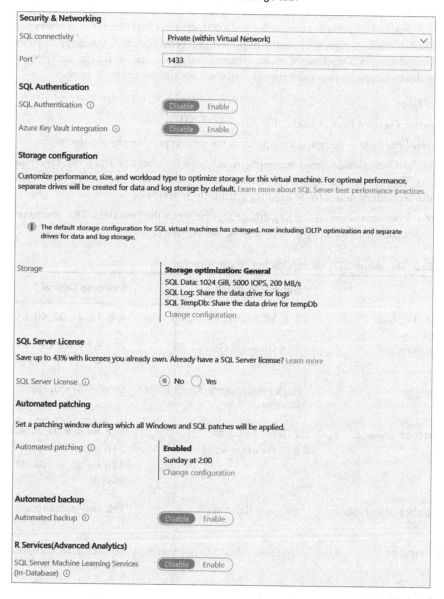

While Azure SQL MI can host SSISDB and SSRS catalog databases, it cannot host SSIS packages or SSRS. If you wish to host these services on Azure, they will need to be hosted on a virtual machine. Another alternative is to use a more modern approach by migrating SSIS packages to Azure Data Factory and hosting SSRS paginated reports in Power BI.

The Azure SQL MI database engine uses the latest version of SQL Server Enterprise Edition, with updates and patches applied by Microsoft as they are made available. Azure SQL MI is nearly 100 percent compatible with on-premises SQL Server and offers support for instance-scoped features such as the SQL Server Agent, common language runtime (CLR), linked servers, Database Mail, and distributed transactions. It also includes a native VNet implementation to provide network isolation for the databases it hosts.

Service Tiers

There are two service tiers available for Azure SQL MI:

- *General Purpose* is designed for applications with typical performance requirements.
- *Business Critical* is designed for applications with low latency and strict HA requirements. This tier uses a SQL Server Always On availability group for HA and enables one of the secondary nodes to be used for read-only workloads.

Table 2.3 outlines some of the key differences between the two tiers. The descriptions listed are for the Gen5 hardware version of Azure SQL MI.

TABLE 2.3   Azure SQL MI service tier characteristics

Feature	General Purpose	Business Critical
Number of vCores	4, 8, 16, 24, 32, 40, 64, 80	4, 8, 16, 24, 32, 40, 64, 80
Max Memory	20.4 GB–408 GB (5.1 GB/vCore)	20.4 GB–408 GB (5.1 GB/vCore)
Storage Type	High Performance Azure Blob storage	Local SSD storage
Max Instance Storage	2 TB for 4 vCores 8 TB for other sizes	1 TB for 4, 8, 16 vCores 2 TB for 24 vCores 4 TB for 32, 40, 64, 80 vCores
Max Number of Databases per Instance	100 user databases	100 user databases
Data/Log IOPS	Up to 30–40K IOPS per instance	16K–320K (4000 IOPS/vCore)
Storage I/O Latency	5–10 ms	1–2 ms

More information on the different Azure SQL MI service categories can be found at `https://docs.microsoft.com/en-us/azure/azure-sql/managed-instance/resource-limits#service-tier-characteristics`. Each of these service tiers falls under the vCore-based purchasing model and can be scaled up or down in the Azure Portal or through an automation script as workload requirements change.

The cost for Azure SQL MI can be reduced using a couple of different methods. First, organizations with existing SQL Server licenses can apply them to Azure SQL MI to reduce its cost. If an organization does not have or decides not to use existing licenses, they can choose to purchase reserved capacity. Like Azure Reserved Virtual Machine Instances for SQL Server on Azure VMs, reserved capacity allows organizations to commit to Azure SQL MI for one or three years. To purchase reserved capacity, you will need to specify the Azure region the Azure SQL MI will be deployed to, the service tier, and the length of the commitment.

Network Isolation

An Azure SQL MI is required to be placed inside a VNet upon creation. On top of this requirement, the subnet that the Azure SQL MI is deployed to must be dedicated to hosting one or more Azure SQL MIs. This requirement restricts access to databases hosted on the Azure SQL MI to only applications that can communicate with that VNet. On-premises networks that host applications connecting to Azure SQL MI can use a VPN or Azure ExpressRoute to communicate with the VNet in Azure.

Deploying an Azure SQL MI to a subnet for the first time creates more than just the database engine. Along with the database engine, the deployment will create the following:

- A virtual cluster to host each Azure SQL MI that is deployed to that subnet. An Azure SQL MI is made up of a set of service components that are hosted on a dedicated set of virtual machines that are abstracted from the user and run inside the subnet. Together, these virtual machines form a virtual cluster.

- A network security group (NSG) to control access to the SQL Managed Instance data endpoint by filtering traffic on port 1433 and ports 11000–11999 when SQL Managed Instance is configured for redirect connections. The NSG will be associated with the subnet once it is provisioned.

- A User Defined Route (UDR) table to route traffic that has on-premises private IP ranges as a destination through the virtual network gateway or virtual network appliance (NVA). The UDR table will be associated with the subnet once it is provisioned.

The subnet will also be delegated to the Microsoft.Sql/managedInstances resource provider. See the section "Azure Resource Manager Templates" later in this chapter for more information on resource providers.

While knowing specific network requirement details for Azure SQL MI is not required for the DP-900 exam, it will be necessary to work with them. You can learn more about Azure SQL MI's network requirements at https://docs.microsoft.com/en-us/azure/azure-sql/managed-instance/connectivity-architecture-overview.

Deploying through the Azure Portal

Use the following steps to create an Azure SQL MI through the Azure Portal:

1. Log into portal.azure.com and search for *SQL managed instances* in the search bar at the top of the page. Click *SQL managed instances* to go to the SQL managed instances page in the Azure Portal.

2. Click *Create* to start choosing the configuration options for your Azure SQL MI.

3. The *Create Azure SQL Database Managed Instance* page includes five tabs with different configuration options to tailor the Azure SQL MI to fit your needs. Let's start by exploring the options available in the Basics tab. Along with the following list that describes each option, you can view a completed example of this tab in Figure 2.9.

    a. Choose the subscription and resource group that will contain the Azure SQL MI and the databases deployed to the instance. You can create a new resource group on this page if you have not already created one.

    b. Enter a name for the Azure SQL MI.

    c. Choose the Azure region you wish to deploy the instance to.

    d. Choose a tier for the instance (i.e., General Purpose or Business Critical), the number of vCores, the storage amount, and the type of redundancy for backup storage.

    e. Set a username and password for the administrator account.

FIGURE 2.9   Create Azure SQL Database Managed Instance: Basics tab.

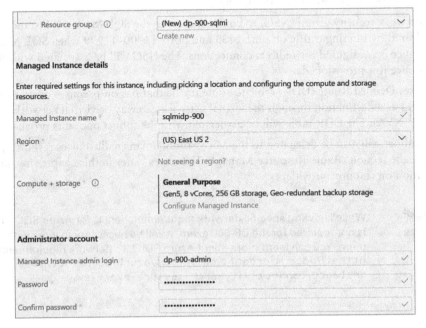

4. The Networking tab provides the following network configuration options for the Azure SQL MI. A completed example of this tab can be seen in Figure 2.10.

   a. Choose the VNet and dedicated subnet that will host the Azure SQL MI.

   b. The next important component will be deciding whether you want to enable a public endpoint for the Azure SQL MI. Public endpoints are disabled by default to limit connectivity to applications that can communicate with the VNet that the Azure SQL MI is in.

   c. Choose the minimum TLS version that will be used to encrypt data in-transit for inbound connections. The default TLS version is 1.2 and should be left as is unless there are specific requirements for a lower version.

FIGURE 2.10 Create Azure SQL Database Managed Instance: Networking tab.

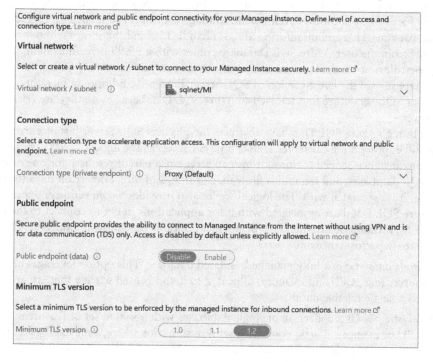

5. The Additional Settings tab provides options to change the collation, time zone, and maintenance window for the Azure SQL MI's underlying SQL Server database engine. It also includes an option to enable the instance as a secondary in an Azure SQL failover group for DR purposes.

6. The Tags tab allows you to place a tag on the Azure SQL MI for cost management.

7. Finally, the Review + Create tab allows you to review the configuration choices made during the design process. If you are satisfied with the choices made for the instance, click the *Create* button to begin provisioning the Azure SQL MI.

Azure SQL Database

Modern applications that are built from the ground up with cloud native best practices rely on database platforms that are flexible and minimize the amount of administrative effort needed to manage the database. Administrators must be able to easily scale performance resources up or down to meet dynamic demand requirements at the most cost-optimal price point. Modern applications are typically designed not to need instance-scoped features that are available in a platform like SQL Server as these features can be implemented using other cloud native offerings. For example, Azure Data Factory, Azure Logic Apps, or Azure Automation can be used to automate when stored procedures or other tasks in the database are run, eliminating the need for SQL Server Agent jobs to perform custom maintenance tasks that are not natively handled by Microsoft.

Azure SQL Database is a fully managed PaaS database engine that is designed to serve cloud native applications. It abstracts both the OS and the SQL Server instance so that users can fully focus on application development. Management operations such as upgrades, patches, backups, HA, and monitoring are also handled behind the scenes without requiring any effort from the user. Azure SQL Database comes with a 99.99 percent availability guarantee, regardless of the deployment option or service tier. Just like Azure SQL MI, Azure SQL Database uses the latest version of SQL Server Enterprise Edition. In fact, the newest features of SQL Server are first released to Azure SQL Database before they are released to SQL Server.

Even though Azure SQL Database abstracts the physical SQL Server instance from the user, it still exposes a logical server. Unlike a physical server, the logical server does not expose any instance-scoped features. It instead serves as a parent resource for one or more Azure SQL databases, and maintains firewall, auditing, and threat detection rules for the databases it is associated with. The logical server also provides a connection endpoint for each Azure SQL Database associated with it for applications to use to connect to them.

Azure SQL Database provides two deployment options that allow organizations to optimize database performance and cost:

- A *single database* is a fully managed, isolated database. This option leverages all the resources (e.g., CPU and memory) allocated to it and is used when a modern application needs a single reliable database.

- An *elastic pool* is a collection of single databases with a shared set of resources, such as CPU or memory. Elastic pools are useful in scenarios where some databases are used more than others during different time periods. This will reduce the cost of these databases since they will be sharing the same pool of resources.

These options can be broken down further by the following purchasing models that are available for Azure SQL Database:

- The *DTU-based* purchasing model offers a fixed blend of CPU, memory, and IOPS. Each blended compute package is known as database transaction units (DTUs). The DTU-based purchasing model comes with a fixed amount of storage that varies for each service tier.

- The *vCore-based* purchasing model lets organizations choose how many virtual cores (vCores) they would like allocated. Service tiers using the vCore-based purchasing model allocate a fixed amount of memory per vCore that varies based on the hardware generation and compute option used. This purchasing model allows organizations to apply their existing SQL Server licenses to reduce the overall cost of the database. Reserved capacity is also exclusively available for the vCore-based purchasing model, allowing organizations to commit to Azure SQL Database for one or three years at a discounted rate. The vCore-based purchasing model provides two options for compute:

  - Provisioned compute allows organizations to deploy a specific service tier with a set amount of compute resources. Provisioned compute can be dynamically scaled manually or through an automation script.

  - Serverless compute allows organizations to specify a minimum and maximum vCore limit for a database. Databases configured to use serverless compute will automatically scale based on workload demand. It will also automatically pause databases during inactive periods and restart them when activity resumes to cut back on compute costs. This option is only available for single databases.

Deciding on which purchasing model to choose comes down to how much control over compute resources you would like to have. The DTU-based purchasing model offers a fixed combination of resources that allow organizations to start developing very quickly. The vCore-based purchasing model allows organizations to choose the amount of compute resources, or a range of compute resources in the case of serverless. This model also includes a more extensive selection of storage sizes as well as more cost-saving options with reserved capacity or existing licenses.

Service Tiers

Azure SQL Database service tiers are different for each purchasing model. The DTU-based purchasing model offers Basic, Standard, and Premium tiers. Table 2.4 lists some of the common characteristics of these tiers.

TABLE 2.4   DTU-based purchasing model service tier characteristics

Characteristic	Basic	Standard	Premium
DTUs	5	S0: 10	P1: 125
		S1: 20	P2: 250
		S2: 50	P4: 500
		S3: 100	P6: 1000
		S4: 200	P11: 1750
		S6: 400	P15: 4000
		S7: 800	
		S9: 1600	
		S12: 3000	

TABLE 2.4   DTU-based purchasing model service tier characteristics *(continued)*

Characteristic	Basic	Standard	Premium
Included Storage	2 GB	250 GB	P1–P6: 500 GB P11 and above: 4 TB
Maximum Storage	2 GB	S0–S2: 250 GB S3 and above: 1 TB	P1–P6: 1 TB P11 and above: 4 TB
Maximum backup retention	7 days	35 days	35 days
CPU	Low	Low, Medium, High	Medium, High
IOPS	1–4 IOPS per DTU	1–4 IOPS per DTU	>25 IOPS per DTU
IO Latency	5 ms (read), 10 ms (write)	5 ms (read), 10 ms (write)	2 ms (read/write)
Columnstore Indexes	N/A	S3 and above	Supported
In-Memory OLTP	N/A	N/A	Supported

The vCore-based purchasing model offers the following three service tiers:

- *General Purpose* is used for most business workloads. This tier offers balanced compute and storage options.

- *Business Critical* is used for business applications that require high I/O performance. It is also the best option for applications that require high resiliency to outages by leveraging a SQL Server Always On availability group for HA.

- *Hyperscale* is used for very large OLTP databases (>4 TB) and can automatically scale storage and compute. Hyperscale databases use local SSDs for local buffer-pool cache and data storage. Long-term data storage is done with remote storage.

Table 2.5 lists the common characteristics for the vCore-based purchasing model service tiers:

TABLE 2.5   vCore-based purchasing model service tier characteristics

Characteristic	General Purpose	Business Critical	Hyperscale
Storage	Uses remote storage. Provisioned Compute: 5 GB–4 TB Serverless Compute: 5 GB–4 TB	Uses local SSD storage Provisioned Compute: 5 GB–4 TB	Supports up to 100 TB
Availability	1 replica, no read-scale replicas	3 replicas, 1 read-scale replica	1 read-write replica, 0–4 read-scale replicas
In-Memory	Not Supported	Supported	Partial Support

> Resource limits for the vCore-based purchasing model such as the number of vCores, amount of memory, IO latency, and maximum IOPS depend on the type of hardware chosen. See https://docs .microsoft.com/en-us/azure/azure-sql/database/ resource-limits-vcore-single-databases for the resource limits related to hardware available in the vCore-based purchasing model.

Network Isolation

Unlike SQL Server on a VM and Azure SQL MI, a logical server for an Azure SQL Database does not come with a built-in private endpoint. This means that an Azure SQL Database is not isolated within a VNet by default. Network isolation for Azure SQL Database can instead be achieved by limiting access to the logical server's public endpoint through the server's firewall, restricting access to only services in a specific VNet or subnet, or explicitly adding a private endpoint that is associated with a subnet in a VNet.

Public endpoint access can be limited using the following settings:

- *Allow Azure Services* allows all resources hosted on Azure, such as an Azure VM or Azure Data Factory, to communicate with databases associated with the logical server. This setting is turned off by default, as turning it on typically provides database access to more resources than what is needed.

- *IP firewall rules* open port 1433 (the default port SQL Server listens on) to a specific IP address or a range of IP addresses. Firewall rules can be set at the server level to allow access to all databases associated with a logical server or at the database level to only allow access to a specific database.

> Server-level IP firewall rules can be created using the Azure Portal, Azure PowerShell, the Azure CLI, the Azure REST API, and T-SQL. Database-level firewall rules can only be created and managed with T-SQL.

Private access to the logical server can also be enabled so that database connectivity is restricted to specific VNets. This type of access can be enabled using one of the following settings:

- *Virtual network firewall rules* restrict access to databases associated with a logical server to traffic using the private IP range of a VNet. Application traffic coming from a specific subnet in a VNet can be switched from using public IP addresses to private IP addresses by adding the Microsoft.Sql service endpoint to the subnet. The subnet can then be added as a virtual network rule in the logical server to allow traffic from that subnet to connect to databases associated with the logical server.

- *Private Link* is a service in Azure that allows you to add a private endpoint to a logical server. Private endpoints are private IP addresses within a specific subnet in a VNet. Once a private endpoint is attached, connectivity will be limited to other applications in the VNet or applications that can connect to the VNet through VNet peering, VPN, or Azure ExpressRoute.

Relational databases covered later in this chapter use the same methods for network isolation as Azure SQL Database. IP or virtual network firewall rules can be set at the logical server level or private endpoints can be attached to the logical server to provide network isolation for all databases associated to that logical server. However, unlike with Azure SQL Database, these rules can only be applied at the server level and not at the individual database level. These services include Azure Synapse Analytics dedicated SQL pools, Azure Database for MySQL, Azure Database for PostgreSQL, and Azure Database for MariaDB.

Deploying Through the Azure Portal

Use the following steps to create an Azure SQL Database through the Azure Portal:

1. Log into portal.azure.com and search for *SQL databases* in the search bar at the top of the page. Click *SQL databases* to go to the SQL databases page in the Azure Portal.

2. Click *Create* to start choosing the configuration options for your Azure SQL Database.

3. The *Create SQL Database* page includes six tabs with different configuration options to tailor the Azure SQL Database to fit your needs. Let's start by exploring the options available in the Basics tab. Along with the following list that describes each option, you can view a completed example of this tab in Figure 2.12.

   a. Choose the subscription and resource group that will contain the Azure SQL Database. You can create a new resource group on this page if you have not already created one.

   b. Enter a name for the Azure SQL Database.

   c. Choose the logical server you wish to deploy the database to. You can create a new logical server on this page if there is not one already available. The logical server chosen will dictate which region the database will be deployed to. Note that creating a new logical server will also require you to set a username and password for the administrator account.

   d. Choose whether the database will be a part of an elastic pool.

   e. Click *Configure database* to choose the purchasing model and service tier. If you choose one of the vCore-based purchasing model service tiers, you will be given the option to apply existing SQL Server licenses, choose the number of vCores, and set the maximum amount of storage allocated for data. Choosing a DTU-based purchasing model service tier will give you options to change the number of DTUs allocated to the database and the maximum amount of storage allocated for data. Figure 2.11 is an example of completed configuration for a General Purpose database. As you can see, the database configuration comes with a monthly cost estimate.

FIGURE 2.11   Configuring an Azure SQL Database

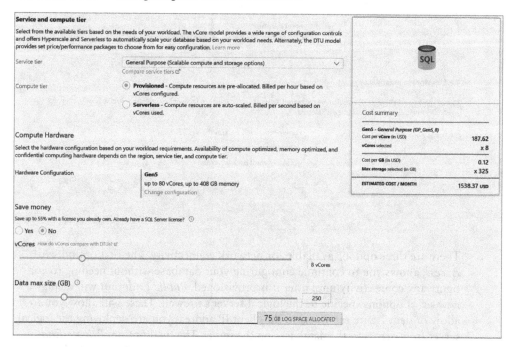

   f. Choose the redundancy tier for database backups.

4. The Networking tab allows you to configure network access and connectivity for your logical server if you are creating a new one. If you are deploying the database to an existing logical server, then most of the options will be grayed out as it will be taking on the existing state of the server. A completed example of configuring a new logical server can be seen in Figure 2.13.

FIGURE 2.12   Create Azure SQL Database: Basics tab.

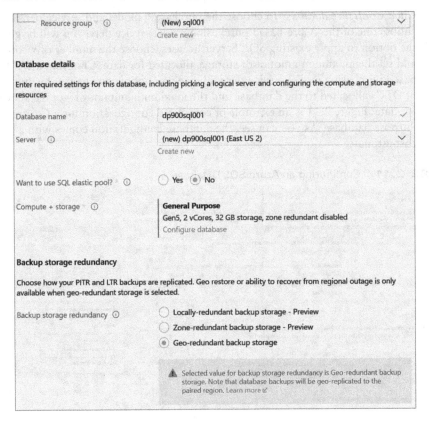

a. There are three options available for network connectivity. The first option, *No Access*, allows you to continue configuring your database without needing to configure any connectivity until after it is provisioned. *Public Endpoint* will display a new set of options specific to the logical server's firewall. These will allow you to allow or deny Azure services and the client IP address you are deploying the logical server from access to the databases on the server. The final option, *Private Endpoint*, will allow you to associate a private IP address from a VNet to the logical server. This will isolate the databases within a VNet, allowing connectivity only to applications that can communicate with the VNet.

b. Choose how client applications will communicate with the logical server.

c. Choose the minimum TLS version that will be used to encrypt data in-transit for inbound connections. The default TLS version is 1.2 and should be left as is unless there are specific requirements for a lower version.

FIGURE 2.13 Create Azure SQL Database: Networking tab.

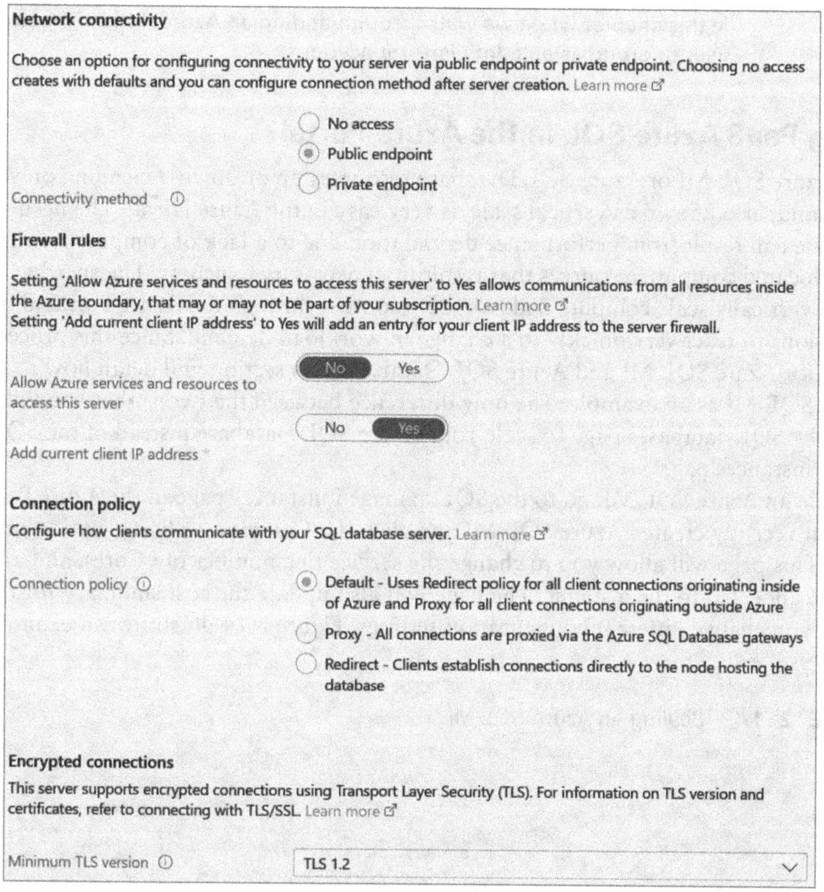

Network connectivity

Choose an option for configuring connectivity to your server via public endpoint or private endpoint. Choosing no access creates with defaults and you can configure connection method after server creation. Learn more ↗

Connectivity method ⓘ
- ○ No access
- ◉ Public endpoint
- ○ Private endpoint

Firewall rules

Setting 'Allow Azure services and resources to access this server' to Yes allows communications from all resources inside the Azure boundary, that may or may not be part of your subscription. Learn more ↗
Setting 'Add current client IP address' to Yes will add an entry for your client IP address to the server firewall.

Allow Azure services and resources to access this server *   No | Yes

Add current client IP address *   No | Yes

Connection policy

Configure how clients communicate with your SQL database server. Learn more ↗

Connection policy ⓘ
- ◉ Default - Uses Redirect policy for all client connections originating inside of Azure and Proxy for all client connections originating outside Azure
- ○ Proxy - All connections are proxied via the Azure SQL Database gateways
- ○ Redirect - Clients establish connections directly to the node hosting the database

Encrypted connections

This server supports encrypted connections using Transport Layer Security (TLS). For information on TLS version and certificates, refer to connecting with TLS/SSL. Learn more ↗

Minimum TLS version ⓘ | TLS 1.2   ⌄ |

5. The Security tab allows you to choose if you would like to use Azure Defender for SQL to provide advanced threat protection for your data.

6. The Additional Settings tab allows you to start your database as a blank database, from a backup, or from a sample provided by Microsoft. You can also choose if you would like to change the default collation for the database and the default maintenance window.

7. The Tags tab allows you to place a tag on the Azure SQL Database for cost management.

8. Finally, the Review + Create tab allows you to review the configuration choices made during the design process. If you are satisfied with the choices made for the instance, click the *Create* button to begin provisioning the Azure SQL Database.

Keep a note of the name of the logical server. This will be important later in this chapter when we walk through adding an Azure Active Directory user or group as an administrator account.

Scaling PaaS Azure SQL in the Azure Portal

Scaling Azure SQL MI or Azure SQL Database resources up or down depending on workload demand, also known as vertical scale, is very easy in the Azure Portal. The need to vertically scale can result from performance degradation due to a lack of compute resources or overallocated compute resources that result in unnecessary expenses. The speed at which users can vertically scale compute and storage resources through the Azure Portal allows organizations to react very quickly to a change in workload demand. Since this process is the same for Azure SQL MI and Azure SQL Database, this section will detail how to scale an Azure SQL MI as an example. The only difference between the two is that you will need to go to the SQL databases page to scale your Azure SQL Database instead of the SQL managed instances page.

To scale an Azure SQL MI, go to the SQL managed instances page in the Azure Portal. Click your recently created Azure SQL MI and click the *Compute + storage* option under *Settings*. This page will allow you to change the service tier, number of vCores, and amount of storage allocated to the instance. The page will also update the cost summary for the instance as you change different configuration settings. Figure 2.14 illustrates an example of this process.

FIGURE 2.14   Scaling an Azure SQL MI

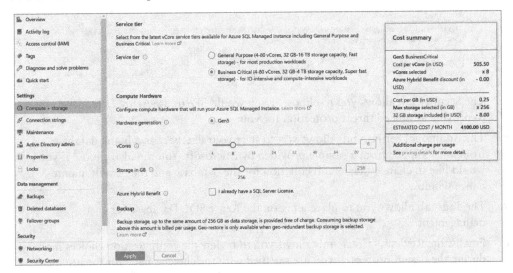

Business Continuity for PaaS Azure SQL

Azure manages backups for Azure SQL Database and Azure SQL MI databases by creating a full backup every week, differential backups every 12 to 24 hours, and transaction log backups every 5 to 10 minutes. These backups are stored in geo-redundant Azure Blob storage and are replicated to a separate Azure region. Backups are kept for 7 to 35 days, depending on the service tier and the retention settings set by an administrator. Long-term backup retention (LTR) can also be enabled to retain full database backups for up to 10 years.

Database backups can be restored to Azure SQL Database or Azure SQL MI by performing a *point-in-time restore (PITR)*. PITR can restore a backup from an existing database or a deleted database. Database backups taken from Azure SQL MI can be restored to the same Azure SQL MI with a different database name or a different Azure SQL MI. This can be done through the Azure Portal, the Azure command-line interface (CLI), or Azure PowerShell.

High availability for Azure SQL Database and Azure SQL MI differs depending on the service tier being used. The following sections outline the high availability architectures used by each service tier of Azure SQL Database and Azure SQL MI.

Basic, Standard, and General Purpose

High availability for the Basic, Standard, and General Purpose tiers of Azure SQL Database and the General Purpose tier of Azure SQL MI is accomplished through the standard availability model. This includes the following two layers:

- A stateless compute layer that runs the `sqlservr.exe` process and contains only ephemeral data such as data stored in tempdb. This is operated by Azure Service Fabric, which will move `sqlservr.exe` to another stateless compute node in the event of a database or OS upgrade or a failure. This process guarantees 99.99 percent availability but could result in performance degradation since `sqlservr.exe` will start with a cold cache after a failover.

- A stateful data layer with the data files stored in Azure Blob storage which has built-in HA.

Premium, Business Critical, and Hyperscale

High availability for the Premium and Business Critical tiers of Azure SQL Database and the Business Critical tier of Azure SQL MI is accomplished through the Premium availability model. This model uses a SQL Server Always On AG for HA and deploys an additional three or four nodes behind the scenes to act as secondaries in the AG. The AG synchronously replicates compute and storage from the primary node to each of the secondaries. This ensures that the secondaries are in sync with the primary node before fully committing each transaction. Azure Service Fabric will automatically initiate a failover to one of the secondaries if the primary node experiences any downtime. This will ensure that anyone using the database will not notice the failover. An added benefit of this configuration is that one of the secondaries can be used for read-only workloads. This increases performance by eliminating resource contention between read-only and write operations.

NOTE

Disaster recovery for Azure SQL database is achieved by zone redundancy. This process replicates the HA model used to three different availability zones in the same region. Disaster recovery for Azure SQL MI can be achieved by adding the Azure SQL MI to a failover group with another Azure SQL MI that is hosted in a different region. More information on failover groups can be found at https://docs.microsoft.com/en-us/azure/azure-sql/database/auto-failover-group-overview?tabs=azure-powershell#best-practices-for-sql-managed-instance.

Azure Synapse Analytics Dedicated SQL Pools

Azure Synapse Analytics dedicated SQL pools is a PaaS relational database engine that is optimized for data warehouse workloads. Dedicated SQL pools use a *scale-out* MPP architecture to process very large amounts of data. This means that data is sharded into multiple distributions and processed across one or more compute nodes. To do this, dedicated SQL pools separate compute and storage by using a SQL engine to perform computations and Azure Storage to store the data. Even though data is stored in Azure Blob storage, dedicated SQL pools serve data to users in a relational format as tables or views.

Dedicated SQL pools shard data into 60 distributions across one or more compute nodes. There are three different distribution patterns to consider when creating tables or materialized views. The most optimal choice is going to depend on the size and nature of the table or materialized view. They include the following distribution patterns:

- Hash distribution uses a hash function to deterministically assign each row to a distribution. In the table or view definition, one of the columns is designated as the distribution column. The most optimal distribution columns have a high number of distinct values and an even amount of data skew. Hash distribution is the best option for large fact and dimension tables as it provides the best performance for joins and aggregations on large tables.

- Round-robin distribution is the simplest distribution pattern as it evenly shards data randomly across distributions. Data is loaded quickly to a table or view using round-robin distribution but it can cause performance issues as data is not organized in the most optimal manner across each distribution. Typical use cases for round-robin distribution include staging tables or using it if there are no columns with highly distinct values.

- Replicated tables or materialized views cache a full copy of the table or materialized view on the first distribution on each compute node. This provides the fastest query performance as data does not need to shuffle from one distribution to another when aggregated or joined. Because extra storage is required, replicated tables and materialized views are recommended for small tables or tables that contain static values.

Distribution design should be carefully considered since data distribution results in data being physically stored in different locations. For example, round-robin distribution tables or poorly chosen distribution columns on hash distributed tables could result in a lot of data *shuffling* when the data is queried. The more that data needs to be shuffled, the more time the query will take to complete.

Just as with Azure SQL Database, it is easy to scale a dedicated SQL pool up or down depending on workload demands through the Azure Portal, PowerShell, or T-SQL. Service level objectives (SLOs) represent the scalability setting of a dedicated SQL pool and determine the cost and performance level as well as the number of compute nodes allocated. These are measured by compute Data Warehouse Units (cDWUs) which are bundled compute units of CPU, memory, and I/O. Table 2.6 lists the available dedicated SQL pool SLOs.

TABLE 2.6   Dedicated SQL pool service level objectives

Performance Level	Compute Nodes	Distributions per Compute Node	Memory (GB)
DW100c	1	60	60
DW200c	1	60	120
DW300c	1	60	180
DW400c	1	60	240
DW500c	1	60	300
DW1000c	2	30	600
DW1500c	3	20	900
DW2000c	4	15	1,200
DW2500c	5	12	1,500
DW3000c	6	10	1,800
DW5000c	10	6	3,000
DW6000c	12	5	3,600
DW7500c	15	4	4,500
DW10000c	20	3	6,000
DW15000c	30	2	9,000
DW30000c	60	1	18,000

Dedicated SQL pools are one part of the broader Azure Synapse Analytics suite of analytical components and will be discussed further in Chapter 5, "Modern Data Warehouses in Azure." This includes how to deploy a dedicated SQL pool through the Azure Portal in an Azure Synapse Analytics workspace.

Open-Source Databases in Azure

While SQL Server is a very popular relational database offering, there are several organizations that rely on open-source database platforms to store their relational data. Open-source database platforms can be deployed quickly at very little cost, enabling organizations to stand up a storage platform for their applications with little overhead. However, on-premises open-source database deployments still require organizations to manage hardware, OS, and database engine maintenance. For this reason, Azure offers three PaaS options for hosting open-source databases. These include Azure Database for MySQL, Azure Database for MariaDB, and Azure Database for PostgreSQL. Just like Azure SQL Database, these offerings come with native high availability, automatic patching, automatic backups, and automatic threat protection.

Each of these offerings use the vCore-based purchasing model and includes the following three service tiers:

- *Basic*—Workloads that require light compute and I/O performance, such as development and test environments
- *General Purpose*—Most business workloads that require a balance of compute and memory, with scalable I/O performance
- *Memory Optimized*—Workloads that require high performance and in-memory capabilities

Azure Database for MySQL and Azure Database for PostgreSQL include two deployment options: Single Server and Flexible Server.

- Single Server is a fully managed database service that manages the database engine, handling database and OS patches, automatic backup schedules, and high availability. This option is best suited for modern applications that use cloud native design practices.
- Flexible Server gives users more granular control over the management of the database engine. It allows users to configure high availability within one availability zone or across multiple availability zones. Users can also stop and start the server and set a burstable compute tier for workloads that do not always need a fixed compute capacity.

The following sections will only cover Single Server as Flexible Server is still in preview and is not a focus of the DP-900 exam.

Single Server is the only deployment option available for Azure Database for MariaDB as of the writing of this book.

Discount pricing for each of these options is available by prepaying for compute resources. Reserved capacity allows users to purchase a one-year term for Azure Database for PostgreSQL and one- or three-year terms for Azure Database for MySQL and Azure Database for MariaDB. As with Azure SQL, the number of vCores will need to be known beforehand as these are the resources that are purchased.

Azure Database for MySQL

MySQL is an open-source relational database engine that is very similar to SQL Server. Users can issue queries to a MySQL database using SQL, with some nuanced syntax differences versus how Microsoft SQL Server implements SQL.

Azure Database for MySQL is a PaaS relational database offering based on the MySQL Community Edition. Supported versions of the MySQL database engine include 5.6, 5.7, and 8.0. Azure Database for MySQL includes the resource configuration options for each pricing tier shown in Table 2.7.

TABLE 2.7   Azure Database for MySQL service tier resource options

Feature	Basic	General Purpose	Memory Optimized
Number of vCores	1, 2	2, 4, 8, 16, 32, 64	2, 4, 16, 32
Amount of Memory per vCore	2 GB	5 GB	10 GB
Storage Size	5 GB to 1 TB	5 GB to 16 TB	5 GB to 16 TB

Deploying Through the Azure Portal

Azure Database for MySQL through the Azure Portal is very similar to how you would deploy an Azure SQL Database.

1. Log into portal.azure.com and search for *Azure Database for MySQL servers* in the search bar at the top of the page. Click *Azure Database for MySQL servers* to go to the Azure Database for MySQL servers page in the Azure Portal.

2. Click *Create* to start choosing the configuration options for your Azure Database for MySQL server.

3. The next page will allow you to select which deployment option you would like to use. This example will demonstrate how to configure a Single Server deployment. Click *Create* under the *Single server* option to continue.

4. The *Create MySQL server* page includes six tabs with different configuration options to tailor the Azure Database for MySQL server to fit your needs. Let's start by exploring the options available in the Basics tab. Along with the following list that describes each option, you can view a completed example of this tab in Figure 2.15.

a. Choose the subscription and resource group that will contain the Azure Database for MySQL server. You can create a new resource group on this page if have not already created one.

b. Enter a server name.

c. Choose to start without any databases associated with the server or to restore a database backup to the server as it is being deployed.

d. Choose the Azure region that the server will be located in.

e. Choose the MySQL database engine version.

f. Choose the service tier, number of vCores, storage amount, backup retention period, and backup redundancy. Note that storage cannot be scaled down once the server is deployed.

g. Note that creating a new logical server will also require you to set a username and password for the administrator account.

FIGURE 2.15   Create MySQL server: Basics tab.

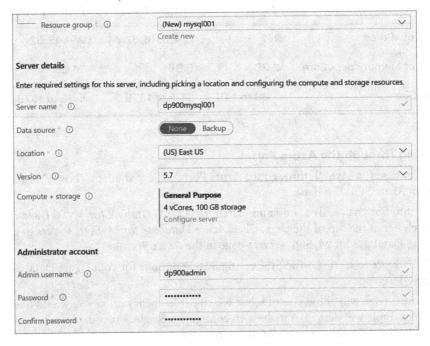

5. The Additional Settings tab allows you to enable double encryption if it is required. This setting will add an additional infrastructure encryption layer on top of the database and database backup encryption layer.

6. The Tags tab allows you to place a tag on the Azure Database for MySQL server for cost management.

7. Finally, the Review + Create tab allows you to review the configuration choices made during the design process. If you are satisfied with the choices made for the instance, click the *Create* button to begin provisioning the Azure Database for MySQL server.

Azure Database for MariaDB

MariaDB is another open-source relational database platform that is a fork of MySQL. In fact, the founders of MariaDB were the original founders of MySQL. There are some performance enhancements made to the query optimizer and the storage engine, but most of the core functionality is the same as MySQL. More information on MariaDB can be found at https://mariadb.org.

Azure Database for MySQL is a PaaS relational database offering based on the MariaDB Community Edition. Supported versions of the MariaDB database engine include 10.2 and 10.3.

Azure Database for MariaDB includes the same service tier resource configurations as Azure Database for MySQL. It also includes most of the same configuration options as Azure Database for MySQL when deploying it through the Azure Portal. The only differences are that Azure Database for MariaDB does not require you to select Single Server or Flexible Server and it does not have an Additional Settings tab.

Azure Database for PostgreSQL

PostgreSQL is an open-source object-relational database system that uses SQL for native queries. It uses a robust feature set with standard and complex data types, including these:

- *Primitives:* Integer, numeric, string, Boolean
- *Document:* JSON/JSONB, XML, key-value pair
- *Geometry:* Point, line, circle, polygon

The PostgreSQL database engine is also highly extensible, allowing users to define their own data types and custom functions with its proprietary language PL/PGSQL or other common development languages like Perl and Python. There are also custom extensions available that solve specific business problems, such as the PostGIS geospatial database extender. This extension adds geospatial-specific functionality that effectively turns PostgreSQL into a spatial database management system. More information about PostgreSQL and PostGIS can be found at www.postgresql.org/about.

Azure Database for PostgreSQL is a PaaS relational database offering based on the PostgreSQL Community Edition. Supported versions of the PostgreSQL database engine include 9.6, 10, and 11 for Single Server as well as 11, 12, and 13 for Flexible Server. Azure Database for PostgreSQL includes the same service tier resource configurations as Azure Database for MySQL for its Single Server and Flexible Server deployment models. It also includes the same configuration options as Azure Database for MySQL when deploying it through the Azure Portal.

Along with the Single Server and Flexible Server deployment models, Azure Database for PostgreSQL also includes a Hyperscale deployment option. Hyperscale (Citus) horizontally scales queries across multiple nodes through data sharding. This deployment option is typically used for multi-tenant applications that require greater scale and performance, such as real-time operational and high throughput transactional workloads. Azure Database for PostgreSQL Hyperscale (Citus) supports versions 11, 12, and 13 of the PostgreSQL database engine.

Management Tasks for Relational Databases in Azure

While Azure removes many of the rigid maintenance demands that come with managing an on-premises relational database environment, there are still several management tasks that must be handled. Failing to give these tasks the proper attention will result in poor database performance or, even worse, potential security risks. These common management tasks are included:

- Managing the deployment of the database through the Azure Portal or with automation scripts

- Migrating existing on-premises relational data to the new environment in Azure

- Maintaining data security through network isolation, access management, threat protection, and data encryption

There are also times that connectivity issues arise and must be troubleshooted. These can be the result of unexpected and expected behavior depending on how the service is configured in Azure. The following sections detail these tasks as well as some of the tools that can be used for database management.

Deployment Scripting and Automation

Cloud environments such as Azure greatly reduce the complexity involved in standing up a relational database. Tasks such as procuring hardware, installing network devices, and reserving capacity in a datacenter that previously required months of planning and implementation are reduced to a matter of minutes. Relational databases in Azure can also be scaled down or deleted just as quickly when they are not needed, allowing organizations to cut costs on services not being used.

In the previous sections we discussed how organizations can leverage the Azure Portal to manually deploy a relational database service. While this makes it easy to get started with a database in a single environment, it is not the most practical solution for deploying databases to multiple environments. Most organizations use several application development life cycle stages such as development, test, and quality assurance to make sure each release of an application meets a specific level of satisfaction before being pushed to production.

Cloud-based services make this process easy by allowing development teams to package their infrastructure requirements in automation scripts that describe each service to be deployed and their desired configuration. These scripts can be parameterized to meet the cost and performance needs of different environments used in an application's development life cycle.

Azure offers three primary options for scripting out service deployments: Azure Power-Shell, Azure CLI, and Infrastructure as Code templates. Azure PowerShell and the Azure CLI are command-line utilities that allow users to script their deployments with PowerShell or Bash. While these tools can be used to deploy services in Azure, the most common use for them is managing automated Infrastructure as Code deployments. Infrastructure as Code templates define the services being deployed and their desired settings. Terraform and Azure Resource Manager (ARM) are the most common Infrastructure as Code services that are used to automate Azure deployments. Building and deploying services with Terraform are outside of the scope for the DP-900 exam and will not be covered in this book. More information can be found at www.terraform.io if you would like to learn more about Terraform.

Azure PowerShell

Azure PowerShell includes a powerful set of PowerShell cmdlets (pronounced command-lets) that can be used to manage and administer Azure services from a command line. Scripts developed with Azure PowerShell can be run in the Azure Portal through the *Azure Cloud Shell* or through the Windows PowerShell command prompt or Integrated Scripting Environment (ISE) on a local machine or VM. Keep in mind that developing and running Azure PowerShell scripts locally requires the *Azure Az* PowerShell module to be installed on the machine. Steps and considerations for installing the Azure Az PowerShell module can be found at https://docs.microsoft.com/en-us/powershell/azure/install-az-ps?view=azps-6.3.0#installation. This module comes preinstalled on the Azure Cloud Shell, allowing users to immediately use the Azure Az module cmdlets in PowerShell scripts.

The Azure Cloud Shell is a web-based interface that allows users to run PowerShell and Azure CLI scripts in the Azure Portal. You can access the Azure Cloud Shell by selecting the Cloud Shell icon in the upper-right corner of the Azure Portal. Figure 2.16 illustrates what this icon looks like in the Azure Portal.

FIGURE 2.16   Azure Cloud Shell icon

Once the Azure Cloud Shell loads at the bottom of the screen, you will be able to develop and run Bash or PowerShell scripts to manage Azure services. Switch from Bash to Power-Shell to run Azure PowerShell commands.

Relational databases can be easily deployed using an Azure PowerShell script. These scripts can define every option related to deploying a relational database, such as where it is deployed, the type of database, the administrator account username and password, network isolation settings, and the service tier. The following code snippet is an Azure PowerShell script that creates the following resources:

- A resource group to logically contain the logical server and its databases
- A logical server and an IP firewall rule that will open port 1433 on the logical server to a defined range of IP addresses
- The username and password for the server's administrator account
- An Azure SQL Database, its initial service tier, and the initial number of vCores it is allocated

```
<#
Sign into your Azure environment. Not
required if running this script in the Azure Cloud Shell
#>
Connect-AzAccount

<#
Set the ID for the Subscription this database
is being deployed to. Also not needed if running in the Azure Cloud Shell
#>
$SubscriptionId = "<Azure Subscription ID>"

# Set the resource group name and location for the logical server
$resourceGroupName = "sql001"
$location = "eastus2"

# Set an admin login and password for your server
$adminSqlLogin = "dp900admin"
$password = "<Admin Password>"

# Set a logical server name
$serverName = "dp900sql001sv"

# Set a database name
```

```
$databaseName = "dp900sql001db"

<#
The IP address range that you want to allow to
access your server. This is optional and can be
set after the deployment has finished.
#>
$startIp = "<First IP Address in Range>"
$endIp = "<Last IP Address in Range>"

# Set subscription
Set-AzContext -SubscriptionId $subscriptionId

# Create the resource group
$resourceGroup = New-AzResourceGroup -Name $resourceGroupName -Location `
$location

# Create the logical server
$server = New-AzSqlServer -ResourceGroupName $resourceGroupName `
 -ServerName $serverName `
 -Location $location `
 -SqlAdministratorCredentials $(New-Object -TypeName System.Management
.Automation.PSCredential
-ArgumentList $adminSqlLogin,
$(ConvertTo-SecureString -String $password -AsPlainText -Force))

<#
Create a server firewall rule that allows
access from the specified IP range
#>
$serverFirewallRule = New-AzSqlServerFirewallRule `
 -ResourceGroupName $resourceGroupName `
 -ServerName $serverName `
 -FirewallRuleName "AllowedIPs" -StartIpAddress $startIp -EndIpAddress `
$endIp

# Create a blank database that uses the General Purpose service tier
$database = New-AzSqlDatabase -ResourceGroupName $resourceGroupName `
 -ServerName $serverName `
 -DatabaseName $databaseName `
 -Edition "GeneralPurpose" `
 -Vcore 2
```

Azure Command-Line Interface

The Azure CLI is a command-line tool that allows users to create and manage Azure resources. As with Azure PowerShell, scripts developed using the Azure CLI can be executed through the Azure Cloud Shell or through an interactive shell on a local machine or VM. Azure CLI commands can be run through a command prompt such as cmd.exe or through PowerShell on a Windows machine or a Bash shell in a Linux or macOS environment. Steps and considerations for installing the Azure CLI on a local machine or VM can be found at https://docs.microsoft.com/en-us/cli/azure/install-azure-cli.

The following code snippet is an Azure CLI script that performs the same actions as the previous Azure PowerShell script:

```bash
#!/bin/bash

# Set the subscription. Not required if being run in the Azure Cloud Shell
az account set-subscription <replace with your subscription name or id>

# Set the resource group name and location for your database
resourceGroupName=sql001
location=eastus2

# Set an admin login and password for the logical server adminlogin=dp900admin
password=<Admin Password>

# Set a logical server and database name
servername=dp900sql001sv
databasename=dp900sql001db

<#
The IP address range that you want to
allow to access your server. This is optional and
can be set after the deployment has finished.
#>
startip=<First IP Address in Range>
endip=<Last IP Address in Range>

# Create a resource group
az group create \
-name $resourceGroupName \
```

```
-location $location

# Create a logical server in the resource group
az sql server create \
-name $servername \
-resource-group $resourceGroupName \
-location $location \
-admin-user $adminlogin \
-admin-password $password

# Configure a firewall rule for the server
az sql server firewall-rule create \
-resource-group $resourceGroupName \
-server $servername \
 -n AllowYourIp \
-start-ip-address $startip \
-end-ip-address $endip

# Create a database in the server
az sql db create \
-resource-group $resourceGroupName \
-server $servername \
-name $databasename \
-edition GeneralPurpose \
-capacity 2
```

Azure Resource Manager Templates

Before diving into how Azure Resource Manager (ARM) templates are defined, we first need to establish what ARM is. ARM is the deployment and management service that enables users to create, update, and delete resources in Azure. It receives, authenticates, and authorizes all requests made by APIs, the Azure Portal, Azure PowerShell, Azure CLI, or applications using one of the Azure SDKs.

ARM uses *resource providers* to know which Azure resources are involved in a request. Resource providers supply different resource types in Azure as well as all the configuration details that they require. One common resource provider is Microsoft.Sql, which includes the Azure SQL Database, Azure SQL MI, and Azure Synapse Analytics resource types. These resources can be specified using the syntax {resource provider}/{resource type}. Examples include Microsoft.Sql/servers or Microsoft.Sql/managedInstances. Resource providers are also the fundamental building blocks of ARM templates, as all other items in the template will be related to the configuration requirements of the resources defined in the template.

While many resource providers are registered to an Azure subscription by default, there are several that must be registered manually through the Azure Portal, Azure PowerShell, or Azure CLI. Steps to manually enable a resource provider can be found at https://docs.microsoft.com/en-us/azure/azure-resource-manager/management/resource-providers-and-types#azure-portal.

ARM templates are JSON files that define the resources and configuration requirements for a deployment to Azure. Templates are defined using a declarative syntax, meaning that they are written in a way that describes what resources are needed and each one's desired configuration without needing to worry about the programming commands that will create them. Resources defined in an ARM template can also have dependencies on other resources. Dependencies will prevent the template from attempting to deploying a resource if a resource it depends on is not available. Templates can then be deployed from Azure PowerShell and Azure CLI scripts, the Azure Portal, and tools like Azure DevOps that manage continuous integration and continuous development (CI/CD) pipelines.

You can think of an ARM template like a food order placed through an online delivery service. When you place an order, you declaratively list what items you want to eat. This may include appetizers, main dishes, side orders, and desserts, depending on what you want included in the order. The size of the order may also vary, depending on whether you are ordering just for yourself or also for other people. Certain items, such as a steak, also require you to state how you would like them to be cooked. Once the order is placed, the restaurant will handle the low-level details involved in preparing, cooking, and packaging the food.

Understanding the full scope of ARM templates and how they can be integrated into continuous integration and continuous deployment pipelines is outside of the scope for the DP-900 exam. If you would like to learn more about customizing ARM templates with parameters, information can be found at the following learning path: https://docs.microsoft.com/en-us/learn/modules/create-azure-resource-manager-template-vs-code.

Defining an ARM Template

The following is a list of required and optional elements that make up an ARM template:

- *schema*—This is a required section that defines the location of the JSON schema file that describes the structure of the JSON data.
- *contentVersion*—This is a required section that defines the version of your template.
- *apiProfile*—This is an optional section that defines a collection of API versions for resource types.
- *parameters*—This is an optional section where you define values that are provided during deployment. Parameters are values that change depending on the environment the resources are being deployed to. These values can be provided by a parameter file, Azure PowerShell, or Azure CLI or in the Azure Portal.

- *variables*—This is an optional section where you define values that are reused in your template.
- *functions*—This is an optional section where you can define user-defined functions that simplify complicated expressions that may be used often in your template.
- *resources*—This is a required section where you define the resources you want to create or update in Azure.
- *output*—This is an optional section where you specify the values that will be returned at the end of the deployment.

The following is an example of an ARM template that will create an Azure SQL Database. The template definition includes the following elements:

- The logical server name.
- The username and password for the server's administrator account.
- An Azure SQL Database, its initial service tier, and its performance SKU.

```
{
  "$schema": "https://schema.management
.azure.com/schemas/2019-04-01/deploymentTemplate.json#",
  "contentVersion": "1.0.0.0",
  "parameters": {
    "serverName": {
      "type": "string",
      "defaultValue": "dp900sql001sv",
      "metadata": {
        "description": "The name of the SQL logical server."
      }
    },
    "sqlDBName": {
      "type": "string",
      "defaultValue": "dp900sql001db",
      "metadata": {
        "description": "The name of the SQL Database."
      }
    },
    "location": {
      "type": "string",
      "defaultValue": "eastus2",
      "metadata": {
        "description": "Location for all resources."
      }
    },
```

```
      "administratorLogin": {
        "type": "string",
        "metadata": {
          "description": "The administrator username of the SQL logical server."
        }
      },
      "administratorLoginPassword": {
        "type": "securestring",
        "metadata": {
          "description": "The administrator password of the SQL logical server."
        }
      }
    },
    "variables": {},
    "resources": [
      {
        "type": "Microsoft.Sql/servers",
        "apiVersion": "2020-02-02-preview",
        "name": "[parameters('serverName')]",
        "location": "[parameters('location')]",
        "properties": {
          "administratorLogin": "[parameters('administratorLogin')]",
          "administratorLoginPassword": "[parameters('administratorLoginPassword')]"
        },
        "resources": [
          {
            "type": "databases",
            "apiVersion": "2020-08-01-preview",
            "name": "[parameters('sqlDBName')]",
            "location": "[parameters('location')]",
            "sku": {
              "name": "GP_Gen5_2",
              "tier": "GeneralPurpose",
            },
            "dependsOn": [
              "[resourceId('Microsoft.Sql/servers',
                  concat(parameters('serverName')))]"
            ]
          }
        ]
      }
    ]
}
```

This template can then be deployed through the Azure Portal, Azure PowerShell, or Azure CLI. The following is an example of an Azure PowerShell script that deploys the preceding ARM template to a new resource group. It also defines the administrator username and password for the logical server and passes the information to the template as it is being deployed. This script also assumes that the template is located in the same folder as the Azure Power-Shell script with the name `azuredeploy.json`.

```
Connect-AzAccount


# Set an admin login and password for your server
$adminSqlLogin = "dp900admin"
$password = "<Admin Password>"


New-AzResourceGroup -Name sql001 -Location eastus
New-AzResourceGroupDeployment -ResourceGroupName `
arm-vscode -TemplateFile ./azuredeploy.json `
-administratorLogin $adminSqlLogin `
-administratorLoginPassword $password
```

There are several commonly used ARM templates available on the azure-quickstart-templates GitHub repository. These templates range from single resource deployments to multiple resource deployments for different application workloads. Feel free to reference these templates as you are building out your own automated deployments in Azure. You can find these templates at `https://github.com/Azure/azure-quickstart-templates`.

Migrating to Azure SQL

There are a variety of methods available for migrating a database from an on-premises SQL Server instance to Azure SQL. Migrating a database to a SQL Server on Azure VM is relatively straightforward unless you are upgrading from an older version of SQL Server and need to update any deprecated features. The following migration options are commonly included:

- Taking a backup of the on-premises database and storing it in Azure Blob storage. Restore the database backup from Azure Blob storage to the SQL Server on Azure VM using RESTORE DATABASE FROM URL.

- If the on-premises instance is a primary in an Always On AG, add the SQL Server on Azure VM as a secondary. Once the data is synchronized to the SQL Server on Azure VM, perform a failover so that the SQL Server on Azure VM is the new primary.

- Configure transactional replication so that the on-premises SQL Server instance is a publisher and the SQL Server on Azure VM is a subscriber. Once the data is replicated to the SQL Server on Azure VM, update application connection strings and point users to the database in Azure.

Migrating to Azure SQL Database or Azure SQL MI requires more planning and consideration due to compatibility differences between on-premises SQL Server and PaaS Azure SQL. Even though Azure SQL MI is nearly 100 percent compatible with on-premises SQL Server, there are still some feature differences between the two that could cause migration issues. The same can be said about the differences between an on-premises instance of MySQL and PostgreSQL and Azure Database for MySQL and Azure Database for PostgreSQL. This is where a service such as the Azure Database Migration Service can provide data that makes the migration planning process much easier.

The *Azure Database Migration Service (DMS)* is a fully managed service that can be used to discover any potential compatibility issues and migrate the database once those issues are addressed. It uses the *Data Migration Assistant (DMA)* to detect compatibility issues and make recommendations on how to address them. DMA is also useful for migrations to a SQL Server on Azure VM by discovering compatibility issues between an older version of SQL Server and a newer version on the Azure VM. DMA can be used to assess versions of SQL Server ranging from SQL Server 2005 to the most up-to-date version. After addressing any compatibility issues, DMA can be used to migrate the database's schema to streamline data migration with DMS.

DMS can be used for offline and online migrations. *Offline* migrations refer to application downtime beginning as soon as the migration starts. Application cutover is a manual process and must be performed by the user. Offline migrations are available for migrations to Azure SQL Database, Azure SQL MI, SQL Server on Azure VM, Azure Cosmos DB, Azure Database for MySQL, and Azure Database for PostgreSQL. DMS can also limit downtime by handling the application cutover process through an *online* migration. Online migrations are only available for migrations to Azure SQL MI, Azure Cosmos DB, and Azure Database for PostgreSQL.

Database Security

Database security is paramount for any RDBMS. For this reason, relational databases in Azure enforce database security through the following methods:

- Network isolation
- Access management
- Data encryption and obfuscation
- Security management

Each of these methods represents a different level of security for protecting data from nonauthorized access. While many of the tasks related to the different security layers are applied the same way across the different relational database offerings in Azure, there are some tasks that are handled differently from one database platform to another. For example, network isolation is implemented very differently on a SQL Server on Azure VM than it is on an Azure SQL Database.

Since network isolation was a core topic in the sections detailing the different relational database offerings in Azure, the following sections will focus on access management, data encryption and obfuscation, and security management capabilities.

Access Management

Access management for relational databases in Azure is centered around the concept of *least-privilege*. This starts at the infrastructure level in Azure with role-based access controls (RBACs), allowing organizations to limit who can manage database operations that are handled in Azure such as changing maintenance windows and scaling compute resources users to only users who need this type of access. The next step is to limit database access to only the users that need access to it, also known as database authentication. Finally, users that can authenticate to a database will need to be granted varying levels of permission to the data and objects in the database, which should be set to the least amount of privilege needed by a user. This is known as a user's authorization level. The following sections explore these different levels of access management.

Role-Based Access Control (RBAC)

Management operations for relational databases that are handled through Azure such as network isolation, scaling compute resources, and changing maintenance windows is controlled through RBAC. RBAC is an authorization system built on ARM that provides fine-grained access management of Azure resources to users and objects in Azure Active Directory. It is important to note that RBAC is decoupled from database-level security, so these roles do not affect database access.

Higher-level RBAC roles such as Owner and Contributor can be used to manage SQL resources but grant additional permissions that may not be necessary. There are built-in RBAC roles specific to Azure SQL that can be granted to Azure Active Directory accounts that eliminate the need for higher-level roles for managing Azure SQL resources. PaaS relational databases include the following built-in roles:

- *SQL DB Contributor*—Lets a user manage Azure SQL Databases but not access them. Also, this role does not allow users to manage the security-related policies or their associated logical servers.

- *SQL Managed Instance Contributor*—Lets a user manage Azure SQL MIs and required network configuration but not access them.

- *SQL Security Manager*—Lets a user manage the security-related policies of Azure SQL Databases and logical servers that manage databases but not access them.

- *SQL Server Contributor*—Lets a user manage Azure SQL Databases and their associated logical servers but not access them. Also, this role does not allow users to manage the security-related policies.

These roles do not apply to SQL Server on Azure VMs because the database engine is managed in the VM. However, there are VM-specific RBAC roles that can be used to manage the VM configuration. More on these and other built-in RBAC roles can be found at https://docs.microsoft.com/en-us/azure/role-based-access-control/built-in-roles.

Authentication

Authentication is the process of validating the identity of users trying to access a database. All versions of Azure SQL support two authentication methods: SQL authentication and Active Directory (AD).

SQL authentication involves storing SQL Server–specific login name and password information in the master database, or in the user database for database contained users. As a matter of fact, the administrator account that is defined when creating a SQL Server on Azure VM, Azure SQL MI, Azure SQL Database, or Azure Synapse Analytics dedicated SQL pool is an example of a SQL login. The administrator can also create additional SQL logins that other users or automation services such as the SQL Server Agent or Azure Data Factory can use to interact with the database.

Active Directory authentication involves adding a user or group stored in Windows AD or Azure AD (AAD) as a login or contained user in SQL. This is the preferred method of authentication as it is more secure than SQL authentication and is easier to manage. SQL Server on Azure VMs can use Windows AD logins for authentication if the VNet that contains the SQL Server on Azure VM is joined to a domain that has AD. As of the writing of this book, SQL Server on Azure VMs cannot use AAD users and groups for authentication. Azure SQL Database and Azure SQL MI, on the other hand, can use AAD objects. The following steps outline how to add an AAD user or group as an administrator for an Azure SQL Database logical server.

1. Log into portal.azure.com and search for *SQL servers* in the search bar at the top of the page. Click *SQL servers* to go to the SQL servers page in the Azure Portal. This page is the home of the logical servers for your Azure SQL Databases.

2. Click on the logical server that was created when you built an Azure SQL Database.

3. Click *Azure Active Directory* under Settings in the left-hand side panel. Click *Set admin* to add an AAD user or group as an administrator on the server. Figure 2.17 illustrates how this page will appear before clicking *Set admin*.

FIGURE 2.17   Adding an AAD Administrator

4. Once you have added an account, click *Save* to save the account as the administrator.

Non-administrator AAD users and groups can also be added using T-SQL. To add additional AAD users and groups as database users, connect to the logical server using a management tool like SQL Server Management Studio (more on management tools later in this chapter) with a login that has permission to create users in the database. This can include the SQL authentication server administrator or the AAD server administrator. Once you're logged in, the following command can be used to add a contained user to a database.

```
CREATE USER [<AAD_User>] FROM EXTERNAL PROVIDER;
```

There are three methods available for using an AAD login to connect to a database. The correct choice depends on how an organization configures AAD. These methods are as follows:

- *Azure Active Directory—Integrated*: This method can be used if the user signed into the Windows machine that they are connecting to the database from with an AAD account.

- *Azure Active Directory—Password*: this method forces the user to enter the AAD login name and password to connect to the database.

- *Azure Active Directory—Universal with MFA*: This is an interactive method that uses multi-factor authentication (MFA) to provide additional access security for the database.

Authorization

Authorization refers to the level of permissions a user has in the database. Some of these permissions include whether they can read or write data in different tables, execute stored procedures, and add or delete other users. Permissions are typically managed by database roles that include a predefined set of permissions. Database roles include fixed-database roles that are included in SQL Server and Azure SQL and user-defined database roles that are created by a database administrator.

There are several fixed-database roles available out of the box with any version of SQL Server or Azure SQL. An extensive list of the available fixed-database roles in Azure SQL can be found at https://docs .microsoft.com/en-us/sql/relational-databases/security/ authentication-access/database-level-roles?view=sql-server-ver15#fixed-database-roles.

User permissions can also be managed by object-level permissions, such as granting or revoking the ability to select, update, or delete data in a specific table or view. Object-level permissions can also go as far as limiting which columns users have access to. An example of denying access to specific columns in a table with T-SQL would look like the following statement:

```
DENY SELECT ON <table_name>(<column_1, column_2>) TO User
```

There is also a special type of database authorization that limits access to specific rows in different tables. *Row-level security (RLS)* allows database administrators to control access to rows in a table based on the characteristics of the user running a query. This is implemented through user-defined table valued functions that block access to rows based on certain security predicates. RLS supports two types of security predicates to prevent user access to specific rows:

- Filter predicates that silently filter the rows available to read operations
- Block predicates that block write operations that violate the predicate

Data Encryption and Obfuscation

Azure provides a variety of methods to protect data from malicious activity by encrypting data in-transit and at rest. These help to ensure that if a disk hosting a database, a data file, a database backup, or connections to a database becomes compromised, then the data is unreadable.

Azure SQL and open-source SQL databases in Azure use *Transport Layer Security (TLS)* to encrypt data in-transit. TLS encrypts data sent over the Internet to ensure that hackers are unable to see the data that is transmitted. Supported versions include 1.0, 1.1, and 1.2. Depending on application requirements, a minimum TLS version can be set so that application connections using the minimum allowed TLS version or higher can connect to that database.

Azure also encrypts data at rest by encrypting the disks that support the various database options. This ensures that if disks involved in hosting a database (e.g., data, log, and tempdb disks) are hacked, the data on those disks will be unreadable. Along with encrypting the physical disk, there are a few additional encryption measures that are native to SQL Server and Azure SQL that ensure a database is encrypted at rest. These are discussed further in the following sections.

Transparent Data Encryption (TDE)

Transparent Data Encryption (TDE) is a SQL Server feature that encrypts all the data within a database at the page level. TDE is available for databases hosted in a SQL Server on Azure VM, Azure SQL Database, Azure SQL MI, and Azure Synapse Analytics dedicated SQL pool. Data is encrypted as it is written to the data page on disk and decrypted when the data page is read into memory. TDE also encrypts database backups since a backup operation is simply copying the data and log pages from the database.

Encryption with TDE is done by using a symmetric key called the Database Encryption Key (DEK). The DEK is managed by default by a service-managed certificate in Azure. Organizations can also use their own certificate, a method known as Bring Your Own Key (BYOK), to manage the DEK. Customer-managed certificates can be managed in Azure Key Vault.

 TDE is enabled by default for Azure SQL Database and Azure SQL MI and can be manually enabled for SQL Server databases that are hosted on a VM.

Always Encrypted

In addition to encrypting entire databases at rest with TDE, SQL Server and Azure SQL allow organizations to encrypt individual columns in tables with *Always Encrypted*. This feature is designed to allow organizations to protect sensitive data such as credit card numbers or personally identifiable information (PII) stored in database tables. Always Encrypted allows client applications to encrypt data inside the application, never revealing the encryption keys to the database engine. This allows organizations to separate who can manage the data, like a database administrator, and who can read it.

Always Encrypted uses a column encryption key to encrypt the column data with either randomized encryption or deterministic encryption, and a master encryption key that encrypts the column encryption key. Neither of these are stored in the database engine and are instead stored in an external trusted key store such as Azure Key Vault. The only values of the two keys that are stored in the database engine are the encrypted values of the column encryption key and the information about the location of the master key.

Client applications accessing encrypted data must use an Always Encrypted client driver. The driver will be able to access the key store where the column and master encryption keys are located and will use them to decrypt the data as it is served to the application. Applications writing data to encrypted columns will also use the Always Encrypted client driver to ensure that data is encrypted as it is written. It is important to reiterate here that the data is never decrypted at the database engine, only at the application level.

Dynamic Data Masking

Dynamic data masking limits the exposure of sensitive data to application users by obfuscating data in specific columns. Applications reading data from tables with masked columns do not need to be updated because dynamic data masking rules are applied in the query results, which does not change the data stored in the database. This means that users can view columns that are masked, but without seeing the actual data stored in the columns.

There are a variety of masking patterns that can be used to obfuscate column data. The following masking patterns are available for SQL Server and Azure SQL:

- *Default*—Fully masks the data in the column. Users will see XXXX for string values, 0 for numbers, and 01.01.1900 for date values.

- *Email*—Masks everything in an email address other than the first letter in the email and the suffix .com (e.g., jXXXX@XXXX.com).

- *Random*—Replaces numeric data with a random value from a specified range of values.

- *Custom*—Exposes the first and last digits of a piece of data and adds a custom padding string in the middle (e.g., 5XXX0).

These masking patterns can be enabled through the Azure Portal or T-SQL. There is also an additional pattern available through the Azure Portal.

Dynamic data masking is designed to limit data exposure to a set of predefined queries without any change needed to application code. However, it is important to note that the data that is masked is not encrypted and can be bypassed using inference or brute-force techniques. It is designed to be complementary to other security features such as TDE, Always Encrypted, and RLS.

Security Management

Once data is secured through network isolation, access management, and data encryption and obfuscation techniques, it is important to make sure data security is maintained on an ongoing basis. The following methods are available through Azure and the database engine to manage database security.

Auditing

Organizations enable auditing for Azure SQL to maintain regulatory compliance, understand database activities, and monitor databases for discrepancies that could indicate suspicious activity. SQL Server on Azure VM and Azure SQL MI use traditional SQL Server auditing through the database engine. This produces audit logs that contain predefined server-level or database-level events. Azure SQL Database and Azure Synapse Analytics dedicated SQL pools use Azure SQL Auditing to write audit logs to Azure Blob storage, Azure Log Analytics, or Azure Event Hubs. Azure SQL Auditing can be enabled through the Azure Portal.

Azure Defender for SQL

Azure Defender provides several SQL security management capabilities. It includes functionality for monitoring and mitigating potential database vulnerabilities and detecting potentially malicious activity. It can be enabled through the Azure Portal at the Azure subscription level for all instances of Azure SQL in a subscription or at the server level for a single instance of Azure SQL. These security capabilities are covered by the following two tools that are packaged in the Azure Defender service: SQL Vulnerability Assessment and Advanced Threat Protection.

The SQL Vulnerability Assessment is a scanning service that provides insight into the state of your database's security. It also provides action items that a database administrator can take to resolve any found security issues. To catch security vulnerabilities in a database, the SQL Vulnerability Assessment employs several rules that are based on Microsoft best practices for database security. These rules cover database-level and server-level issues, such as firewall settings and excessive permissions for logins. The full list of rules that are used by the SQL Vulnerability Assessment can be found at `https://docs .microsoft.com/en-us/azure/azure-sql/database/sql-database- vulnerability-assessment-rules`.

Advanced Threat Protection is a tool that enables organizations to detect and respond to potentially malicious attempts to access a database. The tool will send alerts and recommended action items to users when it detects harmful database activities such as SQL injection, data exfiltration, anonymous logins, and brute force access. It is available for all versions of Azure SQL as well as Azure Synapse Analytics dedicated SQL pools.

Common Connectivity Issues

There will be times when connectivity issues occur with a database. These issues can be related to network or firewall configuration, authentication timeouts, or transient fault errors related to Azure dynamically reconfiguring a database to meet heavy workloads. The following sections list common connectivity issues and how to troubleshoot them.

Network-related or Instance-specific Issues

The "A network-related or instance-specific error occurred while establishing a connection to your server" error message indicates that an application cannot find the database server it is trying to connect to. The most common methods for troubleshooting this issue are as follows:

1. Making sure that TCP/IP is enabled as a client protocol on the application server. On servers that have SQL tools installed, such as a SQL Server on Azure VM, TCP/IP can be enabled by using the following steps in SQL Server Configuration Manager:

    a. Expand *SQL Server Native Client Configuration* and click on *Client Protocols*.

    b. Double-click *TCP/IP* and change *Enabled* from *No* to *Yes*.

    Application servers that do not have SQL tools installed can also be checked to see if TCP/IP is enabled by running the SQL Server Client Network utility (`cliconfig.exe`).

2. Make sure that the connection string specifies the right port (1433 by default) and is using the fully qualified server name. An example of a fully qualified logical server name for Azure SQL Database would be `dp900sql001.database.windows.net`.

3. Connection timeout can be the root cause for applications that are connecting over a slow network. This can be alleviated by increasing the connection timeout in SQL. The Microsoft recommended connection timeout is at least 30 seconds.

Firewall-related Issues

The "Cannot connect to server due to firewall issues" error message indicates that the the client application's IP address is not whitelisted by the server-level or the database-level firewall. Add the IP address as a server-level or database-level firewall rule to alleviate this issue.

Keep in mind that if the database is hosted on an Azure SQL MI or is an Azure SQL Database that is using a private endpoint, then an application trying to communicate with the database will need to be able to communicate with the VNet the database is in. This would include the following applications:

- Applications that are hosted in the same VNet as the database.

- Applications that are hosted in a network that can communicate with the VNet hosting the database. This can be done through VNet peering, a VPN, or Azure ExpressRoute.

- Applications that are allowed to communicate with resources in a VNet hosting a database through an NSG or Azure Firewall. More on network security rules in NSGs can be found at `https://docs.microsoft.com/en-us/azure/virtual-network/network-security-groups-overview`.

Log In Failure with a Database Contained User

The "Cannot open database "master" requested by the login. The login failed" error occurs because the account logging into the server does not have access to the master database. This is typical for database contained users that are trying to connect to the database with SQL Server Management Studio (SSMS). Use the following steps to resolve this issue:

1. When establishing a connection to a SQL instance in SSMS, click *Options* in the bottom left-hand corner of the Connect to Server page and select *Connection Properties*.

2. In the *Connect to database* field, type the name of the database the user is contained in and click *Connect*. Figure 2.18 is an example of the *Connection Properties* tab connecting to a specified user database.

FIGURE 2.18   Connecting to a user database with SSMS

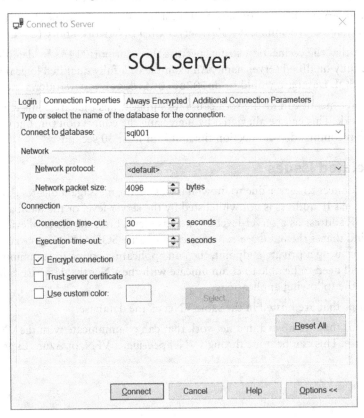

Transient Fault Errors

Transient fault errors occur when Azure dynamically reconfigures the infrastructure on which the database is hosted. These can include planned events such as database upgrades and unplanned events such as load balancing. Reconfiguration events that cause transient fault errors are typically short-lived and last less than 60 seconds. However, this can still cause problems since applications connecting to databases during this time may experience some connectivity issues. For this reason, applications should be built with retry logic to repeat a transaction if it fails due to a transient error. Transient errors are raised by the throw of a *SqlException* and are identified as one of a few error codes. This allows error handling logic to include a retry policy for exceptions that include a transient error code. The full list of transient error codes can be found at `https://docs.microsoft.com/en-us/azure/azure-sql/database/troubleshoot-common-errors-issues#transient-fault-error-messages-40197-40613-and-others`.

> More information on transient fault errors and other common connectivity issues can be found at `https://docs.microsoft.com/en-us/azure/azure-sql/database/troubleshoot-common-errors-issues`.

Management Tools

In previous sections, we established that tools like the Azure Portal and Azure PowerShell are powerful mechanisms for managing relational database deployments in Azure. However, there are other tools that developers use to write, test, and optimize queries before adding them to applications. These tools are also used by database administrators to perform tasks such as managing table design, indexes, and user permissions. The following sections provide a brief overview of the three most popular database management tools.

SQL Server Management Studio

SQL Server Management Studio, or SSMS for short, has been used by database administrators and developers for years. It can connect to any type of SQL Server–based infrastructure, including SQL Server, Azure SQL, and Azure Synapse Analytics dedicated SQL pools. Once connected to a database, SSMS can be used to administer and develop all components of SQL, including the following tasks:

- Building and managing database objects such as tables, stored procedures, functions, and triggers
- Developing and optimizing queries
- Managing security operations
- Performing database backup and restore operations
- Building HADR solutions such as an Always On availability group

Many of these activities can be done through either the GUI or a T-SQL script that is written and executed in SSMS's Query Editor.

> You can download the latest edition of SSMS at https://docs
> .microsoft.com/en-us/sql/ssms/download-sql-server-
> management-studio-ssms?view=sql-server-ver15#download-ssms.

After opening SSMS, you will be prompted to connect to a database server. Connections to Azure SQL Database and Azure SQL MI will use the endpoint created for the server. This can be found in the *Overview* page listed next to *Server Name for Azure SQL Database and Host for Azure SQL MI*. Once you have entered the server name, you will need to choose which type of authentication you will be using and enter the credentials. Remember that if you are logging in with a user that does not have access to the master database, you will need to specify the database you are connecting to in the *Connection Properties*.

Once connected, users can begin writing queries by clicking *New Query* in the top ribbon. This will open a new page in the Query Editor, with results being displayed at the bottom of the Query Editor after a query is run. SSMS also enables users to script out any object in a database by right-clicking on them in the Object Explorer, hovering the mouse over *Script <object> as*, and choosing one of the "script as" options. Figure 2.19 illustrates an example of how to script out an ALTER VIEW statement for an existing database view in SSMS. This example opens the script in a new Query Editor window.

FIGURE 2.19   Script View as ALTER To statement

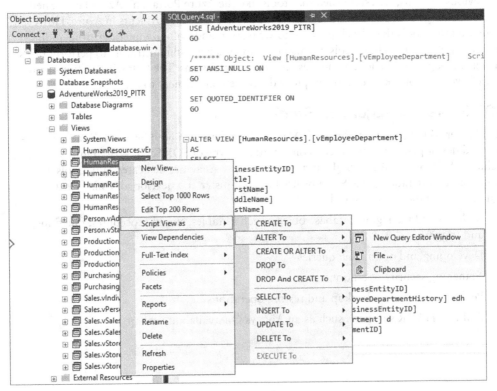

There are several administrative features that are native to SSMS, including the ability to optimize a query based on its execution plan. An *execution plan* is a graphical interpretation of the steps the database engine's query optimizer takes to execute a query. It is read right to left and displays metrics for each step, including the operation that was performed. SSMS will also display resource usage for a step if you hover your mouse over it. Figure 2.20 illustrates an example of an execution plan and includes the pop-up infographic for one of the steps.

FIGURE 2.20 SSMS execution plan

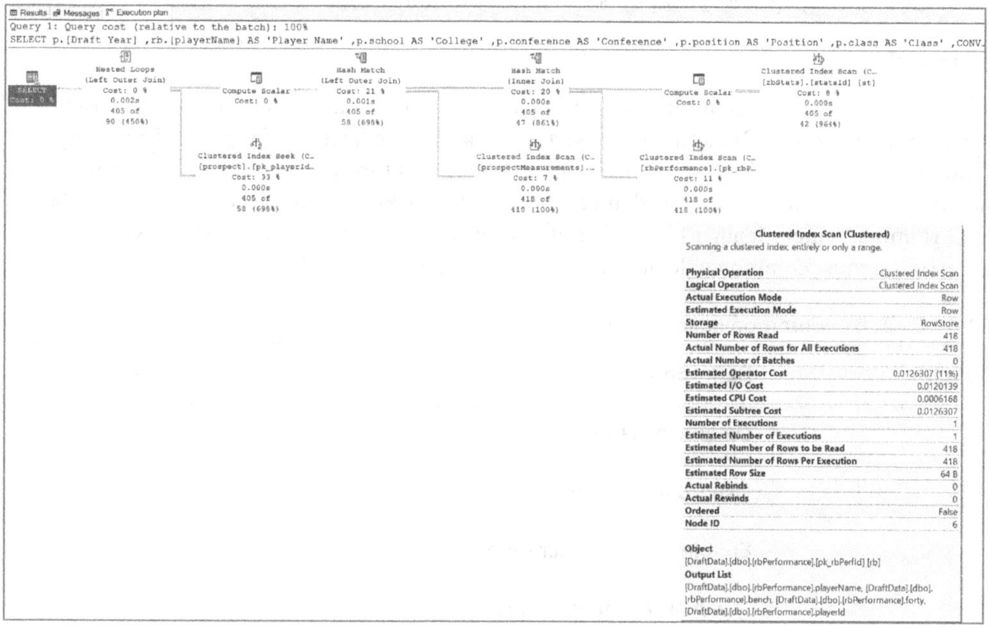

Azure Data Studio

Azure Data Studio is an open-source database management tool that can be used on a Windows, macOS, or Linux machine. Like SSMS, it can connect to SQL Server, Azure SQL, and Azure Synapse Analytics dedicated SQL pools. Azure Data Studio provides a modern developer experience with features such as IntelliSense, source control integration, and an integrated terminal. Not only does it display results for queries, but it also comes with built-in charting to allow users to visualize trends and data skew.

> **NOTE** You can download the latest edition of Azure Data Studio at https://docs.microsoft.com/en-us/sql/azure-data-studio/download-azure-data-studio?view=sql-server-ver15.

Once it's launched, you can connect to a database with Azure Data Studio by clicking *New Connection*. This will open a new window to the right where you can add the server name, authentication type, and credentials. There is also an option to change the database from <Default> to a user database if you are logging in with a database contained user.

After you click *Connect*, Azure Data Studio will display the type (e.g., Azure SQL Database, Azure SQL MI, etc.), SQL Server version, and the databases that are hosted on the server. Users can then choose *New Query* or *New Notebook* to begin developing code. Clicking *New Query* opens a query window that provides a similar experience to the SSMS Query Editor. Clicking *New Notebook* opens a Jupyter Notebook that allows users to write queries using SQL, Python, Julia, R, Scala, and PowerShell code.

Sqlcmd

Sqlcmd is a command-line utility that can be used to connect and query databases hosted in SQL Server, Azure SQL, and Azure Synapse Analytics dedicated SQL pools. The utility allows users to enter T-SQL statements or run script files through a command prompt. It includes several built-in switches that can be used for tasks such as authenticating to a database, running a query from a file, and configuring what information is returned with a query. Some of the most common sqlcmd switches are listed in Table 2.8.

TABLE 2.8 Common sqlcmd switches

Switch	Definition
-d	Database Name
-E	Use Trusted Connection
-g	Enable Column Encryption
-G	Use AAD Authentication
-i	Input File
-K	Set Application Intent (useful for read-only workloads)
-l	Login Timeout
-m	Error Level
-N	Encrypt Connection
-o	Output File
-P	Password
-S	Server Name

Switch	Definition
-t	Query Timeout
-U	Username
-V	Error Severity Level
-z	New Password
-Z	New Password and exit

 You can download the latest edition of sqlcmd at https://docs
.microsoft.com/en-us/sql/tools/sqlcmd-utility?view=sql-
server-ver15#download-the-latest-version-of-sqlcmd-
utility.

To use sqlcmd, open a command prompt and type **sqlcmd** followed by the server information and authentication details. The following is an example of a sqlcmd command connecting to an Azure SQL Database:

```
sqlcmd -S <server_name>.database.windows.net
-d <database_name> -U <user_name> -P <password>
```

Running a query from the command prompt with sqlcmd can be easily performed by entering the sqlcmd command followed by the query. The following is an example of a query in sqlcmd that returns every row in a table:

```
sqlcmd
USE <database_name>;
GO
SELECT * FROM <table_name>;
GO
```

Query Techniques for SQL

As mentioned in Chapter 1, SQL is the development language used to build, access, and manipulate relational databases. The American National Standards Institute (ANSI) and the International Organization for Standardization (ISO) recognizes SQL as a standard language. While ANSI SQL is the standard that all major relational database vendors adhere to, most of them extend the language with functionality custom to their relational database products. For example, T-SQL is the Microsoft extension of ANSI SQL that is native to SQL Server, Azure SQL, Azure SQL Database, Azure SQL MI, and Azure Synapse Analytics.

DDL vs. DML Commands

Standard ANSI SQL commands can be broken down into two primary categories: Data Definition Language (DDL) and Data Manipulation Language (DML). DDL commands are used to define relational database objects such as databases, tables, views, stored procedures, and triggers. DML commands are used to manipulate data stored in a relational database. The following sections describe common commands and statement structure used by these categories.

Chapter 1 describes two additional SQL categories with DDL and DML commands that are specific to T-SQL. These include Data Control Language (DCL) commands that can be used to manage permissions and Transaction Control Language (TCL) commands that are used to control transaction execution.

Data Definition Language (DDL)

DDL statements are used to define database objects. They can be used to create new objects, modify existing ones, or remove objects that are no longer required. DDL statements start with a command that indicates which of these actions the statement is performing. Table 2.9 includes a list of these commands and the common statement structures associated with each of them.

TABLE 2.9   DDL commands

Command	Description	Statement Structure
CREATE	Create a new object in a database.	CREATE TABLE <table name> (<list of columns>)
ALTER	Modify the structure of an existing database object.	ALTER TABLE <table name> ADD COLUMN <column name>
DROP	Remove an object from a database.	DROP TABLE <table name>
RENAME	Rename an existing object.	EXEC sp_rename <old name>, <new name>
TRUNCATE	Remove all rows from a table.	TRUNCATE TABLE <table name>

SQL Server and Azure SQL do not have a RENAME command. Instead, user-defined objects can be renamed using the sp_rename system stored procedure.

Along with the database objects, DDL statements can also define what type of data can be stored in object columns. *Data types* specify the type of data a column can store, which also defines what kind of actions can be performed on that column. For example, columns defined as numeric data types can be aggregated in ways that a string data type cannot. Table 2.10 includes a list of some of the most popular SQL data types and their descriptions.

TABLE 2.10 Common SQL data types

Data Type	Description
INT	Used to define numeric data that rounds to a whole number.
DECIMAL(p, s)	Used to define numeric data that has fixed precision (p) and scale (s).
FLOAT(n)	Used to define numeric data that has approximate, or floating, decimal places.
BIT	Used to define numeric data that can take a value of 1, 0, or NULL.
DATE	Used to define a date.
DATETIME	Used to define a date that is combined with a time of day.
VARCHAR(n)	Used to define string data that has variable size. n is used to define the number of characters that can be stored.
NVARCHAR(n)	Unicode version of the VARCHAR(n) data type. The storage size is two times the number of characters.
CHAR(n)	Used to define string data that has a fixed size. n is used to define the number of characters that can be stored.
NCHAR(n)	Unicode version of the CHAR(n) data type. The storage size is two times the number of characters.

Data types are not the only way DDL commands can define table data. Constraints are used in conjunction with data types to limit the type of data that can be stored in a column. If a statement inserting or updating data violates the constraint, then the action is immediately canceled. Table 2.11 includes a list of some of the most used constraints.

TABLE 2.11 Common SQL constraints

Command	Description
NOT NULL	Ensures that a column has a value for every row.
UNIQUE	Ensures that all values in a column are different.
PRIMARY KEY	Uniquely identifies each row in a table. Also uses NOT NULL and UNIQUE constraints to ensure there are unique values for every row.
FOREIGN KEY	Used to create relationships with other tables. Prevents any action from breaking a relationship.
CHECK	Used to specify what data values are acceptable in one or more columns.
DEFAULT	Sets a default value for a column if a value is not specified when new data is inserted.
INDEXES	Used to enhance the performance of queries. Depending on the index type, they can physically order data in an object or provide pointers to the physical location of data.

Now that we have discussed DDL commands, data types, and constraints, let's explore how these can be used to construct a DDL statement. The following statement creates a table called DimProductCategory.

```
CREATE TABLE [dbo].[DimProductCategory](
.....[ProductCategoryKey] [int] IDENTITY(1,1) NOT NULL,
.....[ProductCategoryAlternateKey] [int] NULL,
.....[EnglishProductCategoryName] [nvarchar](50) NOT NULL,
.....[SpanishProductCategoryName] [nvarchar](50) NOT NULL,
.....[FrenchProductCategoryName] [nvarchar](50) NOT NULL,
CONSTRAINT [PK_DimProductCategory_ProductCategoryKey] PRIMARY KEY CLUSTERED
(
.....[ProductCategoryKey] ASC
)ON [PRIMARY],
CONSTRAINT [AK_DimProductCategory_ProductCategoryAlternateKey]
 UNIQUE NONCLUSTERED
(
.....[ProductCategoryAlternateKey] ASC
)ON [PRIMARY]
)
GO
```

The statement begins by declaring that it is going to create a new table in the database. Columns, their data types, and constraints are then defined between the open and close parentheses. Indexes defined in the table statement also include the columns on which they are based and the ascending or descending sort direction for the column.

Note that the ProductCategoryKey column definition also includes the IDENTITY key word. This property is used to ensure that primary key or unique constraint columns have unique values generated for every new row that is inserted. Unless this property is turned off by using the SET IDENTITY_INSERT ON command at the beginning of a transaction, identity columns do not allow user modifications. Instead, values for identity columns are generated based on the *seed* and *increment* arguments defined in the CREATE TABLE statement. For example, the first row inserted in the DimProductCategory table will generate the value 1 in the ProductCategoryKey column since the *seed* argument is set to 1. The second argument represents the incremental value that is added to the previous row that was loaded. In this case, the second row inserted will generate the value 2 in the ProductCategoryKey column since the *increment* value is set to 1 and the first row's Product-CategoryKey column equals 1.

Data Manipulation Language (DML)

DML statements are used to manipulate data stored in a database. They can be used to retrieve and aggregate data for analysis, insert new rows, or edit existing rows. Table 2.12 lists the four main DML commands and the common statement structures associated with each of them.

TABLE 2.12   DML commands

Command	Description	Statement Structure

SELECT	Read rows from a table or view	SELECT
		 `<list of columns>`
		 FROM
		 `<table name>`
		 WHERE `<filter condition>`
		 GROUP BY `<group by expression>`
		 HAVING `<search condition>`
		 ORDER BY `<columns to sort by>`

INSERT	Insert new rows into a table	INSERT INTO `<table name>`
		 (
		 `<list of columns>`
		)
		 VALUES
		 (
		 `<values to insert>`
		)

TABLE 2.12 DML commands *(continued)*

Command	Description	Statement Structure
UPDATE	Update existing rows	UPDATE *<table name>* SET *<column>* = *<new value>* WHERE *<filter condition>*
DELETE	Remove existing rows	DELETE FROM *<table name>* WHERE *<filter condition>*

Select statements are often more sophisticated than the example structure illustrated in Table 2.12. Queries can retrieve data from multiple tables, convert column data types, and perform aggregations. The UNION, EXCEPT, and INTERSECT operators can also be used to combine or contrast results from multiple queries into one result set. There will be more sophisticated query examples in the following sections, but it is important to note that processing order of operations in a select statement does not match the order they are written. This order, also known as the *logical processing order*, determines when the results from one step are made available to subsequent steps. The logical processing order is defined as follows:

1. FROM
2. ON
3. JOIN
4. WHERE
5. GROUP BY
6. WITH CUBE or WITH ROLLUP
7. HAVING
8. SELECT
9. DISTINCT
10. ORDER BY
11. TOP

More information on the structure of a T-SQL select statement can be found at https://docs.microsoft.com/en-US/sql/t-sql/queries/select-transact-sql?view=sql-server-ver15.

Query Relational Data in Azure SQL, MySQL, MariaDB, and PostgreSQL

While most RDBMSs implementations of SQL use the same core functionality, there are some subtle differences. The following sections explore the syntax used to query data in Azure SQL, Azure Database for MySQL, Azure Database for MariaDB, and Azure Database for PostgreSQL and highlights some of the key differences.

Querying Azure SQL with T-SQL

The first set of queries discussed are constructed using T-SQL. As mentioned previously, T-SQL is the Microsoft extension of ANSI SQL used to communicate with a SQL Server–based relational database. All the examples in this section can be used to query tables in the AdventureWorksDW2019 database. Use the following link to download a backup of the database: https://docs.microsoft.com/en-us/sql/samples/adventureworks-install-configure?view=sql-server-ver15&tabs=ssms#download-backup-files. The link also provides instructions on how to restore the database to an instance of SQL Server or Azure SQL.

Retrieving data from a relational database all starts with a select command. The following is an example of a select statement that returns all data from every column in a single table:

```
SELECT *
FROM [dbo].[FactInternetSales]
```

The asterisk (*) symbol is a wildcard character that indicates "all." In this case, the * is used to represent every column in the FactInternetSales table. While this saves users time when writing queries with long column lists, it can result in poor query performance by returning more data than what is required. Also, applications that use SELECT * statements are liable to break when new columns are added to the table or view being queried. For these reasons, it's always better to explicitly list the columns needed in a select statement.

Queries are often written to return a filtered list of data. The following is an example that returns sales information only for products that cost more than $1,000. The result set is also sorted by sales amount in descending order.

```
SELECT ProductKey
    ,ProductStandardCost
    ,TotalProductCost
    ,SalesAmount
    ,OrderDate
FROM [dbo].[FactInternetSales]
WHERE ProductStandardCost > 1000
ORDER BY SalesAmount DESC
```

Rarely do applications and reports use data from only one table. Instead, applications querying relational databases will often build result sets from two or more tables with the same select statement. Queries can do this by using a *join* operation. Join operations leverage the logical relationships between tables to build rows of data with columns from different tables. There are different types of join operations available that can return different combinations of data. The following is a list of the four most common join types and their T-SQL implementations:

- Inner joins retrieve data from both tables that meets the join condition. Inner joins can be defined with the INNER JOIN or JOIN expressions.

- Left outer joins retrieve all data from the table on the left-hand side of the join condition and data from the right table that meets the join condition. Left outer joins can be defined with the LEFT OUTER JOIN or LEFT JOIN expressions.

- Right outer joins retrieve all data from the table on the right-hand side of the join condition, and data from the left table that meets the join condition. Right outer joins can be defined with the RIGHT OUTER JOIN or RIGHT JOIN expressions.

- Full outer joins retrieve all data from both the left and right tables. Full outer joins can be defined with the FULL OUTER JOIN or FULL JOIN expressions.

Figure 2.21 illustrates how the different join types retrieve data from two tables (represented as table A and table B).

FIGURE 2.21 Types of SQL joins

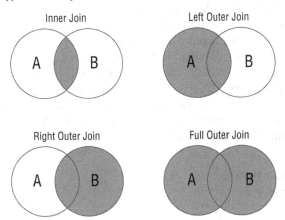

In addition to these join types, SQL Server–based database engines also enable users to develop queries using *cross joins*. Cross joins are special types of joins that return the Cartesian product of rows from both tables. Cross joins can be defined with the CROSS JOIN expression.

The following query builds on the previous example with added data from the DimProduct table. Since it uses a JOIN command without any additional adjectives, the query will perform an inner join, only returning data from both tables that meet the join condition defined in the ON clause.

```
SELECT P.EnglishProductName
      ,FIS.ProductKey
      ,FIS.ProductStandardCost
      ,FIS.TotalProductCost
      ,FIS.SalesAmount
      ,FIS.OrderDate
FROM [dbo].[FactInternetSales] AS FIS
    JOIN [dbo].[DimProduct] AS P
        ON FIS.ProductKey = P.ProductKey
WHERE ProductStandardCost > 1000
ORDER BY SalesAmount DESC
```

Note that the query uses the AS command in the FROM clause to give each table a short form alias. This alias can be used to specify which tables the selected columns are in and how the join condition is defined. Aliases can also be given to columns, allowing users to give names to columns that are the result of aggregations.

SQL provides several built-in functions that can be used to infer insights out of relational data. Built-in functions can be categorized based on the actions they perform on data. For example, aggregate functions such as SUM(), MAX(), and MIN() perform calculations on a set of values and return a single value. They can be used in combination with the GROUP BY clause to calculate aggregations on categories of rows.

The following query revises the previous one so that it returns the total quantity sold and the total sales dollars for products that cost more than $1,000. It also groups the sales totals by product name and monthly sales per year.

```
SELECT P.EnglishProductName
      ,SUM(FIS.OrderQuantity) AS TotalQuantity
      ,SUM(FIS.SalesAmount) AS TotalSales
      ,MONTH(FIS.OrderDate) AS [Month]
      ,YEAR(FIS.OrderDate) AS [Year]
FROM [dbo].[FactInternetSales] AS FIS
    JOIN [dbo].[DimProduct] AS P
        ON FIS.ProductKey = P.ProductKey
WHERE ProductStandardCost > 1000
      AND YEAR(FIS.OrderDate) > 2010
GROUP BY P.EnglishProductName,
        MONTH(FIS.OrderDate),
        YEAR(FIS.OrderDate)
ORDER BY [Year], TotalSales DESC
```

You may be wondering why the WHERE and GROUP BY clauses are not using the column aliases that were defined at the beginning of the statement. This is due to the T-SQL logical processing order that was discussed previously in this chapter. Since the WHERE and GROUP BY clauses are processed by the database engine before the SELECT is, these clauses do not know how to resolve column aliases.

The final T-SQL example in this section describes how to limit the result set to the first 10 rows the query returns. This is one key difference between T-SQL and other versions of SQL, as T-SQL uses the TOP command and other versions use LIMIT. We will demonstrate how other relational database platforms implement the LIMIT command.

```
SELECT TOP(10) P.EnglishProductName
    ,SUM(FIS.OrderQuantity) AS TotalQuantity
    ,SUM(FIS.SalesAmount) AS TotalSales
FROM [dbo].[FactInternetSales] AS FIS
    JOIN [dbo].[DimProduct] AS P
        ON FIS.ProductKey = P.ProductKey
WHERE ProductStandardCost > 1000
GROUP BY P.EnglishProductName
ORDER BY TotalSales DESC
```

Querying MySQL, MariaDB, and PostgreSQL

Queries written to interact with MySQL, MariaDB, and PostgreSQL databases are very similar to ones written in T-SQL. The following example is nearly identical to the previous T-SQL query, with one key difference.

```
SELECT P.EnglishProductName
    ,SUM(FIS.OrderQuantity) AS TotalQuantity
    ,SUM(FIS.SalesAmount) AS TotalSales
FROM [dbo].[FactInternetSales] AS FIS
    JOIN [dbo].[DimProduct] AS P
        ON FIS.ProductKey = P.ProductKey
WHERE ProductStandardCost > 1000
GROUP BY P.EnglishProductName
ORDER BY TotalSales DESC
LIMIT 10
```

The SQL dialects used by MySQL, MariaDB, and PostgreSQL do not use the TOP(n) command to retrieve the first n number of rows that are returned by a query. Instead, these dialects use the LIMIT command to limit the number of rows returned.

Keep in mind that queries written to retrieve and manipulate data stored in one of these database engines will need to be done from a tool that can connect to them. MySQL Workbench is a graphical tool that is like SSMS that can be used to connect to MySQL and MariaDB databases. Queries developed for PostgreSQL databases can be done using the graphical tool pgAdmin.

Summary

The "relational data on Azure" objective of the DP-900 exam focuses on building a foundational understanding of common relational database workloads and database structures. It focuses on the different types of relational database offerings in Azure, along with deployment, security, and development considerations for them.

This chapter covered the following concepts:

Describe relational data workloads.   Relational data workloads can be split between transactional and analytical. Transactional, or OLTP, workloads store interactions that are related to an organization's activities, such as retail purchases. Databases such as SQL Server and Azure SQL Database include mechanisms for managing concurrent transactions to maintain ACID compliancy. Unlike OLTP workloads that are focused on optimizing database writes, analytical workloads are optimized for read-heavy applications. Analytical databases are flattened for this reason, so that users reading data do not have to write overly complex queries to query data.

Describe relational Azure data services.   There are several relational database options on Azure that are designed to meet any organizational need. The Azure SQL portfolio of products include relational database offerings that use the Microsoft SQL Server database engine. These include SQL Server on Azure Virtual Machine, Azure SQL Managed Instance, and Azure SQL Database. Organizations needing horizontal scale for data warehouse and big data analytics workloads can use an Azure Synapse Analytics dedicated SQL pool. Azure Database for PostgreSQL, Azure Database for MariaDB, and Azure Database for MySQL enable organizations to offload infrastructure and management of their on-premises open-source relational database footprint to Azure.

Describe common management tasks for relational databases in Azure.   Relational databases hosted in Azure remove tedious activities associated with managing infrastructure, allowing organizations to spend more time on building solutions that provide valuable insights. However, there are still several management activities that need to be maintained by an administrator, such as automating environment deployments and managing security. For this reason, Azure provides various options for organizations to automated database deployments that are both flexible and highly scalable. Security is also provided at multiple layers in both Azure and in the database engine. These can be categorized by network isolation, access management, data encryption and obfuscation, and security management. There are also several tools provided by Microsoft that allow database administrators and developers to easily perform the activities required to maintain a highly performant relational database solution.

Describe common query techniques.   The Structured Query Language, or SQL for short, is an ANSI/ISO-compliant development language that is used to interact with relational data. SQL commands can be categorized into four different types: Data Definition Language (DDL), Data Manipulation Language (DML), Data Control Language (DCL), and

Transaction Control Language (TCL). Of these, DDL and DML statements are the most important to understand for the DP-900 exam. While ANSI SQL is the standard that all major RDBMSs use, most of them extend the language with some custom functionality. For example, Transact-SQL (T-SQL) is the implementation of SQL that is used by SQL Server–based relational databases.

Exam Essentials

Identify the right data offering for a relational workload.   For this topic, be sure to know when to use an SMP database such as Azure SQL, a MPP database such as Azure Synapse Analytics dedicated SQL pools, and an OLAP tool such as Power BI. SMP databases are typically used for transactional workloads and smaller data warehouses. MPP databases are used for large analytical workloads. OLAP tools are used as data marts or the semantic layer for analytical workloads and include predefined aggregations that are ready to be reported against.

Describe relational data structures.   Be able to identify relational database structures such as tables, views, indexes, stored procedures, functions, and triggers. Tables are the basic storage object for a relational database and store elements of data as rows with one or more attributes stored as columns. Views are virtual objects whose contents are defined by a query returning data from one or more tables. Indexes optimize queries by sorting data physically and providing pointers to where data is stored. Stored procedures and functions encapsulate regularly used T-SQL code to minimize the code footprint needed for applications. Triggers are code blocks that are executed in response to DML, DDL, or login-based events.

Describe IaaS and PaaS Azure SQL services.   Azure has multiple options for hosting relational databases with different levels of abstraction and administrative effort. Of these options, SQL Server on Azure VMs is most like an on-premises SQL Server instance as it gives organizations the most control over the OS and the database engine. This is an example of an Infrastructure as a Service, or IaaS, offering. Organizations looking to offload the management of the OS and features of the database engine can take advantage of Platform as a Service, or PaaS, offerings such as Azure SQL Managed Instance and Azure SQL Database.

Describe Azure Synapse Analytics dedicated SQL pools.   Azure Synapse Analytics dedicated SQL pools is an MPP relational database offering in Azure that is designed for large-scale data warehouses. It uses a scale-out architecture that separates the computational engine and where data is stored so that it can efficiently process big data workloads. Data warehouse practitioners can choose how their data is distributed by configuring their tables to use hash distribution or round-robin distribution or replicating to the first distribution of each compute node.

Describe open-source options in Azure such as Azure Database for PostgreSQL, Azure Database for MariaDB, and Azure Database for MySQL.   Organizations can migrate their existing PostgreSQL, MariaDB, and MySQL footprints to Azure to offload many of the management requirements that are associated with an on-premises environment. Like Azure SQL, Azure manages common tasks such as upgrades, patches, database backups, high availability, and threat protection for these databases without requiring any user intervention. Each of these options includes three service tiers that are designed to meet different performance requirements.

Describe automated deployment options for relational databases in Azure.   While organizations can manually deploy relational databases in Azure through the Azure Portal, it is common to use a technology such as a scripting language or an Infrastructure as Code template to automate database deployments. Automation technologies specific to Azure include Azure PowerShell, Azure CLI, and ARM templates.

Describe database security components.   Security for relational databases hosted in Azure can be broken down into four categories: network isolation, access management, data encryption and obfuscation, and security management. It's important to understand the different methods and technologies that are available in each of these categories. Also, be able to distinguish between authentication and authorization for access management.

Describe common relational database management tools.   There are several tools available for database administrators and developers to build and manage database solutions. The three most common tools available from Microsoft are SQL Server Management Studio (SSMS), Azure Data Studio, and sqlcmd.

Describe DDL and DML commands.   Standard ANSI SQL commands can be broken down into two categories: Data Definition Language (DDL) and Data Manipulation Language (DML). DDL commands refer to SQL operations used to create new objects, modify existing ones, or remove objects that are no longer required. DDL commands include CREATE, ALTER, and DROP. DML commands refer to SQL operations that read and write data in a database. DML commands include SELECT, INSERT, UPDATE, and DELETE.

Describe techniques used to query relational data in Azure SQL, Azure Database for PostgreSQL, and Azure Database for MySQL.   SQL is a highly flexible language that allows developers to perform operations that retrieve data from multiple tables in the same query, filter data, and perform computations on data. Different SQL dialects, such as T-SQL, have several built-in functions that can be used to perform calculations and manipulate data retrieved by a query. While most SQL dialects use the same core functionality, there are some subtle differences, such as the way T-SQL and other SQL dialects limit the number of rows returned in a query.

Review Questions

1. Which of the following isolation levels may result in queries running into the nonrepeatable read issue?

   A. Snapshot

   B. Read Committed

   C. Repeatable Read

   D. Serializable

2. Is the italicized portion of the following statement true, or does it need to be replaced with one of the other fragments that appear below? "The best practice for storing data in analytical systems such as data warehouses and OLAP models is to *normalize data using 2NF.*"

   A. Normalize data using 1NF

   B. Normalize data using 3NF

   C. De-normalize the data and use a star schema

   D. No change necessary

3. You are the database administrator for a company that sells bicycles. One of the developers at the company has expressed a concern with the performance of queries that perform specific filters on columns that are not the primary key. Which of the following types of indexes should you use to increase the performance of these queries?

   A. Nonclustered index

   B. Clustered index

   C. Clustered columnstore index

   D. Filtered index

4. Is the italicized portion of the following statement true, or does it need to be replaced with one of the other fragments that appear below? "Azure SQL Managed Instance is an example of a *PaaS* solution."

   A. IaaS

   B. SaaS

   C. DbaaS

   D. No change necessary

5. You are a consultant for a company that is moving many of its applications from on-premises infrastructure to Azure. Each database must be hosted on a database platform that requires the least amount of administrative effort. One of the applications has a relatively short migration timeline, greatly reducing the amount of time to update deprecated features or fix

any compatibility issues. The databases serving this application run on SQL Server 2019 and have a few SQL Server Agent jobs. Which of the following database offerings provides the fastest time to Azure while maintaining the administrative requirement?

A. Azure SQL MI

B. SQL Server on Azure VM

C. Azure SQL Database Single Database

D. Azure SQL Database Elastic Pool

6. Which Azure virtual machine category is the recommended choice for most SQL Server workloads?

A. Compute optimized

B. Memory optimized

C. Storage optimized

D. General purpose

7. As the lead database administrator for a large retail company, you have been tasked with designing the HADR strategy for your SQL Server on Azure VM footprint. While every database needs to be replicated to a separate server in the same region, only some databases need to be replicated to another server in a different region. During a planned outage, the databases should immediately failover to the server in the same region. If there is a datacenter-wide outage, then the database will need to immediately failover to the server in the other region. Which of the following HADR options should you recommend for this approach?

A. SQL Server Database Mirroring

B. SQL Server Always On availability groups

C. Azure Site Recovery

D. SQL Server Failover Cluster Instances

8. Is the italicized portion of the following statement true, or does it need to be replaced with one of the other fragments that appear below? "A *virtual network* is a networking service in Azure that provides network isolation for relational database services such as SQL Server on Azure VM and Azure SQL MI."

A. Route table

B. Azure ExpressRoute

C. Network security group

D. No change necessary

9. Which of the following components are deployed with Azure SQL MI and exposed to the end user?

A. Network security group

B. SQL database

C. VNet

D. Virtual machine

10. You are designing a database solution in Azure that will serve as the storage engine for an OLTP workload. The chosen database option will need to minimize the amount of administrative effort. Along with supporting several write operations, the solution will also be used by many analysts who will be reading data to build daily summaries of the data. The solution will need to route these read-only workloads so that they do not affect the performance of the write operations. Which of the following is the best option for this scenario?

A. Design the solution to use a SQL Server on Azure VM as the database solution. Create multiple virtual machines and cluster them so that they can participate in an availability group for HADR. Enable one of the instances to serve read-only workloads and set the application the analysts are using to use a read-only application intent. This will route their queries to the read-only secondary.

B. Design the solution to use Azure SQL MI as the database solution. Choose the Business Critical tier and set the application the analysts are using to use a read-only application intent. This will route their queries to the read-only secondary that is deployed with the Business Critical tier of Azure SQL MI.

C. Design the solution to use Azure SQL MI as the database solution. Choose the General Purpose tier and set the application the analysts are using to use a read-only application intent. This will route their queries to the read-only secondary that is deployed with the General Purpose tier of Azure SQL MI.

D. Design the solution to use Azure SQL Database as the database solution. Choose the Standard tier and set the application the analysts are using to use a read-only application intent. This will route their queries to the read-only secondary that is deployed with the Standard tier of Azure SQL Database.

11. What is the maximum number of user databases that can be deployed to a single Azure SQL MI?

A. 1,000

B. 50

C. 100

D. 500

12. Which of the following services allow users to attach a private IP address to an Azure SQL Database logical server?

A. VNet

B. Network Security Group

C. Private Link

D. Azure Firewall

13. You are designing a data warehouse with an Azure Synapse Analytics dedicated SQL pool that analysts will use to power their reporting dashboards. One of the requirements is that users must be able to query data without needing to write complex T-SQL code to retrieve data. These result sets will perform aggregations over a common set of tables. Which object native to dedicated SQL pools is the most performant option for this use case?

A. View

B. Materialized view

C. Temporary tables

D. Stored procedure

14. Azure Synapse Analytics dedicated SQL pool shards data into how many distributions when performing computations?

A. 30

B. 100

C. 45

D. 60

15. You are the lead DBA of an organization that hosts its mission-critical OLTP databases on Azure SQL MI. The development team for an application using one of these databases has requested an older copy of the database be placed on a separate Azure SQL MI to perform tests on data that has since been deleted. They are asking for a version that is two days older than the current date. Which of the following options should you use to copy the database to the other Azure SQL MI?

A. Azure Blob storage automatically stores Azure SQL MI database backups. Use a RESTORE FROM URL command to restore a backup of the database from two days ago on the second Azure SQL MI.

B. Azure manages backups for Azure SQL MI with automated backups. Perform a point-in-time restore to restore a backup of the database from two days ago on the second Azure SQL MI.

C. Azure manages backups for Azure SQL MI with automated backups. Perform a point-in-time restore to restore a backup of the database from two days ago on the first Azure SQL MI using a different name. Then, configure transactional replication to replicate the restored database from the first Azure SQL MI to the second.

D. Azure manages backups for Azure SQL MI with automated backups. Perform a point-in-time restore to restore a backup of the database from two days ago on the first Azure SQL MI using a different name. Then, use Azure Data Synch to replicate the restored database from the first Azure SQL MI to the second.

16. The General Purpose service tier that is available for Azure SQL Database uses which purchasing model?

A. vCore-based

B. DTU-based

C. DWU-based

D. DBU-based

17. Is the italicized portion of the following statement true, or does it need to be replaced with one of the other fragments that appear below? "*Azure Database for MySQL* offers three deployment models, including a Hyperscale deployment model that uses a scale-out architecture to support large OLTP workloads."

    A. Azure Database for MariaDB

    B. Azure Database for PostgreSQL

    C. Azure Database for HBase

    D. No change necessary

18. When running an Azure PowerShell script from a local machine or VM, which of the following Azure PowerShell commands must be run at the beginning of a script to establish a connection with an Azure environment?

    A. Connect-AzSession

    B. Connect-AzAccount

    C. Connect-AzureRmAccount

    D. Connect-AzureRmSession

19. You are designing an Azure Synapse Analytics dedicated SQL pool data warehouse that will be used to serve as the single source of truth for an e-commerce company. There are several large fact tables, each of which includes columns that are used to identify each row. These columns have many distinct values. Which of the following table distribution designs is most appropriate for these fact tables?

    A. Round-robin

    B. Replicated table

    C. Hash

    D. Broadcast

20. Which of the following resource provider and resource type combinations is used by Azure to manage the deployment of an Azure SQL Database?

    A. Microsoft.Sql/managedInstances

    B. Microsoft.Sql/databases

    C. Microsoft.Sql/servers

    D. Microsoft.Sql/servers/databases

21. What Azure PowerShell command can be used to create a new Azure SQL Database?

    A. New-AzSqlDatabase

    B. Create-AzSqlDatabase

    C. New-AzRmSqlDatabase

    D. Create-AzRmSqlDatabase

22. Which of the following RBAC roles lets a user create and manage databases without giving them access? Choose the option that gives the user the least number of privileges.

    A. Azure Active Directory Administrator

    B. SQL DB Contributor

    C. SQL Security Manager

    D. Contributor

23. You are designing an application that will be serving highly sensitive information to a web application. The data must be encrypted so that the only the application can decrypt the data, preventing database administrators from being able to view the raw values. Which of the following options is the best choice for encrypting the columns storing this sensitive information?

    A. Dynamic Data Masking

    B. Denying access to the columns using a DENY statement

    C. Always Encrypted

    D. Transparent Data Encryption

24. Which database management tool is most suited for performing administrative tasks such as managing user permissions, optimizing queries, and building HADR solutions?

    A. Azure Data Studio

    B. Azure PowerShell

    C. Azure Portal

    D. SQL Server Management Studio

25. You are the database administrator for a large e-commerce company. One of the developers is having issues connecting to one of the Azure SQL Databases you manage and has come to you for help. The error message in SSMS indicates a login failure and states that the user cannot open the "master" database. You come to learn that the developer is logging into the database using a database contained user. What step should you tell the developer to take to remediate the issue?

    A. Change the database context on the login screen in SSMS from *default* to the database the user has access to.

    B. Use the SQL administrator credentials to log into the logical server to access the database.

    C. Use an AAD account to log into the database.

    D. Enable TCP/IP for the SQL instance.

26. Which category of SQL statements does a CREATE TABLE statement fall under?

    A. DML

    B. DDL

    C. DCL

    D. TCL

27. What component of Azure Defender for SQL will alert users to malicious activities such as SQL injection and data exfiltration?

   A. SQL auditing

   B. Vulnerability assessment

   C. SQL Server extended events

   D. Advanced Threat Protection

28. What T-SQL statement can be used to add an Azure Active Directory user or group as a user for an Azure SQL Database?

   A. CREATE EXTERNAL PROVIDER AAD; CREATE USER [<AAD_User>] FROM AAD;

   B. CREATE USER [<AAD_User>] FROM EXTERNAL PROVIDER;

   C. CREATE USER [<AAD_User>] FROM EXTERNAL SERVICE;

   D. CREATE USER [<AAD_User>]

29. Which of the following steps comes first in the logical processing order of a T-SQL SELECT statement?

   A. FROM

   B. GROUP BY

   C. ORDER BY

   D. SELECT

30. Which of the following is a Unicode data type that is used to define string data that has variable size?

   A. VARCHAR()

   B. NVARCHAR()

   C. CHAR()

   D. NCHAR()

31. Is the italicized portion of the following statement true, or does it need to be replaced with one of the other fragments that appear below? "A(n) *Full Join* is a join type that is used to retrieve data from both tables that meets the join condition."

   A. Full inner join

   B. Inner join

   C. Outer join

   D. No change necessary

Chapter

3

Nonrelational Databases in Azure

MICROSOFT EXAM OBJECTIVES COVERED IN THIS CHAPTER:

✓ Describe nonrelational data workloads.

- ▪ Describe the characteristics and types of NoSQL data.
- ▪ Recommend the correct NoSQL database.
- ▪ Determine when to use a NoSQL database.

✓ Describe nonrelational data offerings on Azure.

- ▪ Identify Azure data services for NoSQL workloads.
- ▪ Describe Azure Cosmos DB APIs.
- ▪ Describe Azure Table storage.

✓ Identify basic management tasks for nonrelational data.

- ▪ Describe provisioning and deployment of NoSQL data services.
- ▪ Describe method for deployment including the Azure portal, Azure Resource Manager templates, Azure PowerShell, and the Azure command-line interface (CLI).
- ▪ Identify data security components (e.g., firewall, authentication, encryption).
- ▪ Identify basic connectivity issues (e.g., accessing from on-premises, access with Azure VNets, access from Internet, authentication, firewalls).
- ▪ Identify management tools for NoSQL databases.

Nonrelational databases, also commonly referred to as NoSQL databases, allow users to store and query nonrelational data without needing to mold it to fit a predefined schema. NoSQL databases are typically used in scenarios where data needs to be ingested and read very quickly, such as gaming, e-commerce, IoT, and mobile applications. The main categories of NoSQL databases are key-value, document, columnar, and graph. This chapter will discuss the different categories of NoSQL databases, how they can be implemented using Azure Cosmos DB, and basic management tasks for NoSQL databases in Azure.

Nonrelational Database Features

With the boom of data-driven applications over the last several years, organizations have had to reconsider how they store data. Large volumes of data coming in all shapes and sizes needing to be captured in near real time make it nearly impossible for organizations to use traditional relational models for all their data storage needs. Additionally, the advent of cloud computing enabled organizations to easily, and cheaply, scale their data storage solutions horizontally across different geographic regions. This allows organizations to store data in its natural format without needing to apply complex data normalization rules first. For these reasons, NoSQL databases have become a popular choice for software developers who require a dynamic data storage solution.

Instead of forcing data to fit a rigid schema, NoSQL databases use a storage model that is optimized for the requirements of the data being stored. Not needing to focus so much on database management empowers software developers to build applications with a more agile approach, allowing them to adapt to changing requirements more quickly.

While there are several categories of NoSQL databases, they share the following characteristics:

- Ambiguous implementation of ACID principles. This is a benefit for transactional workloads where there are high volumes of data being processed at very fast speeds.

- Easily scaled horizontally across multiple partitions and storage devices since there are no relationships between data, allowing data to reside anywhere.

- Schema flexibility that enables faster and more agile software development. This allows new data records to have different fields and data types than previously stored records. The flexible schema design inherent to NoSQL databases makes them ideal for semi-structured and unstructured data.

Generally, NoSQL databases can be categorized as either key-value stores, document databases, columnar databases, or graph databases. These were summarized in Chapter 1 and are detailed in the following sections.

Key-Value Store

Key-value stores are the simplest type of NoSQL database and store pieces of data as two common elements: a unique key for identification and the value that is captured. Keys can be used by applications to perform lookup operations to retrieve the data values that are associated with them. These data stores are highly scalable, distributing data across all available storage by applying a hash algorithm to the keys. While keys are unique and scalar, values can range from scalar values to complex data objects such as JSON arrays. Figure 3.1 is an example of a key-value store that stores phone directory data.

FIGURE 3.1   Key-Value store

Key	Value
Pete	{(012) 123-4567}
Jim	{(987) 765-4321}
Kate	{(654) 879-1234, (123) 456-7890}

Key-value stores are optimized for ingesting large volumes of data that must be stored and read very quickly. Applications reading data from key-value stores typically perform simple lookups using a single key or a range of keys. Here are two common scenarios where key-value stores are ideal storage solutions:

- Web applications that store user session metadata in real time. These applications can also use key-value stores to make real-time recommendations to users as they are browsing the site.

- Caching frequently accessed data to optimize application performance by minimizing reads to disk-based storage such as Azure SQL Database.

While key-value stores are great at serving data to applications performing simple read operations, they are not ideal storage solutions for applications that need to perform intense search operations. They also do not support scenarios where queries need to filter data by the values. Key-value stores also only support insert and delete operations, requiring users to modify data by completely overwriting existing items.

Azure provides a few different options for implementing a key-value store:

- Azure Table storage

- Azure Cosmos DB Table API

- Azure Cache for Redis

This chapter will focus on Azure Table storage and the Azure Cosmos DB Table API as these are in scope for the DP-900 exam. You can find more information at https://docs.microsoft.com/en-us/azure/azure-cache-for-redis/cache-overview if you would like to learn more about Azure Cache for Redis.

Document Database

Document databases are sophisticated versions of key-value stores that store data as semi-structured *documents*. Individual data fields that are contained in a document can consist of singleton values or a nested group of elements. Documents are assigned unique IDs that can be used by applications to query data. The unique ID, also known as a *document key*, is often hashed to distribute data evenly across available storage. Figure 3.2 illustrates an example of how a document database is structured.

FIGURE 3.2   Document database

Key	Document

1001	`{`
	`  "CustomerID": 101,`
	`  "OrderItems":[`
	`    {`
	`      "ProductID": 500,`
	`      "Quantity": 2,`
	`      "Cost": 350`
	`    },`
	`    {`
	`      "ProductID": 505,`
	`      "Quantity": 1,`
	`      "Cost": 50`
	`    }],`
	`  "OrderDate":"2021-07-14"`
	`}`

1002	`{`
	`  "CustomerID": 102,`
	`  "OrderItems":[`
	`    {`
	`      "ProductID": 450,`
	`      "Quantity": 5,`
	`      "Cost": 650`
	`    }],`
	`  "OrderDate":"2021-07-15"`
	`}`

> While most document databases use JSON format, there are some that encode data in other formats, such as XML, YAML, BSON, or plain text.

Documents contain all the data for a given entity. One example of an entity could be all details related to an order made on an e-commerce site such as the customer's information and the items ordered. This denormalized way of storing data can optimize the performance of queries that need to retrieve data very quickly by eliminating the need to read data from multiple tables.

Each document in a document database can have different sets of fields, like values in a key-value store. Unlike key-value stores, however, queries can filter data by field values. This makes document databases ideal candidates for applications that must store large amounts of data very quickly and need to perform sophisticated filters when querying the data.

Azure provides a couple of different options for implementing a document database:

- Azure Cosmos DB Core (SQL) API
- Azure Cosmos API for MongoDB

Columnar Database

Columnar databases are like relational databases in that they organize data into columns and rows. Unlike relational databases, columnar databases are completely denormalized, dividing data into groups known as *column families*. Column families contain data that would normally be separated into a set of columns if the data was stored in a relational database. However, unlike in a relational database, rows in a column family do not have to share a common schema. One entry can have several columns, while another might only have one or two.

Column families that are a part of the same entity share a common row key. This key is considered the primary key and is used to physically store data in order. Applications can perform lookups using a specific row key or a range of keys. Secondary indexes can also be applied to allow applications to filter by column values.

Figure 3.3 illustrates an example of a columnar database used by a company that sells bicycles and bicycle accessories. This database has two column families, one with product information and another listing quantity information. Related column families are bound by a common product key.

FIGURE 3.3   Columnar database

Row Key	Column Families	
ProductKey	ProductInfo	Quantity Info
500	Category: Bicycle Subcategory: Mountain Bike Color: Matte Black UnitPrice: 700	QuantityOnHand: 10 QuantitySold: 12 ProductRating: 8.2
505	Category: Helmet Subcategory: Standard Helmet Color: Orange UnitPrice: 30	QuantityOnHand: 30 QuantitySold: 40 ProductRating: 9.3

Columnar databases are typically used in analytics scenarios. Grouping data into column families allows queries to jump directly to where specific pieces of data are located. This can result in very fast aggregations since the query does not need to jump from row to row to find the field that is a part of the aggregation. Columns in a column family are also of the same data type, resulting in better data compression and faster queries.

While columnar databases are optimal for analytical workloads that aggregate data, they are not well-suited for transactional workloads where queries perform value-specific lookups. This is where a traditional relational database that stores data in a row-wise format is more performant. Writing data to a columnar database can also take more time than in a row-wise database. While new entries in a row-wise database can be inserted in one operation, columnar databases write new entries to each column one by one.

Azure provides a couple of different options for implementing a columnar database:

- Azure Cosmos DB Cassandra API

- HBase in Azure HDInsight

This chapter will focus on the Azure Cosmos DB Cassandra API. You can find more information at `https://docs.microsoft.com/en-us/azure/hdinsight/hbase/apache-hbase-overview` if you would like to learn more about HBase in Azure HDInsight.

Graph Database

Graph databases are specialized databases that focus on storing the relationships between data entities. Entities in a graph database are stored as nodes, while the relationships between entities are referred to as edges. Nodes and edges can contain attributes specific to them, like tables in a relational database. Edges can also have a direction to indicate the nature of a relationship between two nodes.

Applications that use graph databases run queries that need to traverse the network of nodes and edges, analyzing the relationships between entities. Figure 3.4 demonstrates an example of a graph database that stores information about an organization's personnel chart. The entities represent different job titles and departments, while the edges represent the reporting structure for different employees.

FIGURE 3.4   Graph database

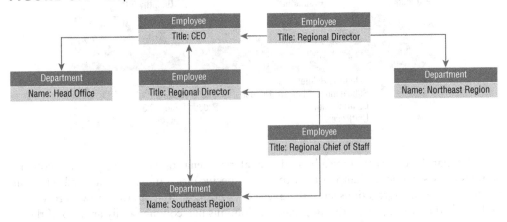

Graph databases are optimal for solutions that ask questions such as "Find all employees that report directly to the CEO." Applications querying large graphs with lots of nodes and edges, such as social media networks, can perform complex analyses very quickly. While relational databases can be used to store the same data as a graph database, queries written for the graph database circumvent any join operations or subqueries that would need to be considered for the relational database.

Graph databases can be implemented in Azure using the Azure Cosmos DB Gremlin API.

Azure Cosmos DB

Azure Cosmos DB is a multi-model PaaS NoSQL database management system. *Multi-model* means that organizations can use Azure Cosmos DB to build key-value, document, columnar, and graph data stores. The different categories are made available as database APIs, including the Table API, Core (SQL) API, API for MongoDB, Cassandra API, and Gremlin API. Users will have the option of choosing one of these APIs when deploying an instance of Azure Cosmos DB.

The highest level of management for Azure Cosmos DB is a database account. Currently, you are allowed to have up to 50 Azure Cosmos DB accounts in an Azure subscription, but that can be increased by submitting a support ticket in the Azure Portal. Each database account can have one or more databases (referred to as a keyspace when using the Azure Cosmos DB Cassandra API), that serve as the unit of management for a set of containers.

Containers are the fundamental unit of scalability for throughput and storage. It is at this level that data is partitioned and replicated across multiple regions. Users can also register stored procedures, user-defined functions, triggers, and merge procedures within a container. Containers are identified by different names depending on which type of NoSQL database is deployed. Table 3.1 lists the naming convention used by each Azure Cosmos DB API.

TABLE 3.1   Azure Cosmos DB API-specific names for containers

API	Container Naming Convention
Table API	Table
Core (SQL) API	Container
Cassandra API	Table
API for MongoDB	Collection
Gremlin API	Graph

Data stored in containers is automatically grouped into logical partitions based on a partition key and is distributed across physical partitions. A *partition key* is a designated data field that is used to efficiently group throughput and related data. Other than choosing an appropriate partition key, partition administration is handled internally by Azure Cosmos DB.

Individual data records stored in a database container are referred to as *items*. When Azure Cosmos DB partitions data, it groups items with the same partition key value into the same logical partition. Items are automatically indexed as they are added to a container. Indexing behavior can also be customized by configuring the indexing policy on the container. Like containers, items are referred to by different names depending on which type of NoSQL database is deployed. Table 3.2 lists the naming convention used by each Azure Cosmos DB API.

TABLE 3.2   Azure Cosmos DB API-specific names for items

API	Item Naming Convention
Table API	Entity
Core (SQL) API	Item
Cassandra API	Row
API for MongoDB	Document
Gremlin API	Node or edge

When choosing a partition key for your container, be sure to select a field that has a high range of values. This will ensure that data is evenly distributed among partitions. Partition key values also cannot be updated, so be sure to select a column that has values that do not change.

Azure Cosmos DB ensures that data is highly available, regardless of which API is being used. As a matter of fact, Azure Cosmos DB guarantees 99.99 percent high availability when deployed to a single region and 99.999 percent high availability when deployed to multiple regions. Reads and writes are also guaranteed within 10 milliseconds across regions wherever the data is being replicated to. The following sections focus on how to optimize performance and availability for Azure Cosmos DB before finishing with an overview of the different database APIs.

High Availability

High availability is a foundational component of Azure Cosmos DB. *Global distribution* in Azure Cosmos DB allows users to easily replicate data to multiple regions by associating one or more additional regions to an Azure Cosmos DB account. Adding new regions can be done through the Azure Portal or programmatically.

New regions can be configured to be read-only or to allow both reads and writes. Read-only workloads such as those produced from reporting applications can be offloaded to the read-only replicas, resulting in better performance for these workloads and those performing write operations. It is recommended to configure at least two different regions to allow writes in case of regional failure. This guarantees that if the primary region goes down, then write operations will automatically be routed to another region.

In addition to global distribution, Azure Cosmos DB maintains four replicas of the data within each region. For example, if you define an Azure Cosmos DB account to use two regions, then eight copies of the data will be maintained. Data resiliency within regions can also be guaranteed by enabling availability zone support. Availability zones ensure that replicas are placed in different zones of a given region, protecting data from in-region zonal failures.

Consistency Levels

Distributed databases such as Azure Cosmos DB that manage multiple write copies across different regions requires a trade-off between data consistency, availability, and performance. Using a strong consistency model results in the most updated data being read by applications but can result in slower performance since data has to replicate and be committed to each associated region before an application is allowed to read data. While eventual consistency offers better performance, applications reading data are at risk of returning dirty data.

Azure Cosmos DB offers five well-defined *consistency levels* to balance the trade-off between consistency, availability, and performance. The following list describes each consistency level, starting with the strictest level of consistency and finishing with the most relaxed:

- *Strong*—This consistency level guarantees that reads return the most recent version of data, regardless of what region an application is reading data from. There is a possibility of slower performance as application connections may experience delays until transactions are committed across every associated region.

- *Bounded staleness*—With this consistency level, applications reading data from the same region that it was written to use strong consistency. For applications reading data from regions outside of where data was written, there is a set "staleness window" for data. This means that data is committed asynchronously to other associated regions in the Azure Cosmos DB account. The staleness window can be configured one of two ways:

  - The number of versions of a record
  - A set time interval between writes

    Whenever either of these two limits is reached, connections are paused, and data is committed to the outside regions. Bounded staleness is a good choice for applications that require low write latency and guaranteed local consistency.

- *Session*—This is the most widely used consistency level for single region and globally distributed accounts. It grants a session token to the application writing data and guarantees that it and any other application sharing the same session token see the most recent version of data. All other reads use eventual consistency.

- *Consistent prefix*—Data is eventually replicated across regions but this level does not provide any guarantees on how long it will take for data to be replicated. However, it does guarantee that applications reading data will read data in order. For example, if an application writes records 100, 101, and 102 to a database in that order, then an application reading the data will see either 100, [100, 101], [101, 102] or [100, 101, 102], but never out-of-order combinations like [100, 102].

- *Eventual*—Much like the consistent prefix consistency level, eventual consistency guarantees that data will eventually be replicated across regions but does not provide any guarantees on how long it will take for data to be replicated. There is also no guarantee that data will not be replicated out of order. While it is the most performant consistency level in terms of read and write latency, it is the least likely to guarantee consistency.

Session consistency is the default consistency level for Azure Cosmos DB. You can change the consistency to be more consistent or more performant with a sliding scale in the Azure Portal or with a deployment script.

Request Units

As with any PaaS offering in Azure, Azure Cosmos DB abstracts compute resources from the end users. Instead, resources such as CPU, IOPS, and memory are bundled into units of measure called Request Units.

Request Units (RUs) represent the throughput required to read and write data in Azure Cosmos DB. One general rule of thumb is that the cost to read and write a 1 KB item is approximately 1 RU and 5 RUs respectively. This is true regardless of what type of Azure Cosmos DB API you are interacting with. Of course, the number of RUs that are required for a given query are going to vary based on the volume of data read or written, how well the data is indexed, the consistency model choice, and the complexity of the query. More information on RU considerations can be found at https://docs.microsoft.com/en-us/azure/cosmos-db/request-units#request-unit-considerations.

 The number of RUs used by a query will vary depending on how evenly distributed data is across partitions. Skewed data caused by a poorly chosen partition key can cause queries to have to perform cross-partition searches, which can take significantly more time and throughput than a query interacting with a single partition.

Since RU usage is measured per second, throughput is set using the Request Units per second (RU/s) measurement. The way throughput is charged depends on the way the RU/s measurement is configured on the Azure Cosmos DB account. These include provisioned throughput, autoscale, and serverless.

Provisioned

Azure Cosmos DB allows users to manually increase or decrease the number of RU/s. With this option, users can allocate RU/s at the database level and at the container level through the Azure Portal or programmatically using the .NET or Java SDK. The minimum throughput that can be allocated for a container or database is 400 RU/s.

Provisioned throughput on an Azure Cosmos DB database is shared across all the containers in the database. This means that all containers share the compute resources that are allocated to a database. There is also an option to dedicate throughput to specific containers. For example, let's say that you create a database with five containers and one of these containers requires dedicated throughput. When provisioning this container, you can enable the *Provision dedicated throughput for your container* option to explicitly allocate RU/s to the container. The rest of the containers will share the throughput allocated to the database.

There are a couple of caveats regarding the 400 RU/s minimum for provisioned throughput. The actual minimum is typically the maximum of the following:

- 400 RU/s
- 10 RU/s per every 1 GB added to storage
- The highest number of RU/s previously provisioned divided by 100

For example, if 50 GB of data is added to a new container, then the minimum RU/s for that container is 500 RU/s.

Provisioned throughput is difficult to calculate when first deploying a database. It's important to understand how much data you will be storing, how many containers you will need, and what type of queries will be interacting with the database. A helpful tool for estimating throughput and throughput cost can be found at `https://cosmos.azure.com/capacitycalculator`. The calculator uses parameters such as the number of regions, whether there are additional write regions, the volume of data stored, and the number of create, read, and delete operations per second to estimate the number of RU/s needed and how much the workload will cost.

Autoscale

Autoscale is a version of provisioned throughput that grants Azure Cosmos DB the ability to automatically scale the throughput of a database or container. Once it's enabled, users can set the maximum number of RU/s that a database or container can scale to. Throughput is then scaled based on usage without impacting the performance of any existing workloads.

Typical use cases for autoscale include workloads with inconsistent or infrequent usage and new applications where the user is not sure how much throughput to provision. Autoscale is a simple, cost-effective solution for most workloads, while still providing high availability.

Serverless

Serverless mode does not require users to provision throughput when creating databases or containers in Azure Cosmos DB. Instead, the Azure Cosmos DB manages throughput for workloads and bills users at the end of their billing period for the number of RU/s that were consumed during that period.

Scenarios that are best suited for serverless include those where you expect unpredictable workload traffic with long periods of downtime. These include development, test, and prototyping scenarios with unknown traffic patterns and applications that have highly random activity.

 Provisioned throughput, autoscale, and serverless are available for all five Azure Cosmos DB APIs.

Azure Cosmos DB APIs

Azure Cosmos DB offers multiple database APIs to create different types of NoSQL databases, including the following options:

- Table API for key-value stores
- Core (SQL) API for document databases
- API for MongoDB for document databases
- Cassandra API for columnar databases
- Gremlin API for graph databases

Users are asked to select an API when creating an Azure Cosmos DB account for the first time. Choosing the most appropriate API depends entirely on the solution(s) that instance of Azure Cosmos DB will be supporting. The following sections will discuss each API and when to use them.

Table API

The Azure Cosmos DB Table API is a key-value store that is based on Azure Table storage. The differences are primarily focused on features that are inherent to the Azure Cosmos DB service such as higher performance and availability, global distribution, automatic secondary indexes, and more options for configuring throughput. However, it is important to know the core components of Azure Table storage to understand how to implement a key-value store with the Azure Cosmos DB Table API.

Azure Table storage is a key-value store that stores nonrelational, structured data. Containers in Azure Table storage are represented as *tables* and can be created in an Azure storage account. Data is stored in tables as a collection of *entities*, like rows in a relational database. Individual data fields in entities are represented as *properties*. Properties are like columns in a relational database.

While the terminology may present Azure Table storage as a relational data store, it is far from it. Tables do not enforce a schema on entities, allowing entities to have different sets of properties. However, there are some entity conditions that must be adhered to. First, each entity must include a set of system properties that specify a partition key, a row key, and a time stamp. Second, there is also a 255-property limit that includes the three previously mentioned system properties.

> Partition keys uniquely identify each partition in a table. Row keys uniquely identify each entity in a partition. Together, the two keys form primary keys that uniquely identify each entity in a table.

Typical use cases for Azure Table storage include caching user data for web applications, address books, device information, or other types of metadata. Applications written in .NET, Java, Python, Node.js, or Go can interact with Azure Table storage using the Azure SDK for those languages. Data can be accessed using OData for all languages and LINQ queries for applications written in .NET.

The Table storage service in Azure is moving from Azure Storage to Azure Cosmos DB to overcome existing limitations with latency, scaling, throughput, availability, and query performance. Keep in mind that Azure Cosmos DB Table API and Azure Table storage share the same data model as Azure Table storage and expose the same query operations through their SDKs. For this reason, applications written for Azure Table storage can easily migrate to the Azure Cosmos DB Table API with minimum code changes.

Table 3.3 includes a list of some of the primary benefits that can be gained by migrating to the Azure Cosmos DB Table API from Azure Table storage.

TABLE 3.3   Azure Table storage vs. Azure Cosmos DB Table API

Feature	Azure Table Storage	Azure Cosmos DB Table API
Maximum Entity Size	1 MB	2 MB
Latency	Fast, but no upper bounds on latency.	Less than 10 ms latency for reads and writes at the 99th percentile, anywhere in the world.
Throughput	Variable throughput model.	Highly scalable with provisioned, autoscale, and serverless throughput options.
Global Distribution	Single region and one optional secondary read region.	Support for multi-region writes and reads with automatic and manual failovers at anytime, anywhere in the world.
Consistency	Strong within the primary region and eventual in the secondary.	Five well-defined consistency levels.

More benefits can be found at https://docs.microsoft.com/en-us/azure/cosmos-db/table/introduction#table-offerings.

Core (SQL) API

The Azure Cosmos DB Core (SQL) API is a document database service and is the default API for Azure Cosmos DB. As the name implies, the Core (SQL) API is the core, or native, API for working with NoSQL data in Azure Cosmos DB. This API is recommended for new applications that require high performance and global distribution and when migrating to Azure from other NoSQL database platforms. The Core (SQL) API is also the recommended migration option for relational databases that require the benefits of a NoSQL database.

The data model for the Core (SQL) API uses the default hierarchy of resources where an account hosts one or more databases, a database hosts a set of containers, and a container stores data as items. Items are formatted as JSON documents and can be interacted with using SQL.

SQL syntax used by the Core (SQL) API is very familiar to T-SQL with some additional functionality that is specialized for interacting with JSON data. For example, an application that is querying the Persons container of a database in an Azure Cosmos DB Core (SQL) API account might want to retrieve information about the user stored in the following JSON document:

```
{
    "firstname": "John",
    "lastname": "Smith",
    "age": 23,
    "favoriteSports": {
        "mostFavorite": "Basketball",
        "secondFavorite": "Baseball"
    },
    "id": "de5760d6-64fd-4dc3-8cb9-cc914ee860b0",
}
```

The application can use the following SQL query to return the user's first name and their most favorite sport:

```
SELECT p.firstname, p.favoriteSports.mostFavorite
FROM Persons AS p
WHERE p.id = 'de5760d6-64fd-4dc3-8cb9-cc914ee860b0'
```

The results from the query are:

```
[
    {
        "firstname": "John",
        "mostFavorite": "Basketball"
    }
]
```

Along with SQL, the Core (SQL) API supports user-defined functions and stored procedures written in JavaScript.

API for MongoDB

MongoDB is a popular document database platform that stores data items as Binary JSON (BSON) documents. Organizations wanting to take advantage of the scalability, performance, high availability, and ease of maintenance that Azure Cosmos DB provides without changing any existing code can do so by migrating their MongoDB databases to the Azure Cosmos DB API for MongoDB.

Data can be migrated to the API for MongoDB using tools such as mongodump, mongorestore, or the Azure native Azure Database Migration Service. Once the data is in Azure, organizations can continue using their existing MongoDB applications by just changing the connection string. Tools that are native to MongoDB such as the MongoDB shell and MongoDB Compass can interact with databases hosted on the API for MongoDB just as they would with MongoDB hosted in an on-premises datacenter.

> MongoDB uses a proprietary query language to perform read and write operations. Syntax and examples of queries written in the MongoDB Query Language can be found at https://docs.mongodb.com/manual/crud.

The Azure Cosmos DB API for MongoDB is compatible with MongoDB server versions 4.0, 3.6, and 3.2. More information about migrating to the Azure Cosmos DB API for MongoDB and estimating throughput can be found at https://docs.microsoft.com/en-us/azure/cosmos-db/mongodb/mongodb-introduction.

Cassandra API

Apache Cassandra is a popular columnar database that stores large volumes of data using a column-oriented schema. Just as with MongoDB and the Azure Cosmos DB API for MongoDB, organizations can migrate their existing Cassandra workloads to the Azure Cosmos DB Cassandra API to take advantage of the premium capabilities that Azure Cosmos DB provides.

Users can query data stored in the Cassandra API using the Cassandra Query Language (CQL) and tools like the CQL shell (cqlsh). Applications can also continue to use existing Cassandra client drivers to interact with Cassandra databases hosted on the Cassandra API.

Gremlin API

The Azure Cosmos DB Gremlin API uses the Apache Tinkerpop graph framework to provide a graph database interface in Azure Cosmos DB. It allows organizations to manage existing and new graph database applications without needing to worry about overhead such as infrastructure, throughput, and availability.

While data is stored as JSON documents as they are with the Core (SQL) API, the Gremlin API enables the data to be queried with graph queries. Applications can query databases hosted on the Gremlin API using the Gremlin query language. More information on the Gremlin query language and using it to query data stored in the Azure Cosmos DB Gremlin API can be found at https://docs.microsoft.com/en-us/azure/cosmos-db/graph/tutorial-query-graph.

Management Tasks for Azure Cosmos DB

Just as with relational PaaS databases in Azure, there are several management tasks that must be taken into consideration for Azure Cosmos DB. These include deploying instances of Azure Cosmos DB, configuring throughput and global distribution, migrating existing on-premises workloads to Azure Cosmos DB, and maintaining data security. The following sections will discuss these tasks in detail, as well as how to troubleshoot common connectivity issues when using Azure Cosmos DB.

Deployment Options

Instances of Azure Cosmos DB can be deployed to an Azure subscription using several methods. Users can manually configure the necessary requirements for their Azure Cosmos DB environment through the Azure Portal or automate the deployment with different scripting languages. As discussed in Chapter 2, Azure PowerShell, Azure CLI, and ARM templates are some of the most common ways to automate Azure resource deployments. Let's discuss in the following sections how to use these different options to configure and deploy Azure Cosmos DB.

Azure Portal

Use the following steps to create an Azure Cosmos DB account through the Azure Portal:

1. Log into portal.azure.com and search for *Azure Cosmos DB* in the search bar at the top of the page. Click *Azure Cosmos DB* to go to the Azure Cosmos DB page in the Azure Portal.

2. Click Create to start choosing the configuration options for your Azure Cosmos DB account.

3. The first requirement for creating an Azure Cosmos DB account is to select the most appropriate API for the workload it will be serving. The Select API Option page allows you to choose from one of the five APIs. Figure 3.5 is a screen shot of what this page looks like. For the purposes of this example, we will select the *Core (SQL)* API.

4. The Create Azure Cosmos DB Account page includes six tabs with different configuration options to tailor the Azure Cosmos DB account to fit your needs. Let's start by exploring the options available in the Basics tab. Along with the following list that describes each option, you can view a completed example of this tab in Figure 3.6.

   a. Choose the subscription and resource group that will contain the Azure Cosmos DB account. You can create a new resource group on this page if you have not already created one.

   b. Enter a name for the Azure Cosmos DB account.

FIGURE 3.5 Select Azure Cosmos DB API.

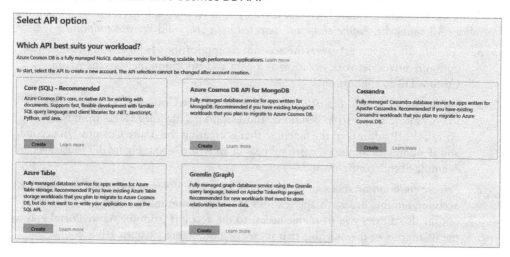

c. Choose the primary Azure region for the account.

d. Choose whether you want to provision throughput for Azure Cosmos DB or have Azure Cosmos DB manage throughput with serverless.

e. The last option allows you to choose whether you would like to apply the free tier discount to this Azure Cosmos DB account. This allows you to get the first 1000 RU/s and 25 GB of storage for free in the account. This option can be enabled for one account per subscription.

FIGURE 3.6 Create an Azure Cosmos DB Account: Basics tab.

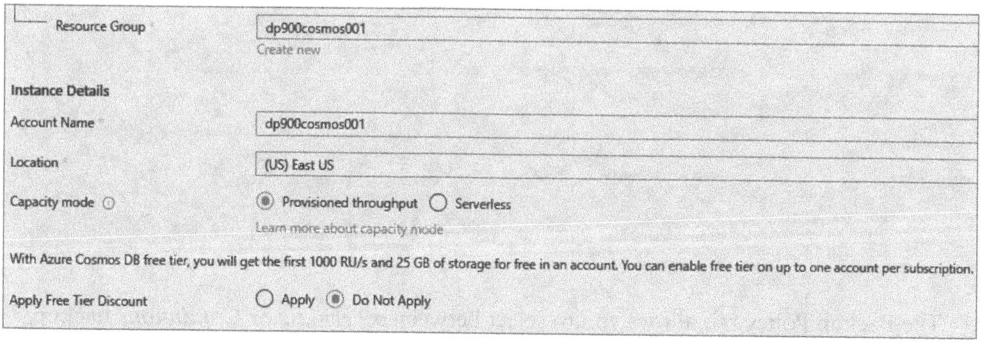

Resource Group	dp900cosmos001
	Create new
Instance Details	
Account Name	dp900cosmos001
Location	(US) East US
Capacity mode ⓘ	● Provisioned throughput ○ Serverless
	Learn more about capacity mode

With Azure Cosmos DB free tier, you will get the first 1000 RU/s and 25 GB of storage for free in an account. You can enable free tier on up to one account per subscription.

Apply Free Tier Discount	○ Apply ● Do Not Apply

5. The Global Distribution tab allows you to enable geo-redundancy, multi-region writes, and availability zones for the account. These options can also be configured post-deployment.

6. The Networking tab allows you to configure network access and connectivity for your Azure Cosmos DB account. There are three options to choose from for network configuration: *All networks*, *Public endpoint (selected network)*, and *Private endpoint*.

   a. *All networks* opens access to the account to applications from any network. This option removes network isolation as a data security component to the Azure Cosmos DB configuration.

   b. *Public endpoint (selected network)* configures Azure Cosmos DB to use a firewall to only allow access from certain IP addresses. This includes access from the Azure Portal, the IP address of the machine that is creating the Azure Cosmos DB account, and IP addresses in one or more subnets in an Azure VNet. Figure 3.7 illustrates an example of this configuration.

   c. *Private endpoint* attaches an IP address in an Azure VNet to the Azure Cosmos DB account, limiting access to applications that can communicate with the VNet. This option also allows you to enable access to the account from the Azure Portal and the IP address of the machine that is creating the Azure Cosmos DB account.

FIGURE 3.7   Create an Azure Cosmos DB Account: Networking tab.

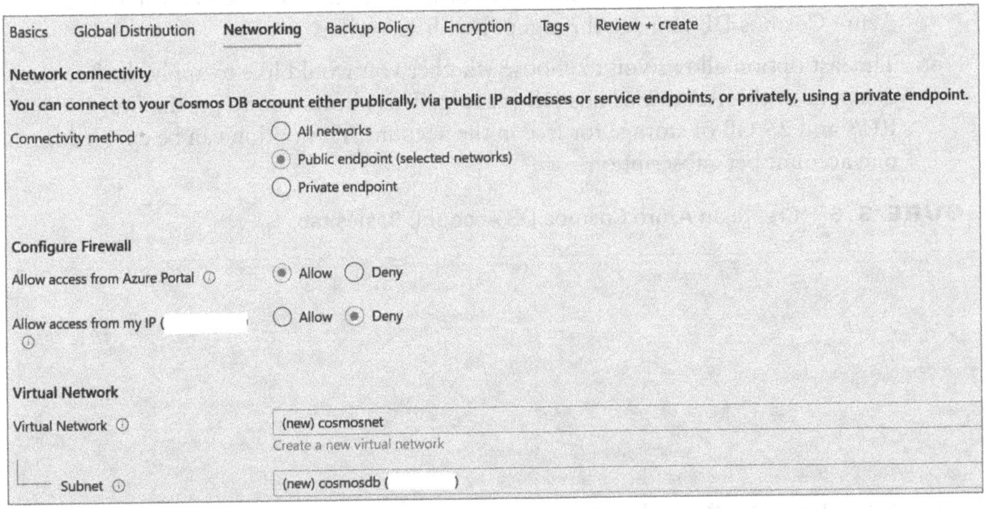

7. The Backup Policy tab allows you to select between a *Periodic* or *Continuous* backup strategy for data stored in this Azure Cosmos DB account. The *Periodic* setting allows you to set the time interval, retention rate, and zone redundancy for data backups. The *Continuous* setting will automatically back up data within 100 seconds of a change in the account, including those made to databases, containers, and items. Figure 3.8 illustrates an example of a *Periodic* backup policy configuration.

FIGURE 3.8   Create an Azure Cosmos DB Account: Backup Policy tab.

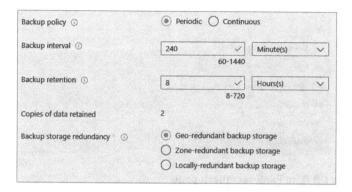

8. The Encryption tab allows you to choose whether data encryption uses a key that is generated and managed by Azure or a custom one that is stored in Azure Key Vault.

9. The Tags tab allows you to place a tag on the Azure Cosmos DB account for cost management.

10. Finally, the Review + Create tab allows you to review the configuration choices made during the design process. If you are satisfied with the choices made for the instance, click the Create button to begin provisioning the Azure Cosmos DB account.

Configuring Databases and Containers

After your Azure Cosmos DB account is deployed, you can start adding databases and containers to store data. You can add these objects using Azure PowerShell, Azure CLI, and Infrastructure as Code templates. There are also SDKs available in .NET, Java, Node.js, Python, and Xamarin that can be used to build Azure Cosmos DB objects. For the purposes of the DP-900 exam, let's focus on configuring these objects using the following steps in the Azure Portal:

1. Go to the Azure Cosmos DB page in the Azure Portal and click on the Azure Cosmos DB account you recently created.

2. In the left-side panel of the Azure Cosmos DB blade, click Data Explorer. Figure 3.9 shows where this button is located.

3. Data Explorer provides a web-based interface to interact with databases, containers, and items in Azure Cosmos DB. The splash page shows all the objects and data in that account, as well as some quick links to creating new tasks such as a new database. This page can be seen in Figure 3.10.

4. To create a new database, click New Database under Common Tasks. The New Database page gives you the option to provision throughput using the autoscale or manual options, as well as the required number of RU/s if using manual or the max database RU/s if using autoscale. Figure 3.11 is an example of a new database using the autoscale option with a maximum RU/s allocation of 4000.

FIGURE 3.9   Azure Cosmos DB Data Explorer button

FIGURE 3.10   Azure Cosmos DB Data Explorer splash page

5. To create a new container for that database, you can either click the New Container button in the upper-left corner of the Data Explorer page or you can click the ellipsis next to the database name and select *New Container*.

6. The New Container page gives you several options for configuring your container. Along with selecting the database that will host the container, you can give the container a name and set a partition key. This page also allows you to set whether the container will use dedicated or shared throughput. When selected, the *Provision dedicated throughput for this container* check box will provision dedicated throughput for the container. Otherwise, the container will share throughput with the other containers hosted by the database. Figure 3.12 shows the configuration for a container that uses dedicated throughput.

FIGURE 3.11   New Database

7.   From here you can start adding new items to the container through Data Explorer or an application.

It is imperative that the partition key is chosen correctly from the start as it cannot be changed after the container is created. The only way to change the partition key is to create a new container with a new partition key and migrate the data from the old container to the new one.

FIGURE 3.12   New Container

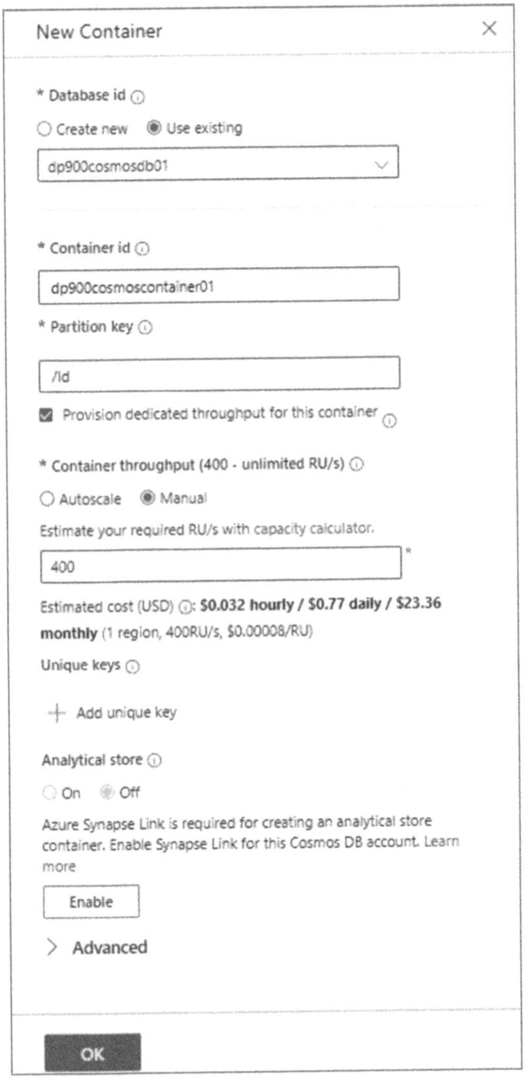

Configuring Global Distribution

Additional regions can be added to an Azure Cosmos DB account to replicate your data for high availability purposes. This can be done through the Azure Portal using the following steps:

1. Click the Replicate Data Globally button under Settings in the left-side panel of the Azure Cosmos DB blade.

2. From this page, you can add regions by either clicking on them in the world map or clicking Add Region and selecting one in the drop-down list. You can also choose to add a new write region using the Add Region button. Figure 3.13 illustrates how to add a new write region replica.

FIGURE 3.13 Adding a new write region replica

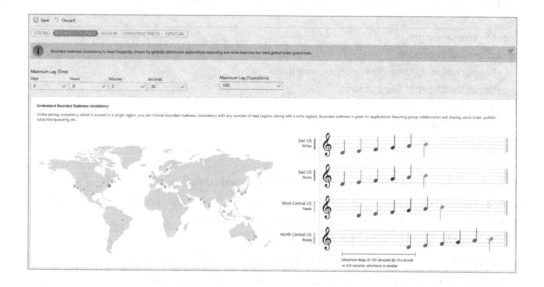

Configuring Consistency

The Azure Portal allows you to change the consistency level from the default session consistency to another. Simply click the Default Consistency button under Settings in the left-side panel and choose a new default consistency level.

If you choose the bounded staleness consistency level, you will be given the option to configure the maximum lag time and maximum lag operations. Figure 3.14 illustrates how you can change the default consistency to bounded staleness through the Default Consistency page.

FIGURE 3.14 Updating the default consistency to bounded staleness

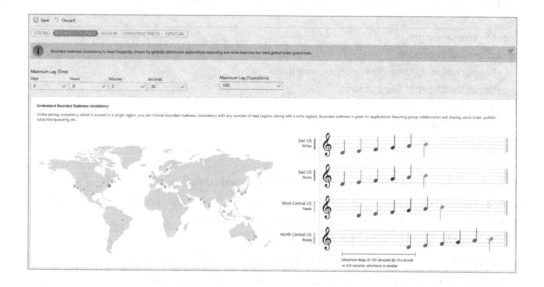

Azure PowerShell

Just as with relational databases in Azure, you can use Azure PowerShell to create and manage all components of Azure Cosmos DB. The following PowerShell script can be run on the Azure Cloud Shell or a PowerShell window to create a new Azure Cosmos DB account:

```
<#
Sign into your Azure environment. Not required
if running this script in the Azure Cloud Shell
#>
Connect-AzAccount

<#
Set the parameters needed to create the account
such as the resource group name, account name,
API type, consistency level, and replica locations
#>
$resourceGroupName = "dp900cosmos001"
$accountName = "dp900cosmos001"
$apiKind = "Sql"
$consistencyLevel = "Session"
$locations = @()
$locations += New-AzCosmosDBLocationObject `
-LocationName "East US" -FailoverPriority 0 -IsZoneRedundant 0
$locations += New-AzCosmosDBLocationObject `
-LocationName "West US" -FailoverPriority 1 -IsZoneRedundant 0

#Create the account
New-AzCosmosDBAccount `
    -ResourceGroupName $resourceGroupName `
    -LocationObject $locations `
    -Name $accountName `
    -ApiKind $apiKind `
    -EnableAutomaticFailover: $true `
    -DefaultConsistencyLevel $consistencyLevel
```

This script includes a few key parameters that are used to define the account:

- **$resourceGroupName**—The resource group that the Azure Cosmos DB account is going to be deployed to. The resource group must already exist.
- **$accountName**—The name for the account.
- **$apiKind**—The Azure Cosmos DB API that will be used for the account.
- **$consistencyLevel**—The default consistency level for the account.

- **$locations**—The replica regions for the account. The region with *FailoverPriority* set to 0 is the write region.

Azure PowerShell can also be used to create an Azure Cosmos DB database and container. The following script is used to create a new database in the newly created account with 4000 RU/s, as well as a container with 400 RU/s:

```
$resourceGroupName = "dp900cosmos001"
$accountName = "dp900cosmos001"
$databaseName = "dp900cosmosdb01"
$containerName = "dp900cosmoscontainer01"
$partitionKey = "/Id"
$databaseThroughput = 4000
$containerThroughput = 400


New-AzCosmosDBSqlDatabase `
    -ResourceGroupName $resourceGroupName `
    -AccountName $accountName `
    -Name $databaseName `
    -Throughput $databaseThroughput

New-AzCosmosDBSqlContainer `
    -ResourceGroupName $resourceGroupName `
    -AccountName $accountName `
    -DatabaseName $databaseName `
    -Name $containerName `
    -PartitionKeyKind Hash `
    -PartitionKeyPath $partitionKeyPath `
    -Throughput $containerThroughput
```

More information about creating and managing Azure Cosmos DB objects with Azure PowerShell can be found at https://docs.microsoft.com/en-us/azure/cosmos-db/sql/manage-with-powershell.

Azure CLI

Azure CLI is an alternative to Azure PowerShell for creating and managing Azure Cosmos DB components via a scripting language. The following Azure CLI script can be run on the Azure Cloud Shell, in a PowerShell window, or in a command prompt to create a new Azure Cosmos DB account, database, and container. This script uses the same parameters as the Azure PowerShell script in the previous section:

```
resourceGroupName='dp900cosmos001'
accountName='dp900cosmos001'
databaseName='dp900cosmosdb01'
```

```
containerName='dp900cosmoscontainer01'
partitionKey='/Id'
dbThroughput=4000
containerThroughput=400

az cosmosdb create \
    -n $accountName \
    -g $resourceGroupName \
    --default-consistency-level Session \
    --locations regionName='West US 2' \
        failoverPriority=0 isZoneRedundant=False \
    --locations regionName='East US 2'
        failoverPriority=1 isZoneRedundant=False \

az cosmosdb sql database create \
    -a $accountName \
    -g $resourceGroupName \
    -n $databaseName \
    --throughput $dbThroughput

az cosmosdb sql container create \
    -a $accountName -g $resourceGroupName \
    -d $databaseName -n $containerName \
    -p $partitionKey --throughput $containerThroughput
```

More information about creating and managing Azure Cosmos DB objects with Azure CLI can be found at https://docs.microsoft.com/en-us/azure/cosmos-db/sql/manage-with-cli.

ARM Template

As mentioned in Chapter 2, ARM templates can be used to define the resources and configuration requirements for Azure deployments. These templates can be used to automate new deployments of Azure Cosmos DB as well as configuration changes for Azure Cosmos DB in different development environments.

One example of an ARM template that creates an Azure Cosmos DB account, database, and container can be found at https://docs.microsoft.com/en-us/azure/cosmos-db/sql/quick-create-template?tabs=CLI. The script can be deployed by clicking the Deploy To Azure button in the link and entering the required parameters or by running the following Azure PowerShell script:

```
Connect-AzAccount
$resourceGroupName = "dp900cosmos001"
```

```
$location = "East US"

New-AzResourceGroup
    -Name $resourceGroupName
    -Location $location

New-AzResourceGroupDeployment
    -ResourceGroupName $resourceGroupName `
    -TemplateUri https://raw.githubusercontent.com/Azure
/azure-quickstart-templates/master/quickstarts
/microsoft.documentdb/cosmosdb-sql/azuredeploy.json
```

Azure Cosmos DB Security

Data security for Azure Cosmos DB is implemented at multiple levels in Azure. Just as with data stored in a relational database in Azure, unauthorized access to Azure Cosmos DB is prevented using network isolation and identity management. Data stored in Azure Cosmos DB is also encrypted at rest and in transit to protect data from malicious activity. The following sections examine the methods Azure uses to secure data stored in Azure Cosmos DB in further detail.

Network Isolation

We briefly examined the two network isolation options for Azure Cosmos DB while going over how to deploy an account using the Azure Portal. These options include the following:

- Using the Azure Cosmos DB firewall to set IP-based access controls that restrict communication to an approved set of IP addresses. This can be taken a step further by allowing access for entire subnets by enabling the Azure Cosmos DB service endpoint on them.
- Assigning a private IP address from a VNet Azure Cosmos DB account with a private endpoint. This will restrict access to only applications that can communicate with the VNet that the private endpoint is associated with.

While there is an option to open Azure Cosmos DB access to requests from any network, it is important to consider the security implications, if any, of that setting. Rarely are security requirements satisfied with just access management and data encryption methods being put in place. Network isolation is an important design consideration and should be discussed when building a data-driven solution that uses Azure Cosmos DB.

Access Management

Azure Cosmos DB provides three approaches to control data access: key-based access control, role-based access control (RBAC), and resource tokens. Not only do each of these options restrict access to only users who should have access, they also determine whether the user has read-write or read-only access to database objects. The following sections provide an overview of these options.

Key-Based Access Control

Azure Cosmos DB provides a primary and a secondary key for read-write access as well as a primary and a secondary key for read-only access. Keys provide access to all resources in an Azure Cosmos DB account. The purpose of having a primary and a secondary key is to allow users to regenerate one key without requiring any downtime.

While keys can be useful when providing access to different applications, they can be cumbersome to manage. Keys also expose more Azure Cosmos DB account objects than what most users need. In most cases, it is better practice to use an identity management model that grants fine-grained permissions to Azure Active Directory (AAD) or native Azure Cosmos DB identities for database authentication and authorization.

Role-Based Access Control (RBAC)

Azure enables organizations to centralize identity management with AAD and RBAC roles. As discussed in Chapter 2, RBAC roles are used to control access to different Azure services. RBAC roles can be assigned to AAD objects (known as identities) such as users, groups, service principals, and managed identities, giving them the ability to perform tasks that are allowed by those roles. There are several RBAC roles specific to Azure Cosmos DB that can be used to perform management and data manipulation operations.

First, let's examine Azure Cosmos DB RBAC roles that control management plane operations. These roles allow AAD identities to manage create/replace/delete operations for Azure Cosmos DB account objects, database backups and restores, and performance monitoring. The following are the Azure Cosmos DB RBAC roles that support management operations:

- The *DocumentDB Account Contributor* role can manage Azure Cosmos DB accounts.

- The *CosmosDB Account Reader* role can read Azure Cosmos DB account data.

- The *Cosmos Backup Operator* role can submit a restore request for a periodic-backup-enabled database or container. It can modify the backup interval and retention through the Azure Portal. This role cannot access any data or use Data Explorer.

- The *CosmosRestoreOperator* role can perform a restore for an Azure Cosmos DB account using the continuous backup mode.

- The *Cosmos DB Operator* role can provision Azure Cosmos DB accounts, databases, and containers. It cannot access any data or use Data Explorer.

More information about Azure Cosmos DB RBAC roles that support management activities can be found at `https://docs.microsoft.com/en-us/azure/cosmos-db/role-based-access-control`.

The next set of Azure Cosmos DB RBAC roles to bear in mind are those that support data plane operations. These allow AAD identities to create, read, update, and delete data from databases and containers. The following are the two built-in Azure Cosmos DB RBAC roles used to manage data plane operations:

- The *Cosmos DB Built-in Data Reader* role can read account metadata, data from specific items (point-reads and queries) and a specific container's change feed.

- The *Cosmos DB Built-in Data Contributor* role can read account metadata and perform create, read, and delete operations on data in specific containers and items.

More information about Azure Cosmos DB RBAC roles that support management activities can be found at `https://docs.microsoft.com/en-us/azure/cosmos-db/how-to-setup-rbac`.

Resource Tokens

Resource tokens allow limited time access to Azure Cosmos DB resources such as containers, partition keys, items, stored procedures, triggers, and user-defined functions. These tokens are initially created when a user is granted permissions to a specific resource and are valid for a preset time limit. The default time limit for a resource token is one hour and can be extended to a maximum of five hours. Resource tokens are re-created when a user makes an API request (GET, PUT, or POST) to Azure Cosmos DB.

Azure Cosmos DB database users are identity constructs that provide permissions to specific objects in a database, much like database contained users in Azure SQL. Users can be granted different levels of access to database resources using a set of permissions, also known as a permission resource. Permissions are authorization tokens associated with a database user that are used to authorize access to different database resources. Permission resources offer the following levels of access for database resources:

- *All*—This mode provides read, write, and delete access to a resource.
- *Read*—This mode provides read-only access to a resource.

Data Encryption

Data encryption at rest and in transit is provided out of the box for Azure Cosmos DB. There are no controls to turn encryption on or off. Azure Cosmos DB supports data encryption in transit with TLS version 1.2 or higher. Data stored in Azure Cosmos DB is encrypted at rest with keys that are managed behind the scenes by Microsoft. Organizations also have the option to add a second layer of encryption with their own keys.

Azure Cosmos DB Common Connectivity Issues

As with any data storage service, there will be times when issues occur when interacting with Azure Cosmos DB. These issues are typically related to bad request exceptions, unauthorized requests, or forbidden exceptions. The following sections include common Azure Cosmos DB connectivity issues and how to troubleshoot them.

Bad Request Exceptions

Errors that return the HTTP 400 status code represent bad request exceptions where the application request contains invalid data or is missing required parameters. These errors are typically caused by the following issues:

- The *missing the ID property* error means that the JSON item that is being inserted is missing the required ID property. Specify the ID property with a string value as a part of the item to resolve this issue.

- The *invalid partition key type* error means that the partition key value is an invalid data type. Make sure the partition key is a string or a numeric value.

- The *wrong partition key value* error means the partition key value being passed in the request does not match the item value in the container. For example, if the partition key path is /Id, the item has a field called Id and has values that do not include the value that was provided in the query. To resolve this issue, make sure the value used in the query is a valid partition key value.

Unauthorized Requests

Unauthorized requests are represented by a 401 HTTP error code, happening when an application request is performing an action with an invalid key. The following is a list of potential causes for unauthorized requests:

- The key is regenerated and the application using the key does not follow best practices for key rotation. This issue can be resolved by rotating the primary key to the secondary key and then regenerating the primary key. More information on key regeneration and rotation can be found at `https://docs.microsoft.com/en-us/azure/cosmos-db/secure-access-to-data?tabs=using-primary-key#key-rotation`.

- The key is misconfigured or was not copied correctly. Simply recopy the primary key or rotate to the secondary key to resolve this issue.

- The application is using a read-only key when trying to perform write operations. Switch the key to a read-write key if the application should be authorized to create or delete data.

- The application is trying to access a container before the container has finished being created. This typically happens when a container is deleted and then re-created with the same name.

Forbidden Exceptions

Forbidden exceptions occur when a data plane request comes from an application whose IP address is not whitelisted by the Azure Cosmos DB firewall or cannot communicate with the VNet the Azure Cosmos DB account is associated with. These exceptions are represented by 403 status codes.

Solutions to this error depend on if the application request comes from an IP address that can communicate with the Azure Cosmos DB account. They will also depend on what type of network isolation the account is using. Use the following recommendations if the application request is coming from an expected path:

- If the Azure Cosmos DB account is using the firewall, check to make sure the request's IP address is whitelisted in the Azure Cosmos firewall or is coming from a subnet with the Azure Cosmos DB service endpoint enabled.

- If the Azure Cosmos DB account is using a private endpoint, then make sure that the request's IP address can communicate with the VNet the private endpoint is associated with.

If the application request is not coming from an expected path, the issue is likely related to the application-side configuration. Use the following guidance to troubleshoot the issue depending on the type of network isolation the account is using:

- If an application request was expected to use a service endpoint but uses the public Internet instead, then check to see if the subnet the application's IP address is in has enabled the Azure Cosmos DB service endpoint.

- If an application request was expected to come through a private endpoint but instead comes from the public Internet, then check to see if the DNS the application is using can resolve the account endpoint to the private IP address associated with the private endpoint.

Management Tools

Azure offers two Azure Cosmos DB management tools that developers can use to write and test queries before adding them to applications. Data Explorer and the Azure Cosmos DB Explorer give developers and administrators the ability to create new resources and manage existing resources as well as optimize the cost-performance ratio for throughput. The following sections describe each of these tools in further detail.

Data Explorer

Data Explorer is a development environment available in the Azure Portal for querying and managing Azure Cosmos DB. It can be used to create and delete resources such as databases, containers, stored procedures, user-defined functions, and triggers. Developers can use query windows, like those in SSMS and Azure Data Studio, to write SQL statements that read, write, or delete data.

Developers using the Azure Cosmos DB Core (SQL) API can create Jupyter notebooks in Data Explorer to analyze and visualize data. Notebook commands can be written in Python or C#.

Administrators can also take advantage of Data Explorer to manage Azure Cosmos DB. Tasks such as scaling throughput, modifying the indexing policy, and setting a Time to Live (TTL) period can be handled using Data Explorer.

Azure Cosmos DB Explorer

Azure Cosmos DB Explorer is a full screen extension of the Data Explorer tool. It offers the same capabilities, such as creating new account objects, authoring queries, and scaling throughput. However, unlike Data Explorer, Azure Cosmos DB Explorer can be used outside of the Azure Portal. Users connecting to an Azure Cosmos DB account will only need one of the read-write or read-only keys that are generated with the account. This allows administrators to restrict who can modify data while still providing an easy-to-use development environment for developers to use.

Use the following steps to open the Azure Cosmos DB Explorer from the Azure Portal:

1. Go to the Azure Cosmos DB account created earlier and click on Data Explorer.

2. Click the Open Full Screen icon on the far right side of the Data Explorer blade. Figure 3.15 shows where you can find this icon.

FIGURE 3.15   Azure Cosmos DB Explorer Open Full Screen icon

3. After clicking this icon, you will be presented with two URL options: *Read and Write* and *Read Only*. You can either copy one of the links or click the Open button to open Azure Cosmos DB Explorer in a separate browser tab. Figure 3.16 illustrates what this pop-up page looks like.

FIGURE 3.16   Azure Cosmos DB Explorer pop-up screen

4. Once Azure Cosmos DB Explorer is opened, you will see the same interface as the Data Explorer.

Summary

This chapter covered NoSQL databases, including key-value, document, columnar, and graph databases. While they specialize in different scenarios, they do share some common characteristics. These include ambiguous implementations of ACID principles, flexible schema design, and the ability to scale horizontally.

Azure Cosmos DB is a fully managed, highly available PaaS NoSQL database that offers multiple database APIs for each type of NoSQL data store, including the Azure Cosmos DB

Table API, Azure Cosmos DB Core (SQL) API, Azure Cosmos DB API for MongoDB, Azure Cosmos DB Cassandra API, and Azure Cosmos DB Gremlin API. Each of these APIs comes with at least a 99.99 percent SLA and can easily be replicated to different regions all around the world. Azure Cosmos DB allows users to choose from five different consistency models to balance the trade-off between consistency, availability, and performance.

Compute is measured in Azure Cosmos DB as the throughput required to read and write data. Throughput is represented as Request Units per second (RU/s). RU/s can be set at the database and the container level by either provisioning a dedicated number of RU/s or setting a maximum number of RU/s that a database or container can scale to. There is also a serverless option that lets Azure Cosmos DB use as many RU/s as it needs for a workload.

Just like relational databases in Azure, Azure Cosmos DB can be deployed manually in the Azure Portal or automated with a script or an Infrastructure as Code template. Data stored in Cosmos DB is also secured at multiple layers, natively encrypting data at rest and in transit and offering flexible network isolation and access management options.

This chapter finishes by providing an overview of the two primary management tools that can be used to administer and query Azure Cosmos DB: Data Explorer and the Azure Cosmos DB Explorer. Data Explorer can be accessed in the Azure Portal. Azure Cosmos DB Explorer is a stand-alone web application that provides the same options and interface as Data Explorer and is typically used by developers who do not have access to the Azure Portal.

Exam Essentials

Describe the characteristics of NoSQL databases. NoSQL databases have become increasingly popular in the last several years due to larger volumes of data being produced at faster speeds. The advent of agile development standards and decreasing storage cost has also led to software developers being more empowered to use database platforms that offer more dynamic storage options.

The common characteristics between the different NoSQL database categories include schema flexibility, ambiguous interpretations of ACID principles, and the ability to scale horizontally.

Describe key-value stores. Key-value stores are the simplest type of NoSQL database. Each entry includes a data value and a unique key. These data stores are optimized for ingesting large volumes of data that must be stored and read very quickly Azure provides several options to implement a key-value store, including Azure Table storage, Azure Cosmos DB Table API, and Azure Cache for Redis.

Describe document databases. Document databases are like key-value stores in that each entry includes a unique key with values of data. There are two options available for implementing a document database in Azure: Azure Cosmos DB Core (SQL) API and Azure Cosmos API for MongoDB.

Describe columnar databases.   Columnar databases organize data in rows and columns like a relational database, but group columns into column families so that data remains denormalized. There are two options available for implementing a columnar database in Azure: Azure Cosmos DB Cassandra API and HBase in Azure HDInsight.

Describe graph databases.   Graph databases are specialized databases that are used to store the relationships between different entities. Graph databases can be implemented in Azure using the Azure Cosmos DB Gremlin API.

Describe Azure Cosmos DB.   Azure Cosmos DB is a PaaS NoSQL database in Azure that can be used to build key-value, document, columnar, and graph data stores. It is highly resilient, providing users with the ability to replicate data globally.

The highest level of management in Azure Cosmos DB is an account. One account can have one or more databases, which serve as the unit of management for a set of containers. Containers are the most fundamental unit of scalability in Azure Cosmos DB, storing database objects such as user-defined functions, stored procedures, and data. Data is referred to as items and is distributed into multiple partitions by running a hash algorithm on a selected partition key.

Describe Azure Cosmos DB consistency levels.   Users can customize the trade-off between read consistency and performance by choosing one of five consistency levels for their Azure Cosmos DB accounts: strong, bounded staleness, session, consistent prefix, or eventual. Session is the default consistency level for Azure Cosmos DB and is suitable for most workloads.

Describe Azure Cosmos DB throughput.   Request Units (RUs) represent the throughput required to read and write data in Azure Cosmos DB. Since RU usage is measured per second, throughput is set using the Request Units per second (RU/s) measurement.

Users can allocate a dedicated number of RU/s at the database level and at the container level or provide a maximum number of RU/s that Azure Cosmos DB can automatically scale to. They can also choose to forgo provisioning throughput and use serverless to enable Azure Cosmos DB to manage RU/s usage without user intervention.

Describe Azure Cosmos DB APIs.   There are five APIs in Azure Cosmos DB that allow users to build key-value, document, columnar, and graph data stores in Azure. They include the Azure Cosmos DB API, Azure Cosmos DB Core (SQL) API, Azure Cosmos DB API for MongoDB, Azure Cosmos DB Cassandra API, and Azure Cosmos DB Gremlin API.

The Azure Cosmos DB Core (SQL) API is native to Azure Cosmos DB and is recommended for new applications that require high performance and global distribution and when migrating to Azure Cosmos DB from other database platforms.

Describe Azure Table storage.   Azure Table storage is a key-value store in Azure that stores nonrelational, structured data. Tables can be created in an Azure storage account and can host one or more entities of data. Remember that the partition key and row key form the primary key for each entity in a table.

Describe deployment options for Azure Cosmos DB.   It is important to understand how to deploy Azure Cosmos DB using the Azure Portal, Azure PowerShell, Azure CLI, and Azure PowerShell. Remember that you can use a free tier discount for one Azure Cosmos DB account per subscription where the first 1000 RU/s and 25 GB of storage are free.

The best way to manage deployments across multiple development environments is to script the deployment using an Infrastructure as Code template. This can be with an ARM, Terraform, or Bicep template.

Describe how to secure Azure Cosmos DB.   Just like relational database offerings in Azure, Azure Cosmos DB has multiple layers of security. Network isolation is achieved by either whitelisting IP addresses or VNets in the Azure Cosmos DB firewall or attaching a private endpoint to the account. Remember that while Azure Cosmos DB provides keys, it is more often better to assign RBAC roles to AAD identities or use permission resources with native Azure Cosmos DB users for access management.

Describe management tools for Azure Cosmos DB.   There are two management tools that can be used to manage account resources, develop queries, and handle administrative tasks: Data Explorer and Azure Cosmos DB Explorer. Data Explorer can be opened after clicking on the Azure Cosmos DB account in the Azure Portal. Azure Cosmos DB Explorer is a web-based tool that offers the same capabilities as Data Explorer.

Review Questions

1. Which of the following services in Azure can be used to build a key-value store?

   A. Azure Table storage

   B. Azure Cosmos DB

   C. Azure Cache for Redis

   D. All of the above

2. Is the italicized portion of the following statement true, or does it need to be replaced with one of the other fragments that appear below? "Queries can return data that is filtered by keys and data fields from *key-value stores*."

   A. Document databases

   B. Graph databases

   C. Azure Table storage

   D. No change necessary

3. What resource is the fundamental unit of scalability for throughput and storage?

   A. Database

   B. Item

   C. Container

   D. Account

4. Which consistency level is the default consistency level for Azure Cosmos DB?

   A. Session

   B. Consistent prefix

   C. Strong

   D. Bounded staleness

5. You are designing a key-value store in Azure that will be used to store user sessions for an e-commerce site. The chosen data store must be able to allow writes to multiple regions to ensure low write latency for global users. Which Azure service is the best choice for this solution?

   A. Azure Table storage

   B. Azure Cosmos DB Graph API

   C. Azure Cosmos DB Table API

   D. Azure Key-Value Storage

6. Which of the following Azure Cosmos DB APIs allows users to host document databases?

    A. Table API

    B. Cassandra API

    C. Gremlin API

    D. API for MongoDB

7. Is the italicized portion of the following statement true, or does it need to be replaced with one of the other fragments that appear below? "The first *100 RU/s and 10 GB of storage* used by an Azure Cosmos DB account are free if you apply the free tier discount to it."

    A. 1000 RU/s and 25 GB of storage

    B. 500 RU/s and 10 GB of storage

    C. 2000 RU/s and 25 GB of storage

    D. No change necessary

8. Which of the following options is the best way to manage Azure Cosmos DB deployments across multiple environments?

    A. Azure PowerShell

    B. Azure CLI

    C. ARM templates

    D. Azure Portal

9. What RBAC role can be used to restrict the data plane access of an Azure Active Directory identity to read-only?

    A. Cosmos DB Built-in Data Contributor

    B. CosmosDB Account Reader

    C. Cosmos DB Built-in Data Reader

    D. DocumentDB Built-in Data Reader

10. You are the administrator of an Azure Cosmos DB account that is used by an e-commerce application. Your manager has asked you to provide read-only access to one of the application developers and to recommend a tool that they can use to develop and test queries that they are adding to the application. The developer does not have access to the Azure Portal. Which of the following tools should you recommend?

    A. Azure Cosmos DB Explorer

    B. Data Explorer

    C. Azure Storage Explorer

    D. Visual Studio Code

Chapter

4

File, Object, and Data Lake Storage

MICROSOFT EXAM OBJECTIVES COVERED IN THIS CHAPTER:

✓ Describe nonrelational data workloads.

  ▪ Describe the characteristics and types of object data storage.

✓ Describe nonrelational data offerings on Azure.

  ▪ Describe the characteristics and types of Azure Storage including Azure Blob storage, Azure Data Lake Storage, and Azure File storage.

✓ Identify basic management tasks for nonrelational data.

  ▪ Describe provisioning and deployment of Azure Storage.

  ▪ Describe method for deployment including the Azure portal, Azure Resource Manager templates, Azure PowerShell, and the Azure command-line interface (CLI).

  ▪ Identify data security components (e.g., firewall, authentication, encryption).

  ▪ Identify basic connectivity issues (e.g., accessing from on-premises, access with Azure VNets, access from Internet, authentication, firewalls).

  ▪ Identify management tools for Azure Storage.

The previous chapter examined nonrelational data that is stored in a NoSQL database. This chapter focuses on nonrelational data that is stored in object storage. Object storage services in Azure are used to store data as files. These services can be used to store binary data such as videos and images, to store files that are used in data processing systems, and as replacements for existing on-premises file servers. Knowing how these services work will not only help you understand object storage services in Azure but will also prepare you for the enterprise data lake aspect of modern analytical solutions covered in Chapter 5, "Modern Data Warehouse in Azure."

File and Object Storage Features

File storage organizes and stores data as flat files in folders under a hierarchy of directories and subdirectories. Data is stored on a local hard drive or a network-attached storage (NAS) device. Shared folders that use a NAS device allow multiple users to share data with each other. While file storage is a good storage solution for small amounts of organized files, it is not ideal for large volumes of files that contain different types of data. Hierarchical folder structures can become bottlenecks when working with large files or unstructured data. Object storage can overcome many of these limitations.

Object storage is used to store large volumes of data in binary and text format. Data stored in object storage can be structured, semi-structured, or unstructured. These data stores are like shared folders on a local network except that they bundle data with custom metadata. APIs can use an object's metadata to retrieve its contents. Cloud-based object data stores are highly scalable, allowing organizations to store exabytes worth of files. Furthermore, these systems are designed to be highly redundant to protect against hardware failures.

Object data stores are useful in the following scenarios:

- Storing images, videos, and audio that are analyzed by deep learning models or served to a website
- Storing raw and processed data in file formats such as Parquet, ORC, or Avro that are optimized for distributed computing solutions
- Serving as the backend storage layer for modern data warehouse scenarios that separate compute and storage with a scale-out architecture
- Capturing IoT data for long-term storage and analysis

- Storing data backups for high availability
- Archiving data for regulatory compliance

Azure offers options for both file and object storage with the Azure Storage platform of services. Let's examine the Azure Storage platform and the core storage options it offers in the following sections.

Azure Storage

Azure Storage is a multi-purpose PaaS storage platform that allows users to create object, file, key-value, and queue data stores. While the ability to host different types of data stores is like Azure Cosmos DB's multi-modal implementation, it differs from Azure Cosmos DB in that a single Azure Storage instance can manage multiple types of data stores.

The highest level of management for Azure Storage is the storage account. *Storage accounts* serve as a container that group the core Azure Storage data services together. It is at this level of management that hardware performance, business continuity, network isolation, and data encryption are managed. Users can create one or more of the following services in the storage account to host their data:

- *Azure Files* can be used to create a fully managed file share in Azure. File shares created using Azure Files are accessible via Server Message Block (SMB) and Network File System (NFS) protocols.

- *Azure Blob Storage* is an object data store that can be used to store exabytes worth of data, including unstructured data, backups, or files used for distributed processing solutions.

- *Azure Data Lake Storage Gen2* is an object data store that is optimized for distributed analytics solutions. It adds a hierarchical namespace on top of the Azure Blob storage service for quick and efficient data access. This service can be enabled when creating a storage account.

- *Azure Table storage* is a NoSQL database that stores data as key-value pairs. Azure Table storage was covered in Chapter Chapter 3, "Nonrelational Databases in Azure," and is being moved to the Azure Cosmos DB Table API.

- *Azure Queue storage* is used to store millions of messages and transfer them between different applications. The specifics of Azure Queue storage are outside of the scope for this book and the DP-900 exam. However, feel free to use the following link if you would like to learn more about Azure Queue storage: `https://docs .microsoft.com/en-us/azure/storage/queues/storage-dotnet-how-to- use-queues?tabs=dotnet`.

Each of the previously mentioned storage services uses different URL endpoints for connectivity. Table 4.1 lists the URL endpoint patterns used for each service.

TABLE 4.1   Storage service URL endpoint patterns

Storage Service	URL Pattern
Azure Files	https://<storage-account-name>.file.core.windows.net/
Azure Blob storage	https://<storage-account-name>.blob.core.windows.net/
Azure Data Lake Storage Gen2	https://<storage-account-name>.dfs.core.windows.net/
Azure Table storage	https://<storage-account-name>.table.core.windows.net/
Azure Queue storage	https://<storage-account-name>.queue.core.windows.net/

Performance Tiers

Storage accounts can be created using one of following two performance tiers depending on the type of storage and hard drive speed required:

- *Standard tier* storage accounts support all the Azure Storage suite of services and is recommended for most scenarios. This tier uses standard hard disk drives (HDDs) for storage. Azure Files created on a standard storage account only support SMB file shares.

- *Premium tier* storage accounts support Azure Files, Azure Blob storage, and Azure Data Lake Storage Gen2 (ADLS). This tier uses solid-state drives (SSDs) for storage. Storage accounts using this tier are typically used in scenarios with high data transaction rates or that require consistently low latency. Azure Files created on a premium storage account support both SMB and NFS file shares.

Standard storage accounts can be categorized as general-purpose v1 or general-purpose v2. General-purpose v1 is a legacy category and is not recommended for any file or object storage scenario. General-purpose v2 storage accounts support the latest Azure Storage features. For the purposes of the DP-900 exam, this book will focus on general-purpose v2 storage accounts when referencing the standard performance tier.

Data Redundancy

Azure Storage maintains HADR by storing multiple copies of the data in the same region, and optionally across different regions. This ensures that data is protected from planned and unplanned downtime. Azure Storage offers the following four options for replicating data:

- *Locally redundant storage (LRS)* creates three copies of the data in a single datacenter. LRS protects data from server rack and driver failures but does not protect against datacenter-wide failures such as a natural disaster.

  Write operations are performed synchronously and will only return successfully once the data is replicated to all three copies.

- *Zone-redundant storage (ZRS)* replicates the data to three different availability zones in the same region. ZRS is recommended for solutions that require high availability, as each availability zone is a separate physical location. For example, ZRS protects against datacenter-wide power outages since data is replicated to other datacenters in the same region.

  As with LRS, write operations are performed synchronously and will only return successfully once the changes have finished replicating to all three availability zones.

- *Geo-redundant storage (GRS)* creates three copies of the data in a single datacenter using LRS. It then creates an additional three copies of data in a secondary region to protect against regionwide failures such as natural disasters.

  Write operations are first committed synchronously in the primary region. Once that is completed, the changes are replicated asynchronously to the secondary region. These changes are then copied synchronously between the three copies in the secondary location using LRS.

- *Geo-zone-redundant storage (GZRS)* replicates the data to three different availability zones in the same region using ZRS. It then creates an additional three copies of data in a secondary region using LRS. GZRS is recommended for solutions requiring maximum HADR.

Storage accounts using GRS or GZRS can also be configured to offload read-only workloads to the secondary region. This is known as read-access geo-redundant storage (RA-GRS) and read-access geo-zone-redundant storage (RA-GZRS). Applications can take advantage of read access to the secondary region by using the secondary URL endpoint. This endpoint simply appends the suffix *-secondary* to the storage account name in the primary URL endpoint (for example, `https://myaccount-secondary.blob.core.windows.net`).

There are some limitations to the level of redundancy that is supported by different storage account types. Table 4.2 lists the redundancy options that are supported by each type of storage account.

TABLE 4.2   Storage account redundancy options

Storage Account Type	Supported Storage Services	Redundancy Options
Standard	Blob storage, ADLS, queue storage, table storage, and Azure Files	LRS, ZRS, GRS, GZRS, RA-GRS, and RA-GZRS
Premium block blobs	Blob storage and ADLS	LRS and ZRS
Premium file shares	Azure Files	LRS and ZRS
Premium page blobs	Page blobs	LRS

Azure Files does not support RA-GRS or RA-GZRS.

The different types of blobs mentioned in Table 4.2 will be detailed later in this chapter in the section "Azure Blob Storage." For now, it is important to understand that replicating data to secondary regions using GRS, RA-GRS, GZRS, and RA-GZRS is only supported by standard storage accounts.

Deploying through the Azure Portal

Storage accounts can be easily deployed through the Azure Portal. Once an account is deployed, users will be able to use it to create the storage service needed for their solution. Use the following steps to create an Azure storage account through the Azure Portal:

1. Log into portal.azure.com and search for *Storage accounts* in the search bar at the top of the page. Click *Storage Accounts* to go to the storage accounts page in the Azure Portal.

2. Click *Create* to start choosing the configuration options for your storage account.

3. The Create a Storage Account page includes six tabs with different configuration options to tailor the storage account to fit your needs. Let's start by exploring the options available in the Basics tab. Along with the following list that describes each option, you can view a completed example of this tab in Figure 4.1.

   a. Choose the subscription and resource group that will contain the storage account. You can create a new resource group on this page if you have not already created one.

   b. Enter a name for the storage account.

c. Choose the primary Azure region for the storage account.

d. Choose the performance tier for the storage account. If you choose premium, you will be asked to choose from the following three account types: block blobs, file shares, and page blobs. This example will continue with the standard tier.

e. Choose the type of redundancy you want the storage account to have. If you choose GRS or GZRS, you will be given the option to enable read access.

FIGURE 4.1   Create a Storage Account: Basics tab.

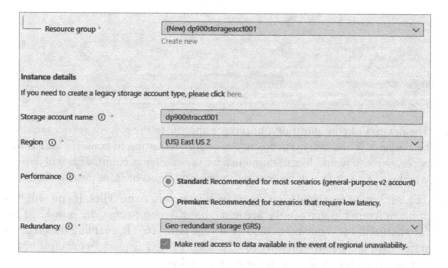

4. The Advanced tab allows you to enable specific security and storage settings. The following describes the configurable settings in this tab.

a. The first set of configuration options relate to security. They include enabling or disabling secure transfer for REST API operations, infrastructure encryption, anonymous public access for blob storage, access via account keys, Azure Active Directory authorization, and the minimum TLS version. We will use the default configuration settings for this example, as shown in Figure 4.2.

b. The next setting will allow you to enable the hierarchical namespace for ADLS. We will cover when to enable this setting later in this chapter in the section "Azure Data Lake Storage Gen2," but for now understand that this option should be enabled if the storage account will be used to store data used by distributed analytics workloads. It's important to note that this setting cannot be changed once the storage account is deployed.

FIGURE 4.2   Create a Storage Account: Advanced tab security configurations.

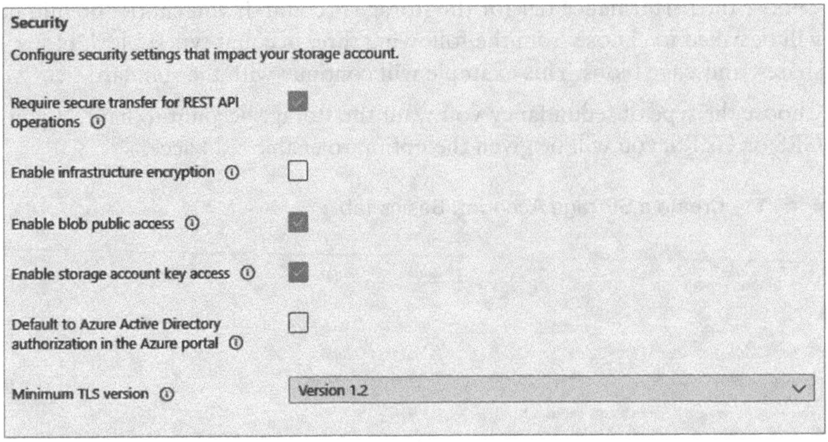

Security

Configure security settings that impact your storage account.

Require secure transfer for REST API
operations ⓘ   ☑

Enable infrastructure encryption ⓘ   ☐

Enable blob public access ⓘ   ☑

Enable storage account key access ⓘ   ☑

Default to Azure Active Directory   ☐
authorization in the Azure portal ⓘ

Minimum TLS version ⓘ | Version 1.2   ⌄ |

    c. The next set of configuration options are specific to the storage services that will be available in the storage account. An important setting to consider here is the access tier you would like to configure for the storage account. This will depend on whether the account will be accessed frequently (Hot) or infrequently (Cool).

    d. The last setting to consider on this page is related to Azure Files. If you will be creating an Azure file share in the account, you will need to consider how large the file share will be. While the standard storage limit is 5 TB, enabling the large files setting will increase the limit to 100 TB. Figure 4.3 illustrates an example of the advanced storage settings with the default options.

5. The Networking tab allows you to configure network access and connectivity for your storage account. There are three options to choose from for network configuration: *Public endpoint (all networks)*, *Public endpoint (selected networks),* and *Private endpoint.*

    a. *Public endpoint (all networks)* opens access to the account to applications from any network. This option removes network isolation as a data security component to the storage account configuration. Figure 4.4 illustrates an example of the Networking tab with this option enabled.

    b. *Public endpoint (select networks)* allows access to specific subnets in a selected VNet.

    c. *Private endpoint* allows you to attach a private IP address from a VNet to the storage account, limiting access to applications that can communicate with the VNet.

FIGURE 4.3   Create a Storage Account: Advanced tab storage configurations.

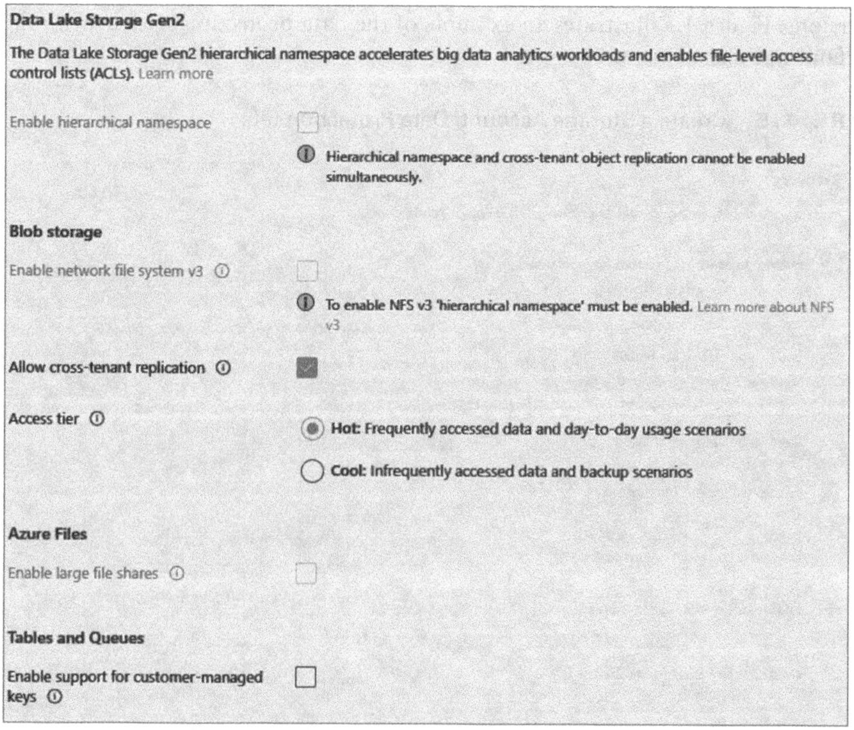

FIGURE 4.4   Create a Storage Account: Networking tab.

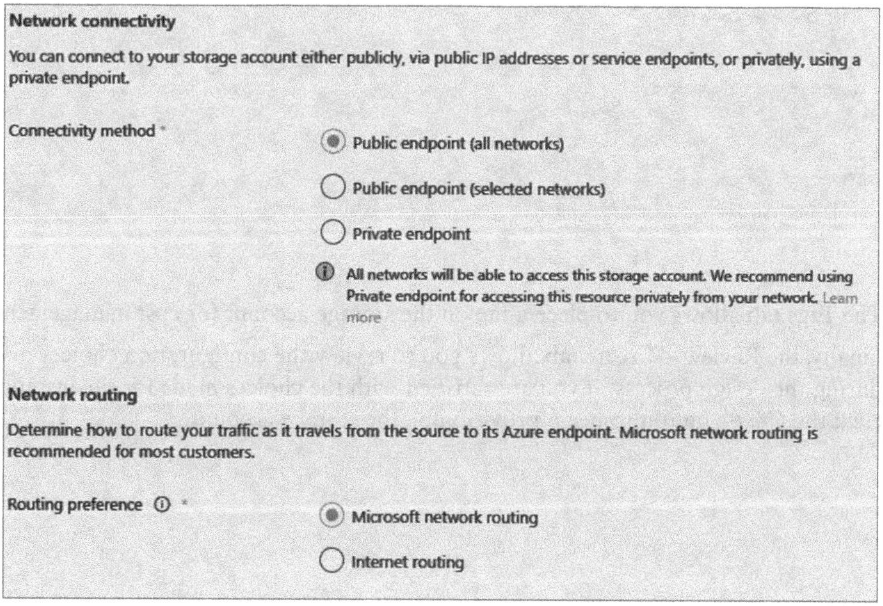

6. The Data Protection tab allows you to protect data from accidental deletes or modifications, enable version management, and set time-based retention policies for blob versions. Figure 4.5 illustrates an example of the data protection settings with the default options.

FIGURE 4.5 Create a Storage Account: Data Protection tab.

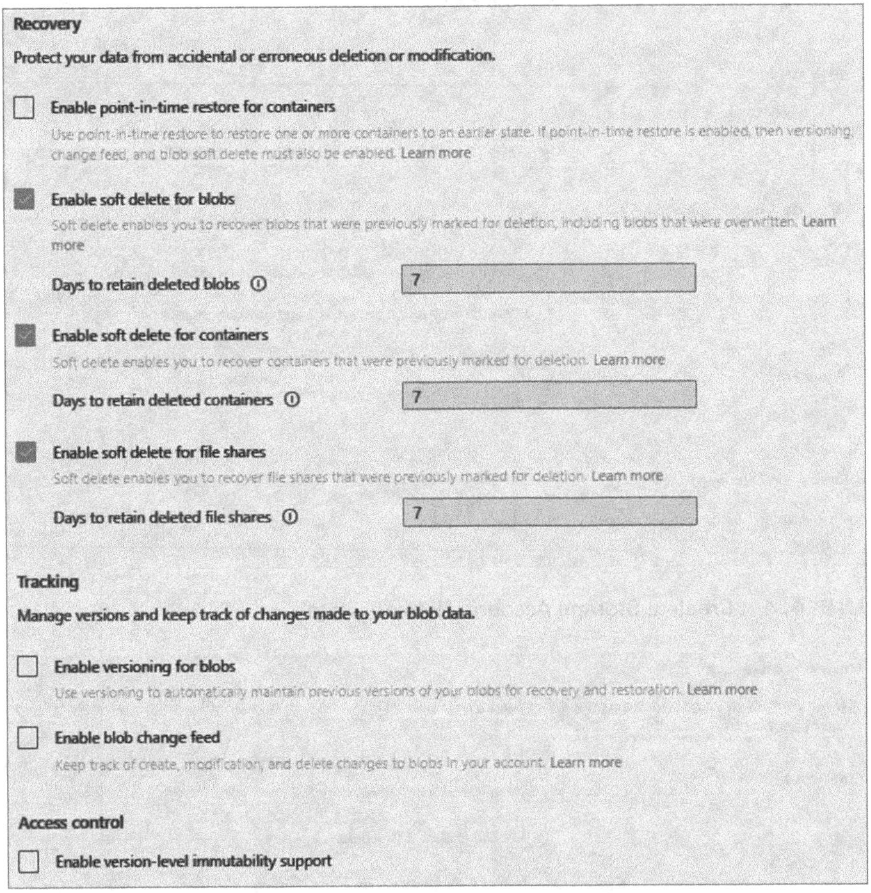

7. The Tags tab allows you to place a tag on the storage account for cost management.

8. Finally, the Review + Create tab allows you to review the configuration choices made during the design process. If you are satisfied with the choices made for the instance, click the *Create* button to begin provisioning the storage account.

Azure Storage Services

The DP-900 exam covers Azure Files, Azure Blob storage, ADLS, and Azure Table storage. Because Azure Table storage was covered in Chapter 3, the following sections will focus on Azure Files, Azure Blob storage, and ADLS.

Azure Files

Azure Files is a storage service that allows organizations to build fully managed file shares in Azure. File shares deployed through Azure Files can be accessed using the SMB protocol on standard and premium storage accounts or the NFS protocol on premium storage accounts. The service organizes data in a hierarchical folder structure and is typically used to replace or complement on-premises file shares. Along with the benefits that are native to Azure storage accounts such as offloading hardware management and global redundancy, data stored in an Azure file share can be accessed from anywhere in the world.

File shares created in Azure Files can be mounted concurrently to a VM in the cloud or on a user's local machine for access. SMB file shares can be mounted to Windows, Linux, or macOS devices. NFS file shares are limited to Linux and macOS devices. In addition to being accessible as a mounted drive, SMB file shares can be synchronized between Azure Files and a local share on a Windows Server device using *Azure File Sync*. This service allows organizations to cache frequently accessed data on the local file share while leaving the least accessed data in Azure.

Access Tiers

Azure Files offers four storage tiers to meet the performance and price requirements of different workloads:

- *Premium* file shares use SSDs for storage, providing high performance and low latency for IO-intensive workloads. This tier is only available in premium storage accounts.

- *Transaction optimized* file shares use standard HDDs for storage, enabling transaction-heavy workloads that do not need the low latency that premium file shares provide. This tier is available in standard storage accounts.

- *Hot* file shares use standard HDDs for storage and are optimized for general-purpose file-sharing scenarios. This tier is available in standard storage accounts.

- *Cool* file shares use standard HDDs for storage and offer cost-efficient storage that is optimized for archive storage scenarios. This tier is available in standard storage accounts.

The premium storage tier is the only tier that users can access via SMB and NFS protocols. Transaction optimized, hot, and cool tiers are only offered in standard storage accounts and do not support the NFS protocol as of this writing.

File shares created on a standard storage account switch between the transaction optimized, hot, and cool tiers without needing to move to a different storage account. Moving from one of the standard storage account tiers to the premium tier will require you to create a new premium storage account and copy the data from the old file share to the new one. The data can be copied from the old share to the new one using the AzCopy utility that is described later in this chapter.

More information about the different storage tiers available for Azure Files can be found at `https://docs.microsoft.com/en-us/azure/storage/files/storage-files-planning#storage-tiers`.

Creating a File Share

File shares in Azure can be created through the Azure Portal, a REST API call, an Azure PowerShell or Azure CLI script, or as a part of an Infrastructure as Code template. The Azure Files client library can be used in custom .NET, Java, C++, or Python applications to manipulate file shares. The following steps describe how to create a file share in the Azure Portal.

1. Navigate to the storage accounts page in the Azure Portal and click on the storage account that was previously created.

2. In the left-side panel of the storage account blade, click *File shares*. Figure 4.6 shows where this button is located.

FIGURE 4.6   File shares button

3. Click the + *File Share* button at the top of the file shares blade to configure a new file share. Figure 4.7 shows what this button looks like and where at the top of the page it is located.

FIGURE 4.7   Create a New File Share button.

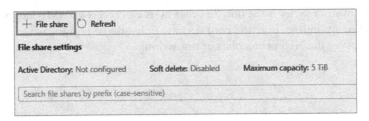

4. Enter a name and select an access tier for the new file share. Figure 4.8 illustrates a completed example of this page.

FIGURE 4.8   New file share

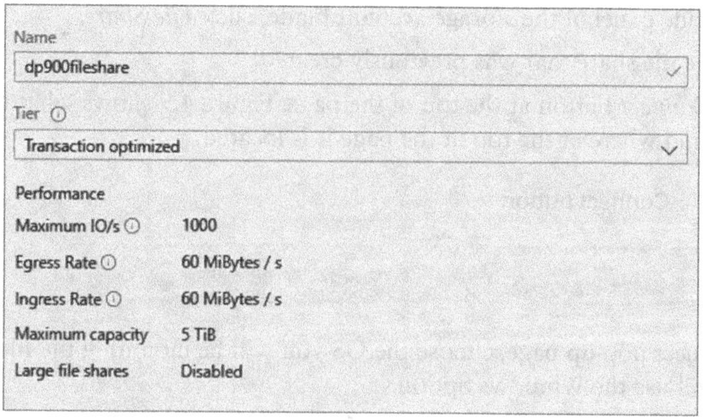

5. Click *Create* to create the file share.

Mounting a File Share

One of the biggest advantages of using an Azure file share is that they can be mounted to any computer in the world. However, there are some considerations that need to be made:

- If you are connecting via SMB, then the OS of the computer that the file share is being mounted to must support SMB 3.0 and higher.

- Ensure that TCP port 445 is open if you are connecting via SMB and using the file share's public endpoint. This is the port that the SMB protocol uses for communication.

- As of this writing, mounting an NFS file share using its public endpoint is restricted to VMs inside of Azure.

Many organizations do not allow public endpoint access and block TCP port 445 for security reasons. In these scenarios, organizations can establish a secure network tunnel between an Azure VNet and their on-premises network using a VPN or ExpressRoute connection. This allows them to attach a private IP address, or private endpoint, from the VNet to the storage account hosting the file share. Using the private endpoint allows users to access the file share using a secure network connection without needing to open TCP port 445. More information about securely accessing an Azure file share can be found at https://docs.microsoft.com/en-us/azure/storage/files/storage-files-networking-overview#accessing-your-azure-file-shares.

The Azure Portal provides scripts that will mount a file share to a machine using a compatible OS. The following steps describe how to access these scripts:

1. Navigate to the storage accounts page in the Azure Portal and click on the storage account that was previously created.

2. In the left-side panel of the storage account blade, click *File Shares*.

3. Click on the file share that was previously created.

4. Click the *Connect* button at the top of the page. Figure 4.9 shows what this button looks like and where at the top of the page it is located.

FIGURE 4.9   Connect button

5. In the Connect pop-up page, choose the OS you will be mounting the file share to. This example will use the Windows option.

6. Choose the drive letter that the mounted file share will use and the authentication method. The example will use *Z* as the drive letter and *Storage account key* for the authentication method.

7. Copy the script provided in the pop-up window. Paste the script into a command prompt or PowerShell window on the host you want to mount the file share to and run it. If all dependencies are configured properly, then the script will mount the file share to the host machine. Figure 4.10 illustrates a completed example of the Connect page.

Azure File Sync

Azure File Sync allows users to use Azure Files as a highly resilient central file repository for their local file shares. It does this by creating a local cache of an Azure file share on one or more local Windows file servers. Content is synchronized between Azure Files and each of the local file servers, thus maintaining a consistent view of data. By enabling the cloud tiering feature, Azure File Sync can control how much local storage is needed for caching by allowing users to only cache frequently accessed files.

To maintain synchronous copies of data between Azure Files and a local file share using Azure File Sync, you will first need to download and install the Azure File Sync agent to the local server. You will be able to map the Azure file share to folders on the local server with sync groups once the agent is installed. Instructions for downloading and installing the Azure File Sync agent, as well as setting up sync groups, can be found at `https://docs.microsoft.com/en-us/azure/storage/file-sync/file-sync-extend-servers#install-the-agent`.

Azure File Sync is only supported on Windows Server 2012 R2 and above.

FIGURE 4.10 Connect page

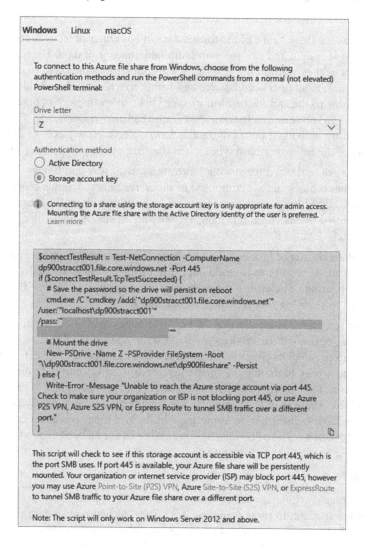

Azure Blob Storage

Azure Blob Storage is a highly flexible object data storage solution in the cloud. It is designed to store massive amounts of data that are used in several different scenarios. The following list includes some common use cases for blob storage:

- Storing unstructured data such as videos, images, and audio
- Storing large amounts of data files that are used in big data solutions
- Storing application log files

- Storing data backups
- Serving as an archive for historical data

Users can manage their Azure Blob Storage data in *container* objects. A container is like a directory in a file system and can store an unlimited amount of data. Users can create as many containers as they want in a single storage account, allowing them to organize data however they want. Containers can be accessed from anywhere in the world by appending the container name to the end of the Blob storage URI (for example, `https://<storage-account-name>.blob.core.windows.net/<container_name>`).

Containers store individual pieces of data as *blob* objects. New pieces of data can be categorized as one of the following blob types when they are uploaded to Azure Blob Storage:

- *Block blobs* are optimized for storing large amounts of text and binary data. Data that is uploaded as a block blob is composed of block segments. A single block blob can contain up to 50,000 blocks, each one identified by a unique block ID. Existing block blobs can be modified by inserting, replacing, or deleting blocks. A single block blob can be approximately 190.7 TB.

- *Append blobs* consist of blocks like block blobs but are optimized for append operations. When an append blob is modified, the additional data is appended to the end of the blob. Updating or deleting existing blocks is not supported. Append blobs are commonly used to store log files from virtual machines.

- *Page blobs* store data as a collection of 512-byte pages, with a maximum blob size of 8 TB. They are optimized for random read and write operations. Writes to a page blob can overwrite up to 4 MB of pages in the blob. Random ranges of bytes can be read from or written to a page blob, making them ideal for storing OS and data disks for VMs and databases. For this reason, virtual data disks that serve Azure VMs are persisted as page blobs. Azure SQL Database also uses page blobs as the underlying storage for its databases. More information about page blobs and their uses cases can be found at `https://docs.microsoft.com/en-us/azure/storage/blobs/storage-blob-pageblob-overview?tabs=dotnet`.

Access Tiers

Azure Blob Storage is regularly used to store data that is frequently and rarely accessed in the same storage account. In these scenarios it is critical to distinguish data that is actively used and data that is archived. For this reason, Azure Blob Storage offers three access tiers that allow users to store blob data in the most cost-effective manner based on how it is used:

- *Hot tier* is an online tier for storing data that is frequently accessed. Data that is configured to use this tier is expected to be read from or written to often. This tier has the highest storage costs but the lowest access latency.

- *Cool tier* is an online tier for storing data that is infrequently accessed and should be stored for a minimum of 30 days. Typical use cases for the cool access tier include storing short-term data backups and older datasets that are not frequently accessed but need to be available at a moment's notice.

- *Archive tier* is an offline tier for storing data that is almost never accessed and should be stored for a minimum of 180 days. This tier has the lowest storage costs but the highest access costs. Data stored with this access tier should have flexible latency requirements as retrieval can take several hours. Typical use cases for the archive tier include storing long-term backups, compliance data that needs to be retained for regulatory reasons, and raw datasets that must be retained but are never used once they are processed.

 Azure Blob storage offers a rule-based life cycle management system that can be used to automatically move blob data from one access tier to another. More details about blob life cycle management can be found at https://docs.microsoft.com/en-us/azure/storage/blobs/access-tiers-overview#blob-lifecycle-management.

Creating a Blob Container

Just like any other Azure Storage service, blob containers can be easily created through the Azure Portal, a REST API call, an Azure PowerShell or Azure CLI script, an Infrastructure as Code template, or a custom application using the Azure Blob Storage client library. The following steps describe how to create a new container in the Azure Portal:

1. Navigate to the storage accounts page in the Azure Portal and click on the storage account that was previously created.

2. In the left-side panel of the storage account blade, click *Containers*. Figure 4.11 shows where this button is located.

FIGURE 4.11 Containers button

3. Click the + *Container* button at the top of the containers blade to configure a new container. Figure 4.12 shows what this button looks like and where at the top of the page it is located.

FIGURE 4.12 Create a New Container button.

4. Enter a name and choose one of the following three public access level options: Private (no anonymous access), Blob (anonymous read access for blobs only), or Container (anonymous read access for containers and blobs).

   a. *Private (no anonymous access)* denies all anonymous requests and only allows authorized requests to access the container and its blobs. This is the default setting for new containers. Figure 4.13 illustrates a completed new container example using this option.

   b. *Blob (anonymous read access for blobs only)* allows anonymous requests to access blobs in the container but denies anonymous requests trying to read container data.

   c. *Container (anonymous read access for containers and blobs)* allows anonymous requests to access container and blob data, except for container permission settings and metadata.

5. The Advanced drop-down list in the New Container page allows you to alter the encryption scope and version-level immutability for container blobs. We will use the default options for this example.

FIGURE 4.13 New Container

6. Click *Create* to create the container.

Uploading a Blob

Uploading blobs to a container can be performed using a variety of different methods. Administrators can write scripts that create and manage blobs using Azure PowerShell and Azure CLI. Developers can implement custom logic in their applications that will upload and manipulate several blobs at a time via the REST API or the Azure Blob Storage client library.

Management tools such as Azure Storage Explorer, AzCopy, Azure Data Factory, and Azure Data Box can be used to migrate massive amounts of data to Azure Blob Storage. These tools will be described later in this chapter in the subsections under "Management Tools."

The following steps explore how to upload a blob through the Azure Portal:

1. Go to the container that was previously created.

2. Click the *Upload* button at the top of the containers blade to upload a new blob. Figure 4.14 shows what this button looks like and where at the top of the page it is located.

FIGURE 4.14   Upload button

3. The Upload Blob pop-up page provides a way to browse your local computer for data to upload. It also provides a setting to overwrite the blob if it already exists.

4. The Advanced drop-down list allows you to define the authentication method used to upload the data as well as configure the blob type, access tier, retention policy, and other optional blob settings. Figure 4.15 illustrates an example of how this page can be used to upload a CSV file using the default options.

Blob Service REST API

The Blob service REST API can be used to upload, manage, organize, and delete containers and blobs. It allows users to manage Azure Blob Storage content using HTTP operations. For example, you can compile a list of all blobs in a specific container by issuing the following GET operation:

```
https://<storage-account-
name>.blob.core.windows.net/<container_name>?resttype=container&comp=list
```

For more information about the different operations that are available through the Blob service REST API, see the following link: `https://docs.microsoft.com/en-us/rest/api/storageservices/blob-service-rest-api`.

Azure Blob Storage Client Library

The Azure Blob Storage client library is a part of the Azure SDK that users can use to build custom application logic for managing Azure Blob Storage. Users can take advantage of this SDK when building applications using different languages, including .NET, Java, Python, JavaScript, and C++. The library contains several classes that can be used to create, replace, list, and delete containers or blobs.

FIGURE 4.15   Upload blob

The following are the most useful classes for interacting with Azure Blob Storage content:

- *BlobServiceClient* allows users to manipulate storage account resources such as blob containers.

- *BlobContainerClient* allows users to manipulate containers and their blobs. This class goes by *ContainerClient* in the Python and JavaScript versions of the Azure Blob Storage client library.

- *BlobClient* allows users to manipulate blobs.

Check out the following tutorial if you would like to learn more about how to get started building custom application logic that manipulates Azure Blob storage: `https://docs` `.microsoft.com/en-us/azure/storage/blobs/storage-quickstart-`

`blobs-dotnet`. While this specific tutorial uses .NET, there are several other tutorials available for the other languages that support the Azure Blob storage client library.

Azure Data Lake Storage Gen2

Azure Data Lake Storage Gen2, or ADLS for short, is an object storage solution that is built on top of Azure Blob Storage. It can be enabled when creating a storage account in the Azure Portal by selecting the *Enable hierarchical namespace* setting in the *Advanced* tab. The hierarchical namespace allows users to easily organize data objects into a hierarchy of directories and subdirectories for efficient data access.

The addition of the hierarchical namespace to Azure Blob storage's existing capabilities makes ADLS an ideal storage solution for big data and distributed analytics solutions. Users can easily organize data into different directories that are specific to where it is in the data processing life cycle. For example, there could be a raw directory that acts as a landing zone for new datasets, a cleansed directory that stores the data once it has been scrubbed of any errors or inconsistencies, and a report-ready directory that stores the data once aggregations and business logic have been applied to it. Furthermore, each of these directories can host several subdirectories that partition data by certain features such as year, month, and date.

ADLS is easily scalable and very cost-effective because it is built on top of Azure Blob Storage. This allows organizations to store data in multiple stages without having to worry about high costs or running out of storage. This allows users to leverage data at different life cycles for several different use cases. For example, data scientists can use raw and processed data to build their models, and analysts can use the report-ready directory to build reports or share aggregated datasets with other business units.

In addition to its performance enhancements, ADLS provides more granular access security to what is available with Azure Blob Storage. Administrators can use POSIX-like access control lists (ACLs) to set user permissions at the directory and file level. Using ACLs to manage access for data stored in ADLS is described further later in this chapter in the section "Access Management."

Azure Blob File System Driver

Perhaps the biggest benefit to using ADLS is its ability to allow users to manage and access data like they would with a Hadoop Distributed File System (HDFS). The Azure Blob File System (ABFS) driver is native to ADLS and is used by Apache Hadoop environments to create and interact with data in ADLS. Typical environments in Azure that access ADLS with the ABFS driver include Azure HDInsight, Azure Databricks, and Azure Synapse Analytics.

The ABFS driver enables access to ADLS resources using a URI-based connection. Applications constructing the URI can use the following format to navigate to specific directories or files in ADLS:

```
abfs://<container-name>@<storage-account-name>.dfs.core.
windows.net/<path>/<file-name>
```

As you can see, the parent directory is a container object. This object can contain several levels of subdirectories depending on how the data is organized. For example, the directory hierarchy for storing product data by date could look like `<product>/<year>/<month>/<day>`, where product is the parent directory and year, month, and day represent different subdirectories. Using this directory structure, let's look at how you would format the ABFS URI to access product data from November 11, 2021:

`abfs://product@dp900adls001.dfs.core.windows.net/2021/November/11/`

This URI will access all the data in the 11 subdirectory. Adding a specific filename at the end of the URI, such as `bicycles.csv`, will redirect access to that one file. There is also support for accessing all files of a specific format by adding the `*` wildcard and the file extension to the end of the URI. The following extends the previous example by accessing all the CSV data produced on November 11, 2021.

`abfs://product@dp900adls001.dfs.core.windows.net/2021/November/11/*.csv`

Data movement with ABFS can be secured using a TLS connection. To use the secure version of the ABFS driver, change the `abfs://` component of the URI to `abfss://`.

Management Tasks for Azure Storage

There are several management activities that administrators and developers must consider when working with Azure Storage. For one, users will need to decide how they will design their Azure Storage deployments to be reusable across multiple environments. Administrators will also need to decide how to secure their storage accounts, as well as how they will provide/restrict access to the different storage services that are created in the account. The following sections will discuss common methods used to perform these tasks as well as the tools users can utilize to manage their storage accounts.

Deployment Scripting and Automation

Automated resource deployments are standard for any multi-environment workload that uses cloud resources. As with any Azure resource, Azure Storage deployments can be scripted using a variety of methods including Azure PowerShell, Azure CLI, and Infrastructure as Code templates. Azure PowerShell and Azure CLI are also common tools that can be used to manage data stored in Azure Storage. The following sections examine how to use Azure PowerShell, Azure CLI, and ARM templates to deploy Azure Storage resources.

Azure PowerShell

Users can easily write Azure PowerShell scripts that will deploy and manage Azure Storage resources. The following is an example of a script that will create a standard general-purpose v2 storage account:

```
<# Sign into your Azure environment. Not required
if running this script in the Azure Cloud Shell #>
Connect-AzAccount

$resourceGroupName = "dp900storageacct001"
$storageAccountName = "dp900stracct001"
$location = "East US"

New-AzStorageAccount -ResourceGroupName $resourceGroup `
  -Name $storageAccountName `
  -Location $location `
  -SkuName Standard_RAGRS `
  -Kind StorageV2
```

> **NOTE**   To enable ADLS using Azure PowerShell, add the EnableHierarchicalNamespace parameter to the script and set it to $True.

The next step after creating the storage account and setting security postures is to begin creating file shares and/or blob containers. The following script creates a new blob container in the previously created storage account:

```
$resourceGroupName = "dp900storageacct001"
$storageAccountName = "dp900stracct001"
$containerName = "dp900container01"


# Retrieve an existing Storage Account reference
$storageContext = Get-AzStorageAccount -ResourceGroupName $resourceGroupName `
    -Name $storageAccountName

# Create the container
New-AzStorageContainer -Name $containerName `
    -Context $storageContext `
```

Once the container is created, you can start uploading data to it using the `Set-AzStorageBlobContent` Azure PowerShell command. The following script demonstrates how to use this command to upload an image stored on a local directory to the container. It also configures the blob to use the hot access tier for quick access.

```
$resourceGroupName = "dp900storageacct001"
$storageAccountName = "dp900stracct001"
$containerName = "dp900container01"


# Retrieve an existing Storage Account reference
$storageAccount = Get-AzStorageAccount -ResourceGroupName $resourceGroupName `
    -Name $storageAccountName

# Get the Storage Account context
$storageContext = $storageAccount.Context

# Upload a file to the Hot access tier
Set-AzStorageBlobContent -File "D:\Images\Image001.jpg" `
  -Container $containerName `
  -Blob "Image001.jpg" `
  -Context $storageContext `
  -StandardBlobTier Hot
```

The script can be modified to upload several files by looping through the local directory. More information about creating and managing Azure Blob storage resources with Azure PowerShell can be found at https://docs.microsoft.com/en-us/azure/storage/blobs/storage-quickstart-blobs-powershell.

Azure CLI

Azure CLI is another scripting environment that administrators can use to create and manage Azure Storage resources. The following Azure CLI script uses the same parameters as the Azure PowerShell script in the previous section to create a storage account and a blob container:

```
resourceGroupName='dp900storageacct001'
storageAccountName='dp900stracct001'
containerName='dp900container01'
location='eastus'

az storage account create \
  --name $storageAccountName \
  --resource-group $resourceGroupName \
  --location $location \
```

```
--sku Standard_RAGRS \
--kind StorageV2

az storage container create \
    --account-name $storageAccountName \
    --name $containerName \
```

More information about creating and managing Azure Blob storage resources with Azure CLI can be found at `https://docs.microsoft.com/en-us/azure/storage/blobs/storage-quickstart-blobs-cli`.

ARM Template

Like other Azure services, Infrastructure as Code templates such as Azure Resource Manager (ARM) templates are the most optimal way to define resources for Azure Storage deployments. These templates can be used to quickly build Azure Storage services in multiple development environments, allowing developers to easily build and test new functionality.

One example of an ARM template that creates a standard storage account can be found at `https://github.com/Azure/azure-quickstart-templates/tree/master/quickstarts/microsoft.storage/storage-account-create`. The template can be deployed using the following Azure PowerShell:

```
Connect-AzAccount
$resourceGroupName = "dp900storageacct001"
$location = "East US"

New-AzResourceGroup
    -Name $resourceGroupName
    -Location $location

New-AzResourceGroupDeployment
    -ResourceGroupName $resourceGroupName `
    -TemplateUri https://raw.githubusercontent.com/Azure/azure-quickstart-templates/master/quickstarts/microsoft.storage/storage-account-create/azuredeploy.json
```

Azure Storage Security

Microsoft provides several layers of security to ensure that data stored in one of the Azure Storage services is protected from unauthorized access. As with any other data service in Azure, there are several network isolation and identity management options that can be used to limit who can access data in a storage account. The following sections examine the methods available for securing data in Azure Storage as well as some of the default security standards such as data encryption and protection from accidental deletes.

Network Isolation

Storage accounts have a public endpoint that provides access over the Internet. Azure allows users to isolate this endpoint by limiting access to certain IP addresses through a firewall, trusted Azure services, or specific Azure subnets. Azure also allows users to attach a private IP address from a VNet to a storage account, restricting communication to traffic that can access the VNet. This is the Microsoft recommended approach for securing storage accounts that store sensitive data such as personally identifiable information (PII).

All these options can be configured through the Azure Portal, or an Azure PowerShell or Azure CLI script after a storage account is created. Let's walk through how to configure one of the network isolation options in the Azure Portal:

1. Navigate to the storage accounts page in the Azure Portal and click on the storage account that was previously created.

2. In the left-side panel of the storage account blade, click *Networking*. Figure 4.16 shows where this button is located.

FIGURE 4.16 Networking button

3. There are three tabs listed at the top of the networking page: Firewalls And Virtual Networks, Private Endpoint Connections, and Custom Domain. We will cover the Firewalls And Virtual Networks and Private Endpoint Connections tabs for the purpose of configuring network isolation on a storage account. Just know that the Custom Domain tab allows you to map a custom domain to a blob or static website endpoint.

4. The Firewalls And Virtual Networks tab enables users to allow access from specific VNets and subnets as well as specific IP addresses. Figure 4.17 illustrates these settings.

   This tab also allows you to configure access from trusted Azure services and read access to storage logging and metrics from any network. There is also an option to determine whether traffic is routed over the Microsoft network or the Internet as it travels from the source application to the storage account's public endpoint. These settings are illustrated in Figure 4.18.

FIGURE 4.17   Virtual Network and Firewall Access

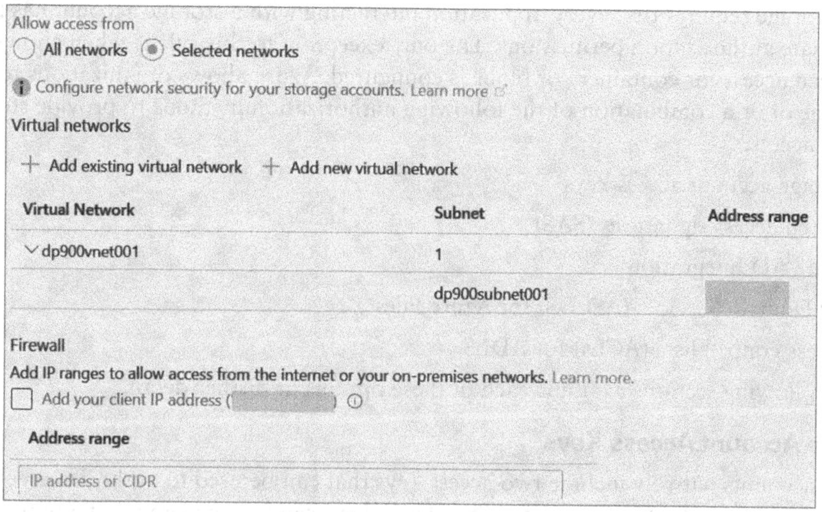

Allow access from
○ All networks ● Selected networks

ⓘ Configure network security for your storage accounts. Learn more ⬚

Virtual networks

╋ Add existing virtual network   ╋ Add new virtual network

Virtual Network	Subnet	Address range
⌄ dp900vnet001	1	
	dp900subnet001	

Firewall

Add IP ranges to allow access from the internet or your on-premises networks. Learn more.

☐ Add your client IP address (▭) ⓘ

Address range

IP address or CIDR

FIGURE 4.18   Exceptions and Networking Routing

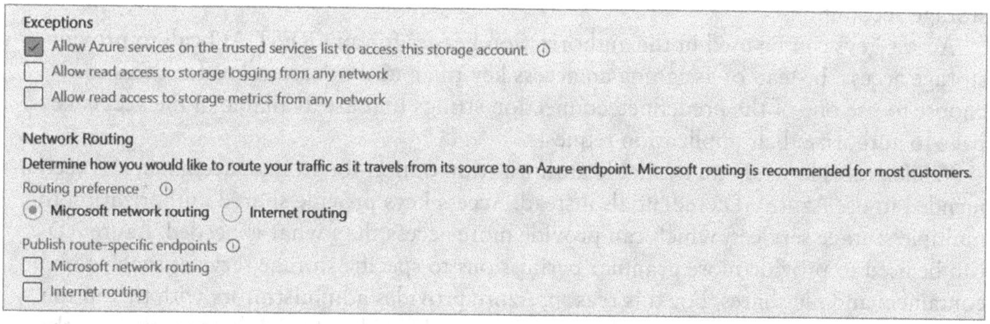

Exceptions

☑ Allow Azure services on the trusted services list to access this storage account. ⓘ
☐ Allow read access to storage logging from any network
☐ Allow read access to storage metrics from any network

Network Routing

Determine how you would like to route your traffic as it travels from its source to an Azure endpoint. Microsoft routing is recommended for most customers.

Routing preference ⓘ
● Microsoft network routing ○ Internet routing

Publish route-specific endpoints ⓘ
☐ Microsoft network routing
☐ Internet routing

You can find an extensive list of trusted Azure services at `https://docs.microsoft.com/en-us/azure/storage/common/storage-network-security?tabs=azure-portal#grant-access-to-trusted-azure-services`.

5. If you click the *Private Endpoint Connections* tab, you will be able create a new private endpoint that will have its very own private IP address from a VNet. This will restrict storage account access to traffic that can communicate with that VNet.

Access Management

Azure Storage requires that every application interacting with a storage account has the appropriate authorization permissions. The only exception to this rule is when anonymous read access for containers or blobs is configured. Azure allows organizations to use either one of or a combination of the following authorization methods to provide storage account access:

- Storage account access keys
- Shared access signatures (SAS)
- Azure AD Integration
- AD Domain Services (AD DS) for Azure Files
- Access control lists (ACLs) for ADLS

The following sections examine each of these options in further detail.

Storage Account Access Keys

Storage accounts natively include two access keys that can be used to authorize access to blob, file, queue, and table storage services. These keys can be regenerated at any point in time and can be kept in a secure location like Azure Key Vault. They can be found by clicking on the *Access keys* button on the left side of the storage account blade for a storage account.

Access keys can be used in the authorization header for any REST API call to provide storage access. Instead of assigning an access key to an authorization header, users can choose to use one of the predefined connection strings that are available in the access keys page to authorize their application requests.

While access keys are an available authorization option for storage accounts, it is recommended to use Azure AD credentials instead. Access keys provide shared authorization to multiple storage services, which can provide more access than what is needed. Azure AD can be used to provide more granular permissions to specific storage services such as blob containers and file shares. For this reason, Azure provides administrators with the option to block storage account requests that use an access key. This can be done by clicking the *Configuration* button (under Settings) on the left side of the storage account blade for your storage account and clicking *Disabled* under the Allow Storage Account Key Access setting.

Shared Access Signature (SAS)

A shared access signature (SAS) delegates access permissions to specific storage account resources over a predetermined period of time. A SAS provides more granular access than an account key, as they allow administrators to restrict what resources a client application can access and what permissions it has on those resources.

Administrators can create a SAS using the Azure Portal, Azure PowerShell, Azure CLI, or the Azure Storage client library for .NET. Creating a SAS results in one or more signed URLs that point to each storage service that the SAS was provided access to. The URL includes a token that indicates what permissions client applications are authorized to use with the SAS.

To create a SAS in the Azure Portal, click on the *Shared Access Signature* button on the left side of the storage account blade for your storage account. Figure 4.19 illustrates the configuration options on the shared access signature page.

FIGURE 4.19 Shared access signature configuration options

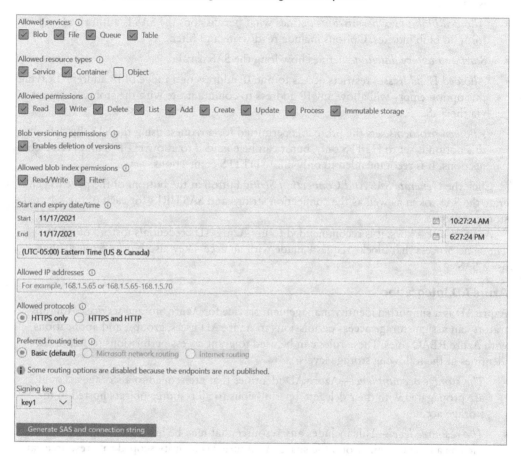

The following list describes each configuration option on this page:

- *Allowed services* defines which storage services the SAS can access. Options include blob, file, queue, and table storage.
- *Allowed resource types* sets the access granularity for the SAS. For example, setting the allowed resource type scope to Service will enable access to the entire blob, file, queue, or table service. Setting the Object resource type scope will limit access to data objects stored in a storage service. Options include service, container, and object types.

- *Allowed permissions* defines what permissions the SAS is authorized to perform. Options include read, write, delete, list, add, create, update, process, and immutable storage.

- *Blob versioning permissions* sets whether the SAS can delete blob versions if versioning is enabled.

- *Allowed blob index permissions* defines what permissions the SAS is authorized to perform on blob indexes. Options include read/write and filter.

- *Start and expiry date/time* defines how long the SAS is valid.

- *Allowed IP addresses* restricts access to one IP address or a range of IP address. Leaving this option empty will allow any IP address to communicate with the storage account via the SAS.

- *Allowed protocols* sets the protocols permitted for a request using the SAS. By default, this option is set to HTTPS only, but it can be changed to allow HTTPS and HTTP connections. It is recommended to only allow HTTPS connections.

Click the *Generate SAS And Connection String* button at the bottom of the page to generate the SAS token as well as the connection strings and SAS URLs for each of the selected storage services.

As with access keys, it is recommended to use Azure AD credentials instead of a SAS. The same process that blocks requests made with an access key also blocks requests that use a SAS.

Azure AD Integration

Azure AD is a supported identity management service for Azure Storage services. Administrators can assign storage access permissions to Azure AD users, groups, and applications with Azure RBAC roles. These roles can be used to grant access permissions to Azure AD identities at the following storage levels:

- *The storage account level*—Azure AD identities that are scoped to a storage account are propagated with their delegated permissions to all resource objects hosted in the storage account.

- *The resource level*—This includes any resource that may be hosted by a storage account, such as a blob container or a file share. An Azure AD identity scoped to a resource can interact with that resource's data, granted the action the identity is trying to perform is allowed by the permissions assigned to it.

ADLS and Azure Files also allow administrators to set permissions at the subdirectory and blob/file level using ACLs. This level of granularity cannot be set with RBAC roles.

Identities can be set using a variety of methods such as through the Azure Portal, Azure PowerShell, and Azure CLI. To add identities through the Azure Portal, click the *Access Control (IAM)* button in the left-side panel of the resource you want to add the identity to.

Click the *Add* button on the Access Control (IAM) page and start adding role assignments to identities. Along with generic RBAC roles such as *Owner, Contributor*, and *Reader* that will grant administrative access to the object, Azure Storage services have built-in roles that grant resource-specific permissions. The following is a list of roles specific to Azure Storage that are relevant to the DP-900 exam:

- *Storage Blob Data Owner*—Identities assigned this role have full access to blob containers and data. It can also be used to assign ACLs to ADLS folders. This role applies to Azure Blob Storage and ADLS.

- *Storage Blob Data Contributor*—Identities assigned this role have read, write, and delete access to blob containers and data. This role applies to Azure Blob storage and ADLS.

- *Storage Blob Data Reader*—Identities assigned this role have read access to blob containers and data. This role applies to Azure Blob Storage and ADLS.

- *Storage File Data SMB Share Elevated Contributor*—Identities assigned this role have read, write, delete, and modify NTFS permission access to file shares over SMB. This role applies to Azure Files.

- *Storage File Data SMB Share Contributor*—Identities assigned this role have read, write, and delete access to files shares over SMB. This role applies to Azure Files.

- *Storage File Data SMB Share Reader*—Identities assigned this role have read access to files shares over SMB. This role applies to Azure Files.

There are also several built-in roles specific to Azure Queue and Azure Table storage, including contributor and reader roles. These roles assign similar permissions to the contributor and reader roles for Azure Blob Storage and Azure Files.

AD Domain Services (AD DS) for Azure Files

Azure Files uses on-premises AD Domain Services (AD DS) and Azure AD Domain Services (Azure AD DS) to manage authentication and authorization through SMB. This is useful in hybrid scenarios where on-premises file servers are migrated to Azure Files but still have to support on-premises AD identities. Azure AD DS enables administrators to assign file share access permissions with one of the built-in RBAC roles for Azure Files to identities hosted in Azure AD.

To enable either on-premises AD DS or Azure AD DS for Azure Files, click on the *File Shares* button in the left-side panel of your storage account. Check to see if AD is configured at the top of the file shares page. Click *Not Configured* if AD is not configured. This setting will look like Figure 4.20 if AD is not configured.

FIGURE 4.20   Configure Active Directory for Azure Files.

The Active Directory page will allow you to set an on-premises Active Directory domain controller or Azure AD DS as an identity provider for the Azure Files instance. Identities can be scoped to file shares and assigned RBAC roles once this step is complete.

Azure Files use Kerberos for authenticating application requests with either on-premises AD DS or Azure AD DS. When an application attempts to access an Azure file share, the access request is routed to AD DS or Azure AD DS for authentication. If the identity the application is using is found and authentication is successful, the on-premises AD DS or Azure AD instance will return a Kerberos token to the application. The application then sends a request to the Azure file share with the Kerberos token, and the file share uses the token to authorize the request.

More information about using on-premises AD DS, Azure AD DS, and Kerberos for authentication and authorization with Azure Files can be found at `https://docs .microsoft.com/en-us/azure/storage/files/storage-files-active-directory-overview#how-it-works`.

ADLS Access Control Lists (ACLs)

While RBAC roles will generally grant the appropriate level of access to a user, they can sometimes grant too much privilege. Identities can be granted access to a storage account or a blob container with an assigned RBAC role such as Storage Blob Data Contributor or Storage Blob Data Reader to limit what that identity can do with data. However, this provides identities access to all of the data in a container. RBAC cannot be used to grant specific permissions to individual blobs in a container. ADLS enables administrators to grant blob-level access with the use of ACLs.

ACLs provide administrators with the ability to grant Azure AD identities *read*, *write*, or *execute* permissions to directories and blobs in ADLS. Table 4.3 details how these permissions can be used.

TABLE 4.3   Blob and Directory ACL Permissions

Permission	Blob	Directory
Read (R)	Read the contents of a blob	Requires read and execute to list the directory's contents
Write (W)	Write and append content to a blob	Requires write and execute to create child items in the directory
Execute (X)	Does not provide any permissions to blobs	Required to traverse the child items (such as additional subdirectories and blobs) in the directory

The key concept to remember about providing blob-level read or write permissions via ACLs to a specific identity is that the identity will need execute permission to each of the directories that lead to the blob. If we use our previous example of product data that is organized in a date hierarchy, then granting read access to an individual blob will require execute access on the product, year, month, and day directories that precede the blob.

ACLs can be set through the Azure Portal, Azure PowerShell, Azure CLI, the REST API, or the Azure Storage client library. To manage ACLs through the Azure Portal, go to an ADLS-enabled storage account and click on a container. Click on the *Manage ACL* button in the left-side panel of the container blade. The Manage ACL page will allow you to add identities and assign them read, write, or execute permissions. Figure 4.21 illustrates an example of this page.

FIGURE 4.21   Manage ACLs in the Azure Portal.

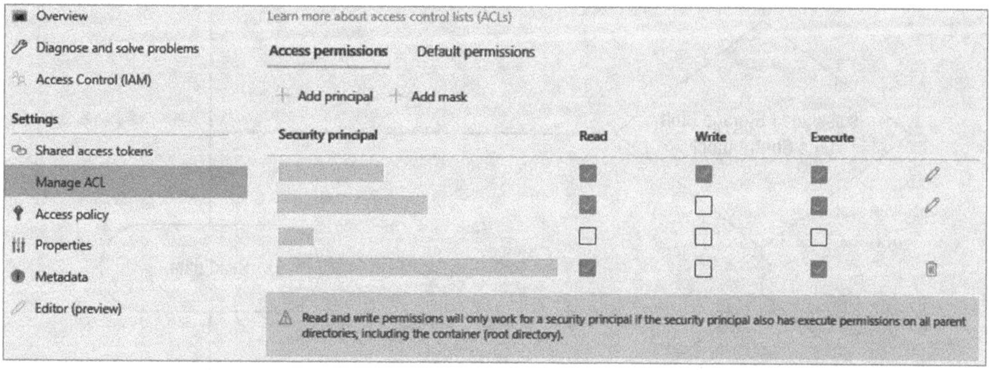

Because ADLS is an add-on to Azure Blob Storage, it has the ability to leverage both Azure RBAC and ACLs to control user access. ADLS uses the following rules when evaluating an identity's RBAC and ACL permissions:

1. Azure RBAC role assignments are evaluated first and take priority over ACL assignments.

2. If the operation is fully authorized based on the identity's RBAC assignment, then any ACL it may be assigned is not evaluated.

3. If the operation is not authorized via RBAC, then the identity's ACLs are evaluated.

Figure 4.22 illustrates the permission flow ADLS uses to evaluate a read request.

FIGURE 4.22 How ADLS evaluates identity access

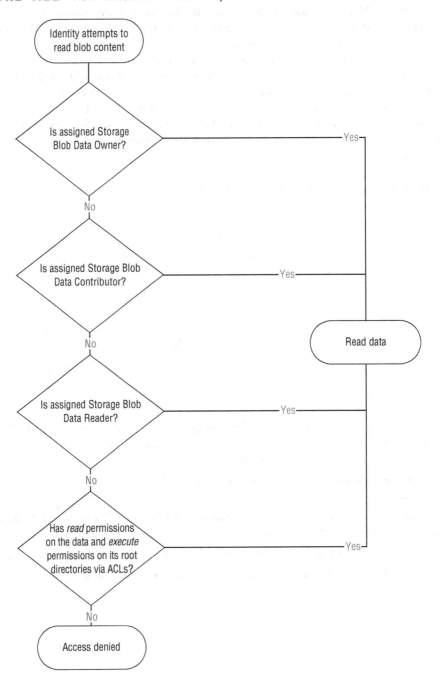

Data Encryption

All data that is stored in an Azure storage account is encrypted at rest by default. Azure Storage also encrypts data in transit using TLS and allows organizations to enforce a minimum required version of TLS for requests made to the storage account.

Data stored in a storage account is encrypted with Microsoft-managed keys by default. This abstracts encryption key management from storage account administrators. While this can be a benefit to some organizations, others require more control of the encryption keys. For this reason, Azure Storage allows organizations to use their own keys to encrypt storage account data. Customer-managed keys must be stored in Azure Key Vault.

A storage account can be configured to use customer-managed keys by changing its encryption type. To do this, click the *Encryption* button on the left side of the storage account blade for your storage account and change the encryption type to Customer Managed Keys. This will prompt you to select an Azure Key Vault and an encryption key.

 Storage accounts using customer-managed encryption keys require soft delete and purge protection to be enabled on the Azure Key Vault instance. Soft delete is automatically enabled for all key vaults and cannot be disabled. Purge protection can be enabled when a new key vault is created or after it is created.

Data Protection

In addition to providing data redundancy for business continuity, Azure Storage protects data from being deleted or modified with the following features:

- *Soft delete* protects data from being accidentally deleted. Storage resources can be recovered when this feature is enabled, within a specified retention period. During the retention period, deleted storage resources can be restored to their state at the time they were deleted. Soft delete can be configured for file shares, containers, and blobs.

- *Blob versioning* captures the state of a blob at a given point in time. When this is enabled, Azure Blob Storage will create a new version of the blob when it is created and every time it is modified. This feature is not available for ADLS or Azure Files.

- *Immutability policies* enable users to restrict data from being modified or deleted once it is written to Azure Blob Storage. With this feature, data can be read as many times as needed but never modified or deleted for a user-specified interval.

  Azure Blob storage supports two types of immutability policies: time-based and legal hold. Time-based retention policies allow users to define the number of days the data is immutable, anywhere between 1 and 146,000 days. Legal hold policies restrict data from being modified or deleted until the legal hold is explicitly removed.

Azure Storage Common Connectivity Issues

Applications interacting with Azure Storage will have to traverse multiple levels of security to establish successful connections. While this is paramount for storing data securely in Azure, it can potentially lead to some connectivity interruptions. These can be expected or unexpected and are typically related to authorization issues, resources not being available, or network failure. The following sections describe some common Azure Storage connectivity issues and how to fix them.

Forbidden Exceptions

Forbidden exceptions typically occur when an application is attempting to authenticate with an access key, SAS, or Azure AD identity that does not have the appropriate access permissions to the storage account. Client applications that experience this issue will throw a 403 exception to indicate that the request was unauthorized.

If the client application is authenticating with an access key, verify that the access key is still valid. There is a chance that the key had been regenerated without it being changed in the application. If the application is using an Azure AD identity to access the storage account, verify that the identity has the correct permissions to perform the action the application is attempting.

While authentication issues with an access key or Azure AD can occur, 403 forbidden exceptions are typically the result of an invalid or expired SAS. Use the following rules to minimize the chances of this issue occurring:

- Do not set a future start time when initially setting up the SAS. It is possible that the SAS will not be valid if there are any clock differences between the time that the client application is sending a request to the storage account and the SAS's start time.

- Do not set a short expiry time on the SAS.

- Make sure that the version parameter in the SAS matches the Azure Storage client library version that the client application is using. Always use the latest version of the Azure Storage client library to mitigate this issue.

Resource Not Found

Resource not found errors imply that the resource the client application was trying to connect to does not exist. Client applications that experience this issue will throw a 404 exception. There are several possible reasons for this error:

- The object the application is trying to access was deleted by a previous operation.

- The application is using a SAS that does not include all of the necessary permissions to perform the attempted operation.

- Unexpected network failures.

There are several third-party tools that can be used to diagnose and troubleshoot network-related issues with Azure Storage, including Fiddler and Wireshark. These tools are outside of the scope for the DP-900 exam, but you can visit https://docs.microsoft.com/en-us/azure/storage/common/storage-monitoring-diagnosing-troubleshooting?toc=%2Fazure%2Fstorage%2Fblobs%2Ftoc.json&tabs=dotnet#appendices to learn more about when and how to use them.

Management Tools

Microsoft provides several tools for uploading and managing data stored in Azure Storage. These also include tools that can be used to migrate data from legacy storage solutions to Azure Storage. The following sections describe some of the most popular tools for interacting with Azure Storage.

AzCopy

AzCopy is a command-line tool that can be used to migrate data into and out of Azure Storage. It includes a set of commands that users can leverage to move data to an Azure storage account from a local file share, Amazon S3, Google Cloud Storage, or another Azure storage account.

Download the most current version of AzCopy from the following link to get started: https://docs.microsoft.com/en-us/azure/storage/common/storage-use-azcopy-v10#download-azcopy. Once it's installed, you will be able to run AzCopy commands through a local command prompt.

Moving data to or from a storage account with AzCopy requires an authorized connection. Table 4.4 lists the authorization methods that AzCopy can use when connecting to Azure Storage:

TABLE 4.4 Supported AzCopy authorization methods

Storage Service	Supported Authorization Method
Azure Blob Storage	Azure AD and SAS
ADLS	Azure AD and SAS
Azure Files	SAS

All AzCopy statements begin with the `azcopy` keyword to indicate that the statement is using the AzCopy executable. Most AzCopy statements use the following format to perform an action:

```
azcopy [command] [source-file-path] [destination-storage-account]
--[optional-flag]
```

For example, the following statement uses this format to upload a local directory of data to Azure Blob Storage:

```
azcopy copy 'C:\myDirectory'
'https://dp900stracct001.blob.core.windows.net/dp900container01'
--recursive=true
```

This example assumes that the statement is being run with an Azure AD identity that is authorized to create data in the storage account. To use a SAS instead of Azure AD to authenticate to the storage account, simply add the SAS token to the end of the blob URL (for example, `https://dp900stracct001.blob.core.windows.net/dp900containe r01<SAS-Token>`).

Azure Storage Explorer

Azure Storage Explorer is a free desktop application that can be used to manage Azure Storage resources across Azure subscriptions. The application uses AzCopy to perform resource management and data movement operations, allowing users to leverage the performance benefits of AzCopy with an easy-to-use GUI.

You can get started with Azure Storage Explorer by downloading the most current version from `https://azure.microsoft.com/en-us/features/storage-explorer`. Here you will find download options for Windows, macOS, and Linux devices. Once it's installed, users can leverage Azure Storage Explorer to perform the following tasks:

- Connect to and manage Azure storage accounts across multiple Azure subscriptions.
- Create, manage, and delete blob containers, ADLS directories, and file shares.
- Upload, manage, download, and delete data and virtual hard disks.

Use the following steps to log into your Azure account and list the subscriptions and storage accounts you have access to:

1. Open Azure Storage Explorer and click the *Connect to Azure Storage* button. Figure 4.23 illustrates where you can find this button.

FIGURE 4.23 Connect to Azure Storage button

2. The Connect to Azure Storage pop-up window provides connection options at the Azure subscription, storage account, and storage service levels. Click the *Subscription* button and follow the prompts to sign into your Azure account.

3. After you successfully log into your Azure account, the account and its associated subscriptions will appear under the Account Management page. Select the subscription that hosts the storage accounts you want to manage and click *Open Explorer*.

4. The Explorer page will list all of the storage accounts and storage resources in the selected subscription(s). Figure 4.24 illustrates how the previously created blob container and file share is listed in Azure Storage Explorer.

FIGURE 4.24   Storage account display

When you click on a blob container or a file share, the main pane will display all of its contents as well as options to upload new items and create a new subfolder. Click on the previously created blob container and click the *Upload* button in the top ribbon. Click *Upload Files* to upload one or more data files. The Upload Files pop-up page allows you to select the files you want to upload, the blob type, and the access tier for the blob. Figure 4.25 shows an example of this page uploading a block blob with the hot access tier.

Once it's uploaded, you will be able to manipulate the data with several options in the top ribbon and by right-clicking the blob.

Azure Data Factory

Azure Data Factory is a PaaS ETL technology that can be used to orchestrate data movement and data transformation activities. With the Azure Data Factory's native data store connectors, users can quickly build connections to on-premises and cloud data stores. Developers can then use those established connections, called *Linked Services*, to build datasets that are used in Azure Data Factory pipelines. Pipelines consist of activities that process datasets, storing them in formats that can be used by data science and reporting applications.

One of the core components of Azure Data Factory is its *Copy Data* activity. Developers can use this activity to move large amounts of data from on-premises and cloud data stores to a central data repository in Azure Storage. The Copy activity is typically the first step used in an Azure Data Factory ETL pipeline, consolidating raw, source data in a single ADLS account. This activity is also used to migrate binary objects such as videos, images, and audio files to Azure Blob Storage.

FIGURE 4.25 Upload Files pop-up page

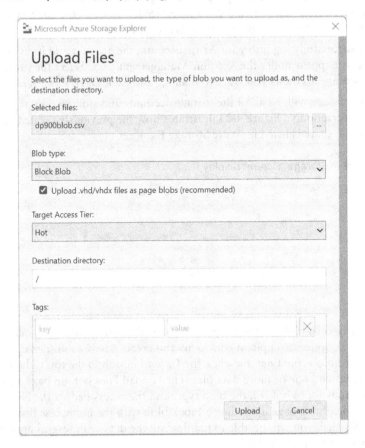

Creating Azure Data Factory resources such as linked services, datasets, pipelines, and pipeline activities is covered in further detail in Chapter 5, "Modern Data Warehouses in Azure."

Azure Data Box

For some organizations, using a programmatic approach to migrating data from an on-premises appliance to Azure can take longer than what is acceptable. Microsoft can support organizations facing this issue with Azure Data Box. *Azure Data Box* is a physical device that lets organizations send large amounts of data to Azure very quickly. It is typically used to migrate datasets that are larger than 40 TBs in scenarios with limited or no network connectivity. Azure Data Box is used in the following scenarios:

- Moving large amounts of media data such as videos, images, and audio files to Azure
- Migrating several VMs to Azure at once
- Migrating large amounts of historical data that is used by distributed analytics solutions

Azure Data Box can also be used to export data from Azure Storage to an on-premises datacenter.

The following steps describe the workflow used to migrate data to Azure with Azure Data Box:

1. Order the device through the Azure Portal. Provide shipping information and the destination Azure storage account for the data.

2. Once the device is delivered, connect the device to your network using a wired connection. Make sure the computer from which you will be copying the data has access to the data.

3. Copy the data to the device.

4. Once the data has finished copying, turn off the device and ship it back to the Azure datacenter that you are migrating the data to.

5. The data is moved to the designated Azure storage account once the device is returned.

More information about procuring and managing an Azure Data Box device can be found at https://docs.microsoft.com/en-us/azure/databox/data-box-overview.

Summary

This chapter covered file and object storage concepts and when to use one over the other. In a nutshell, file storage is used to organize data on a file share and is typically used for network-wide collaboration. File storage is optimized for small amounts of data that can be organized using a hierarchy of directories and subdirectories. Object storage is used to store large volumes of data in binary and text format. This includes images, videos, audio, and data used in distributed analytics solutions.

Azure Storage is a multi-purpose PaaS storage platform that allows users to create object, file, key-value, and queue data stores. A storage account is the highest level of management for Azure Storage and can host one or more storage services. The storage services include Azure Blob storage, Azure Data Lake Storage Gen2, Azure Files, Azure Table storage, and Azure Queue storage.

Depending on the performance requirements for the use case, storage accounts can be configured to one of two account types: standard or premium. Both standard and premium storage accounts replicate their data three times locally for high availability. Standard storage accounts also allow users to configure a secondary region that will replicate the data three more times in a different Azure region for disaster recovery benefits.

Azure Files is a fully managed file share solution in Azure with support for SMB and NFS access protocols. File shares can be easily mounted to network drives or synchronized to a local machine using Azure File Sync. Azure offers the following four storage tiers for file shares to meet the performance and price requirements of different workloads: premium, transaction optimized, hot, and cool.

Azure Blob Storage is Azure's object storage solution. Typical Azure Blob Storage use cases include storing binary data such as images and videos and storing large amounts of textual data for big data processing solutions and as a data archive. Data in Azure Blob Storage is represented as blob objects. Blobs can be stored in one of three access tiers that allow users to store blob data in the most cost-effective manner depending on latency requirements and how frequently they are accessed.

Azure Data Lake Storage Gen2 (ADLS) is an object storage solution that is built on top of Azure Blob Storage. With its hierarchical namespace implementation and native HDFS support, ADLS is an ideal storage solution for big data analytics solutions.

As with any service in Azure, Azure Storage services can be deployed manually in the Azure Portal or automated with a script or an Infrastructure as Code template. Azure Storage provides multiple methods to secure data, including several network isolation and access management techniques. Data is natively encrypted at rest and in transit and is protected from being accidentally deleted or modified.

This chapter ends by describing some of the tools that can be used to manage and move data to Azure Storage. Data movement can be managed through a command line with AzCopy, graphically with Azure Storage Explorer, or as a part of an ETL pipeline with Azure Data Factory. Microsoft also offers Azure Data Box, a physical device that organizations can procure to migrate large amounts of data. Once it's ordered and received, organizations can connect an Azure Data Box device to their local network and upload data to it. The Azure Data Box device can then be shipped back to an Azure datacenter where Microsoft will upload the data to a storage account of the organization's choosing.

Exam Essentials

Describe the characteristics of object storage.   Understand what constitutes object storage. This can range from unstructured data such as videos, images, and audio to semi-structured or structured data files that are used in distributed compute solutions. These data stores are also used to store static content, data backups, and archive data.

Describe Azure Storage.   For the exam, remember that Azure Storage is a multi-purpose storage platform that allows users to create Azure Blob Storage, Azure Data Lake Storage Gen2, Azure Files, Azure Queue storage, and Azure Table storage services. Storage accounts offer two performance tiers, standard and premium, depending on the type of storage and hardware speed needed. There are four redundancy options that storage accounts can use for business continuity, including locally redundant storage (LRS), zone-redundant storage (ZRS), geo-redundant storage (GRS), and geo-zone-redundant storage (GZRS). The secondary GRS and GZRS regions can be configured to be readable.

Describe Azure Files.   Azure Files is a storage service that allows organizations to build fully managed file shares in Azure. File shares deployed through Azure Files can be accessed using SMB on standard and premium storage accounts or NFS on premium storage accounts. Remember that it has four access tiers: premium (only available on premium storage accounts), transaction optimized, hot, and cool. Azure file shares can be mounted to any computer in the world that is running a Windows, Linux, or macOS operating system. Users can also access files by using Azure File Sync to create a local cache of the Azure file share on a machine running Windows Server 2012 R2 or higher. Users can connect to an Azure file share from their local network by either opening TCP port 445 or by attaching a private endpoint to the host storage account and establishing a VPN or ExpressRoute connection between the private endpoint's VNet and the local network.

Describe Azure Blob Storage.   Azure Blob Storage is Microsoft's object storage solution in Azure. It can store any type of file and is optimized for storing videos, images, audio, text formatted files used for big data processing, backups, and archival data. For the exam, remember that a single storage account can have an unlimited number of containers, and a single container can have an unlimited number of blobs. Remember that there are three types of blobs: block blobs, append blobs, and page blobs.

Blobs can be set to use one of three different access tiers, including hot, cool, and archive. The appropriate setting for a given blob depends on how frequently it is accessed and what its latency requirements are.

Describe Azure Data Lake Storage Gen2.   Azure Data Lake Storage Gen2, or ADLS for short, is an object storage solution that is built on top of Azure Blob Storage. It uses a hierarchical namespace to organize data in a structure of directories and subdirectories for efficient data access. This makes it the ideal storage solution for big data and distributed analytics solutions, such as those built with Azure HDInsight, Azure Databricks, or Azure Synapse Analytics. Remember that the Azure Blob File System (ABFS) driver allows Apache Hadoop environments to easily interact with data stored in ADLS.

Describe automated Azure Storage deployments.   As with other Azure data services, the DP-900 exam will include some questions about best practices for Azure Storage deployments. Azure PowerShell, Azure CLI, and Infrastructure as Code templates are commonly used to automate Azure Storage deployments across multiple development environments.

Describe network isolation for Azure Storage.   Like other data services in Azure, storage accounts use a public endpoint that can be secured using an IP firewall or by allowing access to specific Azure VNets or Azure services. Users can also attach private endpoints to a storage account, restricting access to only applications that can communicate with the VNet the IP address is in.

Describe access management for Azure Storage.   Remember that there are three methods that can be used to manage authentication and authorization for storage accounts: access keys, shared access signatures (SAS), and Azure AD identities. Microsoft recommends that access management is done with Azure AD identities as these are easier to manage and they provide more granular levels of permissions than access keys or SAS. Know that there are several Azure RBAC roles that are specific to accessing different types of Azure storage. Also remember that ADLS allows a combination of Azure RBAC and POSIX-like access control lists (ACLs) to provide access at the storage account, container, directory, and blob levels.

Describe data encryption and data protection for Azure Storage.   Azure encrypts data stored in Azure Storage at rest by default. Azure Storage also encrypts data in transit using TLS and allows organizations to enforce a minimum required version of TLS for requests made to the storage account. Azure Storage also protects data from being deleted or modified with the following features: soft delete, blob versioning, and immutability policies.

Describe management tools for Azure Storage.   The DP-900 exam covers several tools that can be used to manage data in Azure Storage. AzCopy is a command-line tool that is used to migrate data from on-premises or cloud storage to an Azure storage account. Azure Storage Explorer is a desktop tool that can be used to manage storage account resources. Remember that Azure Storage Explorer uses AzCopy to upload data. Azure Data Factory is an orchestration tool that can be used to move data to Azure Storage as a part of an ETL pipeline. Finally, Azure Data Box is a physical device that organizations can use to move large amounts of data (more than 40 TB) to Azure Storage.

Review Questions

1. Which of the following types of data can be stored in Azure Storage?

   A. Unstructured

   B. Structured

   C. Semi-structured

   D. All of the above

2. Which of the following redundancy options is not available for premium tier storage accounts?

   A. Local redundant storage.

   B. Geo-redundant storage.

   C. Zone-redundant storage.

   D. All of these are available redundancy options for premium storage accounts.

3. As the Azure administrator for your company, you are responsible for creating a storage system that replaces the existing SMB file share that is used by developers. The solution must be able to provide quick access to files that are frequently used and offload the storage of files that are not frequently used to the cloud. Which of the following solutions meets this requirement?

   A. Create an Azure file share and set up Azure File Sync on a Windows Server device.

   B. Create an Azure file share and mount the share to an on-premises network drive.

   C. Create an Azure Blob Storage container and mount the container to an on-premises network drive.

   D. Create an Azure file share and set up Azure File Sync on a Linux device.

4. What port needs to be opened to allow SMB communication to an Azure file share if there is not an established Azure VPN or ExpressRoute to tunnel SMB traffic to the share?

   A. 445

   B. 443

   C. 1433

   D. 2049

5. Which blob type is used by Azure VMs for disk storage?

   A. Block blob

   B. Append blob

   C. Page blob

   D. Disk blob

6. You are designing an Azure Blob Storage solution to serve as the backend for a big data processing solution. Initially, the data must be available to be processed and analyzed with minimal latency. Once the raw data is processed and is no longer useful, it must be maintained for compliance reasons. Which of the following options should you implement to create the most cost-effective storage solution?

A. Initially store the raw data using the hot access tier and then use a life cycle management policy to move the raw data to the cool access tier once it is processed.

B. Initially store the raw data using the hot access tier and then use a life cycle management policy to move the data to the archive access tier once it is processed.

C. Initially store the data using the transaction optimized access tier and then use a life cycle management policy to move the raw data to the cool access tier once it is processed.

D. Initially store the data using the transaction optimized access tier and then use a life cycle management policy to move the raw data to the archive access tier once it is processed.

7. When selected, which of the following features will enable ADLS for Azure Blob Storage?

A. Hierarchical namespace

B. File share

C. Directory namespace

D. Premium

8. What is the recommended Azure PowerShell command to use when creating a reference to an existing storage account?

A. `Get-AzureRmStorageAccount`

B. `Get-AzStorageAccount`

C. `Get-AzureStorageAccount`

D. `Get-AzRmStorageAccount`

9. You are designing a storage account that will be used to store personally identifiable information. What network isolation solution should you use to ensure that the storage account is properly secured?

A. Use the public endpoint with the IP firewall to restrict access to specific IP addresses.

B. Use the public endpoint and restrict access to specific Azure subnets.

C. Use a private endpoint to attach a private IP address from a VNet to the storage account. This will restrict storage account access to applications that can communicate with the VNet.

D. Use a private endpoint with the IP firewall to restrict access to specific IP addresses.

10. You are an Azure administrator for a sports team and are working with the team's data engineering department to design an Azure Blob Storage repository for all of the team's historical statistics. Analysts must be able to read data from the blob containers but must not be able to write new data or delete existing data. Which of the following access management solutions should you implement?

    A. Storage Blob Data Contributor

    B. Reader

    C. Contributor

    D. Storage Blob Data Reader

11. Your organization is preparing to move its existing data estate to Azure Storage. The scope of the migration will include 50 TBs of historical data and media files. All the data needs to be migrated at once without taking a lot of time. Which of the following solutions should you use to perform this migration?

    A. AzCopy

    B. Azure Data Box

    C. Azure Data Factory

    D. Azure Storage Explorer

12. Which of the following Azure resources can you connect to in Azure Storage Explorer?

    A. Subscriptions

    B. Storage accounts

    C. Blob containers

    D. All of the above

Chapter

5

Modern Data Warehouses in Azure

MICROSOFT EXAM OBJECTIVES COVERED IN THIS CHAPTER:

✓ Describe analytical workloads.

- Describe transactional workloads.
- Describe the difference between a transactional and an analytical workload.
- Describe the difference between batch and real time.
- Describe data warehousing workloads.
- Describe when a data warehouse solution is needed.

✓ Describe the components of a modern data warehouse.

- Describe Azure data services for modern data warehousing such as Azure Data Lake, Azure Synapse Analytics, Azure Databricks, and Azure HDInsight.
- Describe modern data warehousing architecture and workload.

✓ Describe data ingestion and processing on Azure.

- Describe common practices for data loading.
- Describe the components of Azure Data Factory (e.g., pipeline, activities, etc.).
- Describe data processing options (e.g., Azure HDInsight, Azure Databricks, Azure Synapse Analytics, Azure Data Factory).

Chapter 1, "Core Data Concepts," and Chapter 2, "Relational Databases in Azure," examine the fundamental concepts of analytical workloads, including common definitions and design patterns. This chapter expands on these concepts by exploring the various components that can be involved in Azure-based analytical workloads. These components include services that are involved in ingesting and processing data and storage options for a modern data warehouse.

Analytical Workload Features

Throughout this book we have covered the features and design considerations used by different workload types. For this reason, the following sections will only provide a summary of the different workload types. The important takeaway for this chapter is how analytical workloads differentiate from transactional ones and how batch and stream processing are used in a modern data warehouse solution. Understanding these features will set the stage for the rest of the chapter when we examine how to build modern data warehouses in Azure.

Transactional vs. Analytical Workloads

Analytical workloads can be built using many of the same technologies and components as transactional workloads. However, there are several design practices and features that are more optimal for one over the other. When designing a modern data warehouse, it is important to consider what sets analytical and transactional workloads apart.

Transactional Workload Features

As discussed in Chapter 1, "Core Data Concepts," online transaction processing (OLTP) systems capture the business transactions that support the data-to-day operations of a business. Data stores that are used for OLTP systems must be able to handle millions of transactions a day while ensuring that none of the data is corrupted. Traditionally, OLTP systems have always been hosted on relational databases as these platforms implement ACID properties to ensure data integrity.

Relational databases supporting OLTP systems are highly normalized, typically following third normal form (3NF), separating related data into multiple tables to eliminate data redundancy. This design standard ensures that database tables are optimized for write operations. While this level of normalization is ideal for write operations, it is less efficient for analytical workloads that perform read-heavy operations. Analysts who have built reports from databases that are designed for OLTP workloads will inevitably be forced to write complicated queries that use several join operations to create the desired result set. This can lead to bad performance and concurrency issues with write operations.

Before examining features and best practices for analytical workloads, it is important to note that not all OLTP workloads are suitable for highly normalized, relational databases. Transactional data that is produced in large volumes and at high speeds can take a performance hit when being conformed to a fixed, normalized schema. In these cases, organizations can choose to host their transactional workloads on NoSQL document databases such as the Azure Cosmos DB Core (SQL) API. These databases store data in its original state as semi-structured documents, enabling transactions to be written to them very quickly.

While document databases are extremely efficient data stores for large volume and high velocity write operations, the lack of a consistent structure makes them difficult to use with analytical applications like reporting tools. Useful data fields are typically extrapolated from semi-structured NoSQL documents and stored in a format that is optimized for read-heavy operations. Several modern analytical services can also leverage data virtualization techniques to structure data for reporting applications while leaving the data in its source data store.

Analytical Workload Features

Analytical workloads are designed to help business users make data-driven decisions. These systems are used to answer several questions about the business: What has happened over the previous period? Why did particular events happen? What will happen if all things stay the same? What will happen if we make specific changes in different areas? As discussed in Chapter 1, these questions are answered by the different types of analytics that make up the analytics maturity model.

 Remember that the analytics maturity model includes descriptive, diagnostic, predictive, prescriptive, and cognitive analytics.

Data-driven business decisions come from extracting useful information from several source data stores, including OLTP databases. Once extracted, source data will typically undergo several transformation steps to remove extraneous features and remediate data quality issues. Cleansed data is then conformed to an easy-to-use data model for analytics. Data that is ready to be analyzed is stored in a relational data warehouse, an OLAP model, or as files in an enterprise data lake.

Reporting applications and analytical applications used to analyze historical data typically retrieve data from read optimized data stores such as a data warehouse or an OLAP model. Many of these systems offer in-memory and column-based storage capabilities that are optimal for analytical queries that aggregate large amounts of data. Data warehouses and department-specific data marts are built with relational databases like Azure Synapse Analytics dedicated SQL pools or Azure SQL Database. Unlike OLTP data stores that are built with relational databases, data warehouses use a denormalized data model. The section "Data Modeling Best Practices for Data Warehouses" later in this chapter covers this approach in further detail.

While most analytical workloads store processed data used by reporting applications in a relational data warehouse such as Azure Synapse Analytics dedicated SQL pools or an OLAP tool such as Azure Analysis Services, many organizations choose to store data used by data scientists as files in an enterprise data lake. Cloud-based data lakes such as Azure Data Lake Store Gen2 (ADLS) can store massive amounts of data much cheaper than a relational data warehouse. Data lakes can also store large amounts of unstructured data such as images, video, and audio that data scientists can leverage with deep learning techniques. Data architects can take advantage of these capabilities by providing data scientists with large volumes and several types of data that they can use to build insightful machine learning models.

Modern cloud-based analytical workloads typically use a combination of an enterprise data lake and a data warehouse. Relational database engines used to host data warehouses offer faster query performance, higher user concurrency, and more granular security than data lake technologies. On the other hand, data lake services can host unlimited amounts data at a much cheaper cost, allowing users to store multiple copies of data to leverage for several different use cases. Data lakes can also store a wide variety of data, allowing users to interact with semi-structured and unstructured data with relative ease. This is why most organizations store all of their data in an enterprise data lake and only load data that is necessary for reporting from the data lake into a data warehouse.

Separating where data is located so reports retrieve data from a data warehouse or OLAP model and so data scientists use data in a data lake will eliminate concurrency issues that may have been caused by these workloads using data from the same data store. This will help optimize the performance of these workloads.

In recent years, several technologies have been introduced that are optimized for ad hoc analysis with data stored in a data lake. By storing data using a columnar format such as Parquet, analysts can leverage data virtualization technologies such as Azure Synapse Analytics serverless SQL pools to query their data with T-SQL without having to create a separate copy of the data in a relational database. Data engineers can also store data in ADLS with *Delta Lake*. Delta Lake is an open-source storage layer that enables ACID properties on Parquet files in ADLS. This ensures data integrity for data stored in ADLS, perfect for ad hoc analysis and data science initiatives. More information about Delta Lake and the "Lakehouse" concept can be found at `https://delta.io`.

While using a data lake like a data warehouse can serve as a relational database replacement with smaller workloads, large reporting workloads that analyze data from several sources can benefit from the performance of a relational database. You can find more information about the benefits of using a relational data warehouse and a data lake together in the following blog post from James Serra: `www.jamesserra.com/archive/2020/09/data-lakehouse-synapse`.

Data used by analytical workloads have to go through a data processing workflow before it eventually lands in a data lake and/or a data warehouse. Even if the data does not undergo any transformations, it still needs to be extracted and loaded into a destination data store. Data engineers can use one or a combination of the following data processing techniques to create an end-to-end data pipeline: batch processing and stream processing.

Data Processing Techniques

Batch and stream processing are two data processing techniques that are used to manipulate data at rest and in real time. As discussed in Chapter 1, these techniques can be leveraged together in modern data processing architectures such as the Lambda architecture. This empowers organizations to make decisions with a wide variety of data that is generated at different speeds. Let's examine each of these techniques further in the following sections before exploring how they can be used in the same solution.

Batch Processing

Batch processing activities act on groups, or batches, of data at predetermined periods of time or after a specified event. One example of batch processing is a retail company processing daily sales every night and loading the transformed data into a data warehouse. The following list included reasons for why you would want to use batch processing:

- Working with large volumes of data that require a significant amount of compute power and time to process

- Running data processing activities during off-hours to avoid inaccurate reporting

- Processing data every time a specific event occurs, such as a blob being uploaded to Azure Blob storage

- Transforming batches of semi-structured data, such as JSON or XML, into a structured format that can be loaded into a data warehouse

- Processing data that is related to business intervals, such as yearly/quarterly/monthly/weekly aggregations

Data architects can implement batch processing activities using one of two techniques: extract, transform, and load (ETL) or extract, load, and transform (ELT). ETL pipelines extract data from one or more source systems, transform the data to meet user specifications, and then load the data in an analytical data store. ELT processes flip the transform and load stages and allow data engineers to transform data in the analytical data store. Because the ELT pattern is optimized for big data workloads, the analytical data store must be capable of working on data at scale. For this reason, ELT pipelines commonly use MPP technologies like Azure Synapse Analytics as the analytical data store.

Batch processing workflows in the cloud generally use the following components:

- *Orchestration engine*—This component manages the flow of a data pipeline. It handles when and how a pipeline starts, extracting data from source systems and landing it in data lake storage, and executing transformation activities. Developers can also leverage error handling logic in the orchestration engine to control how pipeline activity errors are managed. Depending on the design, orchestration engines can also be used to move transformed data into an analytical data store. Azure Data Factory (ADF) is a common service used for this workflow component.

- *Object storage*—This is a distributed data store, or data lake, that hosts large amounts of files in various formats. Developers can use data lakes to manage their data in multiple stages. This can include a bronze layer for raw data extracted directly from the source, a silver layer that represents the data after being scrubbed of any data quality issues, and a gold layer that stores an aggregated version of the data that has been enriched with domain-specific business rules. ADLS or Azure Blob Storage can be used for this workflow component.

- *Transformation activities*—This is a computational service that is able to process long-running batch jobs to filter, aggregate, normalize, and prepare data for analysis. These activities read source data from data lake storage, process it, and write the output back to data lake storage or an analytical data store. Azure Databricks, Azure HDInsight, Azure Synapse Analytics, and ADF mapping data flows are just a few examples of compute services that can transform data.

- *Analytical data store*—This is a storage service that is optimized to serve data to analytical tools such as Power BI. Azure services that can be used as an analytical data store include Azure Synapse Analytics and Azure SQL Database.

- *Analysis and reporting*—Reporting tools and analytical applications are used to create infographics with the processed data. Power BI is one example of a reporting tool used in a batch processing workflow.

Figure 5.1 illustrates an example of a batch processing workflow that uses ADF to extract data from a few source systems, lands the raw data in ADLS, processes the data with a combination of Azure Databricks and ADF mapping data flows, and finally loads the processed data into an Azure Synapse Analytics dedicated SQL pool.

FIGURE 5.1 Batch processing example

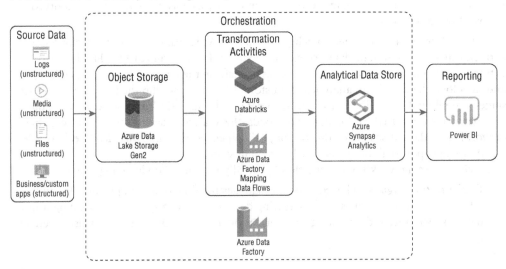

Stream Processing

Stream processing is a data processing technique that involves ingesting a continuous stream of data and performing computations on the data in real time. It is used for processing scenarios that have very short latency requirements, typically measured in seconds or milliseconds. Data that is ready for analysis is either sent directly to a dashboard or loaded into a persistent data store such as ADLS or Azure Synapse Analytics dedicated SQL pool for long-term analysis. Some examples of stream processing are listed here:

- Analyzing click-stream data to make recommendations in real-time

- Observing biometric data with fitness trackers and other IoT devices

- Monitoring offshore drilling equipment to detect any anomalies that indicate it needs to be repaired or replaced

Cloud-based stream processing workflows generally use the following components:

- *Real-time message ingestion*—This component captures data as messages in real time from different technologies that generate data streams. Azure Event Hubs and Azure IoT Hub are two PaaS offerings that data architects can use for real-time message ingestion. Several organizations leverage Apache Kafka, a popular open-source message ingestion platform, to process data streams. Organizations can move their existing Kafka workloads to Azure with the Azure HDInsight Kafka cluster type or the Azure Events for Kafka protocol.

- *Stream processing*—This component transforms, aggregates, and prepares data streams for analysis. These technologies can also load data in persistent data stores for long-term analysis. Azure Stream Analytics and Azure Functions are two PaaS offerings that data engineers can use to receive data from a real-time ingestion services and apply computations on the data.

- *Apache Spark*—This is a popular open-source data engineering platform that supports batch and stream processing. Stream processing is performed with the Spark structured streaming service, a processing service that transforms data streams as micro-batches in real time. Spark structured streaming jobs can be developed with Azure Databricks, the Azure HDInsight Spark cluster type, or an Azure Synapse Analytics Apache Spark pool. The collaborative nature and ease of use with Azure Databricks makes it the preferred service for Spark structured streaming jobs.

- *Object storage*—Data streams can be loaded into object storage to be archived or combined with other datasets for batch processing. Stream processing services can use an object store such as ADLS or Azure Blob Storage as a destination, or sink, data store for processed data. Some real-time ingestion services such as Azure Event Hubs can load data directly into object storage without the help of a stream processing service. This is useful for organizations that need to store the raw data streams for long-term analysis.

- *Analytical data store*—This is a storage service that serves processed data streams to analytical applications. Azure Synapse Analytics, Azure Cosmos DB, and Azure Data Explorer are services in Azure that can be used as an analytical data store for data streams.

- *Analysis and reporting tools*—Processed data can be written directly to a reporting tool such as a Power BI dashboard for instant analysis.

As discussed in Chapter 1, stream processing workflows can use one of two approaches: live or on demand. The "live" approach is the most commonly used pattern, processing data continuously as it is generated. The "on-demand" approach persists incoming data in object storage and processes it in micro-batches. An example of this approach is illustrated in Figure 5.2.

FIGURE 5.2   On-demand stream processing example

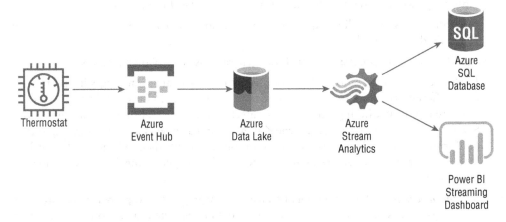

Thermostat → Azure Event Hub → Azure Data Lake → Azure Stream Analytics → Azure SQL Database / Power BI Streaming Dashboard

Modern Data Solutions with Batch and Stream Processing

Azure data services make it easy for data architects to use batch and stream processing workflows in the same solution. This flexibility gives business units the ability to quickly make well informed decisions from their data. These cloud-native solutions are designed with modern data processing patterns like the Lambda architecture.

The Lambda architecture is a data processing pattern that provides a framework for how users can use a combination of batch and stream processing for data analysis. Solutions that use the Lambda architecture separate batch and stream processing operations into a cold and hot path. Figure 5.3 illustrates the components and process flow used by the Lambda architecture.

The cold path, also known as the batch layer, manages all operations that are not constrained by low latency requirements. Batch layer operations typically process large datasets at predetermined periods of time. Once processed, data is loaded into the serving layer (e.g., an analytical data store like Azure Synapse Analytics) to be analyzed by reporting and analytical applications.

The hot path, also known as the speed layer, manages stream processing operations. Data is immediately processed and is either directly sent to a reporting application for instant analysis or loaded into the serving layer and combined with data processed in the batch layer.

FIGURE 5.3 Lambda architecture workflow

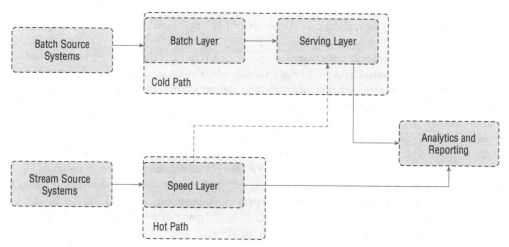

Modern Data Warehouse Components

Modern data warehouse solutions are more than just a simple analytical data store. They are made up of several components that give users flexible options for how they can analyze their data. Technologies used by modern data warehouse solutions are designed to scale horizontally as well as vertically, meaning that they can process and store very large datasets. Modern computing paradigms that enable these technologies to manage large and diverse datasets have also led to more dynamic design patterns. As discussed previously in this chapter, modern data warehouse solutions can combine batch and stream processing workflows with the Lambda architecture.

Cloud platforms such as Azure make building these solutions more accessible than ever before. Instead of having to procure hardware and spend the time configuring distributed services such as Hadoop or Spark to work in an on-premises environment, users can quickly deploy services that are designed to be core components of a modern data warehouse solution. Azure's pay-per-use cost model and the ability to quickly scale or delete services allow organizations to test different modern data warehouse components by completing short projects known as proofs of concept (POCs). POCs enable users to evaluate critical design decisions without having to make any large upfront hardware commitments.

The following sections explore data modeling best practices for the most commonly used Azure services for modern data warehouse solutions.

Data Modeling Best Practices for Data Warehouses

Data warehouses are data management systems that support analytical workloads and business intelligence (BI) activities. Data managed by a data warehouse is derived from several sources, such as OLTP systems, web APIs, IoT devices, and social media networks. Unlike OLTP systems, data warehouses use data models that are read-optimized so analytical queries issued against them can efficiently return aggregated calculations to support business decisions.

As discussed in Chapter 2, data warehouses use denormalized data models that are optimized for analytical queries and read-heavy workloads. The most common design practice for this approach is the star schema. Star schemas denormalize business data to minimize the number of tables in the data model. Tables consist of business entities and measurable events that are related to those entities. This division of data categories is represented by the two types of tables defined in the star schema: dimension tables and fact tables.

Dimension tables contain information that describes a particular business entity. These tables are typically very wide, containing several descriptor columns and a key column that serves as a unique identifier. Some common entities that are stored as dimension tables include date, customer, product category, and product subcategory information. In all of these cases, there could be a relatively small number of rows but a large number of columns to provide as much descriptive information as possible.

Fact tables store quantifiable observations that are related to the dimension tables. These tables can grow to be very large, comprising several millions of rows related to specific measurable events. Some fact table examples include Internet sales, product inventory, and weather metrics. Fact tables also include foreign key columns that are used to establish relationships with dimension tables. These relationships determine the level of granularity that analytical queries can use when filtering fact table data. For example, a query that is filtering an Internet sales fact table by a date dimension can only return time slices for the level of detail contained in the date dimension.

Azure Services for Modern Data Warehouses

In the Azure ecosystem there are several services that can be used to build a modern data warehouse solution. Depending on the scenario and the skillset of the engineers building the solution, most Azure services can be used to build different components of a data processing pipeline. However, there is a set of core Azure data services that are specifically designed to process big data workloads:

- Azure Data Factory
- Azure HDInsight
- Azure Databricks
- Azure Synapse Analytics

Each of these services can perform a variety of different functions in a data processing pipeline. This versatility allows them to be used in various stages of ETL or ELT pipelines. They have the flexibility to manage data in a variety of different formats and can scale horizontally as well as vertically to process very large volumes of data.

First, let's examine how Azure HDInsight, Azure Databricks, and ADF are used in modern data warehouse solutions. End-to-end data processing solutions with Azure Synapse

Analytics will be described in the section "End-to-End Analytics with Azure Synapse Analytics" later in this chapter.

 It is important to note that object storage services like Azure Data Lake Storage Gen2 (ADLS) are critical components to any modern data warehouse solution. While the services described in the following sections are responsible for data transformation and data movement operations, ADLS's scalability, cost-effectiveness, and ease-of-use allow data engineers to use these services to iterate over data several times and store processed data in multiple phases (such as bronze, silver, and gold) without ever worrying about storage constraints.

Azure HDInsight

Azure HDInsight is a managed, open-source analytics service in Azure. With Azure HDInsight, you can deploy distributed clusters for Apache Hadoop, Apache Spark, Apache Interactive Query/LLAP (Live Long and Process), Apache Kafka, Apache Storm, and Apache HBase in Azure. Being able to quickly stand up these environments without having to procure and manage hardware reduces the barriers to entry for organizations who are beginning to build a modern data warehouse.

Open-source frameworks like Hadoop and Spark are designed to handle large-scale data processing activities by using a scale-out architecture. While they can be installed on a single server node for test purposes, most use cases leverage multiple server nodes that are clustered together to perform processing activities at scale. Clusters consist of a head/driver node that divides jobs into smaller tasks and one or more worker nodes that execute each task.

Distributed frameworks also rely on resource managers like Apache Hadoop YARN (Yet Another Resource Negotiator) to manage cluster resources and job scheduling. Resource managers designate compute resources (such as CPU, memory, IO) to cluster nodes and monitor the resource usage. Knowing details of how YARN and other resource managers are designed is beyond the scope of the DP-900 exam and this book, but you can find more information at the following link if you would like to learn more: https://hadoop.apache.org/docs/current/hadoop-yarn/hadoop-yarn-site/YARN.html.

Azure HDInsight makes it easy to manage distributed frameworks like Hadoop and Spark and offers the capability to customize a cluster deployment, such as adding new components and languages. Also, since Azure HDInsight is a PaaS service, you can easily scale the number of worker nodes allocated to cluster up or down to increase compute power or cut back on cost.

It is important to understand the different Azure HDInsight cluster types and when you should use them. Also, keep in mind that after you have deployed an Azure HDInsight cluster, you will not be able to change the cluster type. For this reason, it is critical that you understand the scenarios the cluster will be supporting. The following list describes each of the cluster types supported by Azure HDInsight:

- *Apache Hadoop* is an open-source technology for distributed data processing. It uses the MapReduce parallel processing framework to process data at scale and the Hadoop

Distributed File System (HDFS) as a distributed storage system. MapReduce jobs divide compute jobs into smaller units of work to be run in parallel across the various nodes in a cluster. Users can also leverage Apache Hive with Hadoop to project a schema on data and query data using HiveQL. More information about Apache Hive can be found at `https://docs.microsoft.com/en-us/azure/hdinsight/hadoop/hdinsight-use-hive`.

One drawback to Hadoop is that it only supports batch processing, forcing users to leverage another service like Apache Storm or Apache Spark for distributed stream processing. Hadoop also reads and writes data from and to disk, potentially leading to poorer processing performance than Apache Spark, which supports in-memory processing.

- *Apache Spark* is an open-source, distributed processing framework that supports in-memory processing. Because of its speed, Spark has become the standard framework for batch and stream distributed processing activities over Hadoop. Apache Spark also supports interactive querying capabilities, allowing users to easily query data from distributed data stores like ADLS with popular development languages like Spark SQL. More Spark-specific features such as development languages, workflows, and best practices will be described in the section "Azure Databricks."

- *Apache Kafka* is an open-source, distributed real-time data ingestion platform that is used to build stream processing data pipelines. It offers message broker functionality that allows users to publish and subscribe to data streams.

- *Apache HBase* is an open-source NoSQL database that is built on top of Apache Hadoop. It uses a columnar format to store rows of data as column families, similar to the Azure Cosmos DB Cassandra API. Developers can interact with HBase data using Hive queries.

- *Apache Storm* is an open-source, real-time processing system for processing large data streams very quickly. Similar to Hadoop and Spark, it uses a distributed framework to parallelize stream processing jobs.

- *Apache Interactive Query* is an open-source, in-memory caching service for interactive and faster Hive queries. This cluster type can be used by developers or data scientists to easily run Hive queries against large datasets stored in Azure Blob Storage or ADLS.

As with any service in Azure, you can configure and deploy an Azure HDInsight cluster through the Azure Portal, through an Azure PowerShell or Azure CLI script, or via an Infrastructure as Code template like ARM or Bicep. Creating an Azure HDInsight cluster in Azure deploys the service chosen as the cluster type, the Apache Hadoop YARN resource manager to manage cluster resources, and several popular open-source tools such as Ambari, Avro, Hive, Sqoop, Tez, Pig, and Zookeeper. This greatly reduces the time it takes to get started building distributed solutions.

Most modern data warehouse scenarios leverage Apache Spark over Apache Hadoop, Apache Storm, and Apache Interactive Query to process large datasets due to its speed, ability to perform batch and stream processing activities, number of data source connectors, and overall ease of use. As a matter of fact, ADF mapping data flows use Apache Spark clusters to perform ETL activities. Apache Spark also enables data scientists and data analysts to interactively manipulate data concurrently.

There are a few management aspects that must be considered when deploying an Azure HDInsight cluster:

- Once provisioned, Azure HDInsight clusters cannot be paused. This means that you will need to delete the cluster if you want to save on costs when clusters are not being used. Organizations typically use an automation framework like Azure Automation to delete their clusters with Azure PowerShell or Azure CLI once they have finished running. They can then redeploy the cluster using an automation script or an Infrastructure as Code template.

- The lack of a pause feature for clusters creates a dilemma for metadata management. Azure HDInsight clusters use an Azure SQL Database as a central schema repository, also known as a metastore. The default metastore is tied to the life cycle of a cluster, meaning that when the cluster is deleted, the metastore and all information pertaining to Hive table schemas are deleted too. This can be avoided by using your own Azure SQL Database as a custom metastore. Custom metastores are not tied to the life cycle of a cluster, allowing you to create and delete clusters without losing any metadata. They can also be used to manage the Hive table schemas for multiple clusters. More information about custom metastores can be found at `https://docs.microsoft.com/en-us/azure/hdinsight/hdinsight-use-external-metadata-stores#custom-metastore`.

- Clusters do not support Azure AD authentication, RBAC, and multi-user capabilities by default. These services can be integrated by adding the Enterprise Security Package (ESP) to your cluster as part of the deployment workflow. More information about the ESP can be found at `https://docs.microsoft.com/en-us/azure/hdinsight/enterprise-security-package`.

Later in this chapter we will discuss two other Azure services that can be used to build Apache Spark clusters. Azure Databricks and Azure Synapse Apache Spark pools are two Apache Spark–based analytics platforms that overcome the management overhead presented by Azure HDInsight. Both services allow you to easily pause (referred to as "terminate" in Azure Databricks) Spark clusters and maintain schema metadata without needing a custom external metastore. They are also natively integrated with Azure AD, enabling users to leverage their existing authentication/authorization mechanisms. Because of the ease of use and the additional components that provide a unified development experience for data engineers, Azure Databricks and Azure Synapse Analytics are the preferred choices for Apache Spark workloads. Reasons to use Azure Databricks instead of Azure Synapse Analytics Apache Spark pools and vice versa will be described in the following sections.

Azure HDInsight clusters are typically used in scenarios where Azure Databricks and Azure Synapse Analytics cannot be used or if Apache Kafka is required. The most common example of a scenario where Azure Databricks and Azure Synapse Analytics cannot be used is a solution that requires its Azure resources to come from a region that does not support either of these services. Azure Event Hubs also provides an endpoint compatible with Apache Kafka that can be leveraged by most Apache Kafka applications as an alternative to managing an Apache Kafka cluster with Azure HDInsight. Configuring the Azure Event Hubs Kafka endpoint is beyond the scope of the DP-900 exam, but you can find more information at https://docs.microsoft.com/en-us/azure/event-hubs/event-hubs-for-kafka-ecosystem-overview if you would like to learn more.

 You can use the following site to stay up to date on which regions support Azure Databricks and Azure Synapse Analytics: https://azure.microsoft.com/en-us/global-infrastructure/services/?regions=all&products=databricks,synapse-analytics.

Azure Databricks

Apache Spark was developed in 2009 by researchers at the University of California, Berkeley. Their goal was to build a solution that overcame the inefficiencies of the Apache Hadoop MapReduce framework for big data processing activities. While based off of the MapReduce framework for distributing processing activities across several compute servers, Apache Spark enhances this framework by performing several operations in-memory. Spark also extends MapReduce by allowing users to interactively query data on the fly and create stream processing workflows.

The Spark architecture is very similar to the distributed pattern used by Hadoop. At a high level, Spark applications can be broken down into the following four components:

- A *Spark driver* that is responsible for dividing data processing operations into smaller tasks that are executed by the Spark executors. The Spark driver is also responsible for requesting compute resources from the cluster manager for the Spark executors. Clusters with multiple nodes host the Spark driver on the driver node.

- A *Spark session* is an entry point to Spark functionality. Establishing a Spark session allows users to work with the resilient distributed dataset (RDD) API and the Spark DataFrame API. These represent the low-level and high-level Spark APIs that developers can use to build Spark data structures.

- A *cluster manager* that is responsible for managing resource allocation for the cluster. Spark supports four types of cluster managers: the built-in cluster manager, Apache Hadoop YARN, Apache Mesos, and Kubernetes.

- A *Spark executor* that is assigned a task from the Spark driver and executes that task. Every worker node in a cluster is given its own Spark executor. Spark executors further parallelize work by assigning tasks to a *slot* on a node. The number of worker node slots are determined by the number of cores allocated to the node.

Figure 5.4 illustrates how the components of a Spark application fit into the architecture of a three node (one driver and two workers) Spark cluster.

FIGURE 5.4   Apache Spark distributed architecture

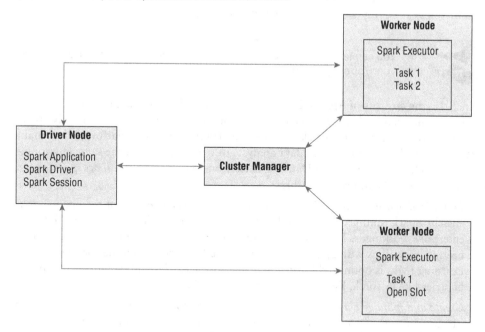

The Spark Core API enables developers to build Spark applications with several popular development languages, including Java, Scala, Python, R, and SQL. These languages have Spark-specific APIs, like PySpark for Python and SparkR for R, that are designed to parallelize code operations across Spark executors. The creators of Spark also developed several Spark-based libraries designed for a variety of big data scenarios, including MLlib for distributed machine learning applications, GraphX for graph processing, Spark Structured Streaming for stream processing, and Spark SQL + DataFrames for structuring and analyzing data.

As mentioned earlier, the Spark RDD API and the Spark DataFrame API are used to create and manipulate data objects. The RDD API is a low-level API that serves as the foundation for Spark programming. An RDD is an immutable distributed collection of data, partitioned across multiple worker nodes. The RDD API has several operations that allow developers to perform transformations and actions in a parallelized manner. While the Spark DataFrame API is used more often than the Spark RDD API, there are still some scenarios where RDDs can be more optimal than DataFrames. More information on RDDs can be found at `https://databricks.com/glossary/what-is-rdd`.

The DataFrame API is a high-level abstraction of the RDD API that allows developers to use a query language like SQL to manipulate data. Unlike RDDs, DataFrame objects are organized as named columns (like a relational database table), making them easy to manipulate. DataFrames are also optimized with Spark's native optimization engine, the catalyst optimizer, a feature that is not available for RDDs. More information on how to get started with the DataFrame API can be found at `https://docs.microsoft.com/en-us/azure/databricks/getting-started/spark/dataframes`.

 You can learn more about the Spark ecosystem at `https://databricks.com/spark/about`.

In 2013, the creators of Apache Spark founded Databricks, a data and artificial intelligence company that packages the Spark ecosystem into an easy-to-use cloud-native platform. The company brands the Databricks service as a "Unified Analytics Platform" that enables data engineers, data scientists, and data analysts to work together in the same environment. Within a single instantiation of a Databricks environment, known as a *workspace*, users can take advantage of the following features:

- *Optimized Spark runtime*—Databricks uses an enhanced version of the open-source Apache Spark runtime, known as the Databricks runtime, that is optimized for enterprise workloads. The Databricks runtime includes several libraries used for engineering operations with Spark. Additionally, the Databricks runtime for Machine Learning (ML) is optimized for machine learning activities and includes popular libraries like PyTorch, Keras, TensorFlow, and XGBoost.

- *Create and manage clusters*—Since Databricks is a cloud-native, PaaS platform, administrators can easily deploy and manage clusters through the workspace UI. Users can choose from several cluster options, including the cluster mode, Databricks runtime version, compute server type, and the number of compute nodes. This UI also lets administrators manually terminate a cluster or specify an inactivity period (in minutes) after which they want the cluster to terminate.

- *Notebooks*—Developers can create notebooks in Databricks workspaces that they can use to author code. Similar to Jupyter Notebooks, notebooks created in a Databricks workspace are web-based interfaces that organize code, visualizations, and text in cells. Databricks notebooks can be easily attached to clusters and support collaborative development, code versioning, and parameterized workflows. Notebook execution can be operationalized and automated with Spark jobs or ADF.

- *Databricks File System (DBFS)*—Like HDFS, DBFS is a distributed file system mounted into a Databricks workspace and available on Databricks clusters. DBFS is an abstraction layer on top of cloud object storage. For example, Azure Databricks uses Azure Blob Storage to manage DBFS. Users can mount external object storage (e.g., Azure Blob Storage or ADLS) so that they can seamlessly access data without needing to reauthenticate. Files can also be persisted to DBFS so that data is not lost after a cluster is terminated.

- *Enterprise security*—Databricks workspaces incorporate several industry-standard security techniques such as access control, encryption at rest and in-transit, auditing, and single sign-on. Administrators can use access control lists (ACLs) to configure access permissions for workspace objects (e.g., folders, notebooks, experiments, and models), clusters, pools, jobs, and data tables.

- *Delta Lake*—Delta Lake is an open-source storage layer that guarantees ACID transactions for data stored in a data lake. Data is stored in Parquet format and Delta Lake uses a transaction log to manage schema enforcement and ACID compliancy. Developers can use Delta Lake as a unified layer for batch and stream processing activities. Delta Lake runs on top of existing cloud object storage infrastructure such as ADLS.

- *MLflow*—MLflow is an open-source Spark platform for managing the end-to-end machine learning model. Databricks workspaces provide a fully managed and hosted version of MLflow that can be used to track experiments, manage and deploy machine learning models, package models in a reusable form, store models in a well-defined registry, and serve models as REST endpoints for application usage.

Visit `https://databricks.com` to learn more about the Databricks platform.

The Databricks platform can be used on Azure with the Azure Databricks service. Azure Databricks is fully integrated with other Azure services such as Azure AD and has connectors for several popular Azure data stores such as ADLS, Azure SQL Database, Azure Cosmos DB, and Azure Synapse Analytics dedicated SQL pools. Because Azure Databricks natively integrates with Azure AD, administrators can use their existing identity infrastructure to enable fine-grained user permissions for Databricks objects such as notebooks, clusters, jobs, and data.

The platform architecture for Azure Databricks can be broken down into two fundamental layers: the control plane and the data plane.

- The *control plane* includes all services that are managed by the Azure Databricks cloud and not the cloud subscription of the organization that deployed the Azure Databricks workspace. This includes the web application, cluster manager, jobs, job scheduler, notebooks and notebook results, and the hive metastore used to persist metadata.

- The *data plane* is managed by a user's Azure subscription and is where data manipulated by Azure Databricks is stored. Clusters and data stores are included in the data plane.

Spark clusters deployed through Azure Databricks use Azure VMs as cluster nodes. As we will discuss in the section "Creating a Spark Cluster with Azure Databricks" later in this chapter, users can choose from several different VM types to serve different use cases.

Azure Databricks allows users to create two types of Spark clusters: *all-purpose* and *job*. All-purpose clusters can be used to analyze data collaboratively with interactive notebooks, while job clusters are used to run automated jobs for dedicated workloads. Job clusters are brought online when a job is started and terminated when the job is finished.

Azure Databricks Cost Structure

Azure Databricks workspaces can be deployed with one of three price tiers: standard, premium, or trial. The primary difference between the standard and premium price tiers is that role-based access control for workspace objects and Azure AD credential passthrough is only available with the premium price tier. The trial price tier is a 14-day free trial of the Azure Databricks premium price tier.

Pricing for Spark clusters created in Azure Databricks consists of two primary components: the cost of the driver and worker node VMs and the processing cost. Processing cost is measured by the number of *Databricks Units (DBUs)* consumed during cluster runtime. A DBU is a unit of processing capability per hour, billed on per-second usage. You can easily calculate the number of DBUs usage by multiplying the total number of cluster nodes by the number of hours the cluster was running. For example, a cluster with 1 driver node and 3 worker nodes that ran for a total of 2 hours consumed 8 DBUs (that is, 4 nodes × 2 cluster runtime hours).

While the Azure VM cost will remain the same regardless of which price tier the Azure Databricks workspace was deployed with, the DBU price will vary. Table 5.1 lists the DBU price differences for the standard and premium price tiers.

TABLE 5.1   Standard and premium tier DBU prices

Workload	Standard Tier DBU Price	Premium Tier DBU Price
All-Purpose Compute	$0.40 DBU/hour	$0.55 DBU/hour
Jobs Compute	$0.15 DBU/hour	$0.30 DBU/hour
Jobs Light Compute	$0.07 DBU/hour	$0.22 DBU/hour

DBUs can be pre-purchased for either one or three years at a discount rate. The purchase tiers and discounts for pre-purchased DBUs can be found at https://azure.microsoft.com/en-us/pricing/details/databricks.

Deploying an Azure Databricks Workspace

You can create an Azure Databricks workspace through any of the Azure deployment methods. The easiest way to get started is by creating a workspace through the Azure Portal with the following steps:

1. Log into portal.azure.com and search for *Azure Databricks* in the search bar at the top of the page. Click Azure Databricks to go to the Azure Databricks page in the Azure Portal.

2. Click Create to start choosing the configuration options for your Azure Databricks workspace.

3. The Create An Azure Databricks Workspace page includes five tabs to tailor the workspace configuration. Let's start by exploring the options in the Basics tab. Just as with other services, this tab requires you to choose an Azure subscription, a resource group, a name, and a region for the workspace. The final option on this tab requires you to choose a price tier. A completed example of this tab can be seen in Figure 5.5.

FIGURE 5.5   Create an Azure Databricks workspace: Basics tab.

4. The Networking tab gives users the ability to configure two optional network security settings: secure cluster connectivity (no public IP) and VNet injection.

- The secure cluster connectivity setting is a simple Yes/No radio dial. If you select Yes, your cluster nodes will not be allocated any public IP addresses and all ports on the cluster network will be closed. This is regardless of whether it's the Databricks managed VNet or a customer VNet configured through VNet injection. This makes network administration easier while also enhancing network security for Azure Databricks clusters.

- The VNet injection setting gives users the ability to use one of their VNets as the network cluster resources are associated with. This enables you to easily connect Azure Databricks to other Azure services in a more secure way using service end-points or private endpoints, connect to on-premises data sources with user-defined routes, and configure Azure Databricks to use a custom DNS. If you select Yes, you will be prompted to select a VNet and delegate two of the VNets' subnets to be exclusively used by Azure Databricks. The first subnet will be used as the host subnet, and the second will be used as the container subnet. The host subnet is the source of each cluster node's IP address, and the container subnet is the source of the IP address for the Databricks runtime container that is deployed on each cluster node. The host subnet is public by default, but if secure cluster connec-tivity is enabled, the host subnet will be private. The container subnet is private by default. Figure 5.6 is an example of the Networking tab with secure cluster con-nectivity and VNet injection enabled. The example subnet ranges have been left for security reasons. A subnet range of /26 is the smallest recommended subnet size for both subnets.

More information about security cluster connectivity and VNet injection can be found at https://docs.microsoft.com/en-us/azure/ databricks/security/secure-cluster-connectivity and https://docs.microsoft.com/en-us/azure/databricks/ administration-guide/cloud-configurations/azure/ vnet-inject.

FIGURE 5.6   Create an Azure Databricks workspace: Networking tab.

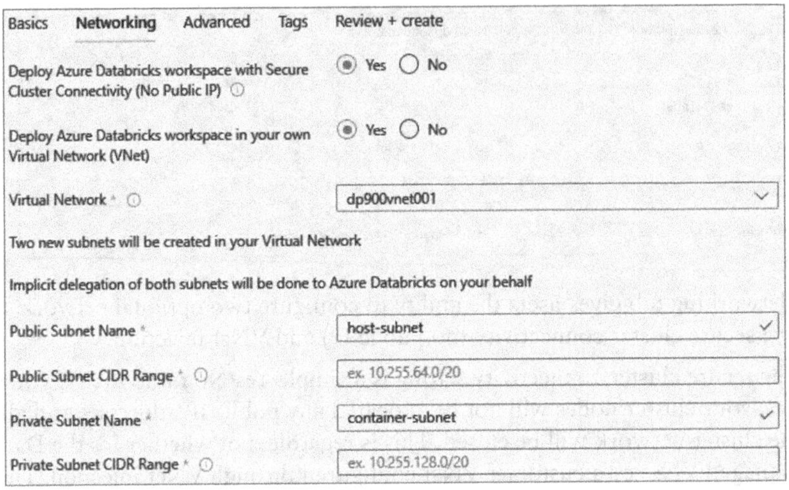

| Basics | **Networking** | Advanced | Tags | Review + create |

Deploy Azure Databricks workspace with Secure Cluster Connectivity (No Public IP) ⓘ   ◉ Yes ◯ No

Deploy Azure Databricks workspace in your own Virtual Network (VNet)   ◉ Yes ◯ No

Virtual Network * ⓘ   `dp900vnet001` ⌄

Two new subnets will be created in your Virtual Network

Implicit delegation of both subnets will be done to Azure Databricks on your behalf

Public Subnet Name *   `host-subnet` ✓

Public Subnet CIDR Range * ⓘ   `ex. 10.255.64.0/20`

Private Subnet Name *   `container-subnet` ✓

Private Subnet CIDR Range * ⓘ   `ex. 10.255.128.0/20`

5. The Advanced tab allows you to enable infrastructure encryption to data stored in DBFS. Keep in mind that Azure encrypts storage account data at rest by default, so this option adds a second layer of encryption to the storage account.

6. The Tags tab allows you to place tags on the resources deployed with Azure Databricks. Tags are used to categorize resources for cost management purposes.

7. Finally, the Review + Create tab allows you to review the configuration choices made during the design process. If you are satisfied with the choices made for Azure Databricks, click the Create button to begin deploying the workspace.

Once the Azure Databricks workspace is deployed, go back to the Azure Databricks page, and click on the newly created workspace. Click on the Launch Workspace button in the middle of the overview page to navigate to the workspace UI and start working within the Databricks ecosystem. Figure 5.7 is an example of what this button looks like.

FIGURE 5.7   Launch Workspace button

A new browser window will open after you click the Launch Workspace button, prompting you to sign in with your Azure AD credentials. Once you are signed in, you will be brought to the Azure Databricks web application where you can begin working with Databricks. The next section describes the key components of the web application.

Navigating the Azure Databricks Workspace UI

The home page for an Azure Databricks workspace serves as a location for users to start working with Databricks. Figure 5.8 is an example of the Azure Databricks web application home page.

FIGURE 5.8   Azure Databricks home page

As you can see in Figure 5.8, there are common task options such as creating a new notebook and importing data. There are also quick navigation links to recently worked on notebooks, Spark documentation, and helpful blog posts.

On the left side of the page is a toolbar with several buttons. The number of buttons in the toolbar varies based on which persona is chosen. Azure Databricks personas include Data Science & Engineering, Machine Learning, and SQL. You can change the persona by clicking the icon below the Databricks logo in the toolbar. Figure 5.9 illustrates this icon and the different options that can be selected from it.

For the purposes of this book and the DP-900 exam, we will only cover the Data Science & Engineering persona. Of the 13 buttons that are under the Data Science & Engineering persona icon, the first 8 buttons are the most relevant to building solutions in Azure Databricks, including the following:

- The Create button opens a pop-up window that allows you to create a new notebook or DBFS table. It also provides quick navigation to pages where you can create a new cluster or a new job.

FIGURE 5.9   Azure Databricks workspace personas

- The Workspace button opens a tab that contains a hierarchical view of the folders and files stored in the workspace. Administrators can use this view to set permissions and import/export folders or files. Usernames act as parent folders (typically Azure AD identities), and users associated with those usernames can add new items to them. Items that users can create from this view include notebooks, libraries, MLflow experiments, and additional subfolders. Figure 5.10 is an example of how the Workspace tab is constructed.

FIGURE 5.10   Azure Databricks Workspace tab

- The Repos button opens a tab that enables developers to create code repositories for their notebooks. Databricks automatically maintains a repository for every user with its native Databricks Repos service. Users can also create shared code repositories for collaborative development efforts. Databricks also supports other Git providers, including GitHub, Bitbucket, GitLab, and Azure DevOps, allowing developers to maintain their code repositories in a single service.

- The Recents button opens a tab that maintains the most recently worked on notebooks.

- The Search button opens a tab that allows users to search for different items in the workspace.

- The Data button opens a hierarchical view of the catalogs, databases, and tables created for each cluster. The metadata for these objects are maintained while a cluster is terminated, allowing developers to easily continue where they left off once the cluster is back online. Depending on how they are defined, tables can be either global or local. Global tables are accessible from any cluster, whereas local tables are only accessible from the cluster they were created from.

- The Clusters button opens the Compute page, displaying the clusters available to the user navigating the workspace. It includes tabs for all-purpose clusters, job clusters, pools, and cluster policies (see Figure 5.11). Users can perform administrative tasks on clusters from this page, such as changing the number and size of cluster nodes and modifying the autoscale setting and changing the inactivity period before clusters are automatically terminated.

FIGURE 5.11   Azure Databricks Compute page

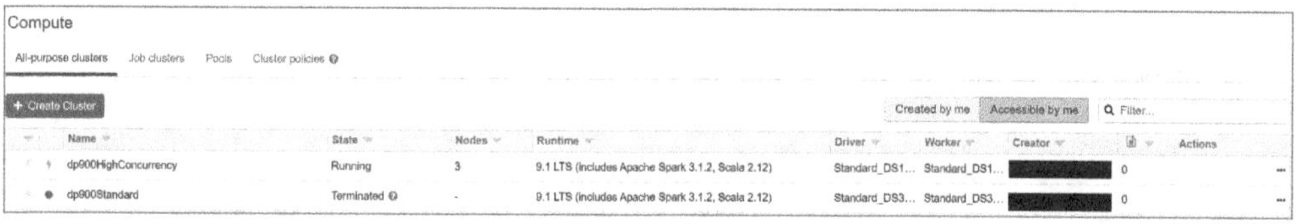

- The Jobs button opens a page that displays the Spark jobs available to the user navigating the workspace (see Figure 5.12). The Jobs page includes a button that allows users to create new jobs that will execute notebooks on a schedule.

FIGURE 5.12   Azure Databricks Jobs page

Jobs							
Create Job					Owned by me	Accessible by me	Q Filter
Name	**Job ID**	**Created by**	**Task**	**Cluster**	**Schedule**	**Last run**	**Actions**
DP900Job	66		Quickstart Notebook	8 workers: Standard_DS3_v2 9.1 LTS (includes Apache Spark 3.1.2, Scala 2...	At 01:00 AM (Amer...		▶ 🗑

Creating a Spark Cluster with Azure Databricks

Spark clusters can be configured and deployed by clicking on the Create Cluster button on the Compute page. Clicking this button will take you to the Create Cluster page, where you will be required to define the following settings (see Figure 5.13):

1. Enter a unique cluster name in the Cluster Name field.

2. Select a cluster mode from the Cluster Mode field. The options include:
   - *Standard*—Optimized for single-user clusters that run batch or stream processing jobs. This cluster mode supports SQL, Python, R, and Scala workloads.
   - *High Concurrency*—Optimized to run concurrent workloads for users performing interactive analysis. This cluster mode supports SQL, Python, and R workloads.
   - *Single Node*—This cluster mode runs a Spark application on a single compute node. It is recommended for single-user workloads that work with small data volumes.

FIGURE 5.13 Azure Databricks Create Cluster page

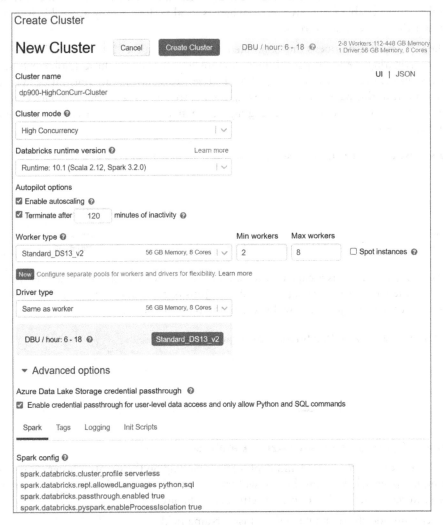

3. Select a Databricks runtime from the Databricks Runtime Version field. This field allows you to select from several Databricks runtimes, including current, older, and beta versions. You can also choose from several Databricks runtimes that are optimized for machine learning workloads.

4. The Autopilot Options field allows you to set two settings: autoscaling and auto-terminate. Selecting the Enable Autoscaling check box will configure the cluster to automatically scale between the minimum and maximum number of cluster nodes, based on the workload. You can also enable and set an inactivity threshold (in minutes) after which a cluster will automatically terminate.

5. Define the size and number of Azure VMs that will be used as cluster nodes in the Worker Type and Driver Type fields. There are several VM types and sizes to choose from, including those that are optimized for compute-heavy workloads, machine learning applications, and deep learning solutions that require GPUs. If autoscaling is enabled, you will also be able to choose a minimum and maximum number of worker nodes.

6. The Advanced Options section allows you to fine-tune your Spark cluster by altering various Spark configuration options, adding libraries or environment-specific settings with init scripts, and defining custom logging. This section also allows you to enable ADLS credential passthrough, which automatically passes the Azure AD credentials of a specific user (when using the Standard or Single Node cluster mode) or the current user (when using the High Concurrency cluster mode) to Databricks for authentication when interacting with an ADLS account.

7. Click Create Cluster at the top of the page to begin creating the cluster.

Creating a Notebook and Accessing Azure Storage

The first step to begin working with data is to create a new notebook. You can do this by clicking the Create button on the left-side toolbar and clicking *Notebook*. This will open a pop-up window that will prompt you to enter a name for the notebook, choose a primary language (Python, Scala, SQL, or R), and select a cluster to attach the notebook to. Once these options are set, click the Create button to create the notebook. You will be guided to the notebook once it is finished being created. Figure 5.14 illustrates how to create a new Python notebook from this window.

FIGURE 5.14   Azure Databricks Create Notebook page

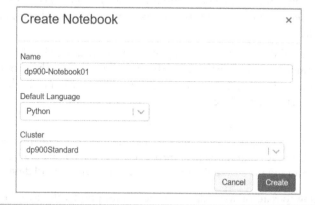

 Regardless of the primary notebook language, developers can set specific notebook cells to user other languages by using the magic % command followed by a language category. For example, if you would like to write a SQL command in a notebook whose primary language is Python, go to a new notebook cell and type **%SQL**. This will configure the cell to accept SQL commands.

The first cell in a notebook is typically used to import any libraries that will be needed to manipulate data or to establish a connection with an external data source. This section will focus on connecting to Azure Storage, more specifically ADLS. There are three ways to establish a connection to ADLS with Azure Databricks:

- Create a mount point in DBFS to the storage account or the desired folder with an access key, a SAS token, a service principal, or Azure AD credential passthrough.
- Access ADLS via a direct path with a service principal.
- Access ADLS directly with Azure AD credential passthrough.

Creating a service principal is out of scope for the DP-900 exam and will not be covered in this book. Refer to the following blog to learn how to create a service principal that can be used to establish a connection with ADLS: https://docs.microsoft.com/en-us/ azure/active-directory/develop/howto-create-service-principal-portal. For now, we will cover how to establish a connection by creating a mount point in DBFS with Azure AD credential passthrough.

To create a mount point in DBFS for an ADLS account, use the dbutils.fs.mount command in the first notebook cell. This command uses three parameters to define a mount point:

- A source parameter that takes the ADLS URI as an argument. If required, the URI can point to a specific subdirectory in ADLS.
- A mount_point parameter that sets the location (in DBFS) and name of the mount point.
- An extra_config parameter that accepts the authorization information required to access the external storage account. You can set a variable to the OAuth and Spark configuration settings for Azure AD credential passthrough and pass it in the extra_ config parameter to make the dbutils.fs.mount command reusable and more readable.

Once the mount point has been created, you can run the dbutils.fs.ls command with the mount point name as an argument to verify that you can view the subdirectories in the dp900-adls-container container. See Figure 5.15 for an illustration of both the dbutils .fs.mount and dbutils.fs.ls commands.

Remember that users who are establishing a connection to ADLS with Azure AD credential passthrough will need to have been assigned the Storage Blob Data Reader role at a minimum to read data.

Users attempting to read or write data via the mount point will have their credentials evaluated. Alternatively, to creating a mount point, users can access data directly from an ADLS account with Azure AD credential passthrough by passing the ADLS URI in a spark.read command. For example, the following PySpark code assumes that the cluster running the command has Azure AD credential passthrough enabled and the user running the command has the appropriate permissions to the products subdirectory of the dp900-adls-container container:

FIGURE 5.15 Creating a mount point with Azure AD credential passthrough

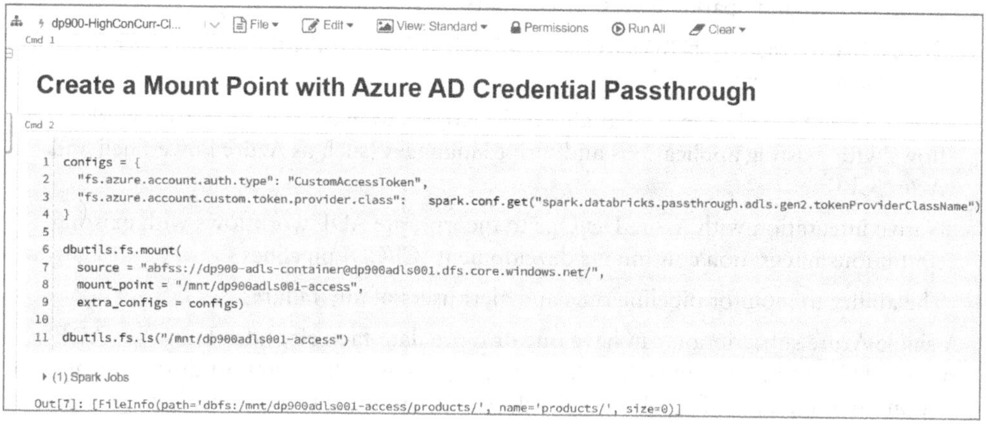

```
readCsvData = spark.read.csv("abfss://dp900-adls-
container@dp900adls001.dfs.core.windows.net/
products/products/*.csv")
```

While Azure AD credential passthrough is the most seamless method for accessing an
ADLS account, there are several scenarios where you will need to use one of the other two
access methods. For example, batch processing jobs that are orchestrated via ADF or an
Azure Databricks job will need to establish a connection to the ADLS path with a service
principal to guarantee a consistent connection. Refer to the following to learn more about
how to use the different access methods to establish a connection with ADLS: https://
cloudblogs.microsoft.com/industry-blog/en-gb/technetuk/2020/07/01/
securing-access-to-azure-data-lake-gen-2-from-azure-databricks.

Azure Data Factory

Azure Data Factory (ADF) is a managed cloud service that can be used to build complex
ETL, ELT, and data integration projects. With ADF, data engineers can create automated
workflows (known as pipelines) that orchestrate data movement and data transformation
activities. The following list includes several strengths that make ADF an integral part of any
data-driven solution built in Azure:

- The ability to author code-free data pipelines with a graphical user interface (GUI) to
  simplify pipeline development and maintenance
- Over 90 native connectors for on-premises and multi-cloud data sources that allow for
  hybrid data movement scenarios
- Integration with several compute services such as Azure HDInsight, Azure Databricks,
  and Azure SQL to orchestrate transformation activities such as Spark jobs and SQL
  stored procedures
- Control flow constructs like loops, conditional activities, variables, and parameters that
  control the customization of a pipeline run

- No-code/low-code data transformations with mapping data flows and Power Query that utilize on-demand Spark clusters for compute
- The ability to trigger pipelines to run at a fixed time, periodic time interval, or in response to an event
- SDK and REST API support that allows developers to manage data factory workflows with existing applications and script languages (such as Azure PowerShell and Azure CLI)
- Native integration with Azure DevOps to incorporate ADF workflows with existing continuous integration/continuous development (CI/CD) pipelines
- The ability to monitor pipeline runs and alert users of any failures

A single Azure subscription can have one or more data factories (also known as ADF instances). This is so users can isolate different projects as well as support different stages of a solution's development life cycle, like development, test, quality assurance, and production.

ADF instances are composed of the following core components:

- *Pipelines* are a logical grouping of activities that perform data transformation or data movement operations. For example, a pipeline can include a group of activities that move data from external data sources to ADLS followed by an Azure Databricks notebook activity to execute an Azure Databricks notebook that processes the data. Pipeline activities can be chained together to run sequentially, or they can operate independently in parallel.

- *Activities* represent a data transformation or data movement step in a pipeline. ADF supports the following three types of activities:

  - *Data movement activities*—These activities move data from one source to another. For example, a copy activity can be used to copy data from one data source to another.

  - *Data transformation activities*—These activities perform transformation operations on the data. Some data transformation activities include an Azure Databricks notebook, a Hive query running on an Azure HDInsight cluster, an Azure Function, and an ADF mapping data flow.

  - *Control activities*—These activities control the flow of an ADF pipeline. For example, ADF supports foreach, filter, if, switch, and until activities to control the flow of a pipeline. Developers can also use the Execute Pipeline control activity to run pipelines as a part of another pipeline.

- *Linked services* define the connection information that is needed for ADF to connect to external resources. ADF supports the following two types of linked services:

  - *Data store*—This linked service type is used to define the connection information for external data sources such as Azure SQL Database, Azure Blob Storage, and Azure Cosmos DB. The full list of supported data stores can be found at `https://docs.microsoft.com/en-us/azure/data-factory/copy-activity-overview#supported-data-stores-and-formats`.

- *Compute resources*—This linked service type is used to define the connection information for external compute resources such as Azure HDInsight, Azure Databricks, and Azure Functions. The full list of support external compute stores can be found at `https://docs.microsoft.com/en-us/azure/data-factory/transform-data#external-transformations`.

- *Datasets* use linked services to represent data structures within data stores, such as a relational database table or a set of files. For example, an Azure Blob Storage–linked service defines the connection information that ADF uses to connect to the Azure Blob Storage account. An Azure Blob Storage dataset can use that linked service to represent a blob container or a specific file within the storage account. Datasets can be used in activities as inputs or outputs.

- *Integration runtimes* provide the compute infrastructure where activities either run or get triggered from. While the location for an ADF instance is chosen when it is created, integration runtimes can be assigned a different location. This allows developers to run activities with compute infrastructure that is closer to where their data is stored. ADF supports the following three integration runtime types:

  - *Azure integration runtimes* can run data flow activities in Azure, copy activities between cloud data stores, and trigger Azure-based compute activities (such as Azure HDInsight Hive operations or Azure Databricks notebooks). The default *AutoResolveIntegrationRuntime* that is created with every ADF instance is an Azure integration runtime. Azure integration runtimes support both public and private connections when connecting to data stores and compute services. Private connections can be established by enabling a managed virtual network for the integration runtime.

  - *Self-hosted integration runtimes* are used to run data movement activities between cloud data stores and a data store in a private or on-premises network. This integration runtime type is also used to trigger compute activities that are hosted in on-premises or Azure virtual networks. Self-hosted integration runtimes require that a self-hosted integration runtime client application is installed on one or more machines that are associated with a private or on-premises network and connected to the self-hosted integration runtime in ADF. More information about creating and configuring a self-hosted integration runtime can be found at `https://docs.microsoft.com/en-us/azure/data-factory/create-self-hosted-integration-runtime?tabs=data-factory`.

  - *Azure-SSIS integration runtimes* are used to execute legacy SQL Server Integration Services (SSIS) packages in ADF. This allows users to lift-and-shift existing SSIS workloads to Azure without having to completely rebuild their control flows and data flows in ADF. When an Azure-SSIS integration runtime is configured, users can leverage it to power an Execute SSIS Package activity. This activity will run the deployed SSIS packages. More information about configuring an Azure-SSIS integration runtime can be found at `https://docs.microsoft.com/en-us/azure/data-factory/concepts-integration-runtime#azure-ssis-integration-runtime`.

Azure and Azure-SSIS integration runtimes package compute resources (CPU, memory, and network IO) as Data Integration Units (DIUs). Self-hosted integration runtimes leverage the compute resources that are allocated to the node the integration runtime is installed on. More information about DIUs can be found at https://docs.microsoft .com/en-us/azure/data-factory/copy-activity-performance-features#data-integration-units.

Now that we have established what the core components of ADF are, let's dive into how to create an ADF instance through the Azure Portal and how to navigate the Azure Data Factory Studio UI.

Deploying an ADF Instance

The following steps describe how to create a new Azure Data Factory instance through the Azure Portal:

1. Log into portal.azure.com and search for *Data factories* in the search bar at the top of the page. Click Data Factories to go to the Data factories page in the Azure Portal.

2. Click Create to start choosing the configuration options for your ADF instance.

3. The *Create Data Factory* page includes six tabs to tailor the workspace configuration. Let's start by exploring the options in the Basics tab. Just as with other services, this tab requires you to choose an Azure subscription, a resource group, a name, and a region for the instance. There is an option to choose an older ADF version, but it is recommended to use the most current version. Figure 5.16 is an example of a completed version of this tab.

FIGURE 5.16   Create an ADF Instance: Basics tab.

Basics	Git configuration	Networking	Advanced	Tags	Review + create

Project details

Select the subscription to manage deployed resources and costs. Use resource groups like folders to organize and manage all your resources.

Subscription * ⓘ	Microsoft Azure Internal Consumption ⌄
└─ Resource group * ⓘ	Wiley ⌄
	Create new

Instance details

Region * ⓘ	East US 2 ⌄
Name * ⓘ	dp900-dataFactory-01 ⌄
Version * ⓘ	V2 (Recommended) ⌄

4. The Git configuration tab allows you to integrate the ADF instance with an existing Azure DevOps or GitHub repository. ADF entities (such as pipelines, activities, linked services, and datasets) are managed behind the scenes as JSON objects, which can be integrated with existing CI/CD repositories. Click the Configure Git Later check box if you would like to configure a Git pipeline later or save your ADF entities to the data factory service (see Figure 5.17).

FIGURE 5.17   Create an ADF Instance: Git configuration tab.

Basics	**Git configuration**	Networking	Advanced	Tags	Review + create

Azure Data Factory allows you to configure a Git repository with either Azure DevOps or GitHub. Git is a version control system that allows for easier change tracking and collaboration.
Learn more about Git integration in Azure Data Factory

Configure Git later ⓘ   ☑

5. The Networking tab allows you to define the networking rules for the auto-resolve integration runtime as well as any self-hosted integration runtimes that you may provision.

6. The Advanced tab allows you to supply your own encryption key for blob and file data. Data is encrypted with Microsoft-managed keys by default, but can be changed to a customer-managed key as long as the key is stored in Azure Key Vault.

7. The Tags tab allows you to place tags on the ADF instance. Tags are used to categorize resources for cost management purposes.

8. Finally, the Review + Create tab allows you to review the configuration choices made during the design process. If you are satisfied with the choices made for the ADF instance, click the Create button to begin deploying the instance.

 While this section describes how to deploy an ADF instance through the Azure Portal, it is important to note that ADF instances can be created with several scripting and development tools such as Azure PowerShell, Azure CLI, the .NET and Python SDKs for Data Factory, and the REST API. They can also be defined within an Infrastructure as Code template and deployed alongside several other services in a CI/CD workflow.

Once the ADF instance is deployed, go back to the Data factories page and click on the newly created workspace. Click on the Open Azure Data Factory Studio button in the middle of the overview page to navigate to the Azure Data Factory Studio and start working within the ADF ecosystem. Figure 5.18 is an example of the overview page with the Open Azure Data Factory Studio button highlighted.

FIGURE 5.18   Azure Data Factory overview page

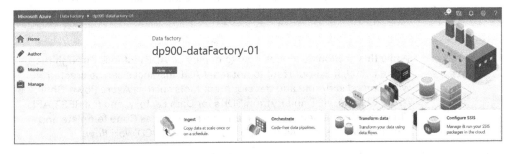

Clicking the Open Azure Data Factory Studio button will open a new browser window, using your Azure AD credentials to log into the Azure Data Factory Studio. Figure 5.19 highlights the main features of the Azure Data Factory Studio home page.

FIGURE 5.19   Azure Data Factory Studio home page

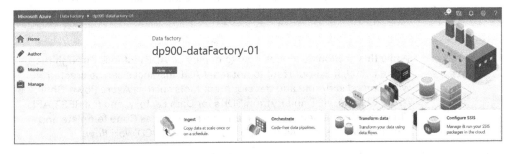

Navigating the Azure Data Factory Studio

The Azure Data Factory Studio is the central tool for authoring ADF resources. There are several buttons on the home page that enable users to start building new workflows very quickly:

- The Ingest button, which navigates users to the Copy Data tool. This tool allows developers to quickly begin copying data from one data store to another

- The Orchestrate button, which navigates users to the Author page where they can begin building pipelines

- The Transform Data button, which opens a new page where developers can build a mapping data flow

- The Configure SSIS button, which navigates users to a new page where they can configure a new Azure-SSIS integration runtime

On the left side of the page there is a toolbar with four buttons, including a Home button that will navigate users back to the Azure Data Factory Studio home page. The following list describes how you can use the other buttons in the toolbar to build and manage ADF resources:

- The Author button opens the Author page where users can build and manage pipelines, datasets, mapping data flows, and Power Query activities. Figure 5.20 is an example of the Author page with a single activity pipeline that copies data from Azure SQL Database to ADLS.

FIGURE 5.20   Azure Data Factory Studio Author page

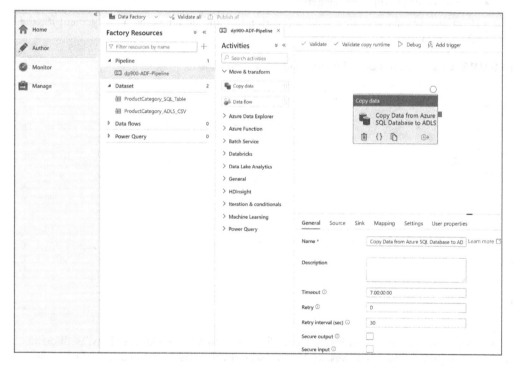

- The Monitor button opens a page that provides performance metrics for pipeline runs, trigger runs, and integration runtimes. Figure 5.21 is an example of the Monitor page.

FIGURE 5.21   Azure Data Factory Studio Monitor page

- The Manage button opens a page (see Figure 5.22) that allows you to perform several management tasks, such as those listed here:

  - Create or delete linked services.

  - Create or delete integration runtimes.

  - Link an Azure Purview account to catalog metadata and data lineage.

  - Connect the ADF instance to a Git repository.

  - Create or delete pipeline triggers.

  - Configure a customer managed encryption key and define access management for the ADF instance.

FIGURE 5.22   Azure Data Factory Studio Manage page

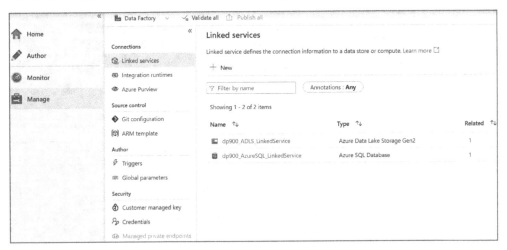

The following section, "Building an ADF Pipeline with a Copy Data Activity," will detail how to create the activity, datasets, and linked services that are associated with the pipeline in Figure 5.20 (shown earlier). More specifically, it will demonstrate how to use the copy activity to copy data from an Azure SQL Database to an ADLS account. The source database is restored from the publicly available AdventureWorksLT2019 database backup. If you would like to build this demo on your own, you can find the database backup at
`https://docs.microsoft.com/en-us/sql/samples/adventureworks-install-configure?view=sql-server-ver15&tabs=ssms#download-backup-files.`

Building an ADF Pipeline with a Copy Data Activity

The first step in creating an ADF pipeline through the Azure Data Factory Studio is to navigate to the Author page by clicking either the Author button on the left-side toolbar or the Orchestrate button on the home page. The left pane on the Author page contains a tree view named Factory Resources. From here, you can create or navigate through existing pipelines, datasets, mapping data flows, or Power Query activities by clicking the + button or the ellipsis (. . .) next to each menu item. Figure 5.23 illustrates how to create a blank pipeline by clicking the + button.

FIGURE 5.23   Creating a blank ADF pipeline

After you click Pipeline, a blank pipeline canvas will open with a new toolbar on the left side of the canvas that contains every activity that can be added to the pipeline. Any of these activities can be dragged from the Activities toolbar and dropped onto the central canvas to build out the pipeline. At the top of the canvas there are buttons to validate the pipeline for any errors, debug the pipeline, and add a trigger to the pipeline. On the right side of the canvas is the Properties tab where you can add a friendly name and a description for the pipeline. At the bottom of the canvas there are options to create new parameters and variables that can make pipeline runs more dynamic. Figure 5.24 illustrates each of these components with a friendly name added in the Properties tab.

FIGURE 5.24   The ADF Pipeline Creation page

To add a copy activity, expand the Move & Transform option in the Activities toolbar and drag the Copy Data activity to the canvas. The new activity will include six configuration tabs that will be located at the bottom of the tab. The first tab (General tab) allows you to provide a friendly name and description for the activity as well as time-out and retry settings. Figure 5.25 is an example of this view with a friendly name that describes the activity's functionality.

FIGURE 5.25 Copy Data Activity: General tab

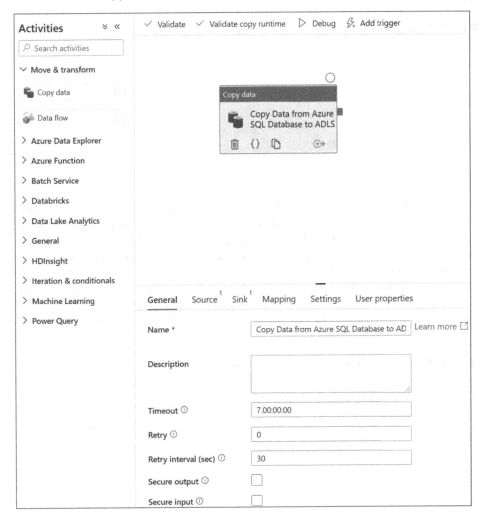

Out of the six copy activity configuration tabs, only two of them require user input: the Source tab and the Sink tab. These two tabs will define the source dataset and the destination, or sink, dataset that the data is being copied to. The Source tab allows you to choose an existing dataset or create a new one. If you click the + New button, a new page will open where you can choose from one of the available data source connectors (see Figure 5.26).

FIGURE 5.26   New Dataset page

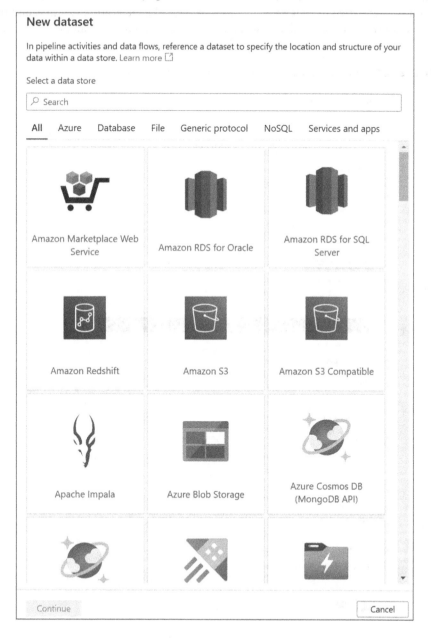

In the search bar, type **Azure SQL Database** and choose the Azure SQL Database connector. Click Continue at the bottom of the page to open the Set Properties page for the dataset. This page allows you to set a friendly name for the dataset and choose/create the linked service that will be used to connect to the data source. Expand the Linked Service drop-down menu and click + New to create a linked service for the database. This will open a new page where you can set a friendly name for the linked service, the integration runtime, and the connection information for the database. Figure 5.27 is a completed example of the New Linked Service page for an Azure SQL Database.

FIGURE 5.27   New linked service page: Azure SQL Database

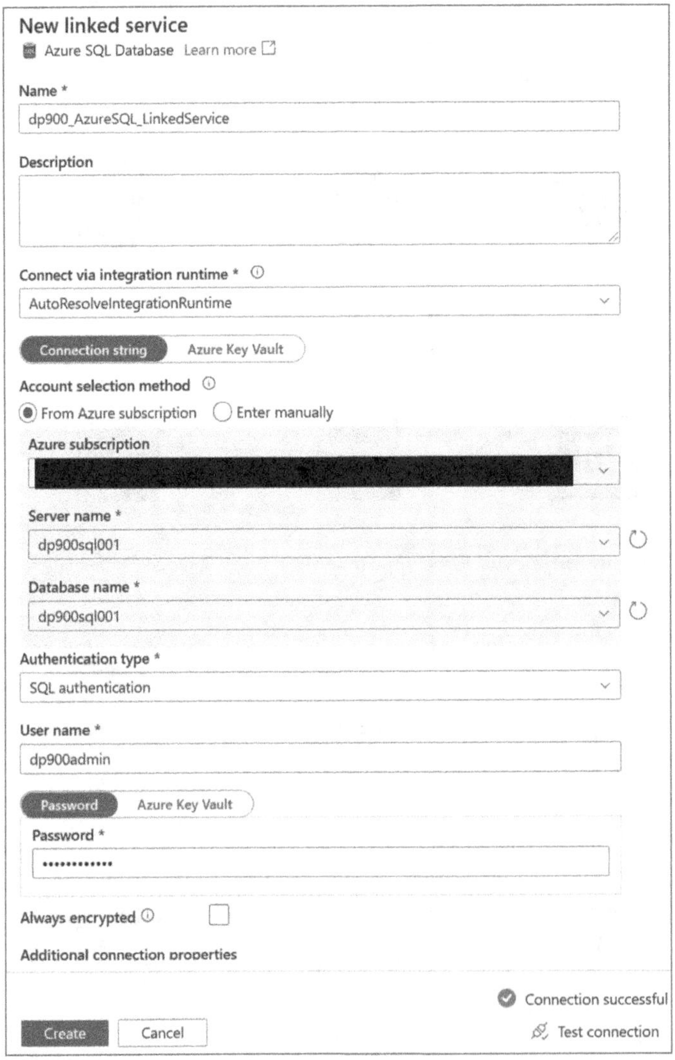

Once the settings for the linked service are properly set, click the Create button to create the linked service and to be redirected to the Set Properties page for the dataset. With the linked service defined, the next step will be to either choose the table or view that the dataset will represent or leave the Table Name setting blank. For the purposes of this example, we will choose the SalesLT.ProductCategory table. Figure 5.28 is a completed example of the Set properties page.

FIGURE 5.28   Set properties page for a new dataset: Azure SQL Database

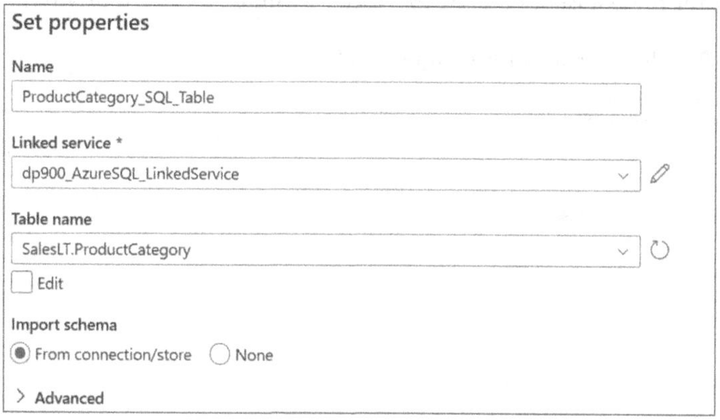

After you click OK at the bottom of the Set Properties page, the dataset will be created and added as the source dataset in the copy activity. Because the source dataset is an Azure SQL Database, the Source tab includes several optional settings that are tailored to relational databases. For example, if you did not choose a table or view in the dataset tab, you can use a query or a stored procedure to define the dataset. You can also parameterize this setting so that the dataset varies based on the value passed to the parameter. Figure 5.29 illustrates the list of options that are available in the Source tab for an Azure SQL Database.

FIGURE 5.29   Copy Data Activity: Source tab

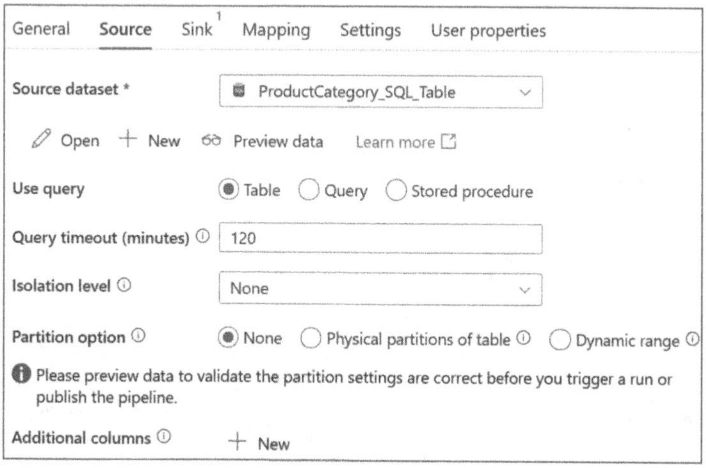

Now that the source dataset is set, the next step is to configure a sink dataset. The Sink tab provides the same options as the Source tab, along with the ability to create a new dataset. Because this example uses an ADLS account as the sink data store, choose the Azure Data Lake Storage Gen2 connector on the New Dataset page. After clicking Continue, you will be prompted to set a file format for the dataset. For this example, choose the Delimited-Text (CSV) option and click Continue.

As with the Azure SQL Database dataset, the Set Properties page allows you to set a friendly name for the dataset and choose/create the linked service that will be used to

FIGURE 5.30 New linked service page: ADLS

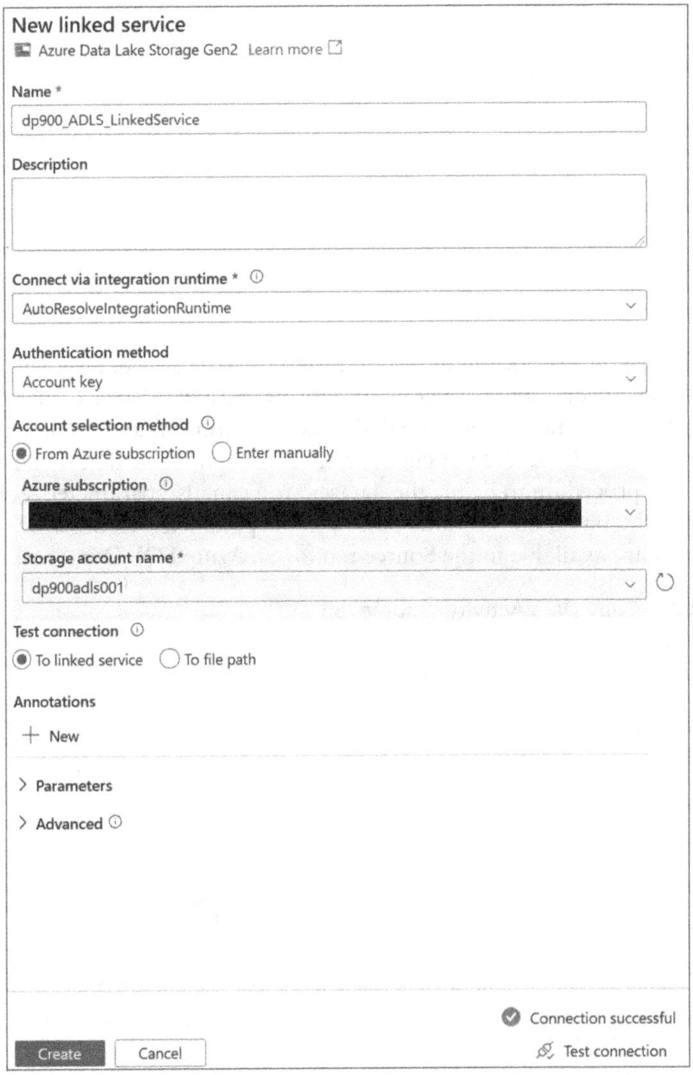

connect to the data source. The new linked service page for ADLS is also similar to the new linked service page for Azure SQL Database as it allows you to set a friendly name for the linked service, the integration runtime, and the connection information for the storage account (see Figure 5.30). Click the Create button to create the linked service and to be redirected to the Set Properties page for the dataset.

With the ADLS linked service defined, the Set Properties page allows you to either set a file path for the dataset or leave it blank. This example uses the `dp900-adls-container/ products/` file path for the sink dataset (see Figure 5.31).

FIGURE 5.31   Set properties page for a new dataset: ADLS

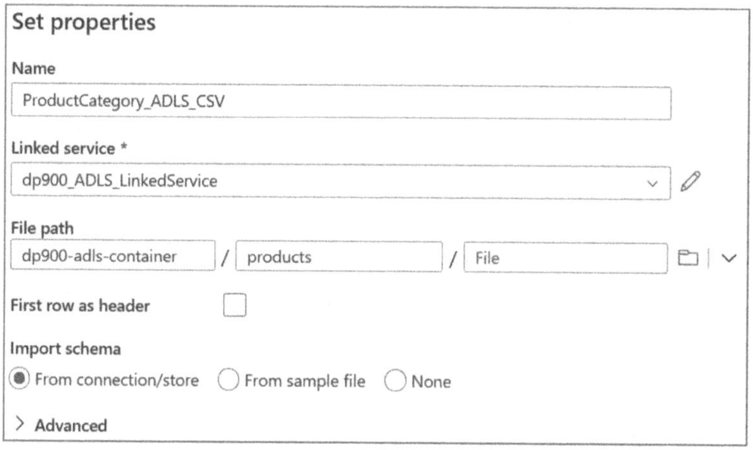

Set properties

Name

ProductCategory_ADLS_CSV

Linked service *

dp900_ADLS_LinkedService

File path

dp900-adls-container   /   products   /   File

First row as header   ☐

Import schema

◉ From connection/store   ○ From sample file   ○ None

> Advanced

After you click OK at the bottom of the Set Properties page, the dataset will be created and added as the sink dataset in the copy activity. Like the Azure SQL Database dataset, there are several additional settings in the Sink tab that will be relevant to the chosen dataset type. The Sink tab (and the Source tab) also allows you to open the dataset with the Open button (next to the Sink dataset setting). This button opens a new page that allows you to make several changes that are specific to the dataset type. Because the sink dataset is CSV data stored in ADLS, the list of settings that can be edited include how the data is compressed, the column and row delimiters for the data, how the data is encoded, and whether the first row should be treated as a header. You can also use this page to define a filename for the dataset. Figure 5.32 illustrates this page with all of the available dataset settings.

Once the dataset settings are properly configured, navigate back to the pipeline by clicking on the pipeline tab at the top of the page. Click on the Mapping tab to map the source dataset columns to the sink columns. This tab also allows you to set datatype settings, such as the date/time format, and whether to truncate data that is longer than what the column definition allows. Figure 5.33 is an example of the Mapping tab.

FIGURE 5.32 Using the Azure Data Factory Studio to edit a CSV dataset

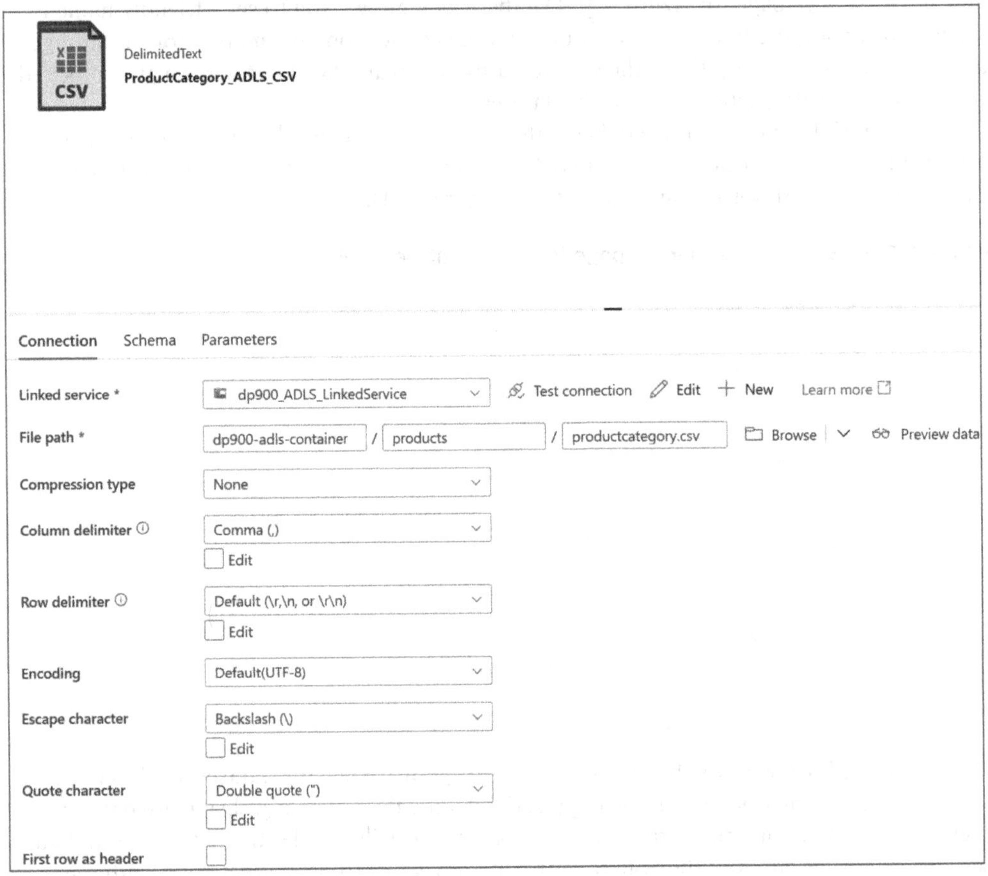

DelimitedText
ProductCategory_ADLS_CSV

Connection   Schema   Parameters

Linked service *	⬛ dp900_ADLS_LinkedService ▾ ⚡ Test connection ✏ Edit ＋ New Learn more ⧉
File path *	dp900-adls-container / products / productcategory.csv ▢ Browse ▾ 👁 Preview data
Compression type	None ▾
Column delimiter ⓘ	Comma (,) ▾ ☐ Edit
Row delimiter ⓘ	Default (\r,\n, or \r\n) ▾ ☐ Edit
Encoding	Default(UTF-8) ▾
Escape character	Backslash (\) ▾ ☐ Edit
Quote character	Double quote (") ▾ ☐ Edit
First row as header	☐

FIGURE 5.33 Copy Data Activity: Mapping tab

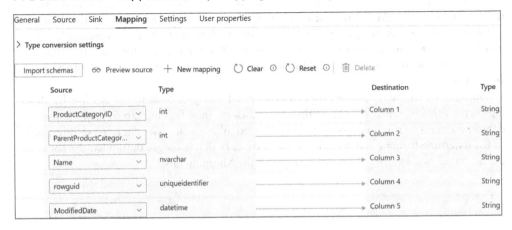

General   Source   Sink   **Mapping**   Settings   User properties

> Type conversion settings

Import schemas   👁 Preview source   ＋ New mapping   ⟳ Clear ⓘ ⟳ Reset ⓘ 🗑 Delete

Source	Type		Destination	Type
ProductCategoryID ▾	int	——————→	Column 1	String
ParentProductCategor... ▾	int	——————→	Column 2	String
Name ▾	nvarchar	——————→	Column 3	String
rowguid ▾	uniqueidentifier	——————→	Column 4	String
ModifiedDate ▾	datetime	——————→	Column 5	String

Navigate to the Settings tab after mapping the source and sink columns. This tab allows you to set how many DIUs you want allocated to the pipeline, or if you want the pipeline to automatically apply the optimal number of DIUs. You can also set the degree of parallelism that the copy activity will use if the volume of source dataset requires a scale-out solution.

The last tab in the copy activity Is the User Properties tab. This allows you to tag and monitor specific ADF resources, such as datasets.

Click the Publish All button at the top of the page to save the pipeline and the datasets. To run the pipeline or schedule the pipeline to run at a later time, click the Add Trigger button at the top of the canvas and choose either Trigger now to begin a pipeline run or New/Edit to create a scheduled or event-based trigger. Figure 5.34 illustrates where the Publish All and Add Trigger buttons are located. Once the pipeline is published, click the Trigger button to either run it right then and there or to create a schedule to run it at a later time.

FIGURE 5.34   Using the Publish all button to save the pipeline and datasets.

Real-Time Azure Data Processing Services

While the previously described set of services can be used in a variety of data processing tasks, it is important to note that there are other Azure data services that are used for niche data processing use cases. For example, Azure Stream Analytics and Azure Data Explorer are almost exclusively used in stream processing workflows. These services are out of scope for the DP-900 exam and will only be covered briefly in the following sections.

Azure Stream Analytics

Azure Stream Analytics is a PaaS stream processing engine that can be used to process high volumes of streaming data from multiple sources. Users can create Azure Stream Analytics jobs through the Azure Portal, Azure CLI, Azure PowerShell, or an Infrastructure as Code template like ARM. Jobs consist of three core components: one or more inputs, a query, and one or more outputs.

Inputs can include real-time message ingestion services like Azure Event Hubs and Azure IoT Hub as well as persistent data stores like Azure Blob Storage and Azure SQL Database. This enables developers to combine streaming data with historical data or with reference data for lookup operations.

Developers can use the Stream Analytics query language to filter, sort, aggregate, or join data from different sources. This language is a subset of standard T-SQL with additional functionality to apply computations over specific time windows. The language can also be extended with JavaScript and C# user-defined functions.

Jobs deliver processed information to one or more outputs. Azure Stream Analytics allows you to customize what happens based on the results of the data that was processed. Here are some common outputs:

- Services like Azure Event Hubs, Azure Service Bus, or Azure Functions to trigger alerts or custom workflows
- Power BI dashboards for real-time dashboarding
- Persistent data stores like Azure Blob Storage, ADLS, Azure SQL Database, or Azure Synapse Analytics dedicated SQL pools for long-term storage or batch processing

If you would like to learn more about Azure Stream Analytics, visit `https://docs`
`.microsoft.com/en-us/azure/stream-analytics/stream-analytics-introduction`.

Azure Data Explorer

Azure Data Explorer is a near real-time processing engine that analyzes structured, semi-structured, and unstructured data across time windows. It uses the Kusto Query Language (KQL) to analyze data and is capable of ingesting and analyzing petabytes of data. Typical use cases for Azure Data Explorer include interactively analyzing logs and conducting time series analytics on metric data from IoT sensors.

If you would like to learn more about Azure Data Explorer, visit `https://docs`
`.microsoft.com/en-us/azure/data-explorer/data-explorer-overview`.

End-to-End Analytics with Azure Synapse Analytics

Azure Synapse Analytics is an enterprise analytics system that integrates multiple services that serve analytical workloads in a single environment. Through the Azure Synapse workspace, users can leverage the following services to build a modern data warehouse solution:

- *Synapse Studio* is a unified environment where users can manage all components of the Azure Synapse Analytics ecosystem. The following tasks can be performed with Synapse Studio:
  - Build ETL and ELT workflows that can be automated to run at predetermined times or after specific events.
  - Configure and deploy dedicated SQL, Apache Spark, and Data Explorer pools.
  - Develop SQL, Spark, or KQL code to analyze data with SQL, Spark, or Data Explorer pools.
  - Monitor resource utilization, query performance, and user access across SQL, Spark, or Data Explorer pools.
  - Integrate with CI/CD and data catalog services such as Azure DevOps and Azure Purview.

- *Dedicated SQL pools* are analytical data stores that use a scale-out, massively parallel processing (MPP) architecture to effectively manage several petabytes of data. Storage and compute are decoupled, allowing users to easily scale compute power without having to move data. Azure Synapse workspaces can have one or more dedicated SQL pools.

- *Serverless SQL pool* is a serverless query service that allows analysts to use T-SQL to interactively query Azure Storage files. It does not have local storage or ingestion capabilities. Every Azure Synapse workspace comes with a serverless SQL pool endpoint that cannot be deleted. Azure Synapse workspaces only support a single serverless SQL pool (named "Built-in").

- *Apache Spark pools* are managed, open-source Apache Spark clusters in the Azure Synapse ecosystem. Users can set the number of compute nodes in a cluster, with an option to automatically scale clusters up and down based on the workload. Cluster nodes can be configured with predefined node sizes, ranging from *small* (4 vCores, 32 GB of memory) to *xxx large* (80 vCores, 504 GB of memory). With Synapse notebooks, data engineers can use an Apache Spark pool to analyze data with Python, SQL, R, Scala, Java, or .NET code. More information about Azure Synapse Analytics Apache Spark pools can be found at `https://docs.microsoft.com/en-us/azure/synapse-analytics/spark/apache-spark-pool-configurations`.

- *Synapse pipelines* are orchestration workflows that define a set of actions to perform on data. This service has the same functionality as ADF but is available through the Azure Synapse workspace, making it more ideal for users who want to manage their analytical data stores, data engineering activities, and orchestration pipelines from the same environment. The concepts covered previously in this chapter for ADF also apply to Azure Synapse pipelines.

- *Synapse Link* is a hybrid transactional and analytical processing (HTAP) tool that enables users to run near real-time analytical queries over transactional data. With Azure Synapse Link, users do not need to build complex ETL workflows that move data from a transactional data store to an analytical one. Instead, Synapse Link synchronizes data from transactional data stores like Azure Cosmos DB and Azure SQL Database with a column-oriented analytical data store that can be explored with the Azure Synapse Analytics serverless SQL pool or an Azure Synapse Analytics Apache Spark pool. More information about Azure Synapse Link can be found at `https://docs.microsoft.com/en-us/azure/cosmos-db/synapse-link`.

- *Data Explorer pools* are optimized for telemetry analytics. Azure Synapse data explorer automatically indexes free-text and semi-structured data that is found in telemetry data, such as logs and time series data. The concepts covered previously in this chapter for Azure Data Explorer also apply to Azure Synapse data explorer.

- *Power BI* is a reporting service that can be used to develop dashboards, reports, and datasets for self-service BI. Azure Synapse Analytics allows users to connect a Power BI workspace to an Azure Synapse Analytics workspace for a seamless development experience. This provides analysts with a single environment for analyzing data, developing insightful reports, and sharing the reports to various business users. Power BI workspaces will be described in further detail in Chapter 6, "Reporting with Power BI."

As you can see, Azure Synapse Analytics allows users to leverage several different technologies to build modern data warehouse solutions in the same environment. The following sections describe how to get started with Azure Synapse Analytics, including how to deploy a workspace and how to navigate Synapse Studio. Afterward, we will examine the two categories of SQL pools, dedicated and serverless, and when to use them.

Deploying an Azure Synapse Analytics Workspace

Like any service in Azure, an Azure Synapse workspace can be deployed though the Azure Portal, Azure PowerShell, or Azure CLI or via an Infrastructure as Code template. The following steps describe how to deploy a new Azure Synapse workspace through the Azure Portal:

1. Log into `portal.azure.com` and search for *Azure Synapse Analytics* in the search bar at the top of the page. Click Azure Synapse Analytics to go to the Azure Synapse Analytics page in the Azure Portal.

2. Click Create to start choosing the configuration options for your Azure Synapse workspace.

The Create Synapse Workspace page includes five tabs to tailor the workspace configuration. Let's start by exploring the options in the Basics tab. Just as with other services, this tab requires you to choose an Azure subscription, a resource group, a name, and a region for the workspace. You will also need to associate an ADLS account to the workspace. Azure Synapse will use this ADLS account as the primary storage account and the container to store workspace data. A completed example of this tab can be seen in Figure 5.35.

The Security tab requires you to create an administrator account for the serverless and dedicated SQL pools managed by the workspace. You can also use this tab to enable network access to the associated ADLS account with the workspace managed identity and enable double encryption with a key that you provide. Figure 5.36 is an example of the security tab.

The Networking tab allows you to choose whether to set up a dedicated, managed VNet for Azure Synapse Analytics. You can also enable access for all IP addresses through this tab or choose to grant access to specific IP addresses after the workspace is deployed.

The Tags tab allows you to place tags on the resources deployed with Azure Synapse Analytics. Tags are used to categorize resources for cost management purposes.

Finally, the Review + Create tab allows you to review the configuration choices made during the design process. If you are satisfied with the choices made for the Azure Synapse Analytics workspace, click the Create button to begin deploying the workspace.

Once the Azure Synapse Analytics workspace is deployed, go back to the Azure Synapse Analytics page, and click on the newly created workspace. From the Azure Portal, administrators can set Azure AD authentication, create new analytics pools (dedicated SQL, Apache Spark, and Data Explorer pools), configure network settings, and monitor performance.

FIGURE 5.35   Create an Azure Synapse Analytics workspace: Basics tab.

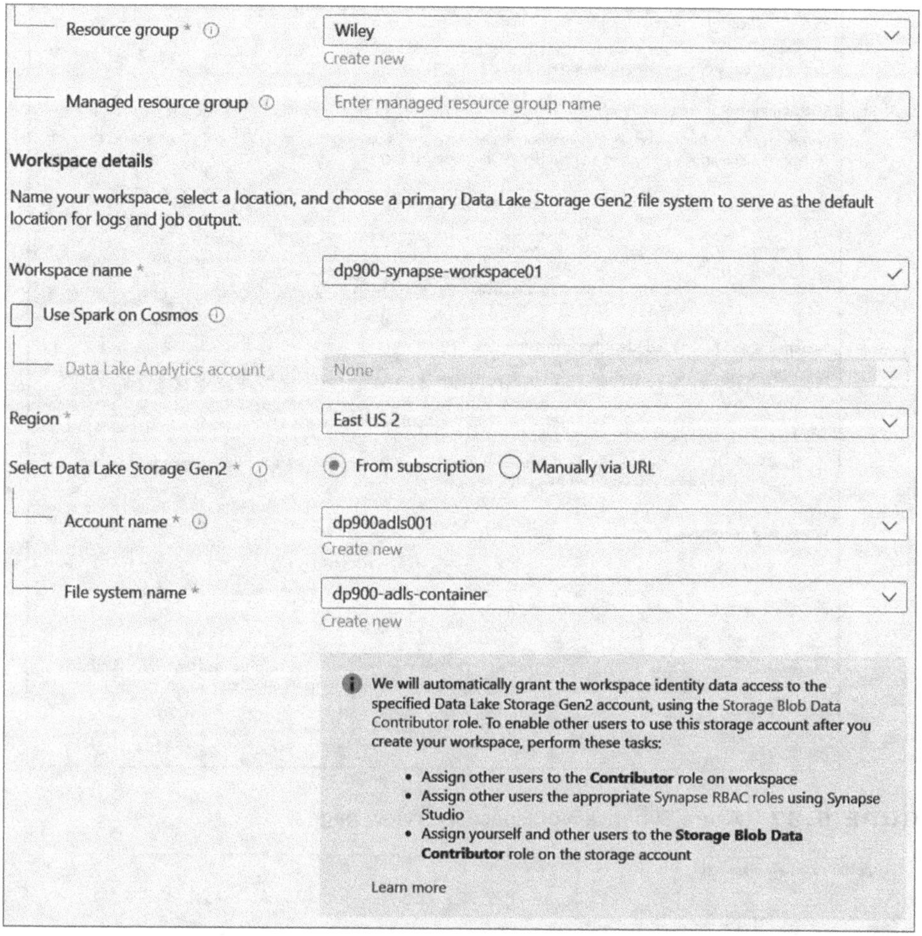

Click on the Open Synapse Studio button in the middle of the overview page to navigate to Synapse Studio UI. Figure 5.37 is an example of the workspace overview page with the Open Synapse Studio button highlighted.

A new browser window will open after you click the Open Synapse Studio button, using your Azure AD credentials to log in to the workspace. Figure 5.38 is an example of the Synapse Studio home page.

Navigating the Synapse Studio UI

Synapse Studio is the central tool for administering and managing all aspects of the Azure Synapse Analytics ecosystem that enable users to start building new Azure Synapse Analytics workflows very quickly, including an Ingest button to begin moving data, an Explore and

FIGURE 5.36   Create an Azure Synapse Analytics workspace: Security tab.

| Basics | **Security** | Networking | Tags | Review + create |

Configure security options for your workspace.

SQL administrator credentials

Provide credentials that can be used for administrator access to the workspace's SQL pools. If you don't provide a password, one will be automatically generated. You can change the password later.

SQL Server admin login * ⓘ   `dp900-synapse-sql-admin`   ✓

SQL Password ⓘ   `•••••••••••••`   ✓

Confirm password   `•••••••••••••`   ✓

System assigned managed identity permission

Select to grant the workspace network access to the Data Lake Storage Gen2 account using the workspace system identity.
Learn more

☐ Allow network access to Data Lake Storage Gen2 account. ⓘ

ⓘ The selected Data Lake Storage Gen2 account does not restrict network access using any network access rules, or you selected a storage account manually via URL under Basics tab. Learn more

Workspace encryption

⚠ Double encryption configuration cannot be changed after opting into using a customer-managed key at the time of workspace creation.

Choose to encrypt all data at rest in the workspace with a key managed by you (customer-managed key). This will provide double encryption with encryption at the infrastructure layer that uses platform-managed keys. Learn more

Double encryption using a customer-   ○ Enable ⦿ Disable
managed key

FIGURE 5.37   Azure Synapse workspace overview page

FIGURE 5.38   Synapse Studio home page

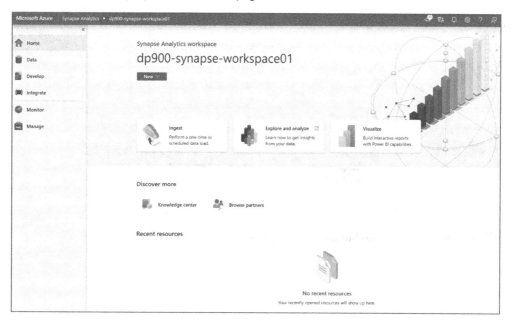

Analyze button to navigate users to Azure Synapse Analytics tutorials, and a Visualize button to connect to a Power BI workspace. On the left side of the page there is a toolbar with six buttons, including a Home button that will navigate users back to Synapse Studio home page. The following list describes how you can use the other buttons in the toolbar to build a modern data warehouse:

- The Data button opens a page that allows you to link external and integrated data-sets to the Azure Synapse Analytics workspace. It has two tabs, the Workspace tab to organize any analytics pools that are associated with the workspace and the Linked tab to organize external storage such as ADLS or Azure Blob Storage. From this page, you can create new blank script pages or predefined scripts that run bulk load operations or select the top 100 rows of a table. Figure 5.39 is an example of the Workspace tab and the external data source options that can be added by clicking the + button.

- The Develop button opens a page that organizes all SQL scripts, KQL scripts, notebooks, mapping data flows, and Apache Spark jobs. Figure 5.40 is an example of the Develop page and the various objects that can be added by clicking the + button.

- The Integrate button opens a page that allows you to build data orchestration and movement pipelines. You can create new pipelines or use the Copy Data tool to perform a one-time or scheduled data load from over 90 data sources. The functionality is similar to ADF, with some additional activities that are specific to Azure Synapse Analytics. Figure 5.41 is an example of the Integrate page and the Synapse-specific activities.

FIGURE 5.39   Synapse Studio Data page

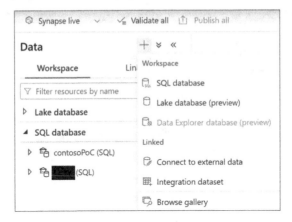

FIGURE 5.40   Synapse Studio Develop page

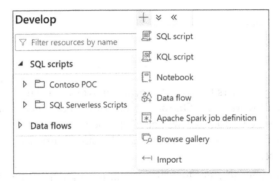

- The Monitor button opens a page that provides a comprehensive view of the performance details and statuses for the different analytics pools, activities, and integration pipelines. Figure 5.42 is an example of the Monitor page with a focus on the SQL pools section.

- The Manage button opens the Manage page (see Figure 5.43). This page allows you to perform several management tasks:

  - Create, configure, pause, and resume analytics pools.

  - Create and delete linked services. Linked services provide the connection information to external data sources that are used in Synapse pipelines.

  - Link an Azure Purview account to catalog metadata and data lineage.

- Create and delete triggers. A trigger is used to automate when a Synapse pipeline is executed. Types of triggers include schedules, storage events, and custom events.
- Create and delete integration runtimes. An integration runtime (IR) is the compute infrastructure used by Synapse pipelines.
- Manage all security access controls and credentials.
- Link a Git repository to your Azure Synapse Analytics workspace.

FIGURE 5.41   Synapse Studio Integrate page

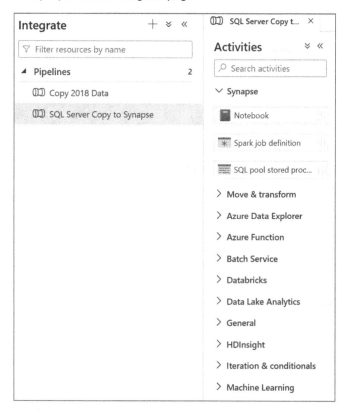

Dedicated SQL Pools

Azure Synapse Analytics dedicated SQL pools (formerly Azure SQL Data Warehouse) are relational data stores that use a massively parallel processing (MPP) architecture to optimally manage large datasets. This can be done by separating compute and storage by using a SQL engine to perform computations and Azure Storage to store the data. Dedicated SQL pools use a relational schema, typically a star schema, to serve data to users as tables or views for business intelligence applications.

FIGURE 5.42 Synapse Studio Monitor page

FIGURE 5.43 Synapse Studio Manage page

In a modern data warehouse architecture, a dedicated SQL pool is at the end of an ETL/ELT process, serving as the *single source of truth* for data analysts and BI applications. Tables using columnstore compression can store an unlimited amount of data, making dedicated SQL pools the ideal destination data store for big data workloads that process several terabytes or even petabytes worth of data. Additional processes can also extract subsets of data that represent specific business segments from a dedicated SQL pool and load them into Azure Analysis Services or Power BI OLAP models for self-service BI scenarios.

As mentioned in Chapter 2, dedicated SQL pools shard data into 60 distributions across one or more compute nodes depending on the dedicated SQL pool's service level objective (SLO). Tables can be defined with one of three distribution patterns to optimize how data is sharded throughout the distributions. The following list is a quick reminder of the three distribution patterns and when to use each one:

- *Hash distribution* uses a hash function to deterministically assign each row to a distribution. When defining a table with this distribution type, one of the columns is designated as the distribution column. This distribution type offers the most optimal query performance for joins and aggregations on large tables. For this reason, large fact tables are typically defined as hash distributed tables. However, keep in mind that the values of a column designated as the distribution column cannot be updated. The column must also have a high number of unique values and a low number of null values. Poorly chosen distribution columns can lead to unacceptable query response times that cannot be resolved without re-creating the table. Use round robin distribution instead of hash distribution if there are no suitable distribution columns for a large fact table.

- *Round robin distribution* evenly and randomly distributes rows across all 60 distributions. Staging tables and fact tables without a good distribution column candidate are typically defined as round robin tables.

- *Replicated tables* cache a full copy of a table on the first distribution of each compute node. This removes the need to shuffle data when querying data from multiple distributions. However, replicated tables can require extra storage, making them impractical for large tables or tables that are frequently written to. For this reason, only small tables (less than 2 GB) or tables that store static data (such as reference data) are defined as replicated tables.

Keep in mind that distribution columns in different tables that are used in join operations must be of the same data type to take advantage of hash distribution benefits and eliminate extraneous data shuffling operations.

Along with classic relational database features such as partitioning, row-store indexes, and statistics, dedicated SQL pools include several features that optimize the performance of analytical queries that aggregate large numbers of rows. These features are especially useful for querying historical data from fact tables, which can quickly become very large. Some of the most important features are as follows:

- *Clustered columnstore indexes (CCIs)* physically organize tables into a columnstore format. With a columnstore format, rows of data are compressed into *rowgroups*, optimizing how large tables are stored (up to 10X data compression versus uncompressed data) and the processing time for queries that perform table scans (up to 10X times the query performance over traditional row-oriented indexes). This is ideal for data warehouses, especially for large fact tables that are subject to analytical queries that scan large amounts of data.

CCIs will not compress data into columnstore format until there are more than 1 million rows per table, or more than 1 million rows per distribution in the case of a dedicated SQL pool. Since a dedicated SQL pool has 60 distributions, a columnstore index will not be beneficial until a table has more than 60 million rows. For this reason, columnstore indexes may not be the most optimal solution for tables with less than 60 million rows. Partitioning data will also increase the number of rows a table needs to benefit from a columnstore index. More information can be found at https://docs.microsoft.com/en-us/azure/synapse-analytics/sql/best-practices-dedicated-sql-pool#optimize-clustered-columnstore-tables.

- *Materialized views* are virtual tables created from a SELECT statement and presented to users as logical tables. Like a standard view, a materialized view abstracts the complexity of the underlying SELECT statement from users so that there is no need to rewrite the statement. Unlike a standard view, materialized views precompute, store, and maintain data in a dedicated SQL pool just like a table. Because recomputation is not needed each time a materialized view is used, queries running against a materialized view are much faster than a standard view. Materialized views improve the performance of complex queries with several joins and aggregations while simplifying query maintenance. The query optimizer in a dedicated SQL pool can also use a materialized view to improve a query's execution plan without the query needing to make a direct reference to the materialized view. Queries used to build a materialized view must include an aggregation in its definition.

- *Result set caching* improves query performance by automatically caching query results in a dedicated SQL pool user database for later use. This allows subsequent runs of the query to get results directly from the cache instead of recomputing the results. Result set caching can be enabled for a database by running the following T-SQL command:

```
ALTER DATABASE dp900dedicatedSQLpool
SET RESULT_SET_CACHING ON;
```

Unlike OLTP database engines like Azure SQL Database, dedicated SQL pools are not suitable for transactional workloads, which are characterized by frequent, small write operations and queries that interact with only a few rows of data (such as a query with a WHERE clause that performs a seek operation to a specific set of rows). Instead, it is best used for bulk write operations and queries that perform aggregations over large amounts of data.

Dedicated SQL pools are optimized for large workloads that are larger than 1 TB. However, there are scenarios where the data warehouse size will be less than 1 TB. For smaller workloads, Azure SQL Database should be considered. Azure SQL Database can provide similar performance while being more cost-efficient in these scenarios.

In addition to Synapse Studio, dedicated SQL pools support several management tasks and tools that are commonly used by other Microsoft SQL offerings (such as SQL Server and Azure SQL Database). SQL developers can connect to a dedicated SQL pool with Azure Data Studio or SQL Server Management Studio (SSMS). Database administrators can also leverage security postures that are common to Azure SQL, such as the following:

- Network isolation with an Azure VNet or an IP firewall

- Access management with SQL authentication and Azure AD

- Data encryption and obfuscation with TDE and TLS, Always Encrypted, row-level encryption, column-level encryption, and dynamic data masking

- Security management with the SQL Vulnerability Assessment and Advanced Threat Protection services

More information about the different security components available for Azure SQL can be found in Chapter 2.

Deploying and Scaling a Dedicated SQL Pool

In addition to the methods described previously in this book for deploying Azure resources, users can deploy a new dedicated SQL pool through Synapse Studio with the following steps:

1. Click on the Manage button on the left-side toolbar in Synapse Studio and click on SQL pools. Click + New to begin creating a new dedicated SQL pool. You can see an example of the SQL pools page in Figure 5.43 (shown earlier).

2. The New dedicated SQL pool page includes four tabs to tailor the workspace configuration. Let's explore the options in the four tabs.

   - The Basics tab requires that you set a name and an initial performance level (SLO) for the dedicated SQL pool. The performance level can be set by dragging the scale to the left or to the right. Figure 5.44 is a completed example of the Basics tab.

FIGURE 5.44   New dedicated SQL pool: Basics tab

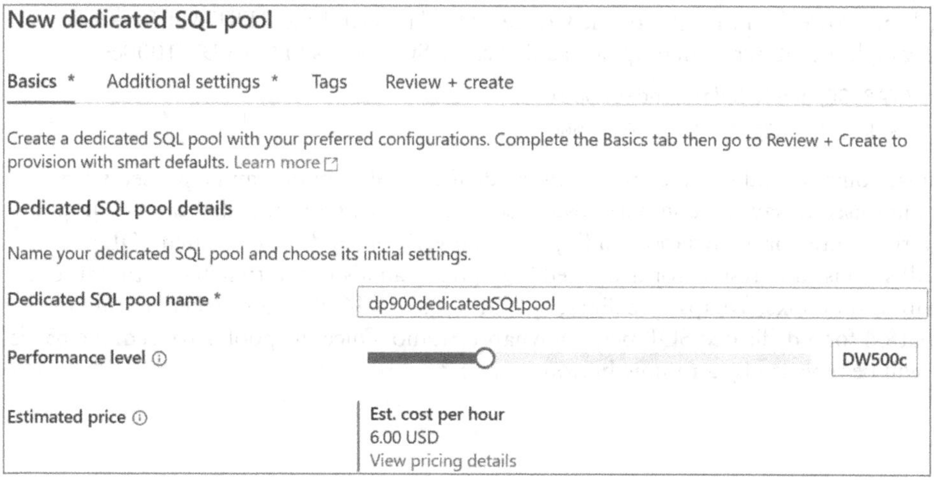

New dedicated SQL pool

Basics *   Additional settings *   Tags   Review + create

Create a dedicated SQL pool with your preferred configurations. Complete the Basics tab then go to Review + Create to provision with smart defaults. Learn more

Dedicated SQL pool details

Name your dedicated SQL pool and choose its initial settings.

Dedicated SQL pool name *   dp900dedicatedSQLpool

Performance level ⓘ   DW500c

Estimated price ⓘ   Est. cost per hour
                           6.00 USD
                           View pricing details

- The Additional settings tab allows you to set the initial state of the dedicated SQL pool, including whether to start with a blank database or from a database backup. Figure 5.45 is a completed example of the Additional settings tab.

FIGURE 5.45 New dedicated SQL pool: Additional settings tab

New dedicated SQL pool

Basics *   **Additional settings ***   Tags   Review + create

Customize additional configuration parameters including collation.

Data source

Start with a blank dedicated SQL pool or restore from a backup to populate your new dedicated SQL pool.

Use existing data *   (None)   Backup   Restore point

SQL pool collation

Collation defines the rules that sort and compare data, and cannot be changed after SQL compute creation. The default collation is SQL_Latin1_General_CP1_CI_AS. Learn more ⬚

Collation * ⓘ   SQL_Latin1_General_CP1_CI_AS

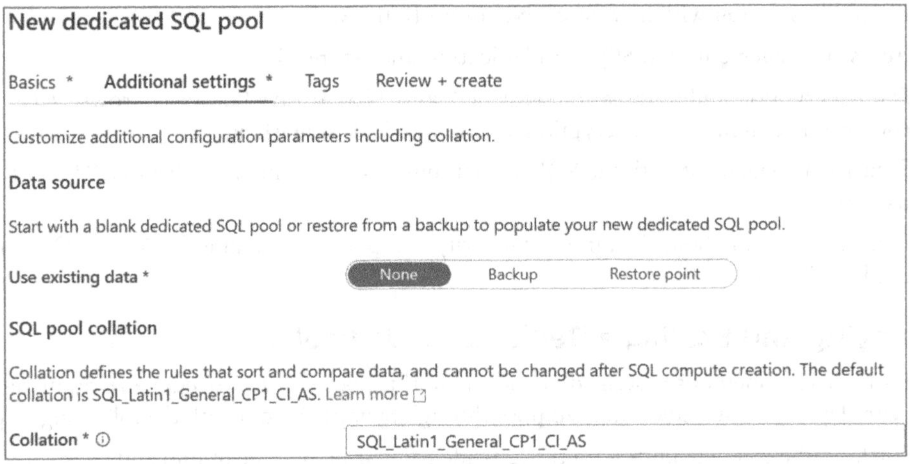

- The Tags tab allows you to place a tag on the dedicated SQL pool. Tags are used to categorize resources for cost management purposes.

- Finally, the Review + Create tab allows you to review the configuration choices made during the design process.

3. If you are satisfied with the choices made for the dedicated SQL pool, click the Create button on the Review + Create tab to begin deploying the new dedicated SQL pool.

As with any PaaS database in Azure, the SLO of a dedicated SQL pool can be easily scaled up or down to meet different workload needs. This can be done through the Azure Portal, Azure PowerShell, T-SQL, or the Create or Update Database REST API. The following is a sample T-SQL script that updates a dedicated SQL pool's SLO to DW1000c:

```
ALTER DATABASE dp900dedicatedSQLpool
MODIFY (SERVICE_OBJECTIVE = 'DW1000C');
```

Because compute and storage are separated, dedicated SQL pools can be paused when they are not used to save on compute costs. Users can pause and restart dedicated SQL pools through the Azure Portal, Synapse Studio, Azure PowerShell, and the dedicated SQL pool REST APIs. Pause and restart for dedicated SQL pools can also be automated with Azure Automation runbooks, Synapse pipelines, or ADF. Figure 5.46 illustrates where to find the pause button for a dedicated SQL pool in Synapse Studio. Once the pool is paused, the pause button will be replaced by a resume button.

FIGURE 5.46   Pausing a dedicated SQL pool

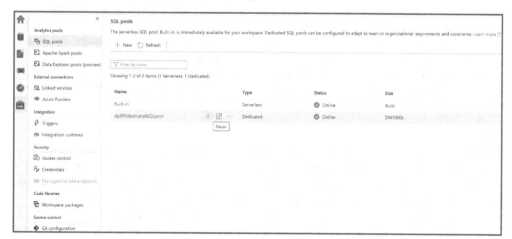

Data Loading Methods for Dedicated SQL Pools

Traditional relational databases that use a symmetric multiprocessing (SMP) design such as SQL Server or Azure SQL Database use an ETL process for data loading. Distributed platforms that use a MPP design like Azure Synapse Analytics dedicated SQL pools can process and store large amounts of data at-scale, allowing them to leverage ELT patterns to load and transform data within the same service. This allows developers to perform data processing activities without having to rely on additional services for data transformation prior to loading.

Dedicated SQL pools support several data loading methods, including popular SQL Server methods such as the bulk copy program (bcp) utility and the SQLBulkCopy API. However, the fastest and most scalable way to load data is through the PolyBase or the COPY statement. In fact, when loading data into a dedicated SQL pool via ADF, it is recommended to set the Copy Method setting in the Sink tab to use either the Copy command or PolyBase. With PolyBase and the COPY statement, developers can access data stored in Azure Blob storage or ADLS via T-SQL commands.

Generally, both of these data loading options are best when used to load data into staging tables. Staging tables are usually defined as heap tables, or tables without any indexes. The lack of an index means that data will not be reordered as it is being written, allowing the data to be written very quickly. Staging tables can be predefined before the external table is created with a normal CREATE TABLE command or created after the external table is established with a CREATE TABLE AS SELECT (CTAS) statement. More information about the CTAS statement can be found in the section "PolyBase" later in this chapter.

Once data is loaded into the staging tables, developers can use different techniques to update production tables with the staging data. Some techniques include using the MERGE statement to insert, update, or delete data in the production table based on differences in the staging table or replacing a section of the production table with the updated staging table through a process called partition switching. More information about partition switching can be found at https://docs.microsoft.com/en-us/azure/synapse-analytics/ sql-data-warehouse/sql-data-warehouse-tables-partition#partition- switching. New production tables that are based off of the staging table, but use a different distribution method and index design, can be created with a CTAS operation.

While the COPY statement offers the best performance and most flexibility for loading data, it is still important to understand how to use PolyBase to load data into a dedicated SQL pool. The following sections describe how to use PolyBase and the COPY statement to load data from Azure Storage into a dedicated SQL pool.

PolyBase

PolyBase is a data virtualization technology that enables dedicated SQL pools to query Azure Storage data while allowing the data to stay in its original location and format. PolyBase uses *external tables* to shape and access Azure Storage data. External tables overlay a schema on top of the data so that it can be easily queried with T-SQL commands.

Defining external tables involves specifying the data source, the format of files in Azure Storage, and the table definition. These can be defined with the following T-SQL commands:

- CREATE EXTERNAL DATA SOURCE

- CREATE EXTERNAL FILE FORMAT

- CREATE EXTERNAL TABLE

External data sources are used to establish a connection with an Azure storage account, such as one that supports Azure Blob Storage or ADLS. The CREATE EXTERNAL DATA SOURCE command that is used to create an external data source requires the following arguments:

- LOCATION—This provides the connectivity protocol and path to the data source, such as abfss://dp900-adls-container@dp900adls001.dfs.core.windows.net/.

- CREDENTIAL—This specifies the database-scoped credential used to authenticate to the external data source. This argument is only required if the storage object does not allow anonymous access. Storage account access keys, service principals, and managed identities are the only support authentication mechanisms for Azure Storage. Developers can create a database-scoped credential with the CREATE DATABASE SCOPED CREDENTIAL T-SQL command.

- TYPE=HADOOP—This specifies the external data source type that is being configured. It is required when the external data source is ADLS and Azure Blob Storage.

The following example creates an ADLS external data source that uses an access key to authenticate to the storage account:

```
/* The following creates a database master key that is used to encrypt
the credential secret created in the CREATE DATABASE SCOPED CREDENTIAL step. */

CREATE MASTER KEY ENCRYPTION BY PASSWORD = '<password>';

/* Use the following command to create the database-scoped
```

```
credential with the storage account key. */

CREATE DATABASE SCOPED CREDENTIAL dp900StorageCredential
WITH
    IDENTITY = 'dp900adls001' -- This is the storage account name.
    SECRET = '<storage_account_access_key>'

CREATE EXTERNAL DATA SOURCE dp900_ADLS_Ext_Source
WITH
(
  LOCATION = 'abfss://dp900-adls-container@dp900adls001.dfs.core.windows.net/',
  CREDENTIAL = dp900StorageCredential,
  TYPE = HADOOP
);
```

The next step in using PolyBase is to define the file format of the data stored in the external data source. External file formats created for Azure Synapse Analytics SQL pools (both dedicated and serverless SQL pools) support delimited text (such as CSV or TSV) and Parquet file formats. The CREATE EXTERNAL FILE FORMAT command accepts a required FORMAT_TYPE argument that defines the file format and several optional arguments such as how the data is compressed. Several of these optional arguments apply only to delimited text files, including:

- FIELD_TERMINATOR—This specifies what character in a delimited text file marks the end of each field (column). The default field terminator is the pipe character (|).

- STRING_TERMINATOR—This specifies the field terminator for words or string data in a delimited text file. The default string terminator is an empty string ("").

- FIRST_ROW—This specifies the row number that is read first by all files.

- DATE_FORMAT—This specifies a specific format for date and time data in a delimited text file.

The following example creates an external file format for CSV files:

```
CREATE EXTERNAL FILE FORMAT dp900_CSV_File_Format
WITH
(
    FORMAT_TYPE = DELIMITEDTEXT,
    FIELD_TERMINATOR = ',',
    STRING_TERMINATOR = '"'
);
```

Now that the external data source and external file format is defined, we can finally create the external table. The CREATE EXTERNAL TABLE command allows developers to define column names and data types for external data. It also accepts arguments for the external data source and the external file format. It also enables developers to specify the folder or the file path and filename for the data in the external data source with the optional LOCATION argument.

The CREATE EXTERNAL TABLE command also allows developers to specify reject parameters that will determine how PolyBase handles dirty records. This information is stored as metadata when the external table is created and is used when a SELECT statement is issued against the table to determine the number or percentage of rows that can be rejected before the query fails. The query will return partial results until the reject threshold is exceeded, after which the query will fail with the appropriate error message. The following arguments can be used to set the reject threshold:

- REJECT_TYPE—Clarifies if the REJECT_VALUE option is specified as a literal value or a percentage. When *value* is chosen, a query issued against the external table will fail when the number of rejected rows exceeds the defined value. When *percentage* is chosen, a query issued against the external table will fail when the percentage of rejected rows exceeds the defined threshold.

- REJECT_VALUE—This specifies the value or the percentage of rows that can be rejected before the query fails. When *value* is chosen, the argument must be an integer between 0 and 2,147,483,647. When *percentage* is chosen, the argument must be a decimal value between 0 and 100.

- REJECT_SAMPLE_VALUE—This determines the number of rows to attempt to retrieve before PolyBase recalculates the percentage of rejected rows. It is only available when *percentage* is chosen for the REJECT_TYPE and must be an integer between 0 and 2,147,483,647.

The following example creates an external table for the SalesLT.ProductCategory CSV file that was created in ADLS by the ADF copy activity described previously in this chapter:

```
CREATE EXTERNAL TABLE [dbo].[ProductCategory_External]
(
    ProductID INT,
    ProductSubcategoryID INT,
    ProductName VARCHAR(50)
)
WITH
(
    LOCATION = '/products/productcategory.csv',
    DATA_SOURCE = dp900_ADLS_Ext_Source,
    FILE_FORMAT = dp900_CSV_File_Format,
    REJECT_TYPE = VALUE,
    REJECT_VALUE = 0
);
```

With the external table defined, developers can issue queries against the data without having to move the data from Azure Storage to the dedicated SQL pool. If they would like to create a copy of the data in the dedicated SQL pool, then they can do so with a CTAS statement. CTAS statements allow developers to create new tables based on the output of a SELECT statement. In a dedicated SQL pool, developers can define the distribution method and index design within the context of a CTAS statement. The following example uses a CTAS to create a dedicated SQL pool staging table based on the previously created external table:

```
CREATE TABLE [dbo].[ProductCategory_Staging]
WITH (DISTRIBUTION = ROUND_ROBIN)
AS SELECT * FROM [dbo].[ProductCategory_External]
```

Once the data is stored in the staging table, data engineers can perform transformations with native T-SQL queries that leverage the built-in distributed query processing capabilities of the dedicated SQL pool. Transformed data can then be moved from the staging table to a production table through a variety of methods, such as a MERGE statement, partition switching, or with an INSERT INTO SELECT statement. New production tables can also be created with a CTAS statement where the SELECT statement retrieves data from the staging table.

COPY Statement

The COPY statement is a T-SQL construct that provides the most flexibility and best performance for parallel data ingestion into an Azure Synapse Analytics dedicated SQL pool. It provides several data loading feature enhancements over PolyBase:

- Allow lower privileged users to load data without needing to grant them CONTROL permissions on the data warehouse.

- Execute a single T-SQL statement without having to create any additional objects, (i.e., external file formats, external data sources, and external tables).

- Parse and load CSV files with a more extensive list of field, string, and row delimiters.

- Access data with a finer permission model without exposing storage account access keys using a shared access signature (SAS).

- Specify a custom row terminator for CSV files.

- Use SQL Server Date formats for CSV files.

- Leverage automatic schema discovery to simplify the process of defining and mapping source data into target tables.

- Use the automatic table creation argument to automatically create the target table. This works alongside the automatic schema discovery feature.

The COPY command uses several arguments to determine how to ingest data:

- FILE_TYPE—This specifies the format of the external data. Supported file formats include CSV, Parquet, and ORC.

- CREDENTIAL—This specifies the identity mechanism used to access the Azure storage account.

- MAXERRORS—This optional argument specifies the maximum number of reject rows allowed before the COPY statement is cancelled. If not specified, the default value for this argument will be 0.

- COMPRESSION—This optional argument specifies the data compression method for the data.

- FIELDQUOTE—This argument applies to CSV files and specifies the character that will be used as the quote character in the file. If not specified, the quote character (") will be used as the default value for this argument.

- FIELDTERMINATOR—This argument applies to CSV files and specifies the field terminator that will be used in the CSV file. If not specified, the comma character (,) will be used as the default value for this argument.

- ROWTERMINATOR—This argument applies to CSV files and specifies the row terminator that will be used in the CSV file. By default, the row terminator is \r\n.

- FIRSTROW—This argument applies to CSV files and specifies the row number that is read first in all files by the COPY statement.

- DATEFORMAT—This argument applies to CSV files and specifies the date format of the date mapping using SQL Server date formats. Supported date formats include *mdy, dmy, ymd, ydm, myd,* and *dym.*

- ENCODING—This argument applies to CSV files and specifies the data encoding standard for the files. The default for this argument is UTF8, but it can be changed to UTF16 depending on the encoding standard used by the files loaded by the COPY statement.

- IDENTITY_INSERT—This argument is specific to values that map to an identity column in the target table. If the argument is set to *off* (this is the default), then the values are verified but not imported. If the argument is set to *on,* then the values will be imported into the identity column.

- AUTO_CREATE_TABLE—This argument specifies if the table could be automatically created by working alongside the automatic schema discovery feature.

A more extensive list of the arguments that can be used with the COPY statement can be found at https://docs.microsoft.com/en-us/sql/t-sql/statements/copy-into-transact-sql?view=azure-sqldw-latest&preserve-view=true#syntax.

The following example uses the COPY statement to load the SalesLT.ProductCategory CSV file from ADLS into the [dbo].[ProductCategory_Staging] dedicated SQL pool table. It assumes that the table has already been created and is empty.

```
COPY INTO [dbo].[ProductCategory_Staging]
FROM 'https://dp900adls001.dfs.core.windows.net/
dp900-adls-container/products/productcategory.csv'
```

```
WITH (
    FILE_TYPE = 'CSV',
    CREDENTIAL = (IDENTITY='Shared Access Signature', SECRET = '<SAS_TOKEN>'),
    FIELDQUOTE = '"',
    FIELDTERMINATOR = ',',
    ROWTERMINATOR = '0X0A'
)
```

With this command, developers can quickly load data from ADLS into a dedicated SQL pool staging table and perform any computations required before moving the staging data into a production table.

Serverless SQL Pools

Azure Synapse Analytics serverless SQL pool is a serverless query service that enables users to analyze files in Azure Storage with T-SQL queries. Every workspace comes with a serverless SQL endpoint (named "Built-in") that data analysts and developers can use to quickly begin querying data in a variety of different formats, including Parquet, CSV, and JSON. Additionally, serverless SQL pools can be used to query Azure Cosmos DB with Azure Synapse Link and Spark tables that are created with Azure Synapse Analytics Apache Spark pools.

Typical use cases for serverless SQL pools are as follows:

- Basic discovery and exploratory analysis with SQL queries. Analysts can use the OPENROWSET function in the FROM clause of a SELECT statement to access data in several different formats (Parquet, CSV, JSON, and Delta) from Azure Storage without having to persist the connection information in a separate object.

- Creating a logical data warehouse to provide a relational schema on top of raw data in Azure Storage without moving or creating a second copy of the data. Logical data warehouses in serverless SQL pools are complete with familiar relational database constructs such as databases, tables, and views.

- Streamlining data transformation activities with T-SQL and loading the transformed data back into Azure Storage or into a persistent relational data store (such as a dedicated SQL pool or Azure SQL Database). Transformed data can also be served directly to BI tools like Power BI.

Logical data warehouses that are built with serverless SQL pools use similar data virtualization techniques as those that are used with dedicated SQL pools, including external data sources to connect to storage accounts, external file formats that define the format of the data in Azure Storage, and external tables that define a schema for your external data sources. The primary difference is that external data sources are native to synapse SQL pools and do not require (or support) the TYPE=HADOOP argument. More information about using these constructs to create a logical data warehouse with a serverless SQL pool can be found at https://docs.microsoft.com/en-us/azure/synapse-analytics/sql/tutorial-logical-data-warehouse.

Just like dedicated SQL pools, serverless SQL pools support several management tasks and tools that are common to the Microsoft suite of SQL offerings. Developers can choose to run ad hoc queries against a serverless SQL pool endpoint from Synapse Studio or via common client tools like Azure Data Studio and SQL Server Management Studio (SSMS). Furthermore, database administrators can manage authentication and authorization with SQL authentication and Azure AD.

While serverless and dedicated SQL pools both leverage distributed processing architectures that are designed to manage large datasets, when to use one or the other depends on use case requirements and the acceptable cost-to-performance threshold. Serverless SQL pools use a pay-per-query cost model, only charging users for the amount of data processed by each query. This cost model provides a cheap alternative to dedicated SQL pools for quickly analyzing data with ad hoc queries. However, because storage is not local to the serverless SQL pool and compute is automatically scaled, queries tend to run slower (a factor of seconds or minutes) than queries executed against a dedicated SQL pool. For this reason, dedicated SQL pools are a better option for workloads that require optimized and consistent performance requirements.

Exploratory Analysis with Serverless SQL Pools

Synapse Studio makes it easy to start analyzing data with the serverless SQL pool by creating a new SQL script. To do this, click on the Develop button on the left-side toolbar and click on the + icon. Select *SQL script* to open a new SQL script window. Within the script window, you can write SQL scripts that use the serverless SQL pool or one of the dedicated SQL pools associated with the workspace. The properties pane on the right side of the script window allows you to rename the script and add a description that explains the functionality of the script. You can also save scripts in Synapse Studio or to an associated Git repository by clicking Publish All at the top of the script window. Figure 5.47 illustrates the layout of the SQL script window.

FIGURE 5.47   Synapse Studio SQL script window

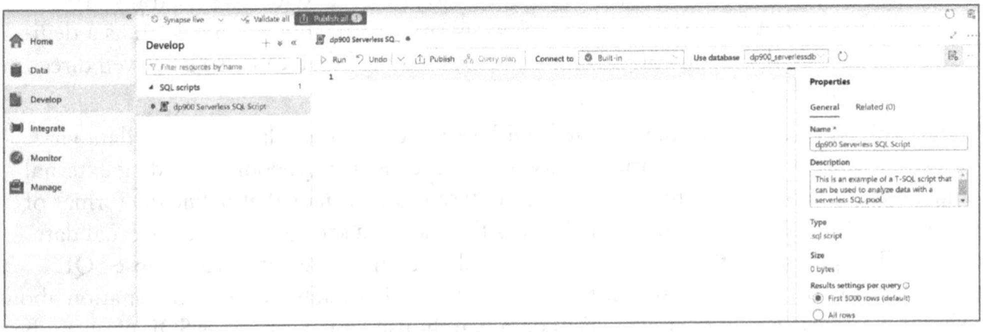

The ribbon at the top of the SQL script window includes several options for running a script, viewing a query's execution plan (exclusive to dedicated SQL pools), connecting to a SQL pool, and setting the database context. To execute queries with the serverless SQL pool endpoint, make sure the "Built-in" SQL pool is chosen in the Connect To drop-down menu (see Figure 5.48).

FIGURE 5.48   Choosing the Built-in SQL pool

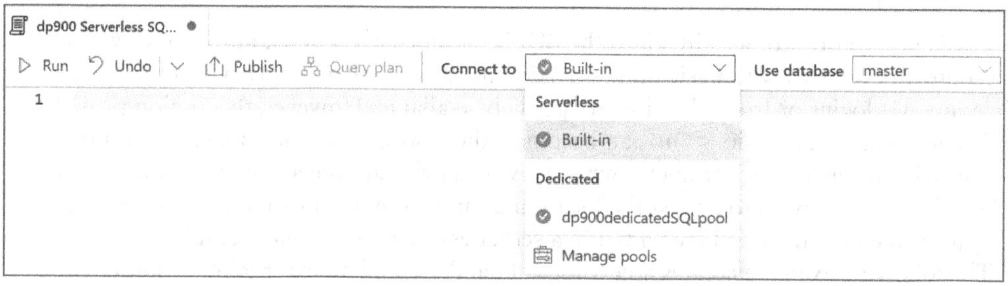

Before going over how to run queries in Synapse Studio, let's briefly discuss the basic structure of a serverless SQL pool query. Serverless SQL pool queries that perform exploratory analysis rely heavily on the OPENROWSET function to read data from external storage devices. For example, the following query uses the OPENROWSET function to retrieve the first 100 entries of the publicly available New York City yellow taxicab dataset.

```
SELECT TOP 100 * FROM
    OPENROWSET(
        BULK 'https://azureopendatastorage.blob.core.windows.net/
nyctlc/yellow/puYear=*/puMonth=*/*.parquet',
        FORMAT='PARQUET'
    ) AS [nyc]
```

The BULK parameter specifies the location of the data while FORMAT specifies the file format of the data being read. The URL location used by the query also uses wildcards (*) to read all of the Parquet files in all of the year and month folders.

This query also uses the column metadata in the Parquet files to infer the column names and data types of the result set. Queries can also automatically infer the column names of data from CSV files if there is a header row. However, there are times where you will want to explicitly define a schema to have more control of the data. Explicitly defining a schema also allows you to specify what columns you want to read from the files. You can define a schema for your data by adding a WITH clause with the column names and data types at the close of the OPENROWSET command. The following example uses the WITH clause to explicitly return three columns from the New York City yellow taxicab dataset.

```
SELECT TOP 100 * FROM
    OPENROWSET(
        BULK 'https://azureopendatastorage.blob.core.windows.net/
```

```
nyctlc/yellow/puYear=*/puMonth=*/*.parquet',
     FORMAT='PARQUET'
  ) WITH (
       tpepPickupDateTime DATETIME2,
       passengerCount INT,
       tripDistance FLOAT
  ) AS [nyc]
```

Passing the entire storage URL into the BULK parameter is a quick and easy way to read the content of the files with basic authentication methods such as Azure AD authentication for Azure AD logins or from files that are publicly available. However, this option provides limited authentication options and can become tedious as it forces developers to add the storage URL to the BULK parameter when they query the storage account. A more repeatable and secure option is to persist the location as an external data source and the access credential as an external scoped credential in a serverless SQL pool logical database.

The following example creates a new logical database and an external data source that references the location of the New York City yellow taxicab dataset. You can then pass the external data source name to the optional DATA_SOURCE parameter in the OPENROWSET command. This allows you to alter the argument passed to the BULK parameter to only the folder path that needs to be queried.

```
CREATE DATABASE dp900_serverlessdb;

USE dp900_serverlessdb
GO;
CREATE EXTERNAL DATA SOURCE nyc_yellowcab
WITH
(
    location = 'https://azureopendatastorage.blob.core.windows.net/
nyctlc/yellow/'
);

SELECT TOP 100 * FROM
    OPENROWSET(
        BULK 'puYear=*/puMonth=*/*.parquet',
        DATA_SOURCE='nyc_yellowcab',
        FORMAT='PARQUET'
    ) WITH (
        tpepPickupDateTime DATETIME2,
        passengerCount INT,
        tripDistance FLOAT
    ) AS [nyc]
```

This script can be executed in the Synapse Studio SQL script window by clicking the Run button at the top of the window. Figure 5.49 shows the SQL script window and the results from the executed script.

FIGURE 5.49   Executing Serverless SQL Pool Queries in Synapse Studio

More information about how to use OPENROWSET to query external data with a serverless SQL pool can be found at https://docs.microsoft.com/en-us/azure/synapse-analytics/sql/develop-openrowset.

Summary

This chapter started by discussing different types of data workflows. Transactional systems, also known as online transaction processing (OLTP) systems, capture business transactions such as sales in a point-of-sale system. They are optimized to handle write-heavy workloads, often handling millions of transactions a day. Analytical systems differ from transactional systems in that they are optimized for read-heavy operations. Data is gathered from several source systems and consolidated in one or a few data stores that users can use for reports, ad hoc analysis, and data science projects.

Analytical systems can process data in batches or as a continuous stream of data. Batch processing involves processing large amounts of data at predetermined periods of time or after a specified event. Stream processing ingests and transforms data in real time as it is generated. Modern data architectures like the Lambda architecture make it easy to use both batch and stream processing in the same solution.

There are several services offered through Azure that data engineers can use when building a modern data warehouse solution. Azure HDInsight is a PaaS resource that can be used to build data processing pipelines with several popular open-source frameworks such as Apache Hadoop, Apache Spark, Apache Kafka, Apache HBase, Apache Interactive Query, and Apache Storm. Azure Databricks is another PaaS resource that provides a unified platform for data engineers building data processing pipelines with Databricks Spark. Databricks Spark is a highly optimized version of Apache Spark, making it the most ideal service for most Spark applications.

Azure HDInsight, Azure Databricks, and several other data movement and data transformation activities can be orchestrated with Azure Data Factory (ADF). ADF enables data engineers to build data engineering pipelines with the Azure Data Factory Studio, a drag-and-drop, low-code/no-code development environment. Developers can author data movement and data transformation activities to run in parallel or chain them together so that they run sequentially. Because ADF is a PaaS offering, compute infrastructure is abstracted from the user in the form of an integration runtime. However, users can choose to use their own compute infrastructure by installing a self-hosted integration runtime on a virtual machine. This allows users to leverage data sources that are located in on-premises and private networks.

Organizations that want to use a single platform to achieve end-to-end analytics can do so with Azure Synapse Analytics. With Azure Synapse Analytics, users can use the Synapse Studio to manage all aspects of the data processing life cycle. Developers can author low-code/no-code data integration pipelines to move and transform data, leverage the serverless SQL pool to explore operational and object data stores with T-SQL without moving the data, build scale-out data engineering solutions with Apache Spark pools, and store report-ready data in relational tables that are optimized to serve analytical queries with a dedicated SQL pool.

Exam Essentials

Describe the difference between transactional and analytical workloads. Transactional systems are used to capture the business transactions that support the day-to-day operations of a business, while analytical systems turn transactional data and other data sources into information that is used to make decisions. Remember that transactional data is highly normalized to support write operations, and analytical data is denormalized to support read operations. Depending on the use case, analytical workloads can store data in a relational data warehouse such as Azure Synapse Analytics dedicated SQL pool or as files in an enterprise data lake such as ADLS.

Describe batch and stream processing. Data engineers can build data processing pipelines with one or a combination of two techniques: batch processing and stream processing. For the DP-900 exam, remember that batch processing workflows process data in batches during a predetermined period of time or after a specific event. Stream processing workflows ingest and transform continuous streams of data in real time. Know the technologies that were listed for each component of the two processing types. Also remember that modern, cloud-based architectures make it easy to implement batch processing and stream processing workflows in the same solution.

Describe data warehouse features. Remember that data warehouses store data that is optimized for analytical queries and are commonly used as the *single source of truth* for data that is important to a business department's decision making. Data models follow the star schema design pattern, where business entities and descriptors related to them are stored in dimension tables and measured events related to business entities are stored in fact tables.

Describe Azure HDInsight. Azure HDInsight is a managed, open-source analytics service in Azure that can be used to deploy distributed clusters for Apache Hadoop, Apache Spark, Apache Interactive Query/LLAP, Apache Storm, Apache Kafka, and Apache HBase. Remember that unlike Azure Databricks and Azure Synapse Analytics Apache Spark pools, Azure HDInsight clusters cannot be paused. You will need to destroy the cluster and build a new one with an automation script to manage Azure HDInsight costs. For this and other management reasons, it is recommended that you use other Azure services like Azure Databricks, Azure Synapse Analytics, and the Azure Event Hubs Kafka endpoint for distributed analytics.

Describe Azure Databricks. Azure Databricks is a unified analytics platform that supports optimized Spark clusters for batch and stream processing. The platform is a PaaS resource that provides a native notebook environment that developers can use to build Spark workflows with SQL, Python, Java, or R. Remember that Databricks clusters use Azure VMs for compute nodes and that processing is measured as Databricks Units (DBUs). Databricks clusters can be configured as dedicated compute for single user, prescheduled processing jobs (Single Node or Standard), or to run concurrent workloads for multiple users performing interactive analysis (High Concurrency). Remember that you can establish a connection with an Azure storage account by creating a mount point or by using a service principal to connect via a direct path. ADLS accounts can also be accessed directly with Azure AD credential passthrough.

Describe Azure Data Factory.   Azure Data Factory (ADF) is a managed cloud service that can be used to build complex ETL, ELT, and data integration projects. ADF instances provide data engineers with a platform to author no-code data movement and data transformation activities and run them sequentially or in parallel with pipelines. ADF pipelines can be executed manually or automatically via a schedule or an event-based trigger. Users can define connections to over 90 data sources and compute resources as linked services. Linked services that are created for data sources can be used to represent specific data structures within data stores, such as a relational database table or a set of files. Remember that integration runtimes are the compute infrastructure that power pipeline activities. Integration runtimes come in three types: one for Azure resources that are accessible via a public endpoint, a self-hosted integration runtime for on-premises resources or Azure resources that are only accessible through a private network, and an SSIS specific integration runtime that allows users to run legacy SSIS packages in an ADF pipeline.

Describe Azure Synapse Analytics.   Azure Synapse Analytics is an enterprise analytics system that unifies multiple services that serve analytical workloads in a single environment. Within Synapse Studio, data engineers can use Synapse pipelines to automate data movement and processing activities, a dedicated SQL pool as an analytical data store to manage data that will need to quickly serve reports and analytical applications, a serverless SQL pool to interactively query data in Azure Storage, an Apache Spark pool to perform data engineering activities with Spark, and a Data Explorer pool to analyze telemetry data in near real time. Analysts can also link a Power BI workspace to an Azure Synapse Analytics workspace to build reports in the same environment that they manage data and write queries.

Review Questions

1. Is the italicized portion of the following statement true, or does it need to be replaced with one of the other fragments that appear below? Relational databases that serve transactional workloads often use *a star schema* as their data model strategy. This modeling pattern is optimal for write-heavy operations.

   A. 1NF

   B. 3NF

   C. 2NF

   D. No change needed

2. Which of the following data storage options are appropriate for data scientists and analysts to use when analyzing business data?

   A. Data warehouses

   B. OLAP models

   C. Enterprise data lakes

   D. All of the above

3. What open-source technology provides ACID properties on data stored in ADLS?

   A. Delta Lake

   B. Parquet

   C. Apache Spark

   D. Hadoop

4. Which of the following services is not used in a batch processing workflow?

   A. Azure Databricks

   B. Azure Stream Analytics

   C. Azure Synapse Analytics

   D. Azure Data Factory

5. You are designing a data warehouse that will serve as the single source of truth for a venue management company. The data warehouse's data model will use a star schema so that it is optimized for reporting tools and analytical queries. Using this design pattern, what type of tables will store concession and retail sales metrics?

   A. Dimension tables

   B. Materialized views

   C. Fact tables

   D. Composite tables

6. You are designing a stream processing pipeline for an IoT workflow. The solution will use Apache Spark structured streaming to process the data, but it requires a highly scalable service to act as the real-time message ingestion engine. Which of the following Azure HDInsight cluster types is a viable option to ingest large volumes of streaming data?

    A. Apache Hadoop

    B. Apache Spark

    C. Apache Kafka

    D. Apache Storm

7. Which of the following statements about Azure Databricks is false?

    A. Azure Databricks cannot read data from a real-time ingestion engine like Azure Event Hubs or Apache Kafka.

    B. Administrators can leverage their existing Azure Active Directory infrastructure to manage user access control for Databricks-specific objects such as notebooks, clusters, and jobs.

    C. Azure Databricks can read and write data from Azure data stores such as Azure Blob Storage, ADLS, Azure SQL Database, and Azure Synapse Analytics dedicated SQL pools.

    D. When creating a Spark cluster in Azure Databricks, users can set a time period that Azure Databricks will use to automatically terminate the cluster when idle.

8. Which of the following components is not used when calculating the cost of an Azure Databricks cluster?

    A. Azure VM price

    B. Price of DBUs consumed

    C. Azure Databricks workspace price

    D. None of the above

9. You are deploying a new Azure Databricks workspace that will be used by data engineers and data scientists at your company. Clusters deployed to the workspace will need to be able to connect to Azure services that are assigned private endpoints. You are also required to configure Azure Databricks so that cluster nodes do not have public IP addresses. Which of the following options is the recommended solution for meeting the listed requirements?

    A. Enable VNet injection on the workspace so that all cluster nodes run on one of your VNets. This will allow you to easily connect clusters to services using private endpoints. VNet injection uses all private IP addresses by default.

    B. Enable VNet injection on the workspace so that all cluster nodes run on one of your VNets. This will allow you to easily connect clusters to services using private endpoints. Enable secure cluster connectivity to change the public subnet to private.

    C. Enable VNet injection on the workspace so that all cluster nodes run on one of your VNets. This will allow you to easily connect clusters to services using private endpoints. Enable private link to change the public subnet to private.

    D. Use VNet peering to peer the Databricks-managed VNet with the VNet that hosts the private endpoints you are connecting to. VVet injection uses all private IP addresses by default. Enable secure cluster connectivity to ensure that only private IP addresses are used.

10. Which of the following Git providers are supported by Azure Databricks?

A. Bitbucket

B. GitHub

C. Azure DevOps

D. All of the above

11. You are configuring an Azure Databricks cluster that will be used by several analysts and data scientists. Because users will be running interactive workloads sporadically, the cluster must be able to support concurrent requests. Which cluster mode should you define for this cluster?

A. Standard

B. High Concurrency

C. Single User

D. Interactive

12. Which of the following is not a component that can be manually created after an Azure Synapse Analytics workspace is deployed?

A. Serverless SQL pool

B. Dedicated SQL pool

C. Data Explorer pool

D. Apache Spark pool

13. You are designing a solution that will analyze operational data that is stored in an Azure Cosmos DB Core (SQL) API database. The solution must be near real time, but it must also minimize the impact on the performance of the operational data store. Which of the following options is the most appropriate for this scenario?

A. Enable Azure Synapse Link to synchronize your transactional data from Azure Cosmos DB to a column-oriented analytical data store and use an Azure Synapse Analytics serverless SQL pool to analyze the data.

B. Create an Azure Data Factory copy activity to copy the data from Azure Cosmos DB to an Azure Synapse Analytics dedicated SQL pool.

C. Create an Azure Data Factory copy activity to copy the data from Azure Cosmos DB to an Azure Synapse Analytics serverless SQL pool.

D. Enable Azure Synapse Link to synchronize your transactional data from Azure Cosmos DB to a column-oriented analytical data store and use an Azure Synapse Analytics data explorer pool to analyze the data.

14. How many additional Azure Synapse Analytics serverless SQL pools can be added to a single workspace?

A. 1

B. 10

C. 0

D. 5

15. You are the administrator for an Azure Synapse Analytics dedicated SQL pool. Table distribution and index design are optimized to meet the workload needs of the queries that are frequently executed against the database. You have recently been asked to improve the performance of a query that is run regularly. When enabled, which of the following features will immediately improve the query's performance by caching the results for later use?

   A. Result set caching

   B. Query store

   C. Extended events

   D. Clustered columnstore index

16. Which of the following is a common use case for an Azure Synapse Analytics serverless SQL pool?

   A. Performing exploratory analysis of Azure Storage data with T-SQL queries

   B. Creating a logical data warehouse that maintains an up-to-date view of data by providing a relational schema on top of raw data stored in Azure Storage without moving data

   C. Transforming ADLS data with T-SQL and serving the transformed data to Power BI or a persistent data store like Azure SQL Database

   D. All of the above

17. What T-SQL function allows you to read the content of files stored in Azure Storage with a serverless SQL pool?

   A. OPENQUERY

   B. OPENROWSET

   C. OPENDATASOURCE

   D. OPENEXTERNALDATA

18. Is the italicized portion of the following statement true, or does it need to be replaced with one of the other fragments that appear below? A *Serverless SQL pool* is an analytical data store that uses a scale-out architecture to distribute data processing across multiple nodes. It is optimized to serve large amounts of historical data very quickly to data analysts and BI applications and is typically used as the single source of truth for business insights.

   A. Dedicated SQL pool

   B. Data Explorer pool

   C. Apache Spark pool

   D. No change needed

19. What type of Azure Data Factory activity is used to manage the flow of a pipeline?

   A. Data movement activity

   B. Control activity

   C. Data transformation activity

   D. Compute activity

20. Which of the following options can you use with an ADF copy activity to define what data is copied from an Azure SQL Database table?

    A. The entire table

    B. The result set from a query

    C. The result set from a stored procedure

    D. All of the above

21. You are the lead data engineer for a company that is modernizing its existing data platform to Azure. One part of the modernization effort is to lift and shift existing SSIS packages to Azure and use PaaS infrastructure to run the SSIS packages. Which of the following is a valid approach in Azure while minimizing infrastructure overhead?

    A. Deploy the existing packages to an SSISDB database hosted on an Azure SQL Database and execute them with the SQL Server Agent.

    B. First, deploy the existing packages to an SSISDB database hosted on Azure SQL Database. Next, create an Azure-SSIS integration runtime in an Azure Data Factory instance and use the Execute SSIS Package activity with the integration runtime to run the SSIS packages.

    C. Deploy the existing packages to an SSISDB database hosted on a SQL Server Azure VM and execute them with the SQL Server Agent.

    D. First, deploy the existing packages to an SSISDB database hosted on Azure SQL Database. Next, create a self-hosted integration runtime in an Azure Data Factory instance and use the Execute SSIS Package activity with the integration runtime to run the SSIS packages.

22. ADF pipelines can be deployed manually, at a scheduled time, and after which one of the following event types?

    A. After a blob is uploaded to Azure Blob storage

    B. After a new row of data is inserted into a SQL Server database table

    C. After a new item is added to an Azure Cosmos DB database container

    D. All of the above

23. You are designing a data ingestion strategy that uses PolyBase to load CSV data from ADLS into an Azure Synapse Analytics dedicated SQL pool. When defining the external file format, what argument and terminator character should you use to indicate the end of each field in the files?

    A. `FIELD_TERMINATOR = '|'`

    B. `STRING_TERMINATOR = '|'`

    C. `STRING_TERMINATOR = ','`

    D. `FIELD_TERMINATOR = ','`

24. You are building a data ingestion solution that will perform a one-time load of ORC data from ADLS into an Azure Synapse Analytics dedicated SQL pool staging table. Which of the following options provides the best performance for this use case?

   A. Build the solution using PolyBase constructs, creating an external table that provides a schema for the ORC data. Once the external table is created, use a CTAS statement to create the staging table based on the PolyBase external table.

   B. Copy the data into the staging table using the bulk copy program (bcp) utility.

   C. Copy the data into the staging table using a COPY statement.

   D. Copy the data into the staging table using AzCopy.

Chapter

6

Reporting with Power BI

MICROSOFT EXAM OBJECTIVES COVERED IN THIS CHAPTER:

✓ **Describe data visualization in Microsoft Power BI.**

- Describe the role of paginated reporting.

- Describe the role of interactive reports.

- Describe the role of dashboards.

- Describe the workflow in Power BI.

Chapter 1, "Core Data Concepts," introduces different data processing techniques and several popular data visualizations such as tables, matrices, pie charts, column charts, line charts, scatter plots, and maps. Chapter 5, "Modern Data Warehouses in Azure," describes different data processing services and analytical data stores. This chapter builds on these lessons by exploring how Power BI can be used to ingest data from different data stores and analyze data with visualizations, reports, and dashboards.

Power BI at a Glance

Power BI is often thought of as a powerful reporting tool that can be used to analyze data with a rich suite of data visualizations. While this is true, Power BI offers so much more. Analysts and business intelligence (BI) practitioners with varying technical expertise can use Power BI to ingest, cleanse, model, analyze, and visualize data from over 130 different data sources. Citizen data scientists can also use built-in AI-related features such as the *Key Influencers* visualization and *AI Insights* to gain insights beyond what can be gained from traditional descriptive and diagnostic analysis.

The range of scenarios that Power BI can be used for is nearly limitless. Self-service BI developers can ingest data from a large data warehouse like an Azure Synapse Analytics dedicated SQL pool into a Power BI model using the Power BI desktop tool and mold the data into an easy-to-use OLAP model. Analysts can also use the service to ingest operational and analytical data stores into the same Power BI model to discover additional features that can be added to a modern data warehouse. Reports that are ready for wide-scale consumption can be published to a central workspace online or on-premises where they can be shared with any user who needs access to the reports.

While Power BI consists of several core components, the three most basic elements are as follows:

- *Power BI Desktop*—A free Windows desktop application that is used to ingest data, build data models, and author interactive reports. This tool can also be used to publish datasets and reports to the Power BI service or a Power BI Report Server where they can be shared or collaborated on with other users. You can download a free copy of the Power BI Desktop by clicking the Download Free button at `https://powerbi .microsoft.com/en-us/desktop`.

- *Power BI service*—An online Software as a Service (SaaS) platform that can be used to host Power BI resources such as datasets, reports, and dashboards. These resources can be shared with other users so that they can view and interact with them. Analysts and BI practitioners can create workspaces within the Power BI service (also referred to as Power BI online) where they can invite other users to collaborate on reports and dashboards. You can sign up for a free trial of the Power BI service by clicking the Try Power BI for Free button at `https://powerbi.microsoft.com/en-us/getting-started-with-power-bi`.

- *Power BI mobile app*—These are mobile applications where users can view and interact with reports via a mobile device. The mobile app is supported by Windows, iOS, and Android operating systems.

Power BI also consists of two elements that are used to build traditional reporting solutions:

- *Power BI Report Builder*—A free Windows desktop application that is used to create traditional paginated reports. These can be uploaded to either the Power BI service or a Power BI Report Server. You can download a free copy of the Power BI Report Builder by clicking the Download button at `www.microsoft.com/en-us/download/details.aspx?id=58158`.

- *Power BI Report Server*—An on-premises report server where report creators can publish their Power BI reports after creating them in Power BI Desktop or Power BI Report Builder.

Because Power BI is briefly covered on the DP-900 exam, the following sections will only cover the core Power BI components at a high level. However, understanding how and when to use these components will provide the fundamental knowledge necessary to start working with Power BI.

Working with Power BI

Before we explore the use cases for different report types and dashboards, let's examine the common steps that most Power BI workflows follow:

1. Ingest data from one or more data sources.
2. Transform data to fit the specific needs of the reports being built.
3. Build a data model.
4. Define calculations that answer business-specific questions.
5. Author reports.
6. Publish the reports.
7. Create dashboards with visualizations from one or more reports to summarize different business views.
8. Share the reports and dashboards with business users who will consume and make decisions based off of the information presented.

In addition to the conceptual workflow that is used throughout most Power BI use cases, the Power BI service allows BI developers to manage the life cycle of their Power BI content with the deployment pipelines tool. This tool is designed as a pipeline with three stages (development, test, and production) to enable report creators to develop and test Power BI content in the Power BI service before sharing content to business users. More information about Power BI deployment pipelines can be found at `https://docs.microsoft.com/en-us/power-bi/create-reports/deployment-pipelines-overview`.

Although they follow similar workflows, interactive and paginated reports require very different approaches when being built, which will be discussed in the sections "Interactive Reports" and "Paginated Reports" later in this chapter. The tools and methods used to ingest, transform, and visualize data are very different for interactive and paginated reports.

Interactive reports are far and away the most sophisticated and feature-rich of the two Power BI report types. In fact, when first released in 2015, interactive reports were the only type of reports that users could build with Power BI. The ability to author, publish, and share paginated reports with Power BI was not supported until several years later in 2019. For this reason, the steps used by most Power BI workflows are intended for interactive reports.

The following sections will examine the full life cycle of an interactive report, before describing the roles of dashboards and paginated reports in Power BI.

Interactive Reports

Interactive reports are collections of data visualizations and filters that reveal insights from a dataset. As the name implies, they are designed to be "interactive," meaning that users can filter and slice the data by interacting with any of the visuals or filters on the report. A single report can have several pages, each filled with content that focuses on different aspects of the dataset being analyzed. The next two sections explore how to create an interactive report through Power BI Desktop and publish the report to the Power BI service for sharing and collaboration.

Creating Interactive Reports with Power BI Desktop

While it is possible to develop interactive reports through the Power BI service, the preferred tool for authoring interactive reports is Power BI Desktop. This is a completely free tool that can be downloaded from the following link: `https://powerbi.microsoft.com/en-us/desktop`.

You will need a different version of Power BI Desktop if you plan on publishing your reports to Power BI Report Server instead of the Power BI service. This version of Power BI Desktop can be downloaded from the Power BI Report Server web portal. Power BI Report Server can be downloaded from the following link: www.microsoft.com/en-us/download/details.aspx?id=57270.

Once you have downloaded, installed, and opened Power BI Desktop, it will ask you to sign into a Power BI account. Feel free to skip this step if you are not going to publish reports to the Power BI service.

The Power BI Desktop UI has a similar look and feel to Microsoft Office products such as Microsoft Excel. The ribbon at the top of the canvas allows you to connect to different data sources, create custom measures and columns, and perform different tasks that are specific to the different Power BI Desktop views. There are three views available in Power BI Desktop, all of which can be accessed on the left side of the canvas. The following is a list of the views in the order that they appear:

- *Report*—In this view report creators can build and modify interactive reports. This view includes several tool panes on the right side of the UI that report creators can use to build new data visualizations and choose what pieces of data are displayed on the page. At the bottom of this view, there is a tab labeled "Page 1" next to a + sign. Interactive reports can have several pages as a means of organizing content for different topics.

- *Data*—This view displays all tables, measures, data fields that are used in the data model. This view also allows users to transform data for best use by the report's data model.

- *Model*—This view allows users to see and edit the relationships among the tables in the data model.

Figure 6.1 illustrates a blank report on the Report view and highlights where you can access the other views.

FIGURE 6.1   A blank report in the Power BI Desktop Report view. You can switch views by clicking one of the options on the left side of the canvas.

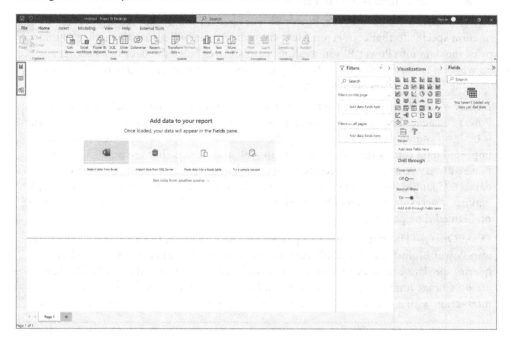

The first step in building an interactive report is to connect to one or more data sources. To do this, click the Get Data button in the Home ribbon at the top of the canvas. This will open the Get Data page (see Figure 6.2), displaying the many data sources that Power BI can connect to. Power BI Desktop groups its data in the following categories:

- *File*—This category includes common file sources, such as Excel, CSV, JSON, and PDF files.

- *Database*—This category includes several popular database services, including SQL Server, Access, Oracle, MySQL, PostgreSQL, SAP HANA, Amazon Redshift, Teradata, and MariaDB.

- *Power Platform*—This category provides connectivity to the Microsoft Power Platform ecosystem, including Power BI datasets and dataflows as well as Dataverse.

- *Azure*—This category contains connectors to the most popular Azure data services, including Azure SQL Database, Azure Synapse Analytics SQL pools (both dedicated and serverless), Azure Blob Storage, ADLS, Azure Databricks, and Azure Cosmos DB.

- *Online Services*—This category contains connectors to popular SaaS platforms like SharePoint Online lists, Microsoft Exchange Online, Dynamics 365, Salesforce, and Google Analytics.

- *Other*—This category contains connectors for services that do not fall in any specific category, such as Active Directory, SharePoint lists, Solver, and Apache Spark. It also includes generic interfaces such as ODBC, OLE DB, OData, and REST APIs to expand Power BI's connectivity options to any service that is accessible via those interfaces. Finally, users can leverage existing R or Python scripts to access data sources through the *R script* or *Python script* connector.

After you select a connector type, Power BI will open a prompt that requests access information specific to that connector. Most connector types will also ask whether to import a copy of the data into Power BI's in-memory data store or leave the data in its source system where it is queried dynamically every time the report is interacted with. Power BI supports the following data connectivity types:

- *Import*—This data connectivity type will load all of the data objects selected into the Power BI cache. This is the most performant data connectivity option as any visual that is built off of imported data will query the cache every time it is interacted with. The imported data is packaged with the data model, and reports that are published to the Power BI service or Power BI Report Server will also publish the imported data as a dataset. Changes that are made to the source data store are not automatically reflected, making it necessary to manually refresh a dataset or scheduling it to be refreshed during predefined time periods.

- *DirectQuery*—This data connectivity type does not load data from the source data store into Power BI. Instead, Power BI creates a reference to the data objects selected and queries the data source every time a data visualization is interacted with. While there are no storage limitations with this option, there are performance implications as every interaction with a data visualization results in a query being issued against the source data store. DirectQuery is usually used instead of importing data when data is changing frequently and near-real-time reporting is needed, and when the volume of data being reported on is very large, making it cumbersome to import all of it.

- *Live connections*—This data connectivity type is similar to DirectQuery but is specific to connectors that use the same storage engine as Power BI, such as Azure Analysis Services and SQL Server Analysis Services.

FIGURE 6.2   Get Data page

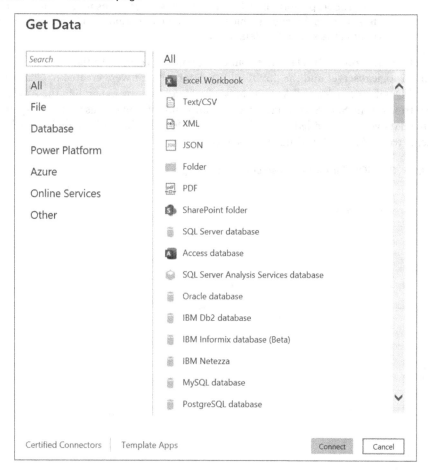

Power BI allows users to mix different connectivity types, resulting in composite data models. *Composite models* consist of two or more data connections from different data sources. For example, a report creator can use DirectQuery to connect to an Azure Synapse Analytics dedicated SQL pool to minimize the size of the Power BI dataset and import reference data from a CSV file to optimize report performance. While this is useful, not all data sources can be used in a composite model. More information about

composite model limitations can be found at `https://docs.microsoft.com/en-us/`
`power-bi/transform-model/desktop-composite-models#considerations-and-`
`limitations`.

> Composite models can also be created by establishing two or more data
> connections to the same data source. This is useful if you are creating
> a data model from a data warehouse that has very large fact tables. By
> creating a composite model, you can import the dimension tables for the
> best report performance (such as dimension features that are used in fil-
> ters and slicers) and establish a DirectQuery connection to the fact tables
> to limit the size of the data model.

By selecting the Azure SQL Database connector, you can connect to the
dp900sql001 logical server and the dp900sql001 database that were created in Chapter 2,
"Relational Databases in Azure." As you can see in Figure 6.3, by expanding the Advanced
Options setting on the SQL Server database pop-up window, you can use a T-SQL query to
retrieve the data you want added to the data model. After clicking OK, you will be asked to
authenticate to the Azure SQL Database instance.

FIGURE 6.3 SQL Server database connection page

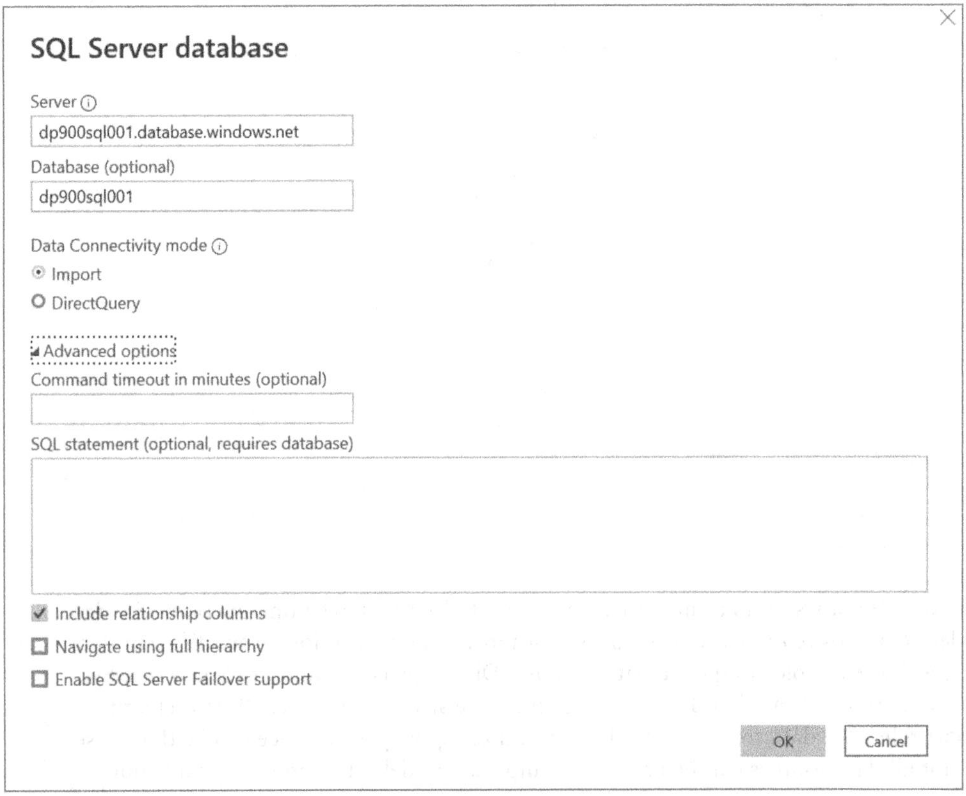

SQL Server database

Server ⓘ

> dp900sql001.database.windows.net

Database (optional)

> dp900sql001

Data Connectivity mode ⓘ

⦿ Import

○ DirectQuery

◢ Advanced options

Command timeout in minutes (optional)

>

SQL statement (optional, requires database)

>

☑ Include relationship columns

☐ Navigate using full hierarchy

☐ Enable SQL Server Failover support

OK   Cancel

If you do not use a query to retrieve data from the database, Power BI will open a new prompt that will allow you to select one or more tables or views to import or reference (see Figure 6.4). This example will import the SalesLT.Product, SalesLT.ProductCategory, and SalesLT.SalesOrderDetail tables from the database into the dataset. Click Transform Data after selecting the tables to use Power BI's *Power Query Editor* to modify data before it is loaded into Power BI.

FIGURE 6.4   Select the tables or views that will be imported into the Power BI data model.

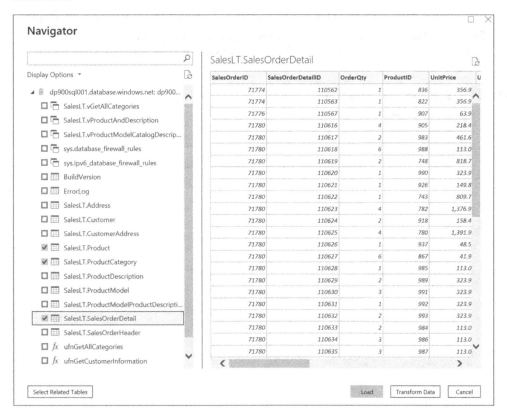

The Power Query Editor enables report creators to preprocess data to meet report requirements. Users can apply several transformations to the data, such as changing column data types, removing rows based on specific criteria, splitting columns, pivoting rows into columns and vice versa, applying mathematical functions to columns, and parameterizing the dataset to make it more dynamic. The Power Query Editor can also apply machine learning transformations by connecting to an Azure Machine Learning model, by invoking an Azure Cognitive Services API, or by running an R or a Python script against the data.

As you can see in Figure 6.5, the Power Query Editor is divided into the following four main components:

- In the ribbon at the top of the page, there are several buttons available to apply transformation steps to the data.
- In the left pane, each table/view selected is presented as a query. Users can switch back and forth between queries to apply different transformations to each one. Keep in mind that if you use a T-SQL query to establish the connection to the data source, then the data source will be presented as a single query in the Power Query Editor.
- In the center pane, data from the selected query is displayed and is available for shaping.
- The Query Settings pane on the right of the page displays all of the transformation steps applied to the query. This pane also allows users to rename the query to a more user-friendly name.

FIGURE 6.5 Power Query Editor

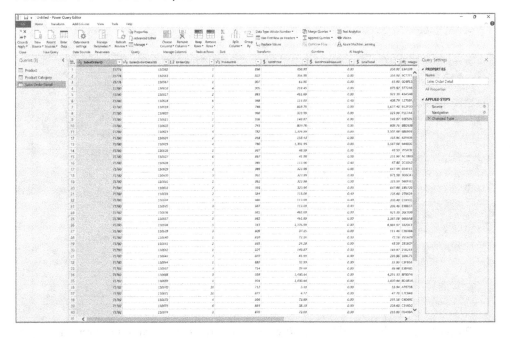

 Keep in mind that data transformations made with the Power Query Editor are not reflected in the source system but are applied as steps over the data as it is imported (or queried if the connectivity type is Direct-Query).

Transformations that are applied through the Power Query Editor are translated to M code. M is the formula language used by the Power Query engines in Analysis Services (both

Azure and SQL Server Analysis Services), Excel, and Power BI to apply data transformations to connected data sources. The Power Query Editor allows users to view the M code by clicking the Advanced Editor button in the ribbon at the top of the page. It also lets users edit the code and add transformation steps or parameters that are not exposed through the Power Query Editor UI. Figure 6.6 is an example of the Advanced Editor and the M code that is generated to connect to the SalesLT.SalesOrderDetail table. The code also applies a single transformation that changes the LineTotal column data type.

FIGURE 6.6 M Code can be viewed and edited through the Power Query Advanced Editor.

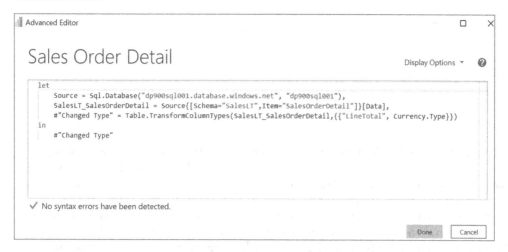

Click Close & Apply in the ribbon at the top of the page to load the data after you are satisfied with the data model. You can revisit the Power Query Editor to add or modify data transformation steps at any time by clicking the Transform Data button in the Home ribbon.

If you go to the *Model* view in Power BI Desktop, you will see that Power BI has inferred a one-to-many relationship between the Product and Sales Order Detail tables and a one-to-many relationship between the Product Category and Product tables (see Figure 6.7). These relationships are proposed based on common field names and can be altered through the Manage Relationships button in the Home ribbon. At the bottom of the view, users can create additional tabs that focus on different subsets of tables. The All Tables tab is created automatically to display the relationships between all tables in the model.

Additional relationships can also be established between tables. Because two tables can only have one active relationship at a time, additional relationships that are not used are configured to be inactive. Inactive relationships can only be made active during the evaluation of the USERELATIONSHIP() DAX function in a custom model calculation. More information on the USERELATIONSHIP() function can be found at https:// docs.microsoft.com/en-us/dax/userelationship-function-dax.

FIGURE 6.7   Power BI Desktop Model view

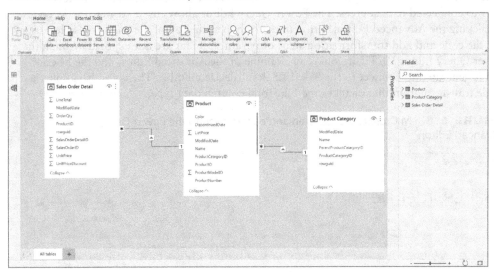

Before moving to the Data view, it is important to note how Power BI manages imported data. Power BI use an in-memory storage engine that stores data as tabular models, just like Azure Analysis Services and the SQL Server Analysis Services tabular mode. *Tabular models* use relational constructs like rows and columns to manage data. The VertiPaq engine used to power tabular models leverages modern compression algorithms to ensure fast performance for data retrieval and custom calculations. Tabular models support Data Analysis Expression (DAX) formulas to create custom calculations such as measures or calculated columns.

> While not in scope for the DP-900 exam, it is important to understand how to create custom calculations with DAX functions if you want to become proficient in Power BI. You can start learning more about these topics by completing the following learning path: https://docs.microsoft.com/en-us/learn/paths/dax-power-bi.

Navigate to the *Data* view to see the imported data in tabular format; it can be broken down into the following components (see Figure 6.8):

- The data grid in the center of the view displays the selected table and all columns and rows in it. You can highlight specific columns in the data grid to apply filters and quick transformations to the data.

- The Fields pane on the right side of the view allows you to choose which table is displayed in the data grid. You can also use the *Fields* pane to add new calculated measures or columns, rename data objects, and hide objects from the report view.

- The formula bar just above the data grid allows you to enter DAX formulas to create new measures and calculated columns. This is grayed out by default, but if you click

New Measure or New Column, the formula bar will become available for you to enter DAX code. Let's take this time to create a new measure that calculates the most popular item sold by order quantity by clicking New Measure and adding the following DAX code to the formula bar:

```
Most Popular Item Sold = TOPN(1, VALUES('Product'[Name]),
    CALCULATE(SUM('Sales Order Detail'[OrderQty])))
```

- At the top of the view there are two contextual ribbons, Table Tools and Column Tools, that contain common transformation activities like changing a column's data type and format.

FIGURE 6.8 Power BI Desktop Data view

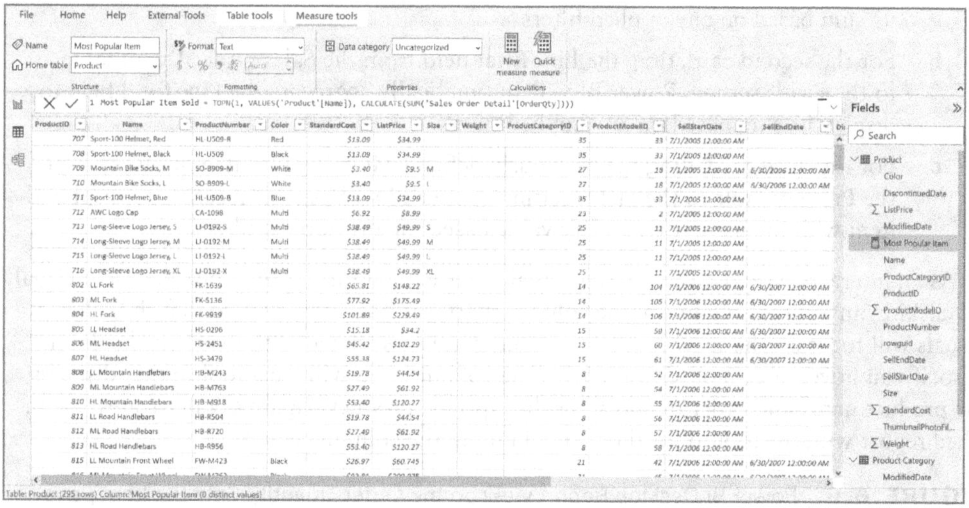

Once the data is modeled and cleansed to meet report specifications, navigate to the Report view to build an interactive report. This view allows report creators to do what they do best: build reports. The following steps can be used to create a report that displays the total order sales and total order quantity for every subcategory of road bikes that were sold.

1. *Create a slicer for product names.* There are two ways to start authoring visualizations with Power BI Desktop. Either you can drag a field from the Fields pane onto the canvas and choose the appropriate visual, or you can drag a visual from the Visualizations pane onto the canvas and drag data fields into the appropriate setting. For this filter, we are going to drag the Names field from the Product Category table onto the canvas and choose the Slicer visual. Select Road Bikes in the slicer to filter every visual on the page to only show data for road bikes.

2. *Create a clustered column chart to display total order quantity for each product category sold.* Select the Clustered Column Chart visual to create a blank clustered column chart. Drag the Name field from the Product table to the Axis setting. Next, drag the

OrderQty field from the Sales Order Detail table to the Values setting. This will create a clustered column chart that displays the number of items sold for each product. Because the slicer is actively filtering the report by the road bike category, the column chart will display the order quantity data for each road bike subcategory. You can modify the visual's format at any time by clicking the Format icon in the Visualizations pane and changing settings such as the bar colors, text font, title, and data labels.

3. *Create three card visuals that display the total sales amount, total order quantity, and most popular item sold.* Select the Card visual three times to create three blank cards on the canvas. Add the following to each card:

    a. For the first card, drag the OrderQty field from the Sales Order Detail table to the Fields setting. Power BI will automatically aggregate the OrderQty field to display its sum based on any applied filters.

    b. For the second card, drag the LineTotal field from the Sales Order Detail table to the Fields setting. Power BI will automatically aggregate the LineTotal field to display its sum based on any applied filters.

    c. For the third card, drag the previously defined Most Popular Item measure from the Product table to the Fields setting. Power BI will use this measure to display the item with the highest OrderQty value based on any applied filters.

As an interactive report, the filtering capabilities extend further than just the slicer visual. By clicking any of the columns in the column chart, the page will filter so that the other visuals will focus on the specific product name that is associated with the clicked column. Also, if you hover your mouse over any of the columns you will see a tooltip that displays the product name and order quantity for that specific product. Figure 6.9 illustrates the finished report with the tooltip for the first column in the column chart.

FIGURE 6.9   Power BI Desktop Report view on the Order Quantity Sold Per Item page

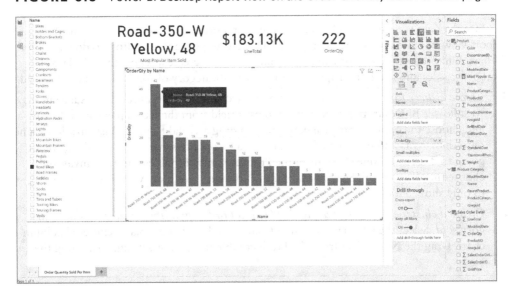

Visuals can be changed at any time by clicking on a visual and then selecting a different visual from the Visualizations pane. Power BI will attempt to rearrange the fields used in the old visual to the most appropriate settings in the new visual.

After you have finished building the report, you can save the file locally as a PBIX file. PBIX files (saved with the .pbix filename extension) can be opened at any time by Power BI Desktop so that report creators can modify the visuals, data model, and query definitions used to power the report. In addition to saving reports as PBIX files, you can save the report as a Power BI report template (PBIT) that other report creators can use as a starting point for a new report's layout, data model, and query definitions. Unlike a PBIX file, PBIT files (saved with the .pbit filename extension) do not include the data used to power the report. More information about Power BI report templates can be found at https://docs .microsoft.com/en-us/power-bi/create-reports/desktop-templates.

Publishing and Sharing Interactive Reports with the Power BI Service

Now that the data model and report are ready to be shared with other users, let's publish the report to the Power BI service. You can do this by clicking the Publish button in the Home ribbon and choosing a destination workspace for the report and data model. Remember that you will need to log into the service first before you can publish the report.

To maintain a connection with data sources that are not publicly accessible from the Power BI service, such as an on-premises SQL Server database or a cloud resource that is only accessible via a private IP address, you will need to install and configure an on-premises data gateway on a machine that is in the same network as the data source. More information on how to use and install the on-premises data gateway can be found at https://docs.microsoft.com/en-us/data-integration/gateway/ service-gateway-onprem.

Workspaces serve as containers in the Power BI service where users can logically organize content and collaborate with colleagues. A single workspace can host several datasets, reports, and dashboards that serve the reporting needs of specific business units or for specific solutions. Content creators with a Power BI Pro or Power BI Premium Per User license can share workspace content to different users and control their level of access by assigning them one of the following roles:

- *Viewer*—Users assigned this role will only be able to view and interact with reports and dashboards contained in the workspace.

- *Contributor*—Users assigned this role will be granted *Viewer* permissions and the ability to create, edit, and delete content. This includes publishing reports to the workspace, downloading a report, and scheduling data refreshes.

- *Member*—Users assigned this role will be granted *Viewer* and *Contributor* permissions as well as the ability to add other users to the workspace with *Viewer* or *Contributor* permissions.

- *Admin*—Users assigned this role will have full control of the workspace, including the ability to update and delete the workspace.

More information about Power BI workspace roles can be found at `https://docs` `.microsoft.com/en-US/power-bi/collaborate-share/service-roles-new-` `workspaces#workspace-roles`.

By default, every Power BI use has a personal workspace called *My work-space* that content creators can use as a private sandbox for learning and testing.

The workspace features that are available to a user, such as the number of times they can schedule a data refresh or the maximum data model size that a workspace can manage, depends on the type of license the user has and the Power BI plan applied to the workspace. While licensing is not covered by the DP-900 exam, it is important to know that users can use a Power BI Pro or Power BI Premium Per User license to manage content and that work-spaces can use shared capacity or premium (dedicated) capacity. The feature and price differences between license and plan types can be found at `https://powerbi.microsoft.com/` `en-us/pricing`.

Workspace content is organized into different sections for dashboards, reports, and data-sets as well as two other objects not discussed so far: workbooks and data flows. Power BI workbooks are Excel workbooks that are imported into a Power BI workspace. Once imported into a Power BI workspace, the workbook is converted to a dataset that can be used to serve new reports. Power BI dataflows offer similar data connection, ingestion, and transformation functionality as the Power BI Desktop Power Query Editor but are instead managed by the Power BI service.

You can navigate to the Power BI service by going to `https://powerbi.com`. Once you are signed in, you will be able to traverse the service by using the buttons in the left-side menu. This menu is divided into two sections, with the top one including buttons that will take the user to commonly browsed pages such as the Power BI service home page, recently viewed objects, Power BI apps, and deployment pipelines. The bottom section of the left-side menu allows users to navigate to the different workspaces that they have access to.

All of the content associated with a workspace is displayed in the center of the page when you select a workspace. The workspace home page also includes options that allow users to manage several administrative activities such as setting a dataset refresh schedule and grant-ing user access. Figure 6.10 shows the home page of the "DP900-PBI-Workspace" workspace that contains the DP900PBI report and dataset.

If you click on the report name, Power BI will open it in the center of the page. This view, known as the "reading view," allows users to interact with visuals and derive insights from the report. Users with the appropriate access can click the Edit button in the top bar to make modifications to the report directly in the Power BI service. Figure 6.11 shows the DP900PBI report in the DP900-PBI-Workspace.

As you can see in Figure 6.11, the top bar includes additional settings that allow you to monitor the usage of your report and share the report to internal and external business users. There are also options that allow users to export the report to a PDF or PowerPoint to serve business users who prefer to consume their reports through those mediums.

FIGURE 6.10   Power BI Service Workspace home page

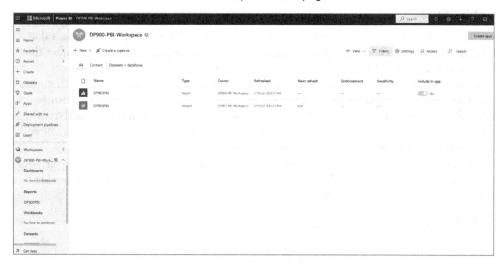

FIGURE 6.11   Power BI Service Report view

Reports, both interactive and paginated, are often too granular for business decision makers who need to monitor the performance of their business in real time. Many times, these decision makers are looking for a clear, summarized view that allows them to monitor their business and see the most important metrics without having to dig through a mountain of reports. Content creators can provide this functionality in Power BI by building dashboards that highlight the most relevant visuals from one or more Power BI reports. The next section, "Dashboards," examines Power BI dashboards in further detail.

Dashboards

Power BI dashboards are single page views that contain a collection of pinned visuals that are taken from reports and other data storytelling objects. It is important to remember that while reports tell a detailed story, dashboards only provide the highlights of that story.

You can think of a pinned visual, known as a *tile*, as a "headline" for the report it comes from. Tiles should summarize the information that a user needs to monitor their business while still being thought-provoking. If a user wants to examine a tile and its underlying information in more detail, or "read the full story," they can click the tile and Power BI will navigate them to the report that the tile comes from.

Report visuals can be added to a dashboard by *pinning* them. To pin a visual, hover your mouse over a report visual and click the pin icon (see Figure 6.12). You will then be able to pin the visual to an existing or new dashboard.

FIGURE 6.12 The pin icon on a report visual

While report visuals are commonly used to compose dashboards, there are other object types that can be pinned to a dashboard. Here is a full list of objects that that can be pinned:

- *Report visuals*—Pinned report visuals maintain the filters that were applied in the underlying report at the time the visual was pinned to the dashboard. Keep in mind that report visuals cannot be filtered once they are pinned to a dashboard, unless you open the tile in focus mode. Even then, the filter will be removed once you exit focus mode.

- *Entire reports*—In addition to being able to pin individual report elements to a dashboard, Power BI allows you to pin an entire report page. When you pin an entire report page, the tile maintains the report's interactivity capabilities. This means that you can interact with the tile as you would the report.

- *Tiles from another dashboard*—You can pin a tile from one dashboard to another. When clicked, the shared tile will still take you to the report that the tile comes from.

- *Excel workbooks*—You can pin a range of cells, an entire table, or a PivotTable from an Excel workbook to a dashboard. The workbook must be located in a OneDrive for Business account, and the account must be linked to a Power BI workspace. You can do this by clicking Get Data in the Power BI workspace, selecting Files, and then selecting OneDrive - Business. From here you will select the workbook file and choose Connect. More information about how to connect to and pin content from an Excel workbook can be found at `https://docs.microsoft.com/en-us/power-bi/create-reports/service-dashboard-pin-tile-from-excel#connect-your-excel-workbook-from-onedrive-for-business-to-power-bi`.

- *Power BI Q&A*—Q&A is a Power BI tool for exploring data with natural language, like "Top 10 product categories by order qty." You can find this tool at the top of any dashboard, with a prompt that states, "Ask a question about your data." As of this writing, Power BI Q&A only supports questions asked in English, with support for Spanish in public preview. If Power BI can translate your question to the features and measures defined in your dataset, Q&A will render a visual that is tailored to answer your question. The generated visual can be pinned to the dashboard.

- *Quick Insights*—The Quick Insights feature in Power BI uses a set of advanced analytical algorithms developed by Microsoft Research to generate visualizations that highlight specific features of a dataset. You can also run the Quick Insights feature on a dashboard tile to discover insightful information from a tile. Once the Quick Insights feature has finished running, you can choose to pin any of the generated visuals to a dashboard.

- *Paginated reports*—Power BI allows you to pin a paginated report that is hosted in the Power BI service, an on-premises Power BI Report Server, or SQL Server Reporting Services (SSRS).

Along with pinned tiles, dashboard designers can incorporate the following five stand-alone tile types into their dashboards:

- *Web content*—With this tile type, you can embed HTML code in a dashboard. This is useful if you would like to add content from social media sites or embed.ly to a dashboard.

- *Image*—This tile type adds an online image to a dashboard. Simply provide the image URL and the image will be displayed. Images stored on a site that requires security credentials, such as OneDrive or SharePoint, are not supported. Also, images that are stored in SVG format are not supported.

- *Text box*—This tile type allows you to add text to a dashboard.

- *Video*—This tile type allows you to add a YouTube or Vimeo video to a dashboard.

- *Streaming data*—This tile type allows you to add a real-time data stream, such as social media feeds or sensor data, to a dashboard. Power BI supports data streams that come from an API, Azure Stream Analytics, or PubNub.

You can add any of these stand-alone tile types by clicking the Edit button at the top of a dashboard and selecting + Add A Tile.

Figure 6.13 illustrates an example of a dashboard with tiles taken from the DP900PBI report. The top three tiles focus on the most popular item sold, the sales total, and the total number of items sold. Below those tiles is the column chart that breaks down the quantity sold for each product subcategory. As you can see, the dashboard tiles reflect the "Road Bikes" filter that was applied in the underlying report.

FIGURE 6.13   Power BI dashboard

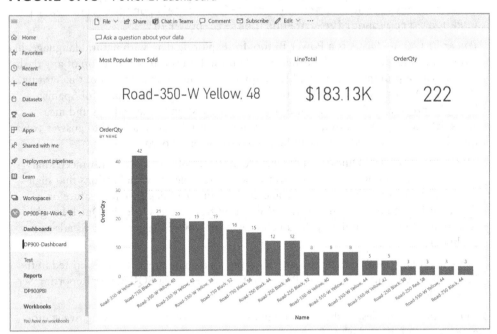

Above the dashboard tiles is the Power BI Q&A text box. If you enter a question like "top 10 product categories by order qty" into the text box, Q&A will generate a clustered bar chart with the Product Category Name field on the y-axis and the Sales Order Detail OrderQty field on the x-axis (see Figure 6.14). If you would like, you can click Pin Visual in the upper-right corner of the Q&A page to pin the visual to the dashboard. You can also change the question to get a new result. Click Exit Q&A to return to the dashboard.

Power BI dashboards can be created and managed only by the Power BI service. Dashboard designers can define two distinct layouts for a dashboard: the *web layout* that is used by computers and tablets and the *mobile layout* that optimizes the dashboard layout for mobile devices. The mobile layout is used when a user is viewing a dashboard through the Power BI mobile app.

Paginated Reports

Paginated reports differ from interactive reports in that they are designed to display every row of data for a given data source and a set of parameters versus aggregating data. They are called *paginated* because they are formatted to fit cleanly on one or more pages, making them easy to print. Just like an interactive report, paginated reports can be shared with business users through the Power BI service, as long as it has Premium capacity, or through an on-premises Power BI Report Server.

FIGURE 6.14   Power BI Q&A output

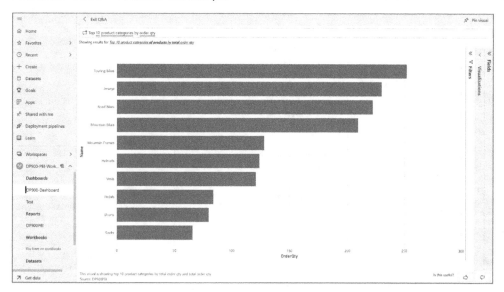

Paginated reports have been a staple of BI solutions for several years now. Prior to paginated reports being available in Power BI, organizations could host their paginated reports in SSRS. While organizations can still host their paginated reports in an SSRS instance, Power BI enables them to consolidate all of their reports in a single ecosystem.

Report creators can use Visual Studio or Power BI Report Builder to create paginated reports. Power BI Report Builder is a free desktop application that is dedicated for building Power BI paginated reports. As mentioned previously in this chapter, you can download a free copy of Power BI Report Builder at `www.microsoft.com/en-us/download/details.aspx?id=58158`.

When you open Power BI Report Builder on your desktop, you will be presented with a pop-up window that provides several options for getting started (see Figure 6.15). Along with being able to open a blank or an existing report, the Getting Started pop-up window allows you to create a new report with one of the following wizards:

- The *Table or Matrix Wizard* will guide you through establishing a data source connection and designing the layout for a table or matrix report.

- The *Chart Wizard* will guide you through creating a column, line, pie, bar, or area chart.

- The *Map Wizard* will guide you through building a report that has a geographical background.

If you click the Blank Report option in the Getting Started pop-up window, you will be taken to a new report page where you can begin building your report. At the top of the page, there are several ribbons that allow you to establish a new data connection and build report visuals. On the left side of the page there are folders for items that can be incorporated into a report, including built-in fields, parameters, images, data sources, and datasets.

FIGURE 6.15 Power BI Report Builder Getting Started window

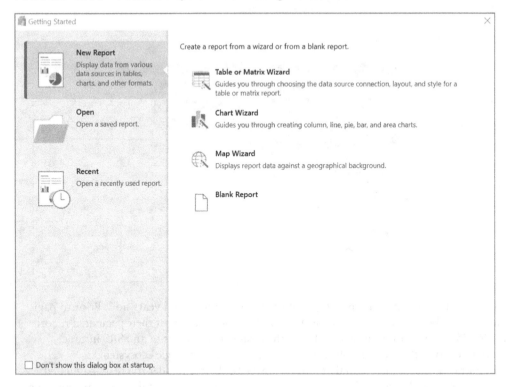

 Unlike interactive reports, datasets that are embedded in a paginated report are only accessible from within that report. If you upload a paginated report to the Power BI service, its underlying dataset will not be displayed under Datasets in the workspace.

In the center of the page is the report canvas, with two prepopulated fields for the report title and the execution time (these can be removed if you do not need them). You can add a new data visualization to the report by navigating to the Insert ribbon at the top of the canvas, selecting a visual, and placing it anywhere on the canvas. Figure 6.16 illustrates a new report in Power BI Report Builder with a focus on the Insert ribbon:

You can establish a connection to a data source by selecting one of the options in the Data ribbon at the top of the canvas. As of this writing, paginated reports support the following data sources:

- Azure SQL Database

- Azure Synapse Analytics

- Azure Analysis Services

- Dataverse

- SQL Server
- SQL Server Analysis Services
- Power BI datasets
- Oracle
- Teradata
- ODBC connections

FIGURE 6.16　A blank report in Power BI Report Builder

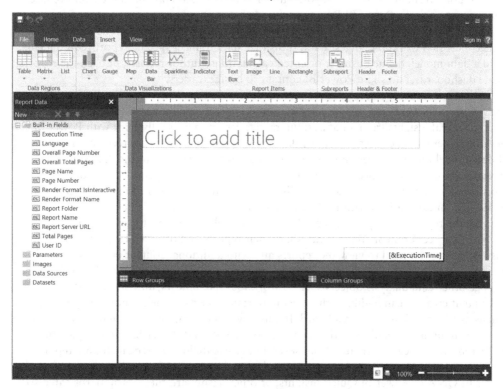

After you have finished building the report, you can save the file locally as a Report Definition Language (RDL) file. RDL files (saved with the .rdl file extension) can be opened at any time by Power BI Report Builder so that report creators can modify the report. You can publish the report to a Power BI workspace that is in a Power BI Premium capacity by clicking the Publish button in the Home ribbon and choosing a destination workspace for the report.

Summary

Power BI is an ecosystem of services that turn data into coherent and visually stimulating insights. BI practitioners and data analysts can build interactive reports from a combination of several data sources with Power BI Desktop and upload those reports to the Power BI service where the reports can be shared with business users. Once a report is published to the Power BI service, users can create a mobile friendly version of the report that business users can view through the Power BI mobile app. Report creators can also create traditional, paginated reports through Power BI Report Builder and host their content in their on-premises environment with the Power BI Report Server.

Regardless of the type of report a user is creating, most Power BI solutions follow the same conceptual workflow: ingest data, transform data to meet specific report requirements, build a data model, define business-oriented calculations, author reports, publish the reports, create dashboards, and share Power BI content to business users.

Of the two report types, interactive reports are far and away the most sophisticated and feature-rich. These reports are a collection of interactive data visualizations and filters that reveal insights from a dataset. Interactive reports are usually built with Power BI Desktop, where users can either import data from one or more data sources into a Power BI data model for fast performance or establish a direct connection to the data source with DirectQuery or a live connection to minimize the data model footprint. Users can apply data transformation activities to the data as it is being ingested with the Power Query Editor and create custom calculations with DAX formulas after the data model is defined.

Once the report is ready to be shared, users can publish the report to a workspace in the Power BI service. Content creators can share their reports and other workspace content to business users who need to view the reports and with additional content creators who will be adding content to the workspace. Along with reports and datasets, Power BI workspaces manage other data analysis objects such as workbooks, dataflows, and dashboards.

Content creators can highlight the most important aspects of their reports by pinning visuals as tiles to a Power BI dashboard. If a user wants to examine a tile and the report it comes from in more detail, then they can click on the tile and Power BI will navigate them to the report. Tiles can be created from several data storytelling objects, including report visuals, entire reports (interactive or paginated), Excel workbooks, visuals generated from Power BI Q&A or Power BI Quick Insights, or other dashboard tiles. Dashboards can also contain several stand-alone tile types that display web content, text, images, videos, or streaming data. Dashboard designers can use the Power BI service to define two distinct layouts for a dashboard: a web layout that is optimal for computers and tablets and a mobile layout that can be used by the Power BI mobile app.

Paginated reports are designed to display tabular data and are formatted to fit cleanly on one or more pages. Just like an interactive report, paginated reports can be shared to business users through the Power BI service, as long as it has Premium capacity, or an on-premises Power BI Report Server. Report creators can build paginated reports with Power BI Report Builder, a desktop tool that provides users with a dedicated environment for building Power BI paginated reports.

Exam Essentials

Describe the Power BI workflow.   Power BI solutions typically follow the same conceptual workflow: ingest data, transform data to meet specific report requirements, build a data model, define business-oriented calculations, author reports, publish the reports, create dashboards, and share Power BI content to business users. Remember that while the workflow is the same, building interactive and paginated reports requires different tools and uses different design approaches.

Describe interactive reports.   Interactive reports, which are commonly created with Power BI Desktop, consist of interactive visuals and filters that can be used to reveal valuable business insights. Report creators can choose to import data from one or more data sources into a single Power BI data model for fast performance or establish a direct connection to the data source to minimize the data model footprint. Remember that you can apply data transformation steps as data is being ingested with the Power Query Editor and that you can create custom calculations with DAX formulas after the data model is defined. Once a report is created and is ready to be shared, you can publish the report and the underlying data model to the Power BI service. From here, you can grant business users access to view the report or grant content creators access to add and modify content.

Describe Power BI dashboards.   Power BI dashboards are single page views that contain a collection of pinned visuals that are taken from reports and other data storytelling objects. They highlight the most important features of a group of reports, giving users a high-level overview of the state of their business. Dashboards can consist of report visuals, entire interactive or paginated reports, Excel workbook objects, Power BI Q&A visuals, Power BI Quick Insights visuals, or tiles from another dashboard. Dashboards can also include standalone tiles that display web content, text, images, videos, or streaming data. A dashboard tile cannot be filtered unless the tile is opened in focus mode or is a pinned report. Remember that Power BI dashboards can only be created through the Power BI service and that you can create a web layout and a mobile layout for a dashboard.

Describe paginated reports.   Paginated reports are formatted to fit cleanly on one or more pages, making them easy to print. Paginated reports can be published and shared through the Power BI Service only if it has Premium capacity. Otherwise, users can publish and share their paginated reports through an on-premises Power BI Report Server instance. Report creators can build paginated reports in Visual Studio or Power BI Report Builder. Power BI Report Builder is a desktop application that provides users a dedicated environment for building paginated reports and publishing paginated reports to a Power BI workspace that is in a Power BI Premium capacity or a Power BI Report Server instance.

Review Questions

1. Is the italicized portion of the following statement true, or does it need to be replaced with one of the other fragments that appear below? The *Power BI service* is a free Windows desktop application that is used to ingest data, build data models, and author interactive reports.

   A. Power BI Report Builder

   B. Power BI Desktop

   C. Power BI Report Server

   D. No change needed

2. Which of the following services cannot be used to create a Power BI interactive report?

   A. Power BI service

   B. Power BI Desktop

   C. Power BI Report Builder

   D. All of the above

3. You are building reports with Power BI Desktop that will use data from a large data warehouse hosted on an Azure Synapse Analytics dedicated SQL pool. You do not want to import all of the fact table data as the volume of data will be too large to upload to the Power BI service. On the other hand, the dimension tables you would like to connect to are small and static in nature. Which of the following options will provide the best performance for this dataset?

   A. Use DirectQuery to create a live connection to the fact tables and import the smaller dimension tables.

   B. Use the live connection connectivity type to connect to the fact tables and import the smaller dimension tables.

   C. Use DirectQuery to create a live connection to the fact and dimension tables.

   D. Use the live connection connectivity type to connect to the fact and dimension tables.

4. What is the minimum role required to allow a user to view existing reports and publish new ones to a Power BI workspace?

   A. Viewer

   B. Member

   C. Contributor

   D. Admin

5. Which of the following scenarios allows you to filter or slice an entire dashboard?

   A. If an entire report page is pinned to a dashboard.

   B. When a filter and a visual from the same report is pinned as separate tiles on a dashboard.

C. When a dashboard tile is opened in focus mode you can filter the tile. The filter will be saved and applied to the other dashboard tiles when you exit focus mode.

D. All of the above.

6. Which of the following can be added as a stand-alone tile to a Power BI dashboard?

A. Text boxes

B. Streaming data

C. Web content

D. All of the above

7. Paginated reports can be published to a Power BI workspace if the workspace is in which of the following Power BI capacity types?

A. Shared

B. Premium

C. Pro

D. All of the above

Appendix

Answers to the Review Questions

Chapter 1: Core Data Concepts

1. C. Azure IoT Hub, Azure Event Hubs, and Apache Kafka are message brokers that can be used to ingest millions of events per second from one or more message producers. They can then queue messages before sending them to either a cold data store such as Azure Data Lake Store Gen2 or a stream processing engine such as Azure Stream Analytics. Azure SQL Database is a relational database that is used to store structured data.

2. B. Data manipulation language commands are used to manipulate data that is stored in a relational database. These commands include SELECT, INSERT, UPDATE, and DELETE.

3. A. Azure Cosmos DB not only supports millisecond reads and writes to avoid lags, but its flexible schema makes for an easy platform to add a player's membership information if they are a part of any gaming or social media communities.

4. D. Azure Databricks Structured Streaming and Azure Stream Analytics can be used to create live and on-demand stream processing solutions. Both technologies can use data stored in Azure Blob Storage as reference data.

5. D. All of these options are nonrelational data stores. While Azure Blob Storage is not a database, it is still a nonrelational data store because of its ability to store nonrelational data such as binary, JSON, and Parquet files.

6. A. Azure Cosmos DB's Gremlin API is the best choice for storing relationships between different department entities. While this can be accomplished with a relational model, graph databases such as the Azure Cosmos DB's Gremlin API are better options since they do not require applications to perform complex queries with several join operations.

7. B. Azure Blob Storage is optimized for storing massive amounts of binary data such as images and can be accessed by several machine learning development platforms.

8. C. The COPY statement provides the most flexibility for high-throughput data loading from external storage accounts into Azure Synapse Analytics.

9. B. Azure Synapse Analytics dedicated SQL pool leverages scale-out architecture by distributing data and data processing to multiple nodes.

10. D. Batch processing is the practice of transforming groups of data at scheduled periods of time.

11. A. Azure Data Factory mapping data flows is a tool that allows data engineers to build data processing pipelines with a graphical user interface. Because there isn't any code involved, this solution is the easiest to maintain and has the least amount of operational overhead.

12. C. Diagnostic analytics answer questions about why things happened, and descriptive analytics answer questions about what has happened.

13. D. Matrices are useful infographics for clearly displaying numerical totals and subtotals over different groups of categories.

14. A. Analysts will need to be able to create and interact with reports as well as be able to pin the most relevant visualizations from those reports to dashboards for executives.

15. B. Line charts are useful for displaying how data has changed over time.

16. A. Cognitive analytics techniques can be used to build machine learning or deep learning models that power conversational bots. Each time they are queried, they become more accurate as these models are designed to learn from each interaction with data.

Chapter 2: Relational Databases in Azure

1. B. While transactions with Read Committed isolation prevent other transactions from reading dirty data, they do not stop other transactions from modifying or inserting data. This can result in nonrepeatable or phantom reads.

2. C. The optimal method for storing data in an analytical system is to flatten data into a star schema. This allows business users to easily write queries that can read data without requiring complex joins.

3. A. Creating a nonclustered index on the column or columns that are included in the filter criteria for commonly used queries will increase their performance.

4. D. No change is needed as Azure SQL Managed Instance falls under the PaaS database options.

5. A. Azure SQL MI is ideal for lift-and-shift scenarios that require a quick migration time to Azure. SQL MI provides nearly 100 percent feature compatibility with SQL Server, all the while providing users with the benefits of a PaaS database.

6. B. Memory optimized virtual machines offer stronger memory-to-CPU ratios that are ideal for SQL Server workloads.

7. B. SQL Server Always On availability groups replicate specific user databases to other SQL Server instances for HADR purposes.

8. D. Virtual networks, or VNets for short, are fundamental building blocks to building an isolated network in Azure. Services such as SQL Server on Azure VM and Azure SQL MI can be added to VNets to limit application connectivity to applications that can connect to the VNet.

9. A. A network security group, or NSG for short, controls access to the SQL Managed Instance data endpoint by filtering traffic on port 1433 and ports 11000–11999 when SQL Managed Instance is configured for redirect connections. The NSG is associated to the subnet hosting the Azure SQL MI once it is created.

10. B. The Business Critical tier of Azure SQL MI automatically creates a SQL Server Always On availability group and multiple secondary nodes for HADR purposes. While these nodes are abstracted from the user, one of them is enabled to serve read-only workloads. This allows users to read data from the database without affecting the performance of the write operations.

11. C. The maximum number of user databases that can be deployed to a single Azure SQL MI is 100.

12. C. Private Link is a service in Azure that allow users to attach a private endpoint to PaaS offerings such as Azure SQL Database. A private endpoint is a private IP address in a specific subnet in a VNet.

13. B. Materialized views consist of aggregations performed on multiple tables, allowing analysts to use simple queries to build reports. Materialized views also compile and store aggregations as data is updated in the underlying tables, making them much faster than traditional views.

14. D. To take advantage of Azure Synapse Analytics dedicated SQL pool's scale-out design, data is sharded 60 distributions across one or more compute nodes.

15. B. Azure SQL MI manages database backups by taking full, differential, and transaction log backups at scheduled time periods. Database backups can be restored to another Azure SQL MI by using a point-in-time restore to specify what version of the database should be restored.

16. A. The vCore-based purchasing model for Azure SQL Database includes the following service tiers: General Purpose, Business Critical, Hyperscale. This purchasing model gives users the ability to choose the number of vCores, the amount of memory, and storage speed.

17. B. Azure Database for PostgreSQL is the only open-source PaaS database option that offers a Hyperscale deployment model for large OLTP workloads.

18. B. Connect-AzAccount is required to establish a connection with an Azure environment before resources can be managed.

19. C. Hash distribution is the best option for large fact tables and provides the best performance for joins and aggregations. This type of distribution distributes data by running a hash function on a column in a table that will deterministically assign each row of a table to a distribution.

20. D. Microsoft.Sql/servers manages the deployment configuration of a logical servers, while Microsoft.Sql/servers/databases manages the deployment configuration for each database associated with a logical server.

21. A. New-AzSqlDatabase is the Azure PowerShell command used to create a new Azure SQL Database.

22. B. The SQL DB Contributor role gives a user the ability to create and manage databases in Azure. While the Contributor role also allows the user to perform the same task, it grants more privileges than what are needed.

23. C. Always Encrypted is a feature in SQL Server and Azure SQL that encrypts sensitive table columns. It allows the client application to manage the encryption and decryption keys, ensuring that only the client app can decrypt the sensitive data.

24. D. SQL Server Management Studio (SSMS) provides tools for configuring, monitoring, and administering instances of SQL Server and Azure SQL.

25. A. Database contained users only have access to the databases they are hosted in. Change the database context in the SSMS Connect To Server screen from *default* to the database the user is contained in to successfully establish the connection.

26. B. `CREATE TABLE` statements fall under the Data Definition Language, or DDL, category of SQL statements.

27. D. Advanced Threat Protection is a component of the Azure Defender for SQL service that enables organizations to detect and respond to potentially malicious attempts to access a database.

28. B. CREATE USER [<AAD_User>] FROM EXTERNAL PROVIDER; is the T-SQL statement that can be used to add an AAD user or group as a user in an Azure SQL Database.

29. A. FROM is the first logical step processed by the database engine.

30. B. NVARCHAR() is a Unicode data type that is used to define string data that has variable size.

31. A. Inner joins are used to retrieve data from both tables that meets the join condition.

Chapter 3: Nonrelational Databases in Azure

1. D. Azure Table storage, Azure Cosmos DB Table API, and Azure Cache for Redis are key-value stores that can be deployed in Azure.

2. A. Key-value stores can only be queried by the keys, not the values. Document databases can be queried by both the keys and fields of data stored in a document.

3. C. Containers are the fundamental resources of scalability for throughput and storage in Azure Cosmos DB. It is at this level that data is grouped into partitions and replicated.

4. A. The session consistency level is the default consistency for Azure Cosmos DB. It grants a session token to the application writing data and guarantees that it and any other application sharing the same session token sees the most recent version of data.

5. C. While Azure Table storage and Azure Cosmos DB Table API are both Azure-based key-value stores, only the Azure Cosmos DB Table API can enable multiple write regions.

6. D. The Azure Cosmos DB API for MongoDB is one of two document database APIs offered in Azure Cosmos DB. The API for MongoDB allows users to migrate existing MongoDB document databases to Azure and take advantage of the premium capabilities provided by Azure Cosmos DB.

7. A. The first 1000 RU/s and 25 GB of storage are free when the free tier discount is applied to an Azure Cosmos DB account. Remember, the free tier discount can only be applied to one Azure Cosmos DB account per Azure subscription.

8. C. Infrastructure as Code files such as ARM templates maintain the infrastructure settings required by development environments. They can be used to quickly provision new Azure Cosmos DB instances across multiple environments, ensuring that each environment is built using consistent standards.

9. C. Cosmos DB Built-in Data Reader is the built-in RBAC role that gives Azure Active Directory identities read access to Azure Cosmos DB data. This role grants the ability to read account metadata, data from specific items (point-reads and queries), and a specific container's change feed. It does not grant permissions to create and delete data.

10. A. Azure Cosmos DB Explorer is a stand-alone web application that can be used to view and manage data stored in Azure Cosmos DB. Developers can connect to an Azure Cosmos DB account using the Azure Cosmos DB Explorer with one of the read-write keys or one of the read-only keys. This allows administrators to restrict developer access to read-only by giving them one of the read-only keys to connect with.

Chapter 4: File, Object, and Data Lake Storage

1. D. Azure Storage accounts are used to store data of all types in multiple file formats. This includes binary data such as videos and images as well as text formats such as CSV, JSON, XML, and Parquet.

2. B. Geo-redundant and geo-zone-redundant storage is only available for standard general-purpose v2 storage accounts.

3. A. Azure Files is a fully managed file share service in Azure that can be used to replace or complement existing on-premises file shares. To create the most performant connection between an Azure file share and an on-premises environment, set up Azure File Sync on a Windows Server machine to create a local cache for frequently accessed items. Azure File Sync is currently only available for Windows Server 2012 R2 and higher.

4. A. SMB uses port 445 for communication and will need to be opened if there is not an established Azure VPN or ExpressRoute to tunnel SMB traffic.

5. C. Page blobs are optimized for random read and write operations, making them ideal for storing data disks for VMs and databases.

6. B. The most cost-effective option for this solution would be to initially store the raw data using the hot access tier and then transition the raw data to the archive access tier once it is processed. The hot access tier for blob data is optimized for storing data that is frequently read from or written to. The archive access tier is for blob data that is rarely accessed, often being used for data that is only saved for regulatory purposes.

7. A. The hierarchical namespace is the fundamental component of ADLS and organizes object data as files in a hierarchy of directories and subdirectories for efficient data access.

This feature also allows users to enable more fine-grained access control on directories or individual files using POSIX permissions.

8. B. The `Get-AzStorageAccount` command gets the information for a specified storage account or all the storage accounts in a resource group or subscription. While the `Get-AzureRmStorageAccount` module will also perform the same function, the AzureRM PowerShell modules are being deprecated in favor of the Az PowerShell modules. AzureRM PowerShell modules will be officially retired in February 2024.

9. C. Using a private endpoint restricts access to only applications that can communicate with the VNet that the private IP address is in. This is the Microsoft recommended solution for securing personally identifiable information.

10. D. The Storage Blob Data Reader role grants read access to blob containers and data to identities that it is assigned to.

11. B. Azure Data Box is a physical device that lets organizations send large amounts of data to Azure very quickly. Microsoft will ship the device to organizations. Once it's received, organizations can upload their data over a wired connection to the device and return the device to the Azure datacenter they would like their storage account to be located in. Microsoft will upload the data from Azure Data Box to the desired storage account once the device is received at the Azure datacenter.

12. D. Azure Storage Explorer can connect at several different levels, including Azure subscriptions, storage accounts, and storage services.

Chapter 5: Modern Data Warehouses in Azure

1. B. Third normal form, or 3NF for short, is a database table modeling approach that is optimal for transactional workloads. It ensures that data is not redundantly stored and reduces the chances of concurrency issues as transactions are written to the database.

2. D. Data warehouses, OLAP models, and enterprise data lakes are all valid data stores for analytical workloads. While most analytical workloads result in clean data being loaded into a data warehouse or OLAP model, data scientists typically use data stored as files in an enterprise data lake to build predictive and prescriptive analysis.

3. A. Delta Lake is an open-source storage layer that brings ACID properties to data stored in ADLS. It is optimized for big data workloads and interactive query engines such as Apache Spark and Azure Synapse Analytics serverless SQL pools.

4. B. Azure Stream Analytics is a real-time analytics engine that is designed to process streaming data. It is not used for batch processing, but it can be used to store data in a persistent data store like ADLS and Azure Synapse Analytics dedicated SQL pools.

5. C. Along with dimension tables, fact tables are core components of the star schema. Fact tables store measurable observations or events such as sales metrics.

6. C. Apache Kafka is a popular open-source framework for large-scale stream processing workflows. It provides message broker functionality that can be used to ingest large volumes of streaming data.

7. A. With Spark Structured Streaming, Azure Databricks can read data in real time from data sources like Azure Event Hubs and Apache Kafka for stream processing workflows.

8. C. The cost of running an Azure Databricks cluster can be calculated by adding the Azure VM and DBU cost.

9. B. VNet injection allows you to deploy Azure Databricks data plane resources such as clusters in your own VNet. This makes it easy to connect to Azure resources that have been assigned private endpoints. Since VNet injection uses a public and a private subnet by default, enable secure cluster connectivity to change the configuration so that it uses two private subnets.

10. D. Azure Databricks supports GitHub, Bitbucket, GitLab, and Azure DevOps integration.

11. B. The High Concurrency cluster mode supports concurrent workloads for users performing interactive analysis.

12. A. Azure Synapse workspaces are automatically deployed with a serverless SQL pool endpoint that can be used to interactively query data in Azure Storage. Serverless SQL pools cannot be deleted, and additional serverless SQL pools are not supported by a single workspace.

13. A. Azure Synapse Link is a hybrid transactional and analytical processing (HTAP) service that enables users to run near real-time analytical queries over transactional data. Data is synchronized with an analytical data store that can be explored with an Azure Synapse Analytics serverless SQL pool or an Azure Synapse Analytics Apache Spark pool.

14. C. There is only one serverless SQL pool allowed per workspace and it is immediately available once the workspace is deployed.

15. A. Result set caching improves query performance by automatically caching query results in a dedicated SQL pool user database for later use. This allows subsequent runs of the query to get results directly from the cache instead of recomputing the results.

16. D. Serverless SQL pools can be used for a variety of analytical workloads, including ad-hoc analysis, building a logical data warehouse, and streamlining data transformations.

17. B. The OPENROWSET function allows you to access files stored in Azure Storage. It reads the content of data and returns the content as rows.

18. A. Dedicated SQL pools use a massively parallel processing (MPP) architecture to optimally manage large datasets. With features such as clustered columnstore indexes (CCIs), materialized views, and result set caching, users can quickly gather insights from running analytical queries over large amounts of historical data.

19. B. Control activities, such as foreach, filter, if, switch, and until activities, control the flow of an ADF pipeline.

20. D. When defining an Azure SQL Database dataset as the source dataset for an ADF copy activity, you can choose to copy an entire table or use the result set of a query or stored procedure.

21. B. Data engineers are able to execute existing SSIS packages with the Azure-SSIS integration runtime and the Execute SSIS Package activity in Azure Data Factory. Packages can be deployed to an SSIS catalog (SSISDB) on an Azure SQL Database and then run as a part of an ADF pipeline.

22. A. ADF triggers can be one of four types: scheduled, a tumbling window, a storage event such as a blob being uploaded to Azure Blob storage, or a custom event that handles custom topics in Azure Event Grid.

23. D. The `FIELD_TERMINATOR` argument specifies one or more characters that mark the end of each field in a delimited text file. Because the data in this use case is formatted as CSV (comma separated values), the field terminator should be set to a comma (`','`).

24. C. The COPY statement provides the best performance and most flexibility for parallel data ingestion into an Azure Synapse Analytics dedicated SQL pool table. The COPY statement requires developers to write and run a single T-SQL statement, unlike PolyBase, which requires users to create additional database objects.

Chapter 6: Reporting with Power BI

1. B. The Power BI Desktop tool is a free Windows desktop application that is used to ingest data, build data models, and author interactive reports.

2. C. Power BI Report Builder can be used to create paginated reports, but not interactive reports. While Power BI Desktop is the preferred tool for creating interactive reports, report creators can quickly author interactive reports through the Power BI service.

3. A. Using DirectQuery to connect to the fact tables will alleviate any issues related to importing data into the Power BI data model. Importing the smaller, static dimension tables will ensure that visualizations and filters using that data will respond quickly to any user interactions.

4. C. Users assigned the Contributor Power BI workspace role are able to view and modify existing workspace content, such as reports and dashboards. They are also able to publish new content to the workspace.

5. A. A dashboard can only be filtered if you pin an entire report page to the dashboard. While you can filter an individual dashboard tile when it is in focus mode, the filter will not be saved when you exit focus mode.

6. D. Along with tiles that come from Power BI reports, Power BI dashboards can incorporate stand-alone tiles that display web content, images, video, text boxes, and streaming data.

7. B. Paginated reports can only be uploaded to a Power BI workspace that is in a Power BI Premium capacity.

Index

B

Online Test Bank

Register to gain one year of FREE access after activation to the online interactive test bank to help you study for your MC Azure Data Fundamentals certification exam—included with your purchase of this book! All of the chapter review questions and the practice tests in this book are included in the online test bank so you can practice in a timed and graded setting.

Register and Access the Online Test Bank

To register your book and get access to the online test bank, follow these steps:

1. Go to www.wiley.com/go/sybextestprep.
2. Select your book from the list.
3. Complete the required registration information, including answering the security verification to prove book ownership. You will be emailed a pin code.
4. Follow the directions in the email or go to www.wiley.com/go/sybextestprep.
5. Find your book on that page and click the "Register or Login" link with it. Then enter the pin code you received and click the "Activate PIN" button.
6. On the Create an Account or Login page, enter your username and password, and click Login or, if you don't have an account already, create a new account.
7. At this point, you should be in the test bank site with your new test bank listed at the top of the page. If you do not see it there, please refresh the page or log out and log back in.